AN INTRODUCTION TO AIR LAW

AN INTRODUCTION TO AIR LAW

I.H.Ph. Diederiks-Verschoor

Sixth revised edition

1997

Kluwer Law International
The Hague • London • Boston

Published by Kluwer Law International
P.O. Box 85889
2508 CN The Hague, The Netherlands

Sold and distributed in the USA and Canada by
Kluwer Law International
675 Massachusetts Avenue
Cambridge, MA 02139, USA

Sold and distributed in all other countries by
Kluwer Law International
Distribution Centre
P.O. Box 322
3300 AH Dordrecht, The Netherlands

Library of Congress Cataloging -in-Publication Data

Diederiks-Verschoor, I. H. Philepina (Isabella Henrietta Philepina) ,
    1915-
     [Inleiding tot het luchtrecht, English]
     An introduction to air law / by I.H. Ph. diederiks-Verschoor. --
6th rev. ed.
       p.   cm.
     Includes bibliographical references and index.
     ISBN 9041104089
     1. Aeronautics--Law and legislation.   2. Aeronautics, Commercial-
-Law and legislation.   I. Title
     K4095.4D5413   1997
     341.7'567--dc21
                                                              97-8413
                                                                 CIP

First reprint, 1998

Cover design: B. Betzema

Printed on acid-free paper

ISBN: 90 411 0408 9

To my husband Kees
for a lifetime of understanding and patience

Preface

Several excellent handbooks on air law have already been available to students and others interested in air law for quite some time now. In recent years, however, a need was increasingly felt for a concise survey which, while not pretending to go deeply into all related issues, could yet provide the reader with a basic insight into this fascinating sector of international law.

Prompted by considerations of this nature I have attempted to fill the gap in the following pages, calling attention, *en passant*, to new technological developments and the legal innovations accompanying them. Besides, it seemed useful to point out some issues that still remain unsolved in the domain of law under review.

In presenting this book, which is a drastically revised and updated version of two earlier editions in the Dutch language, I wish to make it clear that its sole purpose is to furnish practical guidance and orientation: more profound knowledge and understanding can only be acquired from existing standard works and other publications of particular interest to the reader.

I should like to thank Mr. W.A. Frowein for kindly revising the English text. Without his help and inspiration, and the careful checking of the notes by Mr. G.C. van Straaten, to whom I am equally indebted, the publication of the present edition would have taken much longer. I am also grateful to Professor Dr. W.P. Gormley for his most useful suggestions and clarifications, especially on aspects of Anglo-Saxon law. I further wish to mention especially Mr. W.P. Heere and the Institute of Public International Law of Utrecht University for their readiness to assist, as they have done so often in the past. A special word of gratitude is also due to the Netherlands Civil Aviation Administration and KLM Royal Dutch Airlines, who provided interesting data and statistics.

Utrecht, July 1982   I.H.Ph. Diederiks-Verschoor

Preface to the Second Edition

A number of changes, mainly cosmetic or concerned with punctuation, were necessary to improve the text, in addition to some measure of updating in order to keep abreast of the latest developments in air law. Valuable remarks on bilateralism and US deregulation, kindly offered by Prof. Dr. H.A. Wassenbergh, have replaced the relevant paragraphs, a contribution for which I am greatly indebted to him.

Except for the modifications indicated above, design and text of the first edition in English have remained virtually unchanged. Mr. W.A. Frowein and Mr. G.C. van Straaten have, once again, assisted me in reviewing the text, and I wish to express my gratitude for the part they have played in preparing the present edition.

Baarn, April 1985   I.H.Ph. Diederiks-Verschoor

Preface to the Third edition

The text of this edition has been adapted to reflect current developments. Not only has the text been updated and extended with new case law, but the chapter on insurance has undergone major changes. Moreover, a new chapter entitled 'Automation and Air Law' has been added. The case law table now refers to the pages of the book instead of chapters and notes.

It is worth mentioning that in 1987 a Chinese translation has been published, while a Bahasa (Indonesian) version is forthcoming.

Mr. W.A. Frowein and Mr. G.C. van Straaten have, once again, assisted in reviewing the text. Mr. J.E. Jonker, underwriter of the Dutch Aviation Pool, has also given valuable advice in updating the insurance chapter.
I wish to express my deep gratitude for their efficient cooperation in preparing the present edition.

Baarn, March 1988   I.H.Ph. Diederiks-Verschoor

Preface to the Fourth edition

The text of this edition has been adapted again to reflect current developments
I wish to express my deep gratitude to Mr. W.A.Frowein and Mr.

G.C. van Straaten, who have once again given their efficient cooperation and assistance in reviewing the text.

Baarn, January 1991   I.H.Ph.Diederiks-Verschoor

Preface to the Fifth edition

Preparations for the present edition involved a considerable measure of updating, with its main thrust focusing on chapter II, section 14, where important new Regulations of the European Community have found their place and section 16 (Deregulation). A number of significant cases could be added and the Bibliography has been extended with the most recent literature. In addition, some observations could be inserted concerning current problems posed by e.g. non-flight zones and asylum-seekers. Other changes in the text concern improvements of a cosmetic nature.

As in previous years I have enjoyed the cooperation of Mr. W.A. Frowein and Mr. G.C. van Straaten in preparing the text, and Mr. J.E. Jonker has again kindly given his valuable advice concerning insurance matters. To all these persons I owe a deep sense of gratitude.

Baarn, May 1993   I.H.Ph.Diederiks-Verschoor

Preface to the Sixth Edition

The text of this edition has been adapted considerably in view of recent events and current developments. A number of relevant new cases have been added.

I wish to express my heartful gratitude to Mr. W.A. Frowein and Mr. G.C. van Straaten for their faithful and diligent assistence in preparing the revisions and additions.

It may be noted that a companion volume to this book, entitled *An Introduction to Space Law*, has been published by the same publishers in 1993.

Baarn, February 1997   I.H.Ph. Diederiks-Verschoor

Contents

Table of Cases

References in this table relate to pages.

Germany (Federal Republic)

Cases quoted without litigants' names:

Greece

Italy

Table of International Conventions and Other Agreements

In this table the various international Conventions and other agreements cited in this book are listed in their chronological order. The text of many of these is to be found in A.F. Lowenfeld, *Aviation Law* (2nd ed., Documents Supplement, 1981), hereafter cited as *Lowenfeld;* Nicholas M. Matte, *Treatise on Air-Aeronautical Law* (1981), hereafter cited as *Matte; Transport* (looseleaf collection of international Conventions, etc. since 1974); Shawcross and Beaumont, *Air Law* (4th ed., 1977), Volume 2 (1981), hereafter cited as *Shawcross.*

Please note that in this table reference is nearly always made to English texts only; in some cases these are not the authentic texts. It should also be borne in mind that occasionally discrepancies may occur between the official translations used in the United Kingdom and in the United States respectively.

See for the current status of the Conventions and agreements mentioned in this table the latest edition of the ICAO publication named *ICAO Aeronautical Agreements and Arrangements,* and also the tables in *Shawcross* and *Transport.*

July 29, 1899	The Hague: Declaration Prohibiting the Discharge of Projectiles and Explosives from Balloons; AJIL Off. Doc. Suppl. (1907), p. 104.
October 13, 1919	Paris: Convention Relating to the Regulation of Aerial Navigation (Paris Convention); (1922) 11 LNTS 173; *Hudson,* Vol. I. p. 359.
November 1, 1926	Madrid: Ibero-American Convention on Air Navigation ('CIANA'), also known as Madrid Convention; (1927) XI, RJIdeLA 173; *Hudson,* Vol. III, p. 2019; [1937] JAL 263.
February 20, 1928	Havana (Habana): Inter-American International Convention on Commercial Aviation (also known as Pan-American Convention); (1932) 129 LNTS 225; AJIL Off. Doc. Suppl. (1928), p. 124; *Hudson,* Vol. VI, p. 2354; 47 Stat. 1901; [1932] USAvR 298.
October 12, 1929	Warsaw: Convention for the Unification of Certain Rules Relating to International Carriage by Air (Warsaw Convention); ICAO Doc. 7838, 9201; (1933) 137 LNTS 11; *Hudson,* Vol. V, p. 100; *Lowenfeld,* p. 941; *Matte,* p. 706; [1933] JAL 394; [1934] JAL 486; [1937] JAL 298; *Transport,* p. 46; *Shawcross,* p. A-60a; 49 Stat. 3000; TS 876; [1933] USAvR 302; [1934] USAvR 245.
April 12, 1933	The Hague: International Sanitary Convention for Aerial Navigation; (1935) 161 LNTS 65; [1936] JAL 399; *Hudson,* Vol. VI, p. 292; [1935] USAvR 185.
May 29, 1933	Rome: International Convention for the Unification of Certain Rules Relating to Damage Caused by Aircraft to Third Parties on the Surface; *Hudson,* Vol. VI, p. 334; [1937] JAL 312; *Shawcross,* p. A-73; [1933] USAvR 284.
May 29, 1933	Rome: Convention for the Unification of Certain Rules Relating to Precautionary Attachment of Aircraft (also known as the Convention on Precautionary Arrest of Aircraft); (1938) 192 LNTS 289; [1933] JAL 564; [1937] JAL 335; *Transport,* p. 60; *Shawcross,* p. A-70; [1933] USAvR 293.

List of Principal Abbreviations and Acronyms

ACCA	Air Charter Carriers Association
AFCAC	African Civil Aviation Commission
AJIL	American Journal of International Law
ASECNA	Agence pour la Sécurité de la Navigation Aérienne en Afrique et Madagascar
Avi	Aviation Cases (Commerce Clearing House)
CACAS	Civil Aviation Council of Arab States
CITEJA	Comité International Technique des Experts Juridiques Aeriéns
COCESNA	Corporación Centroamericana de Servicios de Navigación Aerea
ECAC	European Civil Aviation Conference
ECSC	European Coal and Steel Community
ECU	European Currency Unit
(E)EC	European Economic Community
EU	European Union
EVR	Europees Vervoerrecht/European Transport Law
FAA	Federal Aviation Administration
GATS	General Agreement on Trade in Services
GATT	General Agreement on Tariffs and Trade
Hudson	International Legislation (Hudson)
IACA	International Air Charter Association
IAEA	International Atomic Energy Agency
IATA ⎫ (ACLR) ⎬	International Air Transport Association (Air Carriers Liability Reports)
ICAO	International Civil Aviation Organization
ICJ Reports	Reports of Judgments, Advisory Opinions and Orders, International Court of Justice (The Hague)
IDA	Il Diritto Aereo
ILA	International Law Association
ILM	International Legal Materials
ILO	International Labour Organization
IMF	International Monetary Fund
ITA	Institut du Transport Aérien
JAL(C)	Journal of Air Law (and Commerce)
LACAC	Latin-American Civil Aviation Commission
LNTS	League of Nations Treaty Series
NACA	National Air Carrier Association
O.J.	Official Journal of the EC
RFDA(S)	Revue Française de Droit Aérien (et Spatial)
RGA(E)	Revue Générale de l'Air (et de l'Espace)
RGDA	Revue Générale de Droit Aérien
RJIdeLA	Revue Juridique Internationale de la Locomotion Aérienne
SDR	Special Drawing Right
Stat	United States Statutes (at Large)
TIAS	Treaties and other International Agreements of the United States
TS	United States Treaty Series
UNTS	United Nations Treaty Series
USAvR	United States (and Canadian) Aviation Reports

USDeptStBull	United States Department of State Bulletin
UST	United States Treaties
WTO	World Trade Organisation
Zfl, ZFL, ZLW	Zeitschrift für Luft(-und Weltraum)recht(sfragen)

CHAPTER I

History and Development of Air Law

1. Introductory note

There is considerable difference of opinion in academic circles around the problem of finding a satisfactory definition of air law. Yet, a study of standard works on the subject will reveal a common formula which has found more or less general acceptance. It runs as follows: 'Air Law is a body of rules governing the use of airspace and its benefits for aviation, the general public and the nations of the world.' In presenting this definition I must stress, however, that it cannot be applied indiscriminately or without exceptions.

Although the term 'aviation law' is still being used in several handbooks it has in fact become obsolete, like its counterpart 'navigation law'. On the other hand, the designation 'air transportation law', which has been employed on occasions, offers the disadvantage of representing only one sector of air law and thus conveying too narrow an interpretation. Currently the term 'aeronautical law' is also being used, especially in the Romance languages, where expressions like *droit aéronautique* and *diritto aeronautico* are commonly employed side by side with *droit aérien* and *diritto aereo*. In the present treatise the term 'air law' has been adopted, which is current practice.[1]

The study of air law is relevant for a number of reasons:

1. Aviation is still in the process of achieving its next phase of development and arouses interest in ever larger circles. For many persons and organisations it is a matter of practical importance to gather at least some basic knowledge of the subject. When a person boards an aircraft as a passenger and reads the small print on his ticket he suddenly realises that he is bound by the provisions of the Warsaw Convention. It will be useful for him to possess some means of appreciating the benefits and disadvantages of the rules to which he has become bound.

2. Air law is intertwined with other areas of law on several points. It involves many aspects of constitutional law, administrative law, civil law, commercial law and criminal law. Its international element, however, is always paramount.

3. Air law offers a striking example of how existing legal rules can be swiftly adapted to the impressive technological progress achieved in recent years.

---

1. See also on the subject of definitions and terminology: E. van Bogaert,'The Relativity of the Notion of the Law of the Air', *Studia Diplomatica* (Brussels, 1979), Vol. XXXII, No. 6, pp. 621-637. Note also the different approach to this subject by Nicolas M. Matte, who uses the term 'air-aeronautical law'; see his *Treatise on Air-Aeronautical Law* (1981), pp. 50 *et seq.*

2. The origin

As early as 1900 the French jurist Fauchille suggested that a code of international air navigation be created by the 'Institut de Droit International', and it is interesting to note, *en passant*, that this was one of the rare instances where legal process went ahead of technology. In 1903 the discussions were given a new impulse: aviation had become a matter of topical interest and concern because the Wright Brothers had just successfully carried out their first engine-powered flight. It is possible to go back even further into the past when one takes into account the national rules and regulations in various countries. In France, for instance, a police directive was issued on April 23, 1784, aimed directly and exclusively at the balloons of the Montgolfier Brothers: flights were not to take place without prior authorisation. The purpose of this measure was of course to protect the population.

The first concerted attempt at codification on an international scale took place before 1910, when German balloons repeatedly made flights above French territory.[2] The French Government was of the opinion that for safety reasons it would be desirable for the two governments involved to try and reach an agreement to resolve the problem. As a result the Paris Conference of 1910 was convened. Contrary to general assumption, this Conference did not adopt the 'freedom of the air' theory. At that time the general tendency was already in favour of the sovereignty of states in the space above their territories. This is borne out by the text of the draft Convention approved at the plenary session of the Conference.[3]

However, due to political (not legal) disagreements the Conference ended without achieving any tangible results. Its only useful effect was that states had had an opportunity of exchanging views on this new area of law. It is apt to recall in this context that in maritime law a long historical evolution and the influential opinion of scholars like Hugo Grotius in his *Mare liberum* had led to a large measure of freedom on the high seas. A similar evolution is conspicuously lacking in air law. The influence of customary law in air law is considerably less evident than in maritime law.

Following the First World War, on February 8, 1919, the first scheduled air service between Paris and London came into operation, and it was considered necessary for existing regulations to be incorporated into a Convention. A choice now had to be made between a free airspace analogous to the principle of maritime law, and an airspace governed by the sovereignty of the underlying states. Due to the

2. Earlier, at the time of the Hague Peace Conference of 1899, aerial warfare — a quite different aspect of aviation which will not be considered in this treatise — had already been the subject of international codification. See the International Declaration Prohibiting the Discharge of Projectiles and Explosives from Balloons (The Hague, July 29, 1899) and also K.W. Colegrove, *International Control of Aviation* (World Peace Foundation, 1930), pp. 46 *et seq.*
3. See on this subject J.C. Cooper, 'The International Air Navigation Conference, Paris 1910', [1952] JALC 127-143 (also in *Explorations in Aerospace Law* (I.A. Vlasic, ed., 1968), pp. 105-124).

aftermath of the War there were strong tendencies to defend the national interest, so that the latter principle prevailed.

3. The autonomy of air law

The point has been raised on several occasions whether it was altogether necessary to introduce a special body of rules to govern the airspace. This line of thinking led, in turn, to the question of whether air law was to be regarded as an area of law *sui generis*, consisting of rules of a typically distinctive nature, or, alternatively, whether it was to be made subject to rules already existent to regulate other means of conveyance such as transport by rail, road or sea. In Italy in particular this issue has caused a considerable amount of controversy, and Italy is now the only country where air law and maritime law are combined in a single code of law entitled *'Il Codice della Navigazione'*, which dates from 1942. Both theories have their own adherents but, whatever their merits, the best approach will be to strike a balance between the two opposing viewpoints. In my submission, air law covers an area which is determined by the special characteristics and demands of aviation, but whenever this implies a departure from existing general law the justification for such departure must be most carefully assessed and weighed. Between those two poles air law will have to find both its range and its limits.

4. Sources of air law

A closer look at the definition recorded above leads almost automatically to the question: what exactly does this 'body of rules', which governs the airspace and makes up air law, consist of? The following classification may provide some useful guidance:

1. multilateral conventions;
2. bilateral agreements;
3. national law;
4. contracts between states and airline companies;
5. contracts between airline companies;
6. general principles of international law

Multilateral conventions are the primary source of air law. In stating this fact I would emphasise that air law has taken on its international character and emerged on an international plane almost from the very beginning, *i.e.* following the first scheduled flight between Paris and London: the Paris Convention was concluded in 1919, the year in which that flight took place. Due to the rapid developments in aviation and with the law-makers attempting to keep pace, custom has largely been bypassed as a source of law, the result being that air law today consists mainly of written law.

3

The most characteristic feature of an aircraft is its speed, in addition to the fact that it moves in three dimensions. Speed enables an aircraft *en route* to a particular destination to pass through the airspace of several countries, each having its own national laws and customs. Consequently, it passes from one legal sphere of influence to another.

It is clearly a matter of prime importance to those involved in aviation — *e.g.* the state, the owner, the operator, the passengers, the owner of the goods carried on board, the mortgage holders — to make sure that their rights are properly safeguarded. Achieving this object is one of the most important elements in air law. The implementing measures are all to be found in international agreements and Conventions. [4]

Another classification which is relevant for air law is that of military and civil aviation. Military aviation, however, is outside the scope of this book and will therefore not be considered.

The classic demarcation between national and international law, and between private law and public law, is also applicable in air law. Private international law, in this context, means the body of rules pertaining to the relations between private persons involved in the operation and use of aircraft, whereas public international law is the corpus of legal norms pertaining to the relations involving states and international organisations in respect of those activities.

Finally, a distinction may be made in matters of aviation between problems of political, technical, economical, financial, social or legal nature. In this book mainly legal aspects will be reviewed.

5. The Paris Convention of 1919

The Paris Convention[5] was the first legal instrument to enter into force in the province of air law. It was ratified by 32 nations. Complete and exclusive sovereignty of states over the airspace above their territory was recognised, in conformity with the Roman adage: *'Cujus est solum, ejus est usque ad coelum et ad inferos'*.

In order to achieve a certain degree of uniformity some technical annexes were added to the Paris Convention, dealing with such matters as standards of airworthiness, certificates of competency for crew members, etc. The Convention also established, in its Article 34, the CINA, the *Commission Internationale de la Navigation Aérienne*, [6] which was granted far-reaching regulatory powers chiefly directed towards

---

4. For references to the full text of air law Conventions and other agreements cited in this treatise see the Table of International Conventions and Agreements on page xxiii.
5. *Convention Portant Réglementation de la Navigation Aérienne* (Convention Relating to the Regulation of Aerial Navigation), Paris, October 13, 1919; hereinafter cited as the Paris Convention. See for this first air law convention I.H.Ph. Diederiks-Verschoor and H.A. Wassenbergh, 'Dr. J.F. Lycklama à Nijeholt (1846-1947)', *Air and Space Law*, vol. XIX (1994), pp. 8-14 and the literature cited there.
6. In English: ICAN, International Commission for Air Navigation.

technical matters. Other functions listed in Article 34 are: centralised gathering and publication of information on air navigation, and the rendering of advice on matters submitted by member states.

The Paris Convention contained the first generally accepted definition of the term 'aircraft', which read as follows: *'Le mot aéronef désigne tout appareil pouvant se soutenir dans l'atmosphére grâce aux reactions de l'air'.* This rather sweeping definition included aircraft, airships, gliders, free balloons, barrage balloons and helicopters. The criterion which should have been given preference is whether the machine has any lift.

Having become outdated, the Convention was eventually replaced, in 1944, by the Chicago Convention,[7] but the latter failed to bring about a change in the definition of 'aircraft', reading: 'Aircraft is any machine that can derive support in the atmosphere from the reactions of the air'.[8] As most other Conventions lacked such a definition altogether the Chicago formula, which had been taken from the Paris Convention, continued to serve as a cornerstone of air law for another few decades, although authoritative opinions were also taken into account on a number of occasions. Eventually, on November 6, 1967, ICAO brought out a new definition reading: 'Aircraft is any machine that can derive support in the atmosphere from the reactions of the air other than the reactions of the air against the earth's surface'[9] Its distinctive feature was that the words 'other than the reactions of the air against the earth's surface' had been added. This addition ensured that hovercraft were excluded from the definition of 'aircraft'.

Other definitions have been suggested, but none were completely satisfactory. According to Riese[10] this is due to their being too loosely worded, together with the fact that air law does not consist exclusively of air transport law, a point he says has been ignored all too often.

Riese's critical comments are not entirely without justification, in my opinion. One should also not minimise the fact that the term 'aircraft' has a different meaning in various air law Conventions.

It is debatable whether rockets fall within the scope of the definition just quoted. Cruise missiles do not derive support in the atmosphere from the reactions of the air, unlike the Second World War flying bombs (V-1). They will not be considered in this treatise as they

---

7. Convention on International Civil Aviation, Chicago, December 7, 1944; hereinafter cited as the Chicago Convention.
8. See, for instance, the original text of Annexes 6 and 7 to the Chicago Convention. In the United States Federal Aviation Act of 1958 an aircraft is defined as 'any contrivance now known or hereafter invented, used, or designed for navigation or flight in the air' (see Shawcross and Beaumont, *Air Law* (1977), Vol. 1, p. 159).
9. Revised and amended text of Annex 7 to the Chicago Convention. See also the *ICAO Lexicon* (5th ed., 1980), ICAO Doc. No. 9294, Vol. II.
10. O. Riese, *Luftrecht* (1949), pp. 186 *et seq.* See also M. Lemoine, *Traité de droit aérien* (1947), para. 209, pp. 15-151.

are subject to special rules of military law. According to the *Multilingual Aeronautical Dictionary* [11] the definition of a rocket(-motor) is as follows: 'device for producing thrust by the ejection of matter, usually in gaseous form, the thrust being generated by a propellant carried in the system'.

6. The Ibero-American Convention and the Pan-American Convention

The Paris Convention was followed by the Ibero-American Convention, concluded at Madrid in 1926.[12] The latter contained provisions largely similar to those of the Paris Convention, provisions which were also recognised, however, by several Latin-American states invited for the purpose by the Spanish Government.

In 1927, the United States initiated the drafting of an air navigation Convention for the Americas, *i.e.* the Pan-American Convention. This Convention was signed at Havana in 1928.[13]

A comparison between the Pan-American Convention and the Paris Convention shows that the former did not provide for a commission like the International Commission for Air Navigation, nor did it contain any technical annexes. Unlike its predecessor, the Pan-American Convention failed to achieve a measure of uniformity in air traffic regulations.

All these Conventions have since been replaced by one single Convention, the well-known Chicago Convention, but it should always be remembered that this comprehensive international agreement owes much to its predecessors.

7. Principal organisations in aviation

7.1. THE 'COMITÉ INTERNATIONAL TECHNIQUE D'EXPERTS JURIDIQUES AÉRIENS' (CITEJA)

During the first International Conference of Private Air Law, which was held in 1925, a *'Comité International Technique d'Experts Juridiques Aériens'* was called into being.[14] CITEJA consisted of numerous legal

---

11. *Multilingual Aeronautical Dictionary* (Advisory Group for Aerospace Research and Development, North Atlantic Treaty Organisation (AGARD/NATO), 1980).

12. Ibero-American Convention on Air Navigation, Madrid, November 1, 1926; hereinafter cited as Ibero-American Convention.

13. Pan-American (or Inter-American) International Convention on Commercial Aviation, Havana, February 20, 1928; hereinafter cited as Pan-American Convention.

14. In English: International Technical Committee of Legal Experts on Air Questions. See *Conférence Internationale de Droit Privé Aérien* (Paris, 1925), published Paris, 1936. For further information see: J.J. Ide, 'The History and Accomplishments of the International Technical Committee of Aerial Legal Experts CITEJA' [1933] JAL 27-49; E. Sudre, *'Le Comité International Technique d'Experts Juridiques Aériens* (CITEJA). *Son origine — son but — son oeuvre — son avenir'* [1946] RGA 49-65; R. Plaisant, *'Le CITEJA et son oeuvre'* [1946/7] RFDA 153-162.

committees, each of them charged with studying a particular subject related to air law, for instance the carrier's liability, mortgage of aircraft, etc. After a preliminary draft Convention had been completed it was submitted to a Diplomatic Conference, and following approval of the text by this body it was opened for signature by the states. CITEJA was concerned in particular with private law issues.

7.2. THE 'COMMISSION INTERNATIONALE DE LA NAVIGATION AÉRIENNE' (CINA)

CINA's important functions have already been outlined briefly under the heading 'Paris Convention'. Both CINA and CITEJA have been instrumental in laying the foundations of air law. They were eventually incorporated in ICAO, the International Civil Aviation Organisation.

7.3. PICAO, ICAO AND IATA

Towards the end of the Second World War, at a time when a spectacular expansion in world air traffic was about to take place, the Provisional International Civil Aviation Organisation (PICAO) was set up as a forerunner of ICAO, the International Civil Aviation Organisation which is still playing an outstanding role in world aviation matters. The latter was created in 1947, and it grew finally to become a body of official representatives of a number of nations now totalling over 170. Note should be taken of the fact that ICAO is quite distinct in nature and origin from IATA, the International Air Transport Association, which is a purely private organisation originally started in 1919 by six private airline companies. Both organisations are mentioned here only in passing, as leading organisations in aviation matters: their main functions and working procedures will be dealt with in Chapter II.

7.3.1. ICAO

ICAO[15] became a Specialised Agency of the United Nations soon after its creation. Its daily business is run by a Council, a permanent body which performs a variety of duties in the legal, technical and recently also in the economic field. It has a membership of 33 at the moment, and operates under the supervision of an Assembly with important budgetary powers. ICAO also has a Legal Committee, which is charged with preparing and drafting international treaties and Conventions on air law prior to their submission to a Diplomatic Conference for final approval. The Legal Committee has since assumed the

---

15. See for information about ICAO's history and accomplishments: G.F. Fitzgerald, 'The International Civil Aviation Organization and the Development of Conventions on International Air Law', *Annals of Air and Space Law*, Vol. III (1978), pp. 51-120.

duties from the former CITEJA and CINA, but there have been important changes in emphasis and working procedures, as will be shown in the next chapter where also other ICAO committees are mentioned.

7.3.2. IATA

Unlike ICAO, which is an organisation of government representatives, IATA[16] is a private organisation of airlines designed to promote safe, regular and economical air transportation. IATA has strong ties with the governments involved in aviation matters and wields considerable influence internationally, for instance in fixing tariffs. Nearly all scheduled airline companies are represented in IATA. Since 1974 charter airline companies can also qualify for admission, but none of them have so far availed themselves of this opportunity: they have, it would seem, preferred to remain members of their own organisations which are listed below.

7.4. CHARTER ORGANISATIONS

1. The National Air Carrier Association (NACA), an association of American air charter companies.
2. The International Air Charter Association (IACA), comprising 13 independent European and American charter companies, established in June 1971.
3. The Air Charter Carriers Association (ACCA), established in September 1971 and in which 12 European companies are represented.

7.5. OTHER ORGANISATIONS

Other organisations worth mentioning in this context are the International Federation of Air Line Pilots Associations (IFALPA), and the International Union of Aviation Insurers,[17] which was founded in 1934 and about which more will be said in the chapter on insurance. Both these organisations, along with others, are represented at the ICAO Legal Committee's preparatory sessions in order to ensure the best possible adaptation of Convention texts to current aviation practice.

A short survey of regional carriers' organisations can be found in Chapter II, section 6.

---

16. See for IATA: J.W.S. Brancker, *IATA and What it Does* (1977).
17. R.D. Margo, *Aviation Insurance*, (1989), p. 43.

The Chicago Convention of 1944 on International Civil Aviation

1. The preparatory stage

On November 1, 1944, in response to a British initiative, US President Roosevelt invited all the allied powers as well as some neutral governments to convene at Chicago for a conference on civil aviation. Expectations were high in anticipation of this conference, in spite of its rather unfortunate timing; there was a feeling of complete uncertainty about the turn of events in international relations at that time.

Four trends of thought may be distinguished in the preparatory work of the Convention:
1. the American trend, advocating complete freedom of competition in air transport;
2. the British trend, suggesting the creation of an international organisation to coordinate air transport and to assume the duties of apportioning the world's air routes and making decisions on frequencies and tariffs;
3. the Canadian trend, recommending support for the British proposals, but in a rather more elaborate version;
4. an Australian and New Zealand plan for the internationalisation of major international airlines under the direction of a single authority in which all states involved would participate.

The Netherlands and the Scandinavian countries followed the American trend. Yet, none of the proposals has exerted a significant influence in determining the ultimate scope and contents of the Convention. On the other hand, the principle of the complete and exclusive sovereignty of a state over the airspace above its territory, which had been articulated as long ago as 1919 in the Paris Convention of that year, remained the legal standard in international civil aviation.

The British proposal did not appear to be feasible: by creating an international high authority the progress of aviation, which was still in the process of development, would be severely hampered. For the same reason the Canadian proposals were also abandoned.[1]

The New Zealand–Australian suggestion was also considered impracticable because international aviation forms an integral part of the larger political issue of world relations. The two areas cannot be

---

1. See for the various proposals W.J. Wagner, *International Air Transportation as Affected by State Sovereignty* (1970), pp. 95 *et seq.*

treated separately. Besides, an important sector of economic and political activity like aviation is not likely to be entrusted by sovereign states to an international organisation without the greatest reluctance.

2. The Convention

On December 7, 1944, some 50 states signed the Chicago Convention,[2] together with two agreements annexed to it, *i.e.* the International Air Services Transit Agreement and the International Air Transport Agreement.[3] At present, over 180 states have ratified or acceded to the Convention, while the Transit Agreement (unlike the Transport Agreement) has also been signed or ratified by a large number of states.

On September 24, 1968, a Protocol was concluded at Buenos Aires and attached to the Chicago Convention, whereby a French and a Spanish text were added with the status of authentic language. In 1977 the same status was accorded to a Russian text, resulting in four texts of equal authenticity.[4]

To the Convention have been added 18 Annexes which give technical rules in implementation of its Articles. They are entitled as follows:
1. Personnel Licensing.
2. Rules of the Air.
3. Meteorological Service for International Air Navigation.
4. Aeronautical Charts.
5. Units of Measurement to be Used in Air and Ground Operations.
6. Operation of Aircraft.
7. Aircraft Nationality and Registration Marks.

---

2. Convention on International Civil Aviation, Chicago, December 7, 1944. Note that a number of Articles of this Convention have been amended since 1944 (some even twice), notably Articles 45, 48(a), 49(e), 50(a), 56, 61 and 93-bis.

Originally, 55 states were invited by the United States Government to the Chicago Conference. Saudi-Arabia did not accept the invitation, while at the last minute the USSR did not participate due to objections against the presence at the Conference of certain other states (Portugal, Spain and Switzerland). The USSR resented the policies followed by these countries during the Second World War not yet ended at that time. See for more information Captain J. Schenkman, *International Civil Aviation Organization* (1955), pp. 73 *et seq.* See also on the subject of the Chicago Convention: D. Goedhuis, 'Problems of Public International Law' (1952-II) 81 *Recueil des Cours* 205–307; M. le Goff, *Manuel de Droit Aérien, Droit Public* (1954); H.A. Wassenbergh, *Post-War International Civil Aviation Policy and the Law of the Air* (1962); W.J. Wagner (see note 1, *supra*); R.L. Thornton, *International Airlines and Politics, a Study in Adaptation to Change*, Michigan International Business Studies, No. 3 (1970); M.R. Straszheim, *The International Airline Industry* (1969).

3. International Air Services Transit Agreement, Chicago, December 7, 1944; hereinafter cited as Transit Agreement (also known as the Two-Freedoms Agreement), and the International Air Transport Agreement, Chicago, December 7, 1944; hereinafter cited as the Transport Agreement (also known as the Five-Freedoms Agreement).

4. See ICAO Doc.8876/LC-160 (Minutes and Documents of the 1968 Buenos Aires Conference) and 9256/LC-181 (1977 Montreal Conference).

8. Airworthiness of Aircraft.
9. Facilitation.
10. Aeronautical Telecommunications.
11. Air Traffic Services.
12. Search and Rescue.
13. Aircraft Accident Investigation.
14. Aerodromes.
15. Aeronautical Information Services.
16. Environmental Protection.
17. Security – Safeguarding International Civil Aviation against Acts of Unlawful Interference.
18. Safe Transport of Dangerous Goods by Air.

Due to Anglo-American influence the Annexes contain a great number of definitions to explain the meaning of terms used in the 'standards' and the 'recommended practices' which, together with the definitions, make up the Annexes. 'Standards' are any specifications 'the uniform application of which is recognized as necessary for the safety or regularity of international air navigation'. 'Recommended practices' are, of course, not of a mandatory nature. Departures from standards must be notified to the ICAO Council under Article 38 of the Convention.

The Chicago Convention, which has been in force for more than 50 years, has come in for some pointed criticism from Milde, especially concerning the differences and deviations which still exist in observing the standards. Milde stresses in particular the lack of international enforcement or even a reference list of the actual implementation of these standards.[5]

While examining the rules of the Convention it should always be borne in mind that they apply solely and exclusively to civil aircraft (Art. 3). State aircraft are explicitly excluded; they will be dealt with in section 11 of this chapter.

One of the fundamental principles underlying the Convention is the fact that all states should be able to participate in air transportation on a basis of equality. The Convention's preamble provides a pointer in that direction, since it refers to the good faith of states in their dealings with each other and to the regard for equal opportunity and participation.[6] The implementation of this principle, however, is

5. See M. Milde, 'Future Perspectives of Air Law', in the proceedings (forthcoming) of the International Colloquium on Perspectives of Air Law, Space Law and International Business Law for the Next Century (Cologne, June 7-9, 1995). See also the proceedings of the conference 'Chicago Revisited' (Montreal, December 3-5, 1994), published as volume XX (1995) of the *Annals of Air and Space Law* and also volume XIX (1994) of this periodical.
6. The Preamble declares: 'Whereas the future development of international civil aviation can greatly help to create and preserve friendship and understanding among the nations and peoples of the world, yet its abuse can become a threat to the general security; and Whereas it is desirable to avoid friction and to promote that co-operation between nations and peoples upon which the peace of the world depends; Therefore, the undersigned governments having agreed on certain principles and arrangements in order that international civil aviation may be developed in a safe and orderly manner and that international air transport services may be established on the basis of equality of opportunity and operated soundly and economically; Have accordingly concluded this Convention to that end'.

hampered by the limitations of rights states can impose upon each other, limitations which find their origin in the principle of sovereignty of the state over the airspace above its territory expressed in Article 1 of the Convention. Governments wish, above all, to urge their own airline companies to satisfy the demand for air transport to and from their countries independently. They therefore show a strong tendency to impose major limitations on foreign airline companies. These may affect the number of passengers to be carried, the flight frequency and other vital matters.

Air law has a lot in common with maritime law, but we may observe that in air law, due to the Chicago Convention's strict provisions and also to bilateral agreements stipulating the requirements of 'substantial ownership and effective control',[7] we do not come across the same problems. For instance, complications resulting from the use of 'flags of convenience' do not occur in aviation because it is governed by a system of permits containing strict rules for all flights. In the United States it is the Department of Transportation which, in its negotiations with airline companies, checks nowadays whether the companies are 'fit, willing and able' to engage in air transport and whether their transport is in the public interest. 'Substantial ownership and effective control' is then regarded as coming under the heading 'fitness'.[8]

3. Freedom and sovereignty

The fact that states can impose limitations on flights of foreign aircraft stems from the principle embodied in the Paris Convention, namely that each state has complete and exclusive sovereignty over the airspace above its national territory. This fundamental rule has been repeated and sanctioned in the Chicago Convention. The possibility of allowing greater freedom of movement has, however, been made explicit in two Agreements annexed to the Convention, which divide the freedom of the air into five categories.

7. Substantial ownership is normally acquired with a minimum of 51% of the shares, although in certain circumstances a lesser amount is required. See H.A. Wassenbergh, *Post-War International Civil Aviation Policy and the Law of the Air* (1962), *passim.* Substantial ownership and effective control are concepts also applied in EC legislation; see H.P.van Fenema, 'Substantial Ownership and Effective Control as Airpolitical Criteria', in *Air and Space Law: De Lege Ferenda* (1992), pp. 27-41. See for the concept of economic ownership Chapter VIII, paragraph 2.2 *infra.*
8. See H.A. Wassenbergh, *Aspects of Air Law and Civil Air Policy in the Seventies* (1970), p. 117, and by the same author *Public International Air Transportation in a New Era* (1976). Originally it was the Civil Aeronautics Board (CAB) who checked these aspects. However, US deregulation resulted in the functions and duties of the CAB being transferred to the Department of Transportation on January 1, 1985.

The first two freedoms are described in the Transit Agreement: they concern the freedom to fly over a country or to make a technical landing. They are also listed in the Transport Agreement, together with three more freedoms. The third freedom enables the state to carry passengers and cargo from its own territory to a foreign state, whereas the fourth concerns the transport of passengers and cargo from a foreign state to its own territory. The right to carry passengers and cargo between two foreign states is contained in the fifth freedom. It is the latter which causes most complications in actual practice, so that many states have been reluctant to adhere to the Transport Agreement.[9]

Occasionally one may come across references to a sixth, a seventh and an eighth freedom, but these may be said to represent only minor variations of the first five.[10]

Apart from the freedoms, the Chicago Convention contains some other provisions clearly related to the principle of sovereignty and worth mentioning in this context. Article 2 of the Convention states: 'For the purpose of this Convention the territory of a State shall be deemed to be the land areas and territorial waters adjacent thereto under the sovereignty, suzerainty, protection or mandate of such State'. The practice of 'cabotage' (Art. 7 of the Convention) needs mentioning at this point as well; it will be examined in section 5 of this chapter. Article 8 deals with pilotless aircraft. It states that 'Each contracting State undertakes to ensure that the flight of such aircraft without a pilot in regions open to civil aircraft shall be so controlled as to obviate danger to civil aircraft'. Article 9 concerns bans and restrictions in exceptional circumstances and for reasons of public safety or military necessity:

Article 9 (a): 'Each contracting State may, for reasons of military necessity or public safety, restrict or prohibit uniformly the aircraft of other States from flying over certain areas of its territory ...';

Article 9 (b): 'Each contracting State reserves also the right, in exceptional circumstances or during a period of emergency, or in the interest of public safety, and with immediate effect, temporarily to restrict or prohibit flying over the whole or any part of its territory...';

Article 9 (c): 'Each contracting State, under such regulations as it may prescribe, may require any aircraft entering the areas contemplated in subparagraphs (a) or (b) above to effect a landing as soon as practicable thereafter at some designated airport within its territory'.

---

9. Bin Cheng, *The Law of International Air Transport* (1962), notably at pp. 21 and 407 *et seq.*

10. Sixth Freedom: the right to fly into the territory of the grantor State and there discharge, or take on, traffic ostensibly coming from, or destined for, the flag-State of the carrier which the carrier has either brought to the flag-State from a third State on a different service or is carrying from the flag-State to a third State on a different service.
Seventh Freedom: the right, for a carrier operating entirely outside the territory of the flag-State, to fly into the territory of the grantor State and there discharge, or take on, traffic coming from, or destined for, a third State or States.
Eighth Freedom (Cabotage): the right to carry traffic from one point in the territory of a State to another point in the same State (Definitions taken from Bin Cheng (note 9, *supra*), at p. 15). See also H.A. Wassenbergh, 'The "Sixth" Freedom Revisited', *Air and Space Law*, vol. XXI (1996), pp. 285-294.

The following case, centering around Gibraltar, provides a perfect illustration of the impact of Article 9.

In April 1967, immediately after the UK had lifted somewhat similar restrictions in a zone around Gibraltar, Spain proclaimed a ban on all flights over and around the Bay of Algeciras for 'fundamental reasons of national security', invoking Article 9 of the Chicago Convention.

The UK first replied to Spain's move by stating that the limits of the territorial waters around Gibraltar had never been defined, and then suggested either negotiating or submitting the case to the International Court of Justice. In a subsequent move, the UK submitted the case of the prohibited zones to the ICAO Council, first *ex* Article 54(n), and later, because the case could not be settled by negotiation, *ex* Article 84. The UK argued that Spain's action constituted an infringement of Article 9, because there was 'unnecessary interference with air navigation'. Spain countered by saying that she alone was in a position to decide on every single aspect of the case, invoking Articles 1, 2 and other Articles of the Chicago Convention. Her attitude reflected unmistakably a political point of view and her insistence on giving a political twist to the dispute.

Given the attitude taken up by Spain, the UK decided that the ICAO Council was not competent to hear the case, a point of view shared by the then President of the Council. Accordingly, on November 28, 1969, consideration of the dispute was deferred *sine die*, at the request of the parties.

Article 9 is interesting in this context because it highlights the tendency of states to put their own interests first in certain circumstances, like political aspirations, military necessity or public safety. This tendency has also prevailed ever since the Paris Convention of 1919, whose Article 3 contained similar provisions, and it has remained alive in spite of all efforts aimed at greater freedom for international air traffic. Such efforts have indeed been successful to a certain extent, as is borne out by the preamble and text of the Convention. Nonetheless, Article 9, like Article 1, clearly and unmistakably reflects both the old principle of the sovereignty of a state over the airspace above its territory and the priority given by states to safeguarding their interests.

However, mention must be made here of a recent important development, namely the introduction of so-called 'no-fly orders' by the UN Security Council. These orders forbid states to make use of the airspace above (parts of) their territory and are issued for certain areas of armed conflict for reasons of humanitarian intervention. Their aim is to prevent or diminish aerial aggression against groups of the population in those areas. By special decision of the UN Security Council military aircraft operating on behalf of the UN may be allowed to enforce the no-fly orders. The legal basis for these orders is to be found in the UN Charter and not in the Chicago Convention.[11]

11. See P. Malanczuk, *Humanitarian Intervention and the Legitimacy of Force* (1993); M. Milde, 'Aeronautical Consequences of the Iraqi Invasion of Kuwait', *Air Law*, vol. XVI (1991), pp. 63–75; and H.A. Wassenbergh, 'Iraq/Kuwait and International Civil Aviation Relations', *ITA Magazine* vol. 63 (Sept.-Oct. 1990), pp. 8-15.

4. Scheduled and non-scheduled air traffic

Another distinction to be made in air transport is that between 'scheduled' and 'non-scheduled' flights. Article 6 of the Chicago Convention provides that 'no scheduled air service may be operated over or into the territory of a contracting State, except with special permission or other authorization of that State, and in accordance with the terms of such permission or authorization'. Therefore, each state is free to impose such limitations as it deems fit on the aircraft of a foreign state. As for non-scheduled flights, which are covered by Article 5, Goudsmit rightly observes that it was drafted to guarantee non-scheduled air traffic freedom and flexibility. In practice, states have been given the possibility of subjecting this freedom to certain restrictions.[12]

Scheduled and non-scheduled air services differ in that the latter are not carried out according to a published timetable, and are not subject to the rates and tariffs applicable to regular scheduled air traffic. Non-scheduled air transport is effected by aircraft not engaged in regular air services.[13]

The sudden rise in the volume of non-scheduled transport after the Second World War may be explained by the greatly disorganised state of land and sea communications. There was a sharp increase in demand for additional air transport services, but the airlines engaged in regular scheduled flights could not meet that demand adequately. Besides, a large number of ex-military transport planes became available for commercial use, as well as many ex-military pilots who were keen to use their wartime experience for practical ends.[14]

In the 1960s, when the jet-age really got under way, there was an even greater demand for charters. In addition, holiday traffic to foreign countries increased considerably, notably the phenomenon of 'inclusive tours', which offer transport and hotel accommodation in

12. J.J. Goudsmit, *Het internationale ongeregelde luchtvervoer en art. 5 van het Verdrag van Chicago* (thesis Utrecht, 1953), at p. 105 in the English Summary. See also on the subject of charter traffic/non-scheduled traffic: J.W.F. Sundberg, *Air Charter, A study in Legal Development* (1961); E. du Pontavice, 'Le statut juridique des affrètements aériens dits "charters"' [1970] RGAE 241–257; Ryohei Itow, *Air Charter Transportation* (1969); J.P. Hari, *Les transports aériens commerciaux non-réguliers en Europe* (thesis Lausanne, 1964); J. Kamp, *Air Charter Regulations, a Legal, Economic Consumer Study* (1975); O.J. Lissitzyn, 'Freedom of the Air: Scheduled and Non-Scheduled Air Services' in McWhinney/Bradley, *Freedom of the Air* (1968), pp. 89-105; J.W.F. Sundberg, 'The Guadalajara Convention Live from Cyprus' *Air Law*, vol. I (1976), pp. 83-98; W. Diersch, *Der internationale 'Gelegenheits' luftverkehr*, published as Volume 8 of the series Bürgerliches, Handels– und Verkehrsrecht (E. Ruhwedel, ed., 1981).

13. See also ICAO Doc. 7278–C/841 (May 10, 1952), Definition of a Scheduled International Air Service.

14. Sundberg uses the name 'irregulars' for these post-war flying veterans, *Air Charter* (1961) (see note 12, *supra*), pp. 24 *et seq.*

a single package deal. The ever-increasing volume of charter flights has posed a great threat to the scheduled air services; so much so that a completely new relationship between scheduled and non-scheduled air transport may lie ahead, as will be shown below.[15]

On March 28, 1952, the ICAO Council adopted the following definition of scheduled international services:

> 'A scheduled international air service is a series of flights that possesses all the following characteristics:
> a. it passes through the airspace over the territory of more than one State;
> b. it is performed by aircraft for the transport of passengers, mail or cargo for remuneration, in such a manner that each flight is open to use by members of the public;
> c. it is operated so as to serve traffic between the same two or more points, either
> 1. according to a published timetable, or
> 2. with flights so regular or frequent that they constitute a recognisable systematic series'[16]

As for charter traffic, the following practices may be noted:

a. the tendency to apply national rules to incoming and outgoing charters unless there is a special agreement abrogating them;
b. the tendency of charter companies to join forces, which has already resulted in the creation of a number of organisations, mentioned in chapter I, section 7 of this book;
c. bilateral charter agreements (the so-called charter bilaterals) along the lines of those concluded for scheduled air transport;
d. scheduled airline companies establishing subsidiary companies solely in order to capture their share of the charter traffic business;
e. increased cooperation between scheduled airline companies and charter companies, especially on the issue of minimum fares and rates. On September 20, 1974, IATA extended its membership to include charter companies, thereby providing a forum for closer cooperation between the two sectors of air transport, but to date no charter company has applied for membership.

On April 30, 1956, the Multilateral Agreement on Commercial Rights of Non-scheduled Air Services in Europe was concluded in Paris.[17]

---

15. See also A. Rudolf, 'Die sogenannten Pauschalreise-(IT)Charter im Spannungsfeld zwischen Fluglinien-und Gelegenheitsverkehr' [1970] ZLW 110–124; J.G. Thomka-Gaszdik, 'Are Inclusive Tour Charters Scheduled or Non-Scheduled Services?' in McWhinney/Bradley, *Freedom of the Air* (1968), pp. 106-122; E.J. Driscoll, 'The Role of Charter Transport in International Aviation' *Air Law*, vol. I (1976), pp. 74-82.
16. See ICAO Doc. 7278-C/841 (see note 13, *supra*), at p. 3.
17. Multilateral Agreement on Commercial Rights of Non-scheduled Air Services in Europe, Paris, April 30, 1956; hereinafter cited as Paris Agreement.

Pursuant to this Convention, facilities were granted for such services on the following conditions:

Article 1:
'This Agreement applies to any civil aircraft
a. registered in a State member of the European Civil Aviation Conference, and
b. operated by a national of one of the Contracting States duly authorised by the competent national authority of that State, when engaged in international flights for remuneration or hire, other than scheduled international air services, in the territories covered by this Agreement...'.

Article 2:
'(1) The contracting States agree to admit the aircraft referred to in Article 1 ... where such aircraft are engaged in
a. flights for the purpose of meeting humanitarian or emergency needs;
b. taxi-class passenger flights of occasional character on request, provided that the aircraft does not have a seating capacity of more than 6 passengers and provided that the destination is chosen by the hirer or hirers and no part of the capacity of the aircraft is resold to the public[18];
c. flights on which the entire space is hired by a single person (individual, firm, corporation or institution) for the carriage of his or its staff or merchandise, provided that no part of such space is resold;
d. single flights, no operator or group of operators being entitled under this paragraph to more than one flight per month between the same two traffic centres for all aircraft available to him.
(2) The same treatment shall be accorded to aircraft engaged in either of the following activities:

---

18. In the 'Hannover Messe' dispute between the Netherlands Civil Aviation Service and the Dutch charter carrier Transavia the situation has been discussed of a trade fair generating sufficient traffic to warrant the operation of a regular service for the duration of that fair, which led the authorities to refuse permission for the simultaneous operation of the 'special event' charter flights on the route in question. The case required an interpretation of the terms 'special event' and 'scheduled air service'. The Netherlands Director-General of Civil Aviation felt that permission could not be granted because such charter flights would divert traffic from scheduled services to the same destination, as KLM Royal Dutch Airlines would operate a scheduled service to Hanover for the duration of the trade fair (*i.e.* two daily return flights during the period from April 25 to May 4, 1974). Transavia lodged an appeal against this decision with the Netherlands Council of State, the competent authority in such a case. The Council ruled against the decision of the Director-General, being of the opinion that he could not reasonably disqualify the Hanover Trade Fair as a 'special event', nor consider KLM's flights to Hanover as 'scheduled air services'. The Council's decision has been criticised by K. Veenstra, see '"Special Event Charter Flights" and "Scheduled Air Service": Some Problems of Interpretation', *Air Law*, vol. I (1976), 294-299.

a. the transport of freight exclusively;
b. the transport of passengers between regions which have no reasonably direct connection by scheduled air service;...'.[19]

The applicability of the above-mentioned Agreement was considered in an interesting case in Norway. Article 2(2) was invoked by the Swedish company Aerocontact when one of its air taxis had made a landing on a lake just inside Norwegian territory without the previous authorisation required by Norwegian law. The landing was in line with the Agreement's provisions. The Court ruled that the relevant provisions of the Norwegian Civil Aviation Act were without effect, since 'customarily' prior authorisation was not insisted upon by Norwegian authorities. The application of the Agreement was thus ruled out by the Court in an indirect manner.[20]

The applicability of the Agreement was again involved on the following occasions:

1. In 1981 France refused to issue a permit to the Cunard shipping company for a charter carrying its passengers from Southampton to Le Havre; in doing so it based its case on a very restrictive interpretation of the 1956 Agreement, arguing that the company's passengers could not be brought under the same heading as its own personnel within the meaning of the Agreement.

2. In 1982 France refused a permit for a charter involving the transport by KLM Royal Dutch Airlines from Southampton to Paris of the personnel of a big foreign company. KLM alleged that the French attitude was without justification in the light of Article 2, para 1(c) and (d) of the Agreement. Following this protest France promised to reconsider its attitude in future.

5. Cabotage

The Chicago Convention also contains provisions on cabotage. In international law, cabotage was originally held to apply to a state reserving to itself the right to restrict all coastal navigation between two points within its territory for the exclusive use of its own subjects. The

---

19. See on this subject: E.A.G. Verploeg, *The Road towards a European Common Air Market* (thesis Utrecht, 1963); W. Stabenow, 'The International Factors in Air Transport under the Treaty establishing the European Economic Community', [1967] JALC 117–131; Bin Cheng, 'Transport Law of the European Communities', (1963) 16 *Current Legal Problems* 197–219; J. Erdmenger. 'A new Dimension to Civil Aviation through European Economic Integration', in Wassenbergh and van Fenema, *International Air Transport in the Eighties* (1981), pp. 35-44.
   See also the reports on aviation subjects to the Xth International Congress (Budapest, 1978) of the International Academy of Comparative Law, notably the General Report by Sundberg (see note 20, *infra*).
20. See for this case: J.W.F. Sundberg, *Chartering of Aircraft*, General Report (section III.D) to the Xth International Congress (Budapest, 1978) of the International Academy of Comparative Law.

objective was of course, to protect the state's own navigation. This concept has also been incorporated into air law. In the Chicago Convention, the scope and application of the term cabotage has acquired a rather broad interpretation; referring to Article 7, a state may reserve to itself the exclusive right of air transport within its own territorial limits and its overseas territories as well as between those two areas of sovereignty.

Bin Cheng gives the following definition: aerial cabotage 'applies to air transport between any two points in the same political unit, that is to say, in the territory of a State as the term is used in air law'.[21] Matte's definition expresses the same principle, but in more precise terms: 'Le terme "cabotage" comprend, en général, toute activité commerciale de transport, caractérisée par le fait que le transporteur embarque des passagers, du courrier ou des marchandises à un certain endroit, à destination d'un autre point, tous les deux points (de départ et de destination) se trouvant à l'intérieur du même pays'.[22]

At present there is a tendency to broaden the interpretation of 'cabotage' in such a manner that it constitutes an obstacle to free aviation.[23] A state may not, according to Article 7, to the exclusion of other states, grant the privilege of cabotage to any other state or to the airline company of any other state. Such an interpretation of cabotage has the effect of making states consider only their short-term interests, which do not always coincide with their long-term ones. The hopes expressed in the preamble to the Convention – equality of opportunity, sound and economical operation – have yet to be fulfilled in practice.

6. Airline co-operation

6.1. POOLING AND OTHER FORMS OF CO-OPERATION

A form of co-operation between airline companies with purely commercial ends are the so-called 'pooling arrangements'. A 'pooling arrangement' involves at least two companies co-ordinating their flight programmes and sharing the proceeds of their services operated on the same route on the basis of a fixed formula, such as each company's share in the total production. When, besides the proceeds, the costs are also shared on such a basis, their co-operation is commonly called a 'joint venture'.

21. Bin Cheng, *The Law of International Air Transport* (1962), p. 314.
22. Nicolas M. Matte, *Traité de Droit Aérien-Aéronautique* (3rd ed., 1980), p. 173. See also his interpretation of the term 'cabotage'. Cf. the English version of this book (*Treatise on Air-Aeronautical Law* (1981)), pp. 171 *et seq.*
23. See on this subject: D. Goedhuis, 'The Cabotage Concept in Aviation', *Interavia* (Review of World Aviation), 1952, No. 1, pp. 41-44 and No. 2, pp. 97-98; W.M. Sheehan, 'Air Cabotage and the Chicago Convention', *Harvard Law Review* 1157–1167 (1980); *Cabotage in International Air Transport. Historical and Present-Day Aspects* (Institut du Transport Aérien (ITA), Paris, Study 1969/7); L. Lewis, 'Air Cabotage: Historical and Modern day Perspectives' [1980] JALC 1059-1088.

Yet another form of co-operation is the consortium, which involves a combination of companies, working together for joint account. They provide capital and other material assets according to a certain ratio, and at the end of the fiscal year profits and losses are shared on the same basis. An example of this form of cooperation is the Scandinavian Airlines System (SAS), in which Sweden, Norway and Denmark participate.

Yet another method of working together is restricted to technical matters, *e.g.* the purchasing of aircraft and their maintenance, with the companies involved retaining their full independence. Such a form of cooperation was exemplified by KSSU, whose membership consisted of KLM, SAS, Swissair and UTA (Union de Transports Aériens) and ATLAS (consisting of Air France, Alitalia, Lufthansa and Sabena).

Currently the practice of interchanging aircraft is becoming more and more popular. This may be done on a long-term basis, and either with a crew (wet lease), or without a crew (dry lease). It may be regarded as a form of leasing.[24]

Organisations like Air Afrique[25] and the East African Airways Corporation[26] should really be classified as multinational organisations, but they may be mentioned here as other examples of international co-operation. The East African Airways Corporation has been dissolved since.

6.2. CODE-SHARING

Each carrier has its own identification code used *inter alia* to identify its flights. This code is assigned by IATA exclusively to one carrier. However, code-sharing by airlines has become an important practice in the course of the past 10 years.

When is it possible to speak of code-sharing? I cannot express it better than Van Houtte who states 'Code-sharing occurs where airlines agree to use a joint airline designator code for flights operated by one of them'.[27]

---

24. See also Dong-Chun Shin, 'Foreign Ownership of Airlines', *Korean Journal of Air Law*, 1993, pp. 207-263; P.V. Mifsud, 'Foreign Investment in Air Transport in the Emerging Multilateral Era', in *The Use of Airspace and Outer Space for All Mankind in the 21st Century*, Proceedings of the International Conference on Air Transport and Space Application in a New World (Tokyo, June 2-5, 1993), Chia-Jui Cheng, ed., pp. 161-166; and H.A. Wassenbergh, 'Future Regulation to Allow Multi-national Arrangements between Air Carriers (Cross-border Alliances), Putting an End to Air Carrier Nationalism', *Air and Space Law*, vol. XX (1995), pp. 164-168. Note that the difference between interchanging, leasing, hire and charter is often difficult to discern: for more information on these subjects see Chapter VIII, paragraph 2.2 *infra.*

25. Air Afrique members are: Benin, Burkina Faso (formerly Upper Volta), the Central African Republic, Chad, Congo-Brazzaville, Ivory Coast, Mauretania, Niger, Senegal and Zaïre. See also *infra*, section 7 of this chapter.

26. East African Airways consisted of Kenya, Tanzania and Uganda, and was dissolved in February 1977 following bankruptcy. See also ICAO Circular 100-AT/21 (1970), Report on the East African Airways Corporation.

27. B. van Houtte, 'Community Competition Law in the Air Transport Sector (II)', *Air and Space Law*, vol. XVIII (1993), pp. 275-287.

Normally, a key element in these co-operative arrangements is that the airlines concerned integrate their operations in varying degrees, so that they can offer, under their own name, a streamlined product which includes flights operated with their partners' aircraft. This practice can take different forms depending on the commercial objectives of the airlines concerned.

According to Weber there are two main variants in code-sharing.[28] In the first variant two successive carriers utilise the same flight number and carrier code in a situation where the passenger has to change plane (and carrier) at a stopover. In the second variant one and the same flight carries two codes and two flight numbers even though the flight is operated by only one of the airlines. In a number of cases variant one can be combined with variant two.

The European Commission observed that customers may be unaware of the existence of a code-sharing operation when they purchase a ticket or be unaware of its implications. Unless they are clearly informed as to the nature of the code-shared flight, including the identity of the actual operating carrier, they may be victims of misrepresentation. In addition, when code-shared flights involve connections between the code-sharing partners, they may be under the illusion that they are purchasing a true on-line service. In either case they may find themselves flying on a carrier which they may not willingly have chosen and/or which they consider to offer a lower quality of service than that of the carrier on which they believed they were purchasing a ticket.

So the fundamental issue in consumer information is one of transparency: the nature of the code-shared flight should be made absolutely clear to the customer, not only at the time of purchasing of the ticket but as early as possible during the customer's travel enquiry process.[29]

Abeyratne points out the advantages of code-sharing in saying that 'By concluding code-sharing arrangements an airline at the same time is able to reduce the operations of its own aircraft and to offer more flight connections under the airline's own designator code and own flight number. In addition to this the economic risk of the operation of a route is reduced as well as handling and air navigation fees are saved. As a result of a codesharing arrangement, an airline might also find it worthwhile to serve points it had not previously served.'[30]

28. L. Weber, 'Legal Activities of the International Air Transport Association (IATA) 1993-1994', *Air and Space Law*, vol. XX (1995), pp. 32-34; see also J.E.C. de Groot, 'Code-Sharing. United States' Policies and the Lessons for Europe', *Air and Space Law*, vol. XIX (1994), pp. 62-74.

29. See *Code Sharing*, A Study into the Consequences for the Internal European Air Transport Market, European Commission, Directorate General for Transport, 1996. See also *infra*, Chapter III, at the end of Paragraph 4.

30. R.I.R. Abeyratne, *Legal and Regulatory Issues of Computer Reservation Systems and Code Sharing Agreements in Air Transport*, Forum for Air and Space Law, vol. 3, 1995, at p. 119.

Being such a relatively new phenomenon code-sharing has not yet found its way into all bilateral air traffic agreements. To which this may lead is summed up by ICAO with regard to the Bermuda II Agreement: 'Since 1988, when the US Department of Transportation (DOT), noted the absence of "automatic authorization for codesharing operations" in the "Bermuda II" air services agreement with the United Kingdom, it has required codesharing operations to receive a specific authorization, as in the case of the wet-lease of an aircraft or a blocked space arrangement, in addition to underlying traffic rights. A "public interest" test is now applied, involving an assessment of the impact of the proposed codeshared service on competition, on the overall balance of bilateral benefits and on the possibility of using the authorization as a regulatory negotiating lever. It is important to note however that the DOT decision did not turn codesharing into a quasi-traffic right. It simply stated that in the absence of a bilateral provision on codesharing, the government is free to regulate and approve such agreements as it wishes. Subsequently, this approach prompted some countries to secure codesharing rights by incorporating a specific codesharing provision in their bilateral air services agreements with the US and other countries.'[31]

As a final note, I would like to point out that in the USA and Canada specific legislation has been enacted for the disclosure of code-sharing agreements.

7. Nationality

How has the concept of nationality evolved in public air law? What has been its impact? The first person of authority to examine these points was the French jurist Fauchille, whose call for international rules to govern aviation finally led to the inclusion of several Articles in the Paris Convention to deal with the matter.

Article 6 of the Paris Convention stipulates that aircraft shall have the nationality of the state in which they are registered. The same rule is to be found in Article 6 of the Ibero-American Convention of Madrid[32] and in Article 7 of the Pan-American Convention of Havana[33] During the Second World War, the nationality of an aircraft proved to be a fully recognised fact, even for aircraft belonging to countries that were not members of the aforementioned Conventions.

However, as regards the question whether an aircraft is part of the territory of the state of nationality the situation is different. An aircraft *may* belong to the national territory and does so in any case when so designated in a Treaty or Convention rule. An example is to be found in Article 23, section 2 of the 1952 Rome Convention which reads as follows:

31. ICAO, Air Transport Committee, *Study on the Implications of Airline Codesharing*, AT-WP/1785, 21/5/96, Appendix. See also H.A. Wassenbergh, *Principles and practices in air transport regulations*, 1993, at pp. 175-168.
32. See Chap. I, note 12, *supra*.
33. See Chap. I, note 13, *supra*.

For the purpose of this Convention a ship or an aircraft on the high seas shall be regarded as part of the territory of the State in which it is registered.

The Chicago Convention lacks such a rule which might have been included in its Article 2.

In international transport it has always been a matter of prime importance for an aircraft or ship to enjoy the protection of the state to which it belongs, while on the other hand the interests of third parties have also been furthered through this link between a state and the ship or aircraft flying its flag. For ships, the principle of nationality is a universally accepted norm. Looking at other types of transport, however, like rail and road transport, one is struck by the fact that nationality does not carry much weight there, notwithstanding the fact that means of transport are often registered in a particular state. Consequently, state attention and protection are lacking.

The nationality issue occupies a prominent place in the Chicago Convention, which underscores once more the fact that the nationality of an aircraft may now be considered as a 'fait accompli'. Now that this fundamental principle has been accepted we may mention *en passant* the problem of jurisdiction in respect of events or incidents on board. Jurisdiction in civil matters (births, deaths, marriages, contracts on board aircraft) has repeatedly come up for discussion, but has not yet been given formal expression in legal rules. For offences committed on board, however, jurisdiction has been provided in the Tokyo Convention, the Hague Convention and the Montreal Convention.[34]

The Chicago Convention settles the nationality issue in Article 17, which states: 'Aircraft have the nationality of the State in which they are registered', the very words used in the Paris Convention quoted above. Article 18 of the Chicago Convention stipulates that 'An aircraft cannot be validly registered in more than one State, but its registration may be changed from one State to another'. According to Article 19, 'The registration or transfer of registration of aircraft in any contracting State shall be made in accordance with its laws and regulations'. Article 20 requires that 'Every aircraft engaged in international air navigation shall bear its appropriate nationality and registration marks'. Finally, Article 21 states that:

'Each contracting State undertakes to supply to any other contracting State or to the International Civil Aviation Organisation, on demand, information concerning the registration and ownership of any particular aircraft registered in that State. In addition, each contracting State shall furnish reports to the International Civil Aviation Organisation, under such regulations as the latter may prescribe, giving such pertinent data as can be made available concerning the ownership and control of aircraft registered in that State and habitually engaged in international air

34. See chapter X, *infra*.

navigation. The data thus obtained by the International Civil Aviation Organisation shall be made available by it on request to the other contracting States'.

The issue of nationality and registration, viewed in conjunction with the joint operation of aircraft by several states, may give rise to both political and legal entanglements.[35] They first arose around the creation of Air Afrique in 1961.[36]

The point at issue was whether this form of multinational airline operation was in keeping with the provisions of Articles 17 to 21 and Articles 77 and 79 of the Convention, all of which are relevant to co-operation, so the Legal Committee of ICAO convened to decide whether Articles 77 and 79 could be applied in this case.[37] The conclusion was that the Chicago Convention did not need modifying, provided that certain conditions were met:

a. the states involved shall create a joint register;
b. this register shall consist of as many sections as there are participating states;
c. aircraft shall always be registered in a section allotted to a particular state;
d. instead of national markings, the registered aircraft shall display a 'communal' marking;
e. the state, designated as the state of registration, shall carry out all the registration procedures imposed by the Chicago Convention; and
f. the states involved are jointly and severally liable.

Yet, for all these conditions which seemingly provide a solution, the fact remains that there still has to be a state of registration.

During the deliberations in the Legal Committee doubts were expressed as to whether Air Afrique should be regarded as an 'operating agency', or not. At present, Air Afrique aircraft are being registered in the Ivory Coast. A similar problem was created by the East African Airways Corporation.

Another point at issue was whether the nationality provisions of the Chicago Convention were also applicable to state aircraft. In raising this question it must be remembered, however, that the Convention's provisions apply only to civil aircraft. In my submission it would be inconsistent with the general rules of air law to assume that state

---

35. See on this subject Dr. Khairy El-Hussainy, 'Registration and Nationality of Aircraft operated by International Agencies in Law and Practice' *Air Law*, vol. X (1985), 15–27. See also I.H.Ph. Diederiks-Verschoor, 'International Co-operation and its Implications for Aircraft Registration and Nationality', *Annals of Air and Space Law*, vol. XIX, Part I (1994), pp. 145-159.
36. See ICAO Circular 98-AT/19 (1970), Treaty relating to Air Transport in Africa (Establishment of Air Afrique).
37. See for the minutes and documents of this 16th session of the ICAO Legal Committee (Paris, 1967): ICAO Doc. 8787-LC/156-1 and ICAO Doc. 8787-LC/156-2.

aircraft are incapable of possessing a nationality. Cooper even goes so far as to insist that it is not the registration that constitutes nationality: it is only a proof of nationality.[38]

Although not directly relevant in this context, it is perhaps interesting to recall that the Convention has been particularly successful in creating uniformity in the rules on matters of a technical nature, thereby furthering the cause of safety. To quote an example, according to Article 25, states are required to provide rescue services to aircraft in distress.[39] Also included are uniform rules relating to the investigation and inquiries into accidents. These are to be found in Article 26 which reads as follows:

> 'In the event of an accident to an aircraft of a contracting State occurring in the territory of another contracting State, and involving death or serious injury, or indicating serious technical defect in the aircraft or air navigation facilities, the State in which the accident occurs will institute an inquiry into the circumstances of the accident, in accordance, so far as its laws permit, with the procedure which may be recommended by the International Civil Aviation Organisation. The State in which the aircraft is registered shall be given the opportunity to appoint observers to be present at the inquiry and the State holding the inquiry shall communicate the report and findings in the matter to that State.'

Closely related to this Article is Annex 13 which contains technical and procedural rules to be applied to accident investigations. Of prime importance is the fact that the investigation must focus exclusively on discovering the cause of an accident and preventing future accidents: establishing criminal or civil liability is not to be its purpose. This arrangement enables those involved in the inquiry to give all information in complete freedom and without any restraint. Publication of the investigation report is also a requirement but Article 26 does not specify a time limit. This is a weakness which is illustrated occasionally by the unwillingness of states to publish reports which throw an unfavourable light on their aviation safety rules or practices.[40]

In October 1994 the eighth edition of Annex 13 became applicable. It inserted into Chapter 7 (Accident Prevention Measures) a recommendation regarding the introduction and use of formal incident-reporting systems for accident prevention. It will be noted that due

---

38. J.C. Cooper, 'National Status of Aircraft' [1950] JALC 292–311 at 307.
39. See Chapter IX, *infra*, on assistance and salvage.
40. See also section 2 of Chapter VI, *infra*, and M.S. Kamminga, 'Some Aspects of Aircraft Accident Inquiries' in *Studi in onore di Antonio Ambrosini* (1957), pp. 577–585; A.A. van Wijk, *Aircraft Accident Enquiry in the Netherlands* (thesis Amsterdam, 1974). See W.H.van Baren, 'Recent aviation case law from the Benelux', *Air and Space Law*, vol. XVIII (1993), pp. 29–35, at pp. 34–35, for a case regarding publication of an accident investigation report. See also D.J. Slijper, 'Standardization of Safety Requirements', in *The Use of Airspace and Outer Space for All Mankind in the 21st Century*, Proceedings of the International Conference on Air Transport and Space Application in a New World (Tokyo, June 2-5, 1993), Chia-Jui Cheng, ed., pp. 185-193.

to the non-mandatory nature of this recommendation, unwillingness of States to comply may prevent the disclosure and dissemination of vital information here as well.

8. Airports

The first indication of the importance of airports in a legal sense is to be found in Annex H, Article 1, of the Paris Convention, which requires foreign aircraft to take off and land on an airfield specially designated for the purpose by the appropriate authorities. Nearly all states have adopted this rule in their legislations. In the experimental phase of aviation a pilot would land wherever he thought fit, but as soon as the initial technical difficulties had been overcome the airport became the only legally sanctioned contact point for an aircraft with the ground. Considering the present stage of technology it would be surprising if the governmental authorities were to permit otherwise.

The Paris Convention provided that airports could be given customs facilities; moreover, sanitary measures were encouraged. Article 10 of the Chicago Convention states that every aircraft 'shall, if the regulations of that State so require, land at an airport designated by that State for the purpose of customs and other examination'. This requirement must be viewed in connection with Article 15 dealing with airport fees and similar charges. All this is subject to the provisions of Article 68 which provides that: 'Each contracting State may, subject to the provisions of this Convention, designate the route to be followed within its territory by any international air service and the airports which any such service may use'. The following decision illustrates the impact of the Convention.

On October 4, 1956, the criminal court of Dakar, Senegal, sentenced a passenger accused of diamond smuggling while making an intermediary stop at Yoff airport to a fine, a prison term and confiscation of the diamonds. The passenger, who was on his way from Monrovia, Liberia to Dakar, Senegal, had failed to declare a large number of diamonds found in his luggage during a customs inspection at Yoff airport. However, the Dakar Court of Appeal decided on May 15, 1957, that pursuant to Annex 9, Chap. 5, para. 3 of the Chicago Convention the luggage of a passenger in transit was not subject to inspection unless for reasons of national security; those reasons did not include the carrying of diamonds. The decision of the criminal court of October 4, 1956, was therefore nullified and the passenger released.[41]

A comparison between airports in Europe and in the United States shows that the US airports are mostly privately owned, whereas in Europe some degree of government control has usually been retained. Consequently, there can be no question of a uniform type of management of airports: each state has its own regulations, in spite

---

41. *Ministère Public et Administration des Douanes* v. *Schreiber et Air France*, Appeal Court of Dakar, May 15, 1957; [1957] RFDA 355 *et seq.*; IATA ACLR No. 57.

of the rules given in Annex 14 of the Chicago Convention. The latter, it must be added, contain technical rather than legal matters.

There are two different kinds of airports: civil airports and military airports. The distinction between military and non-military airports is relevant because their legal status is different: military airports are subject to other rules and jurisdiction than those in force for civil airports.

The following legal points may occur in connection with airports:

a. problems concerning the ownership of the airport, physical obstacles in the surrounding area, easements, etc.;

b. the liability of the airport operator in case of accidents, a liability which in most cases comes under civil law. It must be remembered, though, that this liability is quite distinct from that incurred by the air traffic control services;

c. the juridical form for airport-management (*e.g.* incorporation), and for allied problems such as responsibility for maintenance; and

d. the legal relationship between the users of the airport and the airport management, and their relationship *vis-à-vis* the government authorities, the airport police, etc.

Due to the multitude of national legislations involved these legal problems assume a different character in each country.[42]

9. Aviation personnel

The technical standards required for aircraft and the issuing of certificates of competency and licences for the crew are matters which have been made subject to uniform rules.[43] Annex 1 of the Chicago Convention contains a system of rules on pilot certificates. These rules were introduced for urgent reasons of safety. The Annex constitutes an elaboration of Articles 32 and 33 of the Convention proper.

---

42. See for the latest developments, especially regarding the so-called mega-airports, *Aéroports du Futur/Airports of the Future*, 1996, proceedings of an international symposium (Paris, December 15-17, 1995).

43. Art. 32 of the Chicago Convention reads:
   '(a) The pilot of every aircraft and the other members of the operating crew of every aircraft engaged in international navigation shall be provided with certificates of competency and licences issued or rendered valid by the State in which the aircraft is registered.
   (b) Each contracting State reserves the right to refuse to recognise, for the purpose of flight above its own territory, certificates of competency and licences granted to any of its nationals by another contracting State'.
   Art. 33 reads:
   'Certificates of airworthiness and certificates of competency and licences issued or rendered valid by the contracting State in which the aircraft is registered, shall be recognised as valid by other contracting States, provided that the requirements under which such certificates and licences were issued or rendered valid are equal to or above the minimum standards which may be established from time to time pursuant to this Convention'

27

9.1. THE AIRCRAFT COMMANDER

The aircraft commander occupies a special position within the legal framework. Right from the beginning the importance of his position has been recognised, and it has been given careful consideration since 1926, first by CITEJA and later by ICAO. As early as 1891 a study had been published on the subject in connection with balloon navigation.[44] CITEJA formulated two preliminary drafts during the period before the Second World War. The first concerned the status of the commander; the second examined the position of the crew, and there was a tendency in favour of merging the two drafts. In 1946, the draft convention was reviewed in the light of the latest technological developments and a new draft convention was drawn up, but never adopted.[45] Yet it is most desirable that the rights and duties of a person in such a responsible position should be carefully defined.

One might compare the position of an aircraft commander with that of a ship's captain, but there are notable differences: a journey by aircraft is shorter; passengers and crew are less numerous; the freedom of movement on board is very limited. All these factors affect the relationships amongst those on board an aircraft, and contribute to making the aircraft commander's position quite different from that of a ship's captain.

Since 1947 ICAO has been working on an analysis of the legal status of aircraft personnel. The studies and drafts of the former CITEJA served as a starting-point. Yet ICAO has not made much progress beyond revising an earlier draft dating from 1931.

In a general manner the powers and responsibilities of the aircraft commander may be categorised as follows:

1. The responsibility for the perfect condition of the aircraft and the welfare of the crew, the preparations for the flight and its successful completion. This description, taken from Soviet law, is admirably suited for codification in international law. It includes the commander's duty to obtain the proper flight documents and the cargo manifests, to carry out pre-takeoff checks, etc.[46]

2. The right of the commander to issue strict orders to crew and passengers. This role is especially important in the event of criminal offences being committed on board. Ruhwedel bases this authority over the passengers on a silent agreement between the passengers and the airline company. As regards the status of the crew, Ruhwedel maintains that the employer (the company) delegates part of his powers to the commander, who is thus established in a position of authority over the crew.[47]

44. See A. Wilhelm, 'De la situation juridique des aéronautes en droit international', *Journal du Droit International Privé* (Clunet, 1891), pp. 440-452.

45. See on this subject: M.S. Kamminga, *The Aircraft Commander in Commercial Air Transportation* (thesis Leiden, 1953); Nicolas M. Matte, *The International Legal Status of the Aircraft Commander* (1975).

46. Cf. Art. 29 of the Chicago Convention.

47. E. Ruhwedel, *Die Rechtsstellung des Flugzeugkommandanten im zivilen Luftverkehr*, Schriften zum Deutschen und Europäischen Zivil-, Handels- und Prozessrecht, No. 27 (1964), pp. 109 *et seq.*

3. In addition, the commander has the authority to undertake all necessary measures to ensure the safe completion of the flight. He must have authority, for instance, to have repairs carried out when necessary, and to arrange for fresh supplies on behalf of the company by which he is employed. When no airline officials are present in a particular country, the commander should be empowered to act as the official representative of the company. As the granting of such authority and duties is entirely at the discretion of the company it would be better to draw up international rules to cover this point, making it compulsory for contracting states to adapt their own legislations accordingly.

4. The administrative duties of the commander include the registration of births and deaths on board an aircraft, the authority to perform marriages or to act as the competent authority for drawing up wills.[48]

5. The commander decides whether and in what way to render assistance in search and rescue operations in the event of an accident, in accordance with the provisions of the Convention.[49]

According to Kamminga it would be desirable to include into a future draft dealing with the status of an aircraft commander an obligation for him to ensure the safe completion of the flight. Moreover, his liability should be limited to cases of malicious intent or gross negligence.[50] It should be noted in this context that the commander's civil liability is given only scant attention in the Warsaw and Rome Conventions, but more so in Article 10 of the Tokyo Convention. On the whole, it is mainly governed by general law in the various national legislations. Admittedly, the Annexes of the Chicago Convention contain a number of recommendations regarding the commander's conduct, but although they are usually observed in practice they do not have force of law. This means that the provisions laid down in the Annexes will have to be incorporated into national law if they are to become legally binding. Unification and codification of those rules is therefore a matter of considerable importance.

In April 1980, the legal status of the aircraft commander was examined by a panel of ICAO experts on the basis of a study[51] prepared by the secretariat and in the light of comments by states and international organisations. The panel was also supposed to prepare a list of operational and legal problems related to the subject which in the opinion of the panel required a solution, and to suggest any specific solutions for further consideration by the appropriate bodies of ICAO.

---

48. Cf. Art. 7 of the Draft Convention on the Legal Status of the Aircraft Commander, ICAO Doc. 4006 (1947); the text of this Draft Convention is also to be found in the treatises by Kamminga and Matte referred to in note 45, *supra*.

49. See also Chap. IX, *infra*, on assistance and salvage.

50. Kamminga (see note 45, *supra*), at p. 170.

51. Study on the Legal Status of the Aircraft Commander, ICAO Doc. C-WP/6946 (October 26, 1979). See also the reports in the section entitled 'News from the international organisations' in *Air Law*, notably in Vol. V (1980), pp. 53-54 and 187-188.

In June 1980 the Council acknowledged the report of the panel and decided to submit it to the Legal and Technical Commissions of the Assembly to decide on the further course of action to be taken. The issue was referred back to the panel, which suggested in June 1981 that the matter should be dropped. This suggestion was taken over by the ICAO Council.

In connection with the position of the commander the duties and the liability of the ground control services require our attention as well. As a result of major technological developments like radar, aviation is becoming more and more dependent on the assistance and co-operation of ground control. 'Ground control' is a term covering various groups of persons such as airport management, air traffic control personnel, radio telephonists and meteorologists; yet some governments are not always familiar with all the specific requirements of aviation. The situation in the railways, by way of comparison, is totally different. The entire management and running of the railways is in the hands of the railway company.

In Annex 2 of the Convention entitled 'Rules of the Air', air traffic procedures are set out in detail. In Chapter 3 it is stated that the aircraft commander is responsible for carrying out the directions of air traffic control. It also provides, however, that the aircraft commander is ultimately responsible. How to reconcile these conflicting rules? In general, the commander will be bound by the instructions given by air traffic control. In certain cases, however, the commander may deviate from those instructions, for instance in an emergency. In such a situation air traffic control must be kept informed.[52]

Reading through the relevant provisions one is struck by the fact that the commander's powers in criminal law have been adequately defined in the Tokyo Convention of 1963 and the Hague Convention of 1970.[53] In comparison, the private law aspects of his responsibilities seem to have been rather neglected, in terms of international law.[54] As Matte has recommended, the rights and obligations of the commander should be compiled and integrated into a uniform and mandatory text.[55]

9.2. OTHER PERSONNEL

Leaving aside the aircraft commander with his special position, the other personnel involved in aviation may be divided into two categories, i.e.

---

52. See also the Report on the Liability of Air Traffic Control Agencies, ICAO Doc. 8582-LC/153-2, pp. 11–121, prepared by a sub-committee of the ICAO Legal Committee for the 15th session of this Committee at Montreal in September, 1964. See also on this subject the notes by Early, Garner, Ruegsegger and Schiff, 'The Expanding Liability of air Traffic Controllers' [1973] JALC 599-624.
53. See Chapter X, *infra*.
54. See on this subject Flavio de Planta, *Principes de Droit International Privé Applicables aux Actes Accomplis et aux Faits Commis à Bord d'un Aéronef* (1955). See also J.W.F. Sundberg, 'The aircraft commander in legal turbulence', *Air Worthy*, pp. 169-194.
55. See Matte (note 45, *supra*), at p. 102.

ground personnel and flying personnel, according to their function or assignment.

9.2.1. Ground personnel

Included in this group are employees who, without leaving the ground, are involved in the preparation and guidance of aircraft. The group therefore includes airport personnel, meteorological, safety and other ground services personnel.

9.2.2. Flying personnel

This category includes anyone who normally performs his duties during the flight and whose presence on board throughout the flight is essential: the commander, the co-pilot and the flight attendants.

In most national legislations flying personnel is sub-divided into the following categories:

a. persons in charge of command, the actual flying or technical matters during the flight, and
b. persons performing ancillary services, for instance cabin stewards.

In terms of international law, the civil liability of flying personnel is laid down in the Warsaw Convention, the Hague Protocol (which amended the Warsaw Convention), the Guadalajara Convention, the Guatemala Protocol, the Rome Convention of 1952 and its Montreal Protocol of 1978. Apart from these international agreements, their liability is governed by general law and employment contracts.

Regrettably, the legal status of ground personnel has hardly any base in international law while, on a national level, it enjoys the protection of rules applicable to aviation personnel generally only in isolated cases. Consequently, their position is at best covered merely by general provisions of domestic law and employment contracts. In this context the different interpretations given to the terms 'agent' and 'servant' in domestic and international law respectively must be mentioned here as possible sources of legal problems. Both ICAO and ILO, the International Labour Organisation, have already taken note of this problem in the course of their debates and discussions.

The category of ground personnel deserves a special mention in connection with the vital role played by the air traffic control services, whose duty it is to ensure a safe and orderly flow of traffic. A strike action undertaken by this group of personnel may have the most serious consequences for thousands of people not even remotely involved in the conflict. Liability of their employer, usually a governmental authority, may be assumed and has been upheld in court on a number of occasions. It should be borne in mind, however, that an action against the government is available to the airlines only. The persons suffering damage may sue the carrier on the basis of their contract of carriage.[56]

10. Jurisdiction

In air law the following areas of jurisdiction may be distinguished: the airspace above the national territory, the territorial waters, and the high seas.

State sovereignty extends to the airspace above national territory and the territorial waters. There is an important qualification to this basic rule, however, in respect of the territorial waters, where no right of innocent passage for aircraft exists like there is for ships in the same area.

For air law jurisdiction above the high seas the provisions of Article 12 of the Chicago Convention apply. This Article should be read in conjunction with Annexes 2, 6, 11 and 12 of the Chicago Convention. The Paris Convention, in its Annexes, already contained technical specifications valid in that area.

In general, the law of the state in which the aircraft is registered will be applicable to the aircraft during its flight above the high seas. Disputes concerning the use of the airspace above the high seas may, however, arise in connection with military exercises and nuclear testing; they may also occur in respect of the Air Defence Identification Zones.[57] Mention must be made here that recently a new Article 3-*bis* has been added to the Chicago Convention recognizing among

56. See about this subject H.P. Kehrberger, 'The German Go-Slow Action' *Air Law*, vol. III (1978), pp. 175-178; C.A. Heymann, 'Standards of Care for Air Traffic Controllers', *Annual Survey of American Law* (1979), pp. 85-93; Federico Videla Escalada, 'The international regulation of liability in the field of air traffic control services', *Air Worthy*, pp. 195-213; A.E. du Perron, 'Liability of air traffic control agencies and airport operators in civil law jurisdictions', *Air Law*, vol. X (1985), pp. 203-216; and S.K. Hamalian, 'Liability of the United States Government in cases of air traffic controller negligence', *Annals of Air and Space Law*, Vol. XI (1986), pp. 55-85. Cf. *Musini & Iberia v. France*, Tribunal Administratif de Nantes (France), July 1, 1980; RFDA 1980, pp. 312-321.

57. For literature see H. Drion, 'The Council of ICAO as International Legislator over the High Seas', *Studi in onore di Antonio Ambrosini* (1957), pp. 323-332; E. Pépin, 'The Law of the Air and the Draft Articles concerning the Law of the Sea adopted by the International Law Commission at its Eighth Session', UN Conference on the Law of the Sea, Geneva, 1958, *Official Records*, Vol. I pp. 64-74; J. Carroz, 'International Legislation on Air Navigation over the High Seas' [1959] JALC 158-172; P.P. Heller, 'Flying over the Exclusive Economic Zone' [1978] ZLW 15-17; P.P. Heller, 'French Bomb Tests and International Law', (1978) 8 *Recent Law* 252-256; E. Cuadra, 'Air Defense Identification Zones – Creeping Jurisdiction in the Airspace', 18 *Virginia Journal of International Law* 485-512 (1978/9); and J.T. Murchison, *The Contiguous Airspace Zone in International Law* (thesis McGill, 1955).

other things that every state must refrain from resorting to the use of weapons against civil aircraft in flight.[58]

Apart from the Conventions mentioned above a number of other instruments of international law are relevant to the jurisdiction issue. In the Convention on the High Seas of 1958[59] some rules have been devoted to air law. Article 15 provides that piracy can also be directed against aircraft; Article 23 gives rules for the pursuit and seizure of aircraft. Article 3 of the Continental Shelf Convention[60] relates to the airspace above the shelf.[61] During the Third United Nations Conference on the Law of the Sea, an Informal Composite Negotiating Text was presented. In this proposal the territorial sea limit was extended to 12 miles, and an entirely new concept of an 'economic zone' of 200 miles was introduced. In the latter zone, the freedom of overflight and other freedoms connected with communications (like the laying of submarine cables) were to be respected.[62]

The Conference resulted eventually in the United Nations Convention on the Law of the Sea (Montego Bay, December 10, 1982) which entered into force on November 16, 1994. A salient feature of this convention was the extension of the territorial sea limit to 12 miles (Article 3). Consequently many of the sea straits thus far considered as belonging to the High Seas may now come under the rules and regulations governing the territorial waters: overflying such straits without permission of the States involved will no longer be allowed. In the light of this new situation Article 38 establishes a right of transit passage in the straits for all ships and aircraft, including military vessels and airplanes.

Another effect of the Convention coming into force is that the road is now free to establish an International Tribunal for the Law of the Sea in the Free and Hanseatic City of Hamburg, Germany. This Tribunal will have an important role to play in settling disputes relating, *inter alia*, to rights of overflight within the complex of rules governing tertitorial seas, contiguous zones, archipelagoes, exclusive economic zones, continental shelves and the High Seas.[63]

---

58.   See ICAO Doc. 9436 and *Air Law*, vol. IX (1984), p. 190. See also Bin Cheng, 'The destruction of KAL flight KE007, and Article 3 *bis* of the Chicago Convention', *Air Worthy*, pp. 47-74; Aart A. van Wijk; 'Visual and oral signals between aircraft in flight as a means to convey instructions by a State', *Air Worthy* pp. 235-289; and Ian Awford, 'Civil liability concerning unlawful interference with civil aviation' in *Aviation Security: How to safeguard international air transport* (proceedings of a conference held at the Peace Palace, The Hague, January 22–23, 1987), pp. 47-73. See also A.F. Lowenfeld *et al*, 'Agora: the downing of Iran Air flight 655', *AJIL*, vol. 83 (1989) pp. 318-341.

59.   Convention on the High Seas, Geneva, April 29, 1958.

60.   Convention on the Continental Shelf, Geneva, April 29, 1958.

61.   Art. 3 of the Continental Shelf Convention reads as follows: 'The rights of the coastal State over the continental shelf do not affect the legal status of the superjacent high seas, or that of the airspace above those waters.'

62.   Official Records Third UN Conference on the Law of the Sea, Eighth Session, UN Doc. A/Conf. 62/WP 10 Rev. 1 (April 28, 1979) ICNT Arts. 55–75 (Exclusive Economic Zone).

63.   See J. Bentzien, 'Die Zuständigkeit des Internationalen Seegerichtshofes für Streitigkeiten der internationalen Luftfahrt', ZLW, vol. 45 (1996), pp. 145-161.

11.   State aircraft

The legal status of state aircraft is at present very unsatisfactory, with a corresponding degree of uncertainty. The cause can be traced mainly to Article 3(a) of the Chicago Convention, whereby state aircraft are excluded from its application. The Paris Convention, on the contrary, did contain special provisions for state aircraft in Article 30 *et seq.* Military aircraft, for instance, are, according to Article 32, to enjoy the same privileges as foreign 'men-of-war' (warships) once they have received authorisation to enter the territory of a contracting state.

The term 'state aircraft' is rather vague and often includes many different types of aircraft. The main criterion in the definition of a state aircraft is its being intended for use in public service. According to Meyer there is no universally accepted definition of state aircraft. As a rule, aircraft are recognised as state aircraft when they are under control of the state and used exclusively by the state for state-intended purposes.[64] The following categories of state aircraft may be distinguished:

a. customs aircraft;
b. police aircraft;
c. military aircraft;
d. mail-carrying aircraft;
e. aircraft carrying Heads of State;
f. aircraft carrying high government officials;
g. aircraft on special missions.

Aircraft, when used in customs and police services, are beyond doubt classifiable as state aircraft, and it is generally accepted that military aircraft are also state aircraft. Opinions differ, however, as to how exactly the term 'military aircraft' is to be interpreted in this context.

In the early stages of the development of military aviation much emphasis was placed on the military status of the commander. During the First World War military aircraft had to display external markings so as to make their nationality easily identifiable. Subsequently they were given a legal status in the Paris Convention, and again mentioned in the Chicago Convention.[65]

A definition proposed by de Vlugt would, in my opinion, seem to be the most preferable. According to this author military aircraft are aircraft forming part of, or – by virtue of registration in a military aviation register – destined to form part of, the armed forces.[66] This

---

64. A. Meyer in *Wörterbuch des Völkerrechts* (2nd ed., Berlin, 1962), Vol. III under the reference 'Staatsflugzeuge'; see also on this subject S. Sucharitkul, 'Immunities of Foreign States before National Authorities' (1976-I) 149 *Recueil des Cours* 87–216.
65. See Art. 31 of the Paris Convention and Art. 3(b) of the Chicago Convention.
66. P. de Vlugt, 'Het begrip "Militair Luchtvaartuig"' (1956) 49 *Militair-Rechtelijk Tijdschrift* 81–85. See also on this subject: O.J. Lissitzyn, 'The Treatment of Aerial Intruders in Recent Practice and International Law' (1953) 47 AJIL 559–590; Ming-Min Peng, *Le statut juridique de l'aéronef militaire* (1957); L. Oppenheim, *International Law* (8th ed., 1955), Vol. I, pp. 521 and 851; A. Verdross, *Völkerrecht* (5th ed., 1964), p. 281; K. Hailbronner, *Der Schutz der Luftgrenzen im Frieden*, Beiträge zum ausländischen öffentlichen Recht und Völkerrecht, No. 58 (Köln-Bonn, 1972).

definition may be given either an extensive or a restrictive interpretation, depending on whether one is the requested or requesting party when permission is sought for military flights through the airspace of a foreign state.

11.1. RED CROSS AIRCRAFT

A complicating factor in Red Cross aircraft is that they may be used for both military and civil humanitarian purposes. This puts them in a special position. According to the definition of the term 'military aircraft' given earlier, Red Cross aircraft should be regarded as military aircraft when they belong to the armed forces and are engaged in assisting the casualties of belligerent armies or transporting medicine, food and clothing for the military medical services.

Most of the Red Cross aircraft do, in fact, belong to military medical services. In peacetime, these aircraft follow the rules and regulations governing military aircraft. The status of military Red Cross aircraft in time of war has been defined in the Geneva Convention of 1949.[67]

In 1977 a Protocol[68] was added to this Geneva Convention relating to the protection of victims of international armed conflicts, giving supplementary measures for the protection of people fighting against colonial domination, alien occupation and racist regimes in the exercise of their right of self-determination, in accordance with the principles of the Charter of the United Nations. The terms 'wounded' and 'sick' were extended to cover military personnel as well as civilians; medical units were accorded greater protection.

There are also civil Red Cross aircraft. To these the Chicago Convention is fully applicable. Due to the nationality requirement these aircraft have to be registered in a particular country (Art. 17 of the Chicago Convention). International organisations, such as the United Nations or the International Committee of the Red Cross (CICR),

---

67. Although often referred to in the singular, there were actually four Conventions concluded at Geneva on August 12, 1949: the first and second of these contain Articles relating to the status of medical aircraft, namely The Convention for the Amelioration of the Condition of the Wounded and Sick in Armed Forces in the Field (the so-called First Convention), in Arts. 36 and 37, and The Convention for the Amelioration of the Condition of the Wounded, Sick and Shipwrecked Members of Armed Forces at Sea (the so-called Second Convention), in Arts. 39 and 40. The Third Convention relates to the treatment of prisoners of war; the Fourth Convention relates to the protection of civilians in time of war. See also G.I.A. Draper, *The Red Cross Conventions* (1958).

68. Protocol I, additional to the Geneva Conventions of August 12, 1949, Relating to the Protection of Victims of International Conflicts; adopted at Geneva on June 8, 1977; open for signature at Berne, December 12, 1977 to December 12, 1978. See also K. Hailbronner, 'Der Schutz von Sanitätsflugzeugen im Krieg', *Beiträge zum Luft- und Weltraumrecht*, Festschrift zu Ehren von Alex Meyer (Cologne, 1975), pp. 127-146; 'The Right to Health as a Human Right', Workshop Hague Academy of International Law/United Nations University (The Hague, July 27–29, 1978), edited by R.-J. Dupuy, published 1979 in the *Recueil des Cours* series.

enter their Red Cross aircraft on the national register of some country (according to Art. 18 of the Chicago Convention, registration may be transferred from one state to another). These aircraft follow the rules and regulations of the country of registration.

In Europe a special rule for emergency flights can be found in the Multilateral Agreement on Commercial Rights of Non-scheduled Air Services in Europe,[69] whereby, according to Article 2, para. 1(a), 'flights executed for the purpose of meeting humanitarian or emergency needs' will be admitted freely by the contracting states. In time of war civil Red Cross aircraft enjoy no special protection.

11.2. OTHER STATE AIRCRAFT

Aircraft carrying mail as part of their cargo enjoy no special status.

Aircraft engaged in carrying Heads of State and/or high government officials on missions or public functions are generally regarded as state aircraft.

Finally, state aircraft may include aircraft which, in the light of their mission, display appropriate state markings (for instance aircraft intended for rescue operations, scientific missions, etc.).

It would be desirable and useful to amend and elaborate Article 3 of the Chicago Convention. Four suggestions which might provide a basis for clarification are:

1. to further define the three categories designated as 'state aircraft' in Article 3(b);
2. to insert rules governing public health aircraft;
3. to create rules for aircraft carrying Heads of State (here, one could imagine a situation in which a Head of State uses a civil or a chartered aircraft: What would be the consequences for the legal status of the aircraft?);
4. to avoid introducing a general definition of the term 'state aircraft', because it is impracticable to incorporate all the divergent elements in a satisfactory formula.[70]

Apart from the Paris Convention already mentioned, references to state aircraft and legal provisions affecting them are to be found in the following international agreements:

1. The Warsaw Convention: according to Article 2(1), the Convention is applicable to carriage performed by a state. Nevertheless, an additional protocol (with reference to Article 2) provides that states may reserve to themselves the right to declare that 'the first paragraph of Article 2 of this Convention shall not apply to international carriage by air performed directly by the State'.

---

69. Paris Agreement, see note 17, *supra*.
70. See about this subject Bin Cheng, 'State Ships and State Aircraft' (1958) 11 *Current Legal Problems* 225–257; I.H.Ph. de Rode-Verschoor, W.P. Heere, *et al.*, 'The Legal Status of State Aircraft' (1963) 2 IDA 115–140; S. Sucharitkul in the 1976 *Recueil des Cours* (see note 64, *supra*).

2. The Hague Protocol (concluded to amend the Warsaw Convention): Article 26 stipulates that states may declare this Convention, as amended by the Hague Protocol, to be inapplicable to military transport.

3. The Guadalajara Convention[71] follows, in so far as state aircraft are concerned, the provisions of the Warsaw Convention and the Hague Protocol. The Guatemala Protocol[72] stipulates in Article XXIII that a state may declare 'that the Warsaw Convention as amended at The Hague, 1955, and at Guatemala City, 1971, shall not apply to the carriage of persons, baggage and cargo for its military authorities on aircraft, registered in that State, the whole capacity of which has been reserved by or on behalf of such authorities'.

4. The Convention for the Unification of Certain Rules Relating to the Precautionary Attachment of Aircraft,[73] declares that aircraft used exclusively in the service of a state, including the postal service, but excluding commercial service, are not subject to precautionary arrest (Art. 3).

5. The Convention for the Unification of Certain Rules relating to Assistance and Salvage of Aircraft or by Aircraft at Sea[74] provides in Article 16 that the Convention is applicable to government vessels and aircraft, but with the exception of Article 13 dealing with jurisdiction. The Convention (which, incidentally, never entered into force) is, however, inapplicable to 'military, customs or police vessels or aircraft'.

6. The Convention on the International Recognition of Rights in Aircraft[75] provides in Article XIII that the Convention shall not apply to military, customs or police aircraft. Accordingly the Convention is applicable to other state aircraft.

7. The Convention on Damage Caused to Third Parties on the Surface, Rome 1933,[76] replaced by the Rome 1952 Convention,[77] had a similar provision in Article 21. This Convention is also applicable to other categories of state aircraft. One can only speculate as to what will happen in the event of damage being inflicted by these types of aircraft.

71. Convention Supplementary to the Warsaw Convention, for the Unification of Certain Rules Relating to International Carriage by Air Performed by a Person Other than the Contracting Carrier, Guadalajara, September 18, 1961; hereinafter cited as Guadalajara Convention.
72. Protocol to Amend the Warsaw Convention, Guatemala City, March 8, 1971; hereinafter cited as Guatemala Protocol.
73. The Convention for the Unification of Certain Rules Relating to the Precautionary Attachment of Aircraft, Rome, May 29, 1933. Note that often instead of 'attachment' the term 'arrest' is used.
74. Convention for the Unification of Certain Rules relating to Assistance and Salvage of Aircraft or by Aircraft at Sea, Brussels, September 29, 1938; hereinafter cited as the Brussels Convention.
75. Convention on the International Recognition of Rights in Aircraft, Geneva, June 19, 1948; hereinafter cited as the Geneva Convention.
76. Convention on Damage Caused to Third Parties on the Surface, Rome, May 29, 1933.
77. Convention on Damage Caused by Foreign Aircraft to Third Parties on the Surface, Rome, October 7, 1952; hereinafter cited as the Rome (1952) Convention.

8. The Tokyo Convention,[78] the Hague Convention,[79] and the Montreal Convention[80] do not apply to military, customs or police aircraft either.

12. Measures to facilitate air navigation

The Chicago Convention contains a number of rules designed to facilitate air navigation.

Article 28 gives rules concerning practices recommended for airports, radio and meteorological services, standard systems for communication procedures and other operational matters.

Customs and immigration rules and procedures are items covered by Articles 10, 13, 23 and 24. They have been taken from the Convention Concerning the Exemption from Taxation for Liquid Fuel and Lubricants Used in Air Traffic, signed in London and dated March 1, 1939.[81]

Sanitary measures are another category coming under this heading: considering the rapidity with which epidemics may spread by means of aviation, Article 14 outlines certain provisions aimed at preventing the spread of diseases: among these sanitary measures have found their place, but without prejudice to the application of other international Conventions operative in this field.[82]

According to Article 37, contracting states are bound to collaborate in securing the highest degree of uniformity in these regulations and in any other matters in which uniformity will facilitate and improve air navigation. Whenever a state finds it impracticable to do so, or wishes to adopt different regulations or practices, it must notify ICAO, according to Article 38. The same obligation applies in the case of amendments to international standards which a state is unwilling to apply; ICAO will then inform all other states.

13. International organisations (Worldwide)

The impetus given by the Second World War to aviation in general has already been touched upon earlier in this treatise. It has also given rise to some innovations in the structures of international co-operation and law-making in the field of aviation. The Chicago Convention provides an appropriate starting point for reviewing these post-War developments.

---

78. Tokyo Convention (see chapter X, *infra*), Art. 1(4).
79. Hague Convention (see chapter X, *infra*), Art. 3(2).
80. Montreal Convention (see chapter X, *infra*), Art. 4(1).
81. Convention Concerning Exemption from Taxation for Liquid Fuel and Lubricants Used in Air Traffic, London, March 1, 1939. This Convention is not in force.
82. *E.g.* the International Sanitary Convention for Aerial Navigation, The Hague, April 12, 1933.

An interim Agreement concluded during the Chicago Conference of 1944 saw the birth of the Provisional International Civil Aviation Organisation (PICAO) which was destined to become the predecessor of the prestigious International Civil Aviation Organisation (ICAO), dating from 1947.

13.1. ICAO (THE INTERNATIONAL CIVIL AVIATION ORGANISATION)

ICAO became a Specialised Agency of the United Nations Organisation on May 13, 1947, and is for that reason invested with special powers, pursuant to Article 64 of the Chicago Convention.

13.1.1. The Assembly

ICAO has an Assembly which meets not less than once in three years and is convened by the Council, in accordance with Article 48. All member states have an equal right to representation and each state has one vote. The Assembly's functions are summarised in Article 49: they comprise, among other duties, examining the Council's reports and voting and controlling budgets.

13.1.2. The Council

In addition to the Assembly there is a Council. The ICAO Council is a permanent body which consists of 33 representatives of member states (whose number total over 180 at present) and may be regarded as the organisation's executive committee. The Council is entrusted with numerous duties of a technical, economic and legal nature. To perform its legal functions, ICAO has been assisted, since 1947, by a permanent Legal Committee. Apart from the Legal Committee ICAO also has the following special committees:
   a. the Air Navigation Commission;
   b. the Air Transport Committee;
   c. the Committee on Joint Support of Air Navigation Services;
   d. the Finance Committee; and
   e. the Committee on Unlawful Interference with International Civil Aviation and its Facilities.

The Air Navigation Commission represents the technical element of ICAO. The Convention provides in its Article 56 that the members of this Commission 'shall have suitable qualifications and experience in the science and practice of aeronautics'. The Commission is responsible for drafting and amending the Annexes to the Convention (Art. 57).

13.1.3. The Legal Committee

The ICAO Legal Committee is entrusted with the task of studying and preparing draft Conventions, which it then submits to the Assembly in plenary session for approval. In the next stage the Convention has to be approved by a Diplomatic Conference.

In the former CITEJA, the Legal Committee's predecessor, draft Conventions used to be prepared by legal experts possessing a high degree of scientific competence. The final version was subsequently submitted for approval to a Diplomatic Conference attended by CITEJA's own experts together with official representatives of the various governments.

Attention has already been called in Chapter I to this marked difference in working procedures, and it is perhaps not surprising that objections have been voiced against the ICAO procedure by experts like Goedhuis and Riese: they have both pointed to the danger of undue political influence being exerted in the Legal Committee, as opposed to the purely juridical atmosphere and approach prevailing in CITEJA. Yet one advantage of the present situation is that political arguments are now being tabled right from the beginning, which improves the chances of Conventions being more rapidly adopted. On the other hand the decision-making process is occasionally impeded, due to the large number of states which are members of the ICAO.

13.1.4 The ICAO Council and the International Court of Justice

One of the more important functions performed by the Council lies in its role in settling disputes.[83] ICAO is authorised to request advisory opinions from the International Court of Justice (ICJ) at The Hague on the interpretation of treaties and Conventions. According to Article 96(2), of the UN Charter: 'Other organs of the United Nations and specialized agencies, which may at any time be so authorized by the General Assembly, may also request advisory opinions of the Court on legal questions arising within the scope of their activities'. ICAO has not yet availed itself of this right. On the other hand, several aviation cases have been brought before the Court by interested parties, some of which are worth mentioning here.

On November 19, 1951, a US cargo aircraft drifted off course over Hungary. The four members of the crew were arrested and the aircraft seized. The American Government attempted to lodge a claim with the International Court of Justice against the Governments of Hungary and the Soviet Union, but these refused to submit to the Court's jurisdiction. As a result, the Court was unable to take action and the case was struck off the list.[84] In the Czechoslovakian case of 1953 and the USSR case of 1952, the USA recognised that these Governments had not accepted the Court's jurisdiction.[85] In the Bulgarian case of July 27, 1955, the Court gave a decision in the preliminary phase,

---

83. W.P. Heere, 'Some Observations concerning the Desirability of Creating an International Court for Aeronautical Disputes', *Air Law*, vol. I (1976), pp. 229-252. See also I.H.Ph. Diederiks-Verschoor, 'The Settlement of Aviation Disputes', *Annals of Air and Space Law*, vol. XX (1995), pp. 335-341.
84. *Case of Treatment in Hungary of Aircraft of the USA* [1954] ICJ Reports 99 and 103.
85. *USA* v. *Czechoslovakia*, Aerial incident of March 10, 1953, [1956] ICJ Reports 6; *USA* v. *USSR*, Aerial incident of October 7, 1952, [1956] ICJ Reports 9. Other cases were *USA* v. *USSR*, aerial incident of September 4, 1954, [1958] ICJ Reports 158 and *USA* v. *USSR*, aerial incident of November 7, 1954, [1959] ICJ Reports 146.

but Bulgaria then contested the Court's jurisdiction on the ground that she had not been admitted to the United Nations until after the date of the incident. Proceedings were discontinued.[86] In all cases mentioned the defendant states had successfully challenged the Court's jurisdiction.

Redirecting our attention to the ICAO Council, we note in Article 84 of the Chicago Convention that whenever a state is involved in a dispute which cannot be settled by negotiation, the Council is called upon for a decision.[87] Until now, the Council has never really fully exercised this function, although it has played a mediating role in quite a number of disputes, successfully on occasions.

In 1953 the Council mediated in an incident involving restricted areas. Pakistan had proclaimed an area bordering on Afghanistan to be a restricted zone. On April 21, 1952, India complained to the Council, arguing that the measure was of a discriminatory character since the Iranian airline company had been allowed to continue its service over the restricted area. Afghanistan supported India's position. Pakistan replied that the restricted zones had been in existence for security reasons since 1935, therefore long before 1947, when India and Pakistan became separate states. Thanks to the recommendation of the Council a friendly settlement was reached between the two parties; the Pakistan Government opened two corridors above the restricted area, thereby providing the Indian airline company with a shorter route.

The ICAO Council has been involved in quite a number of cases. They include:

1. *Jordan* v. *UAR*, concerning a ban on overflying UAR territory;
2. *UAR* v. *Lebanon*, concerning an attack on a Mystère aircraft;
3. *UAR* v. *Lebanon*, concerning the establishment of a danger zone;
4. *Lebanon* v. *UAR*, involving a temporary ban on flying and a failure to furnish adequate information;
5. *UAR* v. *Israel*, concerning an attack on an aircraft;
6. *Lebanon* v. *France*, concerning the seizure of passengers and freight of a Lebanese aircraft.

A case of compulsory jurisdiction of the ICAO Council again arose between India and Pakistan in 1971. While flying over Pakistani territory, an Indian aircraft was forced to land at Lahore airport, where it was subsequently destroyed. The Government of India decided, in February 1971, to ban flights by Pakistani aircraft above Indian territory.

On March 3, 1971, Pakistan filed a complaint with the ICAO Council. The Council declared itself competent, because both countries had joined the Transit Agreement annexed to the Chicago Convention,

---

86. Cases concerning the aerial incident of July 27, 1955: *Israel* v. *Bulgaria* (Preliminary Objections), [1959] ICJ Reports 127 *et seq.*, at 142; *United Kingdom* v. *Bulgaria*, [1959] ICJ Reports 264 and *USA* v. *Bulgaria* [1960] ICJ Reports 146.
87. Based on Art. 84 of the Chicago Convention and Art. 2, section 2, and Art. 4, section 3 of the Transit and Transport Agreements respectively.

which allowed contracting states to fly over each other's territory. India lodged an appeal with the ICJ against the Council decision, being of the opinion that the Chicago Convention and the Transit Agreement were no longer in force, since during the war between India and Pakistan in 1965 the regulations of the Chicago Convention had been suspended and never renewed, and that, therefore, the Council had no jurisdiction. Both countries had, however, concluded a special agreement in February 1966 to allow passage through each other's airspace provisionally and on the basis of reciprocity. The issue was decided on August 18, 1972, by the ICJ. It rejected the Government of Pakistan's objections on the question of the ICJ's competence and held that it had jurisdiction to entertain India's appeal; it further considered the Council to be competent to receive the Application and Complaint laid before it by the Government of Pakistan; and, in consequence, the Court rejected the appeal lodged by the Government of India against the decision of the Council to assume jurisdiction in those respects.[88]

The procedure for settlement of disputes is laid down in Articles 84 to 88 of the Chicago Convention. Article 86 is of special interest, for it stipulates that:

'Unless the Council decides otherwise, any decision by the Council on whether an international airline is operating in conformity with the provisions of this Convention shall remain in effect unless reversed on appeal. On any other matter, decisions by the Council shall, if appealed from, be suspended until the appeal is decided. The decisions of the Permanent Court of International Justice and of an arbitral tribunal shall be final and binding.'

One form of settling disputes is, of course, arbitration. However, many arbitrations never become known to the general public since parties to an arbitration may keep it secret.[89] In practice arbitration usually works very fast, which is to the advantage of the parties which have to pay the expenses. Great Britain was the first state to incorporate an arbitration clause in a bilateral treaty, concluded with the Republic of South Africa in October 1945, but no special organ or procedure to deal with disputes was mentioned in this treaty. Most bilateral treaties containing arbitration clauses designate the ICAO Council as the competent body, sometimes without any restrictions. In such cases the arbitral award is binding. An exception to this general practice is occasionally made by parties agreeing that the Council's opinion will only have a purely advisory character.

88. [1972] ICJ Reports 46–179 (Appeal Relating to the Jurisdiction of the ICAO Council), at p. 70.
89. See P.B. Larsen, 'Arbitration of the United States – France Air Traffic Rights Dispute' [1964] JALC 231–247; see for the United States – Italy Air Transport Arbitration, A.F. Lowenfeld, *Aviation Law* (1981), Chap. 2, para. 4, pp. 71-85; see for the second US–France Arbitration [1979] USAvR, 868–876 and [1979] RFDA 399–419 and 460–496. See for a different, one-man arbitration case J. Naveau, 'A New Arbitration Verdict Involving a Bilateral Agreement: Arbitration on the Belgium/Ireland Capacity Clause', *ITA Bulletin* 38/1981, pp. 975-984.

13.2. IATA (THE INTERNATIONAL AIR TRANSPORT ASSOCIATION)

This organisation occupies a most important place in the world of international air transport. Unlike ICAO, IATA is not an official body, but a private organisation of scheduled airlines. It was originally set up by six airline companies, on August 28, 1919, as the 'International Air Traffic Association'. IATA's aims and objectives are clearly set out in its incorporating Act, where they are described as follows:

a. to promote safe, regular and economical air transport for the benefit of the peoples of the world, to foster air commerce and to study the problems connected therewith;
b. to provide means for collaboration among the airline enterprises engaged directly or indirectly in international transport service;
c. to co-operate with ICAO and other international organisations.

IATA's main purpose lies in the technical and commercial sector. Its technical duties were designed from the beginning to achieve safer, more regular and more economical air traffic; in the commercial sector, IATA's activities were expected to create the best possible conditions for all categories of customers. An important function is performed by IATA's Clearing House, which operates under the ultimate responsibility of its Financial Committee. This organisation was originally established in London in 1947, but later transferred to Geneva. It acts as a clearing institute for accounts between airlines, including those accumulated from ticket sales and other sources. Non-IATA members can also qualify for admission to the Clearing House.

As Haanappel mentions: 'Most of IATA's activities find their expression in Resolutions and Recommended Practices adopted by the Traffic Conferences. IATA Traffic Conference Resolutions can be defined as agreements adopted by the *unanimous* vote of the Traffic Conference members. They become binding on the members when approved by interested governments.'[90]

Practically all airline companies involved in scheduled air transport have a seat in the organisation, which maintains close ties with the government authorities of member states. Some companies are supported by public funds, others are even 100 per cent state-owned. It is therefore not surprising that IATA's recommendations to governments are always received with due respect and consideration. Whenever a Convention enjoys IATA support there is a fair chance of it being adopted and successfully applied in practice; conversely, if IATA is opposed to a particular Convention, its chances of securing adoption are greatly reduced.

13.3. CHARTER ORGANISATIONS

Air charter organisations have already been mentioned earlier in this treatise. For an enumeration see chapter I, section 7.4 *supra*.

---

90. P.P.C. Haanappel, *Ratemaking in International Air Transport* (1978), p. 57.

14.   Regional organisations and agreements

Following the conclusion of the Chicago Convention there have been several more efforts seeking internationalisation of civil aviation on a worldwide scale. These attempts were aimed chiefly at achieving greater coordination and freedom, but none has been successful.[91]

What has been achieved, however, is a notable measure of co-operation between European nations, not only through their airlines[92] (although 'Air Union' never got off the ground), but also within the framework of the Council of Europe. This European organisation has been most active in stimulating closer unity in air transport, as will be shown below.

The need for co-operation stressed by the Council of Europe becomes understandable when one considers that Europe has a great many scheduled airline companies, belonging to no less than 18 different countries and using at least seven different types of aircraft between them. To those wishing to encourage the smooth development of civil aviation in Europe the need for more unity in the technical, legal and air-political sector is also quite obvious.

To reach this goal a number of proposals have been put forward in Strasbourg, the seat of the Council of Europe's Parliament.[93] In 1950 it was Bonnefous, a French delegate, who submitted a plan aimed at setting up a European Transport Authority that would comprise railways, highways, inland waterways, coastal navigation, shipping and aviation. Bonnefous sought to create an organisational structure similar to the European Coal and Steel Community,[94] including a High Authority whose jurisdiction would extend over the types of transport mentioned above. This plan was too far-reaching: the proposal to create a High Authority gave rise to strong objections inspired by nationalism.

A second plan, also submitted in 1950, was presented by the Italian Minister of Foreign Affairs, Count Sforza, whose ideas were confined to civil aviation. He suggested that states should surrender part of their sovereignty to further unity in the legal, technical and economical sectors. His plan provided for the creation of a consortium and a High Authority, but it did not define the relationship between the two.

A third plan was presented in May 1951 by the Dutch Cabinet Minister van der Kieft, who suggested founding a European civil aviation organisation in order to achieve greater unity.

---

91. See W.J. Wagner, *International Air Transportation as Affected by State Sovereignty* (1970), Chap. IV.
92. See also section 6, *supra*.
93. Statute of the Council of Europe, London, May 5, 1949.
94. Plan for a European Coal and Steel Community developed by French Minister Schuman in 1950, eventually leading to the Treaty on the ECSC, Paris, April 18, 1951.

14.1. THE EUROPEAN CIVIL AVIATION CONFERENCE (ECAC)

A 'European Civil Aviation Conference' finally emerged in 1955 from all these proposals, sponsored by the Council of Europe. Its aim was to facilitate and unify European air traffic,[95] in co-operation with the International Civil Aviation Organisation (ICAO). Nineteen states took part in ECAC.[96] Its objectives were, generally, to review the development of intra-European air transport, to promote coordination and to achieve more effective unification and orderly development of European air transport, while at the same time considering any special problems that might arise.

Initially, ECAC had an advisory task and its conclusions and recommendations were subject to the approval of governments.[97] In 1968 its structure was overhauled: in addition to the General Assembly and the Co-ordinating Committee for Administration and Budgeting there are now four standing committees:
(1) ECO – I, committee for tariffs and conditions;
(2) ECO – II, committee for regulatory framework of air transport;
(3) TECH, technical committee for the co-ordination and harmonisation of navigation and communication equipment; and
(4) FAL, committee charged with applying the principles and directions of Annex 9 of the Chicago Convention to improve air transport safety.

In June 1976 a permanent body was established consisting of all the Directors General of Civil Aviation.[98] Notable achievements of ECAC were:
(1) the Multilateral Agreement on Commercial Rights of Non-scheduled Air Services in Europe[99];
(2) the Multilateral Agreement Relating to Certificates of Airworthiness for Imported Aircraft[100];
(3) the International Agreement on the Procedure for the Establishment of Tariffs for Scheduled Air Services.[101]

During the past few years ECAC seems to have concentrated its efforts more on the political attitude of Western Europe towards third countries than on co-operation and harmonisation of air traffic within

95. ICAO Doc. 7676 ECAC/1 (1956).
96. Original members were Austria, Belgium, Denmark, Finland, France, German Federal Republic, Greece, Iceland, Ireland, Italy, Luxembourg, The Netherlands, Norway, Portugal, Spain, Sweden, Switzerland, Turkey and the United Kingdom. Cyprus, Malta and Yugoslavia joined later.
97. See K.H. Böhme, *Die internationale Organisation der zivilen Luftfahrt in ihrem geschichtlichen Werdegang* (thesis Göttingen, 1956).
98. *Annals of Air and Space Law*, Vol. II (1977), pp. 461-462.
99. Paris Agreement, see note 17, *supra*.
100. Multilateral Agreement relating to Certificates of Airworthiness for Imported Aircraft, Paris, April 22, 1960. See on this Agreement J.-M. Fobe, *Aviation Products Liability and Insurance in the EU*, 1994, pp. 22-24.
101. International Agreement on the Procedure for the Establishment of Tariffs for Scheduled Air Services, Paris, July 10, 1967.

Europe. As a result of this attitude we would quote the ECAC-USA Memorandum of Understanding (May 2, 1982 and December 17, 1982) relating to fares and tariffs.

Objections have been raised here and there against regional Conventions on the assumption that regional rules are bound to stimulate bloc-formation. This is considered undesirable because bloc-formation is supposed to hamper unification. Besides, some European airlines form part of a much larger world-wide network of airlines.

In assessing the readiness, or lack of it, of states to cooperate in furthering a purely European interest the role played by their national interests cannot be ignored. Proposals seeking the creation of a High Authority for aviation are not easy to reconcile with the concept of the freedom of air transport and there is always the danger of larger states dominating the smaller ones.

Nothwithstanding the fact that the High Authority of the Coal and Steel Community has been highly successful within its own province it seems to me that a similar structure would be both unsuitable and undesirable for aviation.

14.2. THE TREATY OF ROME (EEC TREATY)

The Treaty of Rome of 1957, which created the European Economic Community (EEC),[102] contains a number of provisions relating to transport in its fourth Title, namely in Articles 74 to 84. According to Article 84, para. 1, these provisions are applicable to transport by rail, road, and inland waterways, while paragraph 2 states that the Council of Ministers, acting unanimously, may decide whether, to what extent and by what procedure appropriate provisions may be laid down for sea and air transport.

The fact that no rules of air law or maritime law have been given in this Article is due to their worldwide nature and scope. During the *travaux préparatoires* of the EEC Treaty it was decided that the matter would be dealt with at a later date. By way of comparison the position of maritime transport within the EEC Treaty was defined in a decision of the Court of Justice of the European Communities in Luxembourg.[103] The Court was of the opinion that 'Whilst under article 84, para. 2, therefore, sea and air transport, so long as the Council has not decided otherwise, is excluded from the rules of Title IV of Part Two of the Treaty relating to the common transport policy, it remains, on the same basis as the other modes of transport,

---

102. Original members to the EEC Treaty (Rome, March 25, 1957) were Belgium, France, German Federal Republic, Italy, Luxembourg and The Netherlands; joined in 1972 by Denmark, Ireland and the United Kingdom and in 1981 by Greece. On January 1, 1986 Spain and Portugal became members of the EEC. Due to the Treaty of Maastricht of February 7, 1992 (entered into force November 1, 1993) the EC was transformed into the European Union. Austria, Finland and Sweden joined the by then European Union on January 1, 1995.

103. *EEC Commission v. French Republic (French Seamen case)*, Decision of April 4, 1974, Case 167/73; see [1974] European Courts Reports 359, *et seq.*

subject to the general rules of the Treaty'. This decision offers a distinct possibility for a broader interpretation of the EEC Treaty in relation to navigation and aviation, namely, that the general rules of the Rome Treaty are applicable and that Member States should commence the integration process by applying the general Treaty rules. Prior to this decision, the ambiguous provision of Article 84, para. 2, tended to provide a legal excuse for excluding sea and air transport from the scope of the Treaty.[104]

The last vestiges of doubt whether the competition rules apply to air transport have been dispelled by the European Court ruling in the 1986 'Nouvelles Frontières' case.[105] The Court had to rule on the compatibility of French Government regulations regarding the approval of air tariffs with the Rome Treaty rules on competition. In essence, the Court found that the approval of air tariffs constitutes a violation of Articles 3f, 5 and 85 of the Treaty where such tariffs are the result of an agreement, a decision of an association of enterprises (trade association) or a concerted practice, all of which are prohibited by Article 85. It is not the actual government intervention itself which may be unlawful, but more in particular the approval of tariffs which are the result of what is generally called 'tariff coordination between airlines'.

This case settles once and for all the hitherto unresolved question of whether or not the competition rules of the Rome Treaty apply to air transport: there is no longer any doubt that they do.[106]

The Court also confirmed that the appropriate authorities of the Member States are responsible for the application of the competition rules even if the EC–Commission itself has limited powers of investigation; in addition, that body also has powers to take appropriate measures in order to terminate unlawful practices.

According to EC planning a completely free internal market was to be achieved by January 1, 1993, which would also mean an entirely deregulated market for the airline business. A first step towards this goal was made in December 1987, when the member states agreed to partly liberalise aviation. Under this agreement new possibilities were opened up, especially for aircraft with less than 70 seats. It was also supposed to result in lower air fares in general, fifth-freedom

---

104. See L. Weber, *Die Zivilluftfahrt im Europäischen Gemeinschaftsrecht* (thesis Heidelberg, 1980), published as Vol. 78 of the *Beiträge zum ausländischen öffentlichen Recht und Völkerrecht* (Berlin-Vienna, 1981).

105. Decision of April 30, 1986 (Preliminary Judgment), Cases 209–213/86; see *'Ministère Public* v. *Lucas Asjes et al.',* Annals of Air and Space Law, vol. XI (1986), pp. 385-395, and H.A. Wassenbergh, 'The "Nouvelles Frontières" case', *Air Law,* vol. XI (1986), pp. 161-166.

106. See also Court of Justice of the EEC, April 11, 1989 (Ahmed Saeed Flugreisen), *EVR,* vol. XXIV (1989), p. 229 *et seq.* This judgment forms one of the main topics of the various contributions in *EEC Air Transport Policy and Regulation and their Implications for North America* (Proceedings of a conference held at McGill University, Montreal, September 1989), 1990, P.P.C. Haanappel *et al.,* eds. See also P.P.C. Haanappel, 'The external aviation relations of the EEC and of the EEC Member States into the 21st Century', *Air Law,* vol. XIV (1989), pp. 69-87 and p. 145 *et seq.*

rights for EC airlines within the EC, and finally more flexibility on routes operated by two national carriers.[107]

In the meantime, however, this agreement has already been replaced by a number of new regulations. On June 22, 1992, the EC Council adopted the so-called 'Third Package' of measures to implement the final phase of liberalisation. Under this measures, which are designed to maximise freedom of pricing and market access, the general framework for a single aviation market came also into being on that date. A key element in the regulations of the Third Package is that they have been formulated to cover both scheduled and charter airlines. Bearing in mind that the 40 European charter companies alone carry more than 50 million passengers annually, accounting for 67 per cent of all international EC passenger-kilometers flown in the EC, this integration of non-scheduled operations was long overdue.

The following EC Regulations are specially relevant to civil aviation:

1. Council Regulation No. 2408/92, providing that by January 1, 1993, all capacity-sharing arrangements on routes between EC member states were to be eliminated. All restrictions on airlines operating fifth-freedom flights were to be abolished;

2. Council Regulation No. 2409/92, allowing fares and cargo rates to be set by agreement between carriers and their customers. The only requirement still to be observed is that they must be filed with the governments of the member states, but no more than 24 hours in advance. To prevent anti-competitive behaviour (e.g. carriers cutting fares to force smaller companies out of business), some safeguards against overpricing and predatory practices are included. Governments may intervene if a proposed fare is considered too high or too low. In that case they must take into account other tariffs on the same route and factors like competitive conditions in the market. A low fare may only be suspended if it is unrelated to the carrier's long-term fully allocated costs;

3. Council Regulation No.2410/92, amending Regulation No. 3975/87 laying down the procedure for the application of rules on competition to enterprises in the air transportation sector; and

4. Council Regulation No. 2411/92, amending Regulation No. 3976/87 on the application of Article 85(3) of the EC Treaty to certain categories of agreements and concerted practices in the air transportation sector.[108]

---

107. See for the text of this agreement and related regulations regarding air transport: *Official Journal of the EC*, No. L 374 (December 31, 1987). See also the various contributions in the special issue 'EC – Civil Aviation' of *Air Law*, vol. XV, (1990), pp. 229-336.

108. See for the texts of these and further EC regulations, etc. relating to air transportation, E. Giemulla, R.Schmid and W. Mölls, *European Air Law* (loose-leaf), 1992 (with supplements). See also H. A. Wassenbergh, '"Open Skies"/"Open Markets": The Limits to Competition', in *The Use of Airspace and Outer Space for All Mankind in the 21st Century*, Proceedings of the International Conference on Air Transport and Space Application in a New World (Tokyo, June 2-5, 1993), Chia-Jui Cheng, ed., pp. 195-204; A.F. Lowenfeld, 'Competition in International Aviation: The Next Round', *ibidem*, pp. 175-184; H.A. Wassenbergh, 'De-regulation of Competition in International Air Transport', *Air and Space Law*, vol. XXI (1996), pp. 80-89; B. Adkins, *Air Transport and EC Competition Law*, 1994; J. Balfour, *European Community Air Law*, 1995; and B.J.H. Crans, 'EC Aviation Scene', *Air and Space Law*, vol. XVII (1992), pp. 217-223.

Also worth mentioning are the European Commission's efforts to ensure that the liberalisation of air transport in the European Union is not jeopardized by anti-competitive practices at airports. These are continually monitored and investigated, which has sofar resulted in a gradual opening-up of the market or specific commitments by member states.

A recent development in this matter is an endeavour to come to a Directive relating to liberalisation of ground handling services in Community airports. A transitional market adjustment period will be included; full liberalisation is envisaged between 1998 and 2003.[109]

14.3. EUROCONTROL

Besides the Multilateral Agreement on Commercial Rights of Non-scheduled Air Services in Europe, which was reached within the framework of ECAC, there have been other Conventions which achieved greater unification in Europe. A notable achievement was the Convention for the Safety of Air Navigation, usually called Eurocontrol.[110]

Eurocontrol is an international organisation with regulatory powers relating to the upper airspace of member countries. Article 1 states: 'The contracting Parties agree to strengthen their co-operation in matters of air navigation and in particular to provide for the common organisation of the air traffic services in the upper air space'.

According to Article 3 the expression 'air traffic' covers both civil aircraft and such military, customs and police aircraft as conform to ICAO standards. Due to the speed of modern aircraft air traffic control at high altitude (over 6,000 metres) can no longer be envisaged within the restrictive framework of national frontiers in Europe. It was therefore thought expedient to create an international control organisation operating in the upper airspace and extending beyond the territorial limits of individual member states. For the lower air space it was thought to be useful in certain cases to entrust air traffic control over part of the territory of a member state either to another member state or to entrust it to the Eurocontrol organisation. Moreover, the Convention suggests that coordinated action be taken by states, firstly, in respect of aviation personnel training and, secondly, for study and research of air traffic problems.

To finance the air traffic control performed by Eurocontrol fees are being levied on the basis of the Multilateral Agreement relating to the Collection of Route Charges,[111] in conjunction with bilateral

---

109. *XXV-th Report on Competition Policy*, Doc.COM(96) 126 final, at p. 49.
110. Convention relating to Co-operation for the Safety of Air Navigation – Eurocontrol, Brussels, December 13, 1960. See *'La naissance d'Eurocontrol et les développements à propos des tarifs de cette organisation'* by I.H.Ph. Diederiks-Verschoor *et al*, EVR, (1976), pp. 842-853. Contracting parties were Belgium, France, German Federal Republic, Luxembourg, The Netherlands and the United Kingdom; later joined by Ireland. Agreements for co-operation exist with Austria, Denmark, Italy, Norway, Sweden, Switzerland and the FAA (United States); also there is an association agreement with Spain.
111. Multilateral Agreement relating to the Collection of Route Charges, Brussels, September 8, 1970, signed by the states parties to the aforementioned Eurocontrol Convention.

agreements of the same date. In addition, there is the International Agreement on the Procedure for the Establishment of Tariffs for Scheduled Air Services which needs mentioning.[112]

Finally we note the Protocol to amend the Eurocontrol Convention, signed at Brussels on February 12, 1981. On that occasion a new Multilateral Agreement relating to Route Charges, replacing the 1970 Agreement on the same subject, was concluded. The 1981 Amending Protocol was eventually implemented in 1986.[113]

Eurocontrol's functions continued to undergo changes[114] and in December 1992 it was decided to investigate what further amendments of the Convention would be required. A draft of a revised convention was examined by the Permanent Commission, the highest governing body of Eurocontrol, late in 1995. A final draft was to be submitted for signature to a diplomatic conference, possibly mid-1997. We will have to wait and see how Eurocontrol's status will crystallise.

14.4. OTHER REGIONAL FORMS OF CO-OPERATION

Apart from ECAC and Eurocontrol, we must not fail to mention some more typically regional organisations of ICAO:
- AFCAC, the African Civil Aviation Commission.[115] This Commission is a branch of the Commission on economic, social, transport and communicational affairs, which is itself an affiliation of the Organisation of African Unity (OAU). Membership is open to African States which are members of ECA (the Economic Commission for Africa) or the OAU.
- CACAS, the Civil Aviation Council of Arab States.[116] CACAS has translated the main air law treaties into Arabic and established the Arabic Services Transit Agreement as well as an agreement to created a Pan-Arabic airline.
- LACAC, the Latin American Civil Aviation Commission.[117] LACAC has held a number of conferences,[118] concentrating on non-scheduled

112. See note 101, *supra*.
113. Protocol to Amend the Eurocontrol International Convention relating to Co-operation for the Safety of Air Navigation, Brussels, February 12, 1981.
114. See about this subject J. Moussé, 'Eurocontrol: The Changes effected in International Organisation by the Instruments Signed on 12 February 1981', *Air Law*, vol.VI (1982), pp. 22-40; and also J.F. Bentzien, 'Der europäische Luftverkehr und der EWG- Vertrag' [1981] ZLW 258–277, at 274–275; A.E. du Perron, 'Eurocontrol: Liability and Jurisdiction', *Air Worthy* pp. 135-149.
115. AFCAC was the result of the Addis Ababa Conference of 1969; see *Annals of Air and Space Law*, Vol. II (1977), pp. 202-203 and also I.I. Lessedjina, *La coopération multilatérale interafricaine en aviation civile* (Presses Universitaires de Zaïre, 1977), and Shawcross and Beaumont, *Air Law* (1981), Vol. 2, para. 139 in the section entitled 'Noter-up to Volume 1'.
116. The agreement on the CACAS came into force in October 1967. See Shawcross and Beaumont, *Air Law* (1977), Vol. 1 para. 138 (pp. 117-118).
117. LACAC was founded at a meeting in Mexico City in 1973. See J.C. Bogolasky, 'Air Transport in Latin America: the Expanding Role of LACAC' [1978] JALC 75–107 and also Shawcross and Beaumont, *Air Law* (1977), Vol. 1, para. 139 (pp. 118-119).
118. For instance: Buenos Aires, 1974; Montevideo, 1976; Santiago de Chile, 1978; and Bogotá, 1980.

air transport tariff structures and a 'Code de la navigation aérienne latino-américaine'.[119]

In conclusion we must mention,

- ASECNA, l'Agence pour la Sécurité de la Navigation Aérienne en Afrique et Madagascar,[120] and
- COCESNA, the Corporación Centroamericana de Servicios de Navigación Aerea.[121]

The main effect of intergovernmental co-operation for greater air safety lies in the harmonisation procedures and the standardisation of equipment.

15.   Bilateralism[122]

When it became apparent that achieving more freedom in the air by means of exchanging the five freedoms in a multilateral convention was impossible, states had to turn to reciprocity as a basis for granting each other commercial (traffic) rights. In practice this took the form of bilateral agreements based on Article 6 of the Chicago Convention, and it is exemplified by the Bermuda I Agreement between the United States and Great Britain.[123] The Bermuda I Agreement became of particular importance to civil aviation because it gave a standard formula for exchanging traffic rights and thereby a powerful impetus towards the conclusion of a large number of bilateral agreements (totalling approximately 1,200 in number).[124]

In these bilateral agreements, the text of certain Articles of the Chicago Convention was often incorporated.

The main issues affecting international aviation are routes, tariffs and capacity. The re-establishment of IATA in Havana in 1945 by 31 airlines operating scheduled services had been chiefly aimed at fixing and controlling tariffs; the Parties exceeded the bilateral scope of the air agreements by referring the establishment of tariffs to multilateral coordination within the IATA Traffic Conferences.

---

119.   See notes on LACAC activities by Bogolasky in *Annals of Air and Space Law* (1977), Vol. II, pp. 464-468 and in (1981), Vol. V, pp. 655-657.

120.   ASECNA Convention, Saint Louis du Sénégal, December 12, 1959. See *Yearbook of Air and Space Law* (1965), Vol. I, pp. 116 *et seq.* and also Lessedjina (see note 115, *supra*).

121.   Convention on the Central American Air Navigation Corporation, Tegucigalpa, February 26, 1960.

122.   This paragraph refers mainly to passenger services; for bilateralism with regard to cargo services see R.J. Fennes, *International Air Cargo Services: Economic Regulation and Policy*, thesis Leiden, 1997.

123.   Agreement between the Government of the United Kingdom and the Government of the United States relating to Air Services between their respective Territories, Bermuda, February 11, 1946; hereinafter cited as the Bermuda I Agreement.

124.   See also on this subject J.C. Cooper, 'The Bermuda Plan – World Pattern for Air Transport' (1946) 25 *Foreign Affairs* 59-71; H.A. Wassenbergh, *Aspects of Air Law and Civil Air Policy in the Seventies* (1971); P. van der Tuuk Adriani, 'The "Bermuda" Capacity Clauses' [1955] JALC 406–413.

The Bermuda I Agreement is characterised by liberal route descriptions and flexible capacity arrangements. As there were differences of approach between the United States and Great Britain, the Agreement represented a compromise between liberalism and protectionism involving a quite open route and capacity system but a 'closed' (IATA) tariff-regime.

The spectacular success of the first Bermuda Agreement is probably due to its conciliatory nature and somewhat vaguely worded rules. The Agreement was concluded between two leading powers in aviation at a time when there were conflicting aims and policies between them: Great Britain favoured a restrictive policy, whereas the United States was a champion of freedom. The Agreement's terminology was sufficiently flexible to accommodate both principles to a certain extent. Some experts feel that Bermuda's success stemmed also from the fact that the United States and Great Britain agreed to accept its clauses as standard and not to conclude aviation agreements with third countries that were either more liberal or more restrictive than the agreement they had reached between them.[125]

What were the contents of the Bermuda Agreement of 1946? Its basic principle, in its Article 4 of the Final Act, was that states should have a 'fair and equal opportunity' to operate the agreed international air services, based upon the volume of air traffic to and from their own country. The establishment of tariffs was left to the Traffic Conferences of the International Air Transport Association but the IATA-agreed tariffs were subject to the approval of the aeronautical authorities of both Parties. Parties granted each other the right to designate one or more air companies that were allowed to operate regular international air services over the specified routes (multiple designation).

In addition, Article 5 contains the provision that 'in the operation by the air carriers of either Government of the trunk services described in the Annex to the Agreement, the interest of the air carriers of the other Government shall be taken into consideration so as not to affect unduly the services which the latter provides on all or part of the same routes'.

Furthermore, parties agreed to recognise each other's aircraft documentation and crew licences and to comply with each other's rules regarding health, customs and immigration. Disputes would be settled by consultation, obligatory advice or arbitration. Article 9 mentions that 'it is the intention of both Governments that there should be regular and frequent consultation between their respective aeronautical authorities (as defined in the Agreement) and that there should thereby be close collaboration in the observance of the principles and the implementation of the provisions outlined herein and in the Agreement and its Annex'.

---

125. See also P. van der Tuuk Adriani, 'Some Observations on the newly born Bermuda II', *Air Law*, vol. II (1977), pp. 190-193, at 190.

Article 6 contains the famous clause to the effect that the agreed services shall retain 'as their primary objective' the provision of capacity adequate to the traffic demands between the country of which the air carrier operating the service is a national and the country of ultimate destination of the traffic.

As regards transport capacity based on the so-called Bermuda capacity clauses, all decisions concerning the main flights and the necessary equipment are left to the management of the designated airline companies, with *ex post facto* supervision by the two governments through consultations. The guiding principle in all this was to rule out predetermination of capacity: capacity was to be determined 'after the fact', on the basis of traffic actually carried.

The post-war pattern for international scheduled air services was established along these lines early in 1946. It was based on the Bermuda standard formula for bilateral agreements. In addition, the recognition of IATA as the multilateral fixer of tariffs worldwide made it possible for a fully-integrated air transport system to be established. The public was thus enabled to use one single contract of carriage for transportation over any combination of routes flown by IATA carriers.

This system of interlining worked well for over thirty years, but thereafter difficulties arose mainly because of the US Civil Aeronautic Board's discontent with the level of the agreed IATA fares and rates, which were considered to be generally too high. Meanwhile and in the interest of the travelling public the CAB liberalised the US non-scheduled (charter) regulations. This development caused a tremendous increase of charter operations on the North Atlantic route and put pressure on the tariff–setting for scheduled air services in the IATA Traffic Conferences.

The 1970's were characterized by the oil crisis and the economic recession which seriously affected air transport.

In the USA the International Air Transportation Fair Competitive Practices Act of 1974, the Deregulation Act of 1978, the CAB Show Cause Order of June 9, 1978, directed against the IATA 'cartel', and the International Air Transportation Competition Act of 1979, all contributed to a trend to progressively 'deregulate' not only USA domestic but also international air transportation.[126] The denunciation by the UK of the Bermuda Agreement on June 22, 1976, necessitating a full renegotiation of the bilateral air relationship between the USA and the UK, resulted, at the last possible moment in 1977, in agreement on what is called the Bermuda II agreement.[127]

The UK had become disenchanted with Bermuda I working basically in favour of US carriers and wanted closer regulation of routes,

---

126. See A.F. Lowenfeld, *Aviation Law* (1981), Chap. 4 and 5. The texts of the mentioned Acts are reproduced in the *Documents Supplement* to his book.

127. Agreement between the Government of the United Kingdom of Great Britain and Northern Ireland and the Government of the United States concerning Air Services, Bermuda, July 23, 1977; hereinafter cited as Bermuda II Agreement. See also P. van der Tuuk Adriani (note 125, *supra*) and the various contributions in *Air Law*, vol. III (1978), pp. 2-30.

capacity and frequencies, designation and fifth freedom traffic rights as well as of tariffs. In other words, Great Britain wanted to implement a more restrictive air policy than embodied in the Bermuda I agreement and was partly successful. In the USA strong criticism was voiced against the protectionist provisions of the Bermuda II agreement, which were at variance with the ever stronger call for de-regulation of the air transport industry in the interest of the consumer.

The Agreement virtually abolished the fifth freedom opportunities available to especially US air carriers under Bermuda I, while the multiple designation of air carriers to operate any of the specified routes was severely restricted. Moreover, IATA's role as a tariff-setting machinery was downgraded.

An important clause is anchored in Annex 4: a permanent working group on tariffs has been provided for, whereby a method and a forum have been created for governments to sort out mutual problems. Nevertheless it remains most questionable whether Bermuda II will ever be able to contribute as much to the development of international air transport as its illustrious predecessor.

For one thing, the emphasis placed by the USA on US anti-trust legislation being applicable to international air transport, especially in view of their efforts to deregulate the industry, created a lot of controversy between the USA on the one hand and the UK and other European countries on the other. The UK view was that Bermuda II would become virtually unworkable if it could be overridden by US anti-trust laws, while the USA felt that no international agreement could abrogate basic civil rights of US citizens.

16.   Deregulation

In 1978 a new international aviation policy was enacted in the United States: the policy that was soon to become known under the name of 'deregulation'. It was based on the principle of 'fare and fairer' competition, which meant 'no government intervention in scheduled fares except by mutual agreement' and 'internationalisation of traffic'.

The first agreement embodying these principles was the 'Protocol relating to the US-Netherlands Air Transport Agreement of 1957', which was signed at Washington on March 31, 1978.[128] The Netherlands had always been in favour of more liberalisation in aviation policy.

The Protocol, in Article 2, spoke 'designated airlines', be they schedule-designated, charter-designated, or both. Article 3 provided more route flexibility. According to Article 4(a) charter services rights were based on country of origin rules, and scheduled tariffs subjected to country of origin approval only. the lowest fares, rates or prices were to be

---

128. Air Transport Agreement between the Government of the Kingdom of the Netherlands and the Government of the United States of America, Washington, April 3, 1957. Protocol Relating to United States-Netherlands Air Transport Agreement of 1957, Washington, March 31, 1978. See H.A. Wassenbergh, 'Innovation in international air transportation regulation (the US–Netherlands Agreement of March 10, 1978)' (1978) 3 *Air Law* 138–162.

competitive, but not predatory or discriminatory, and fixed by each designated airline individually with a minimum of government intervention (Article 6(a)). As regards capacity, the only mandatory provision which remained was the requirement that capacity should be related to traffic demand for agreed services (Article 11).

Similar agreements have been concluded between the USA and a number of other countries, e.g. the German Federal Republic, Belgium, Israel, and Jamaica.

The reaction of less competitive and therefore more protectionist countries was to place more emphasis on third- and fourth-freedom operations and markets, which tended to damage their own long-term interests and to counteract the ever-increasing need for sixth-freedom traffic rights and interconnecting routes: a truly international and integrated air transportation system cannot be based on direct, point-to-point third-and fourth-freedom traffic licences alone.

While these developments were taking place the US government continued its drive for more liberalisation, resulting eventually in it adopting an 'open skies' policy. Its objective was to allow designated carriers free access to foreign markets and to create maximum flexibility for them to carry out their business with a minimum of government interference. In the wake of these events the USA-Netherlands Agreement of 1957 and its Protocol of 1978 were amended accordingly in September 1992. These revisions caused quite a stir in Europe as the resulting texts were contrary in a number of aspects to the then just started EC programme: almost simultaneously the European Community enacted a number of important liberalisation measures in a series of Council Regulations (see section 14.2 of this chapter, *supra*).

A comparison with the American effort shows that American-style deregulation was not considered suitable for European consumption: there were too many differences. To name but a few: the USA is one large internal market, Europe has many markets; air transport in the USA is reserved for US carriers while Europe allows many non-European carriers; in the USA, government interference is practically non-existant, whereas in Europe it is quite an important factor; and in the USA there are no state-owned airline companies, unlike in Europe, where there are several.

Considering all the liberalisation trends going on at present it must be realised that they cannot be entirely separated from the clearly identifiable factors and developments in the environment within which aviation fulfills its role. These factors vary considerably in different parts of the world. In the industrial world, for instance, the USA, Canada, Europe and Japan, consumer interests demand a great deal of competition in order to keep tariffs down. On the other hand government charges, airport fees, environmental taxes and restrictions and the constant need for fuel-saving are all elements that must be taken into account when regulatory measures are being considered. And, last but not least, one of the main objectives of the Chicago Convention, namely to afford every nation an opportunity to operate international air services soundly and economically, must be heeded at all times.

Despite all the obstacles yet to overcome on the road to full liberalisation it can be stated without any reservation that the era of bilateralism in aviation policy has come to an end, at least inasmuch the USA and Europe are concerned. Also in Australia important progress in the same direction has already been made.[129]

Apart from the Chicago/bilateral developments described above, attempts have been made during the Uruguay Round of GATT negotiations[130] aimed at establishing a General Agreement on Trade in Services (GATS). This GATS agreement also includes air services, but only in terms of ancillary rights. These were hitherto regulated by the Chicago Convention and also by bilateral agreements. Traffic-related rights will not come under the GATS. States which become parties to GATS will have to record and file their existing commitments established under the Chicago system. Where these are less permissive than GATS rules the latter will have priority.[131]

ICAO discussed GATS and its application to air transport extensively at its World Air Transport Colloquium in April 1992[132] and at its Conference in 1994.[133]

Meanwhile, in October 1993, a revised text of GATS was published.[134] At the end of that year the Uruguay Round was concluded and the GATS agreement signed. Following the rejuvenating of the GATT agreement and organisation the latter will henceforth be entitled the World Trade Organisation (WTO).

129. See also Roderick D. van Dam, 'Licensing as an instrument of deregulation', *Air Worthy*, pp. 75-87; P.P.C. Haanappel, 'Deregulation of air transport in North America and Western Europe', *Air Worthy*, pp. 89–115; Jurgen Reifarth, *Internationale Regelungen der Tarife im Linienluftverkehr*, Europäische Hochschulschriften, Reihe II, Rechtswissenschaft, Bd. 478, 1985; H.A. Wassenbergh, 'The "right to fly" and the "right to carry traffic by air", in international air transportation, after 40 years', *Air Worthy*, pp. 215-233. P.P.C. Haanappel, 'Recent Regulatory Developments in Europe', *Annals of Air and Space Law*, vol. XVI (1991), pp. 107-125; J. Naveau, *Droit Européen: Les Nouvelles Règles du Jeu* (1993); and F. de Coninck, *European Air Law: New Skies for Europe* (1993).

130. The GATT was established in 1948 on the coming into force of the General Agreement on Tariffs and Trade, negotiated and initially signed by 23 countries. The GATT is the principal international negotiating body for reduction of barriers in international trade.

131. See M. Zylicz, 'Key Problems of the Future International Air Transport Regime', *Air and Space Law*, vol. XIX (1994), pp. 185-188 and R. Ebdon, 'A Consideration of GATS and its Compatibility with the Existing Regime for Air Transport', *Air and Space Law*, vol. XX (1995), pp. 71-75.

132. See R.I.R. Abeyratne, *Legal and Regulatory Issues of Computer Reservation Systems and Code Sharing Agreements in Air Transport*, 1995 (Forum for Air and Space Law, vol. 3), p. 51 *et seq.*

133. See A. Gil, 'The Outcome of the 4th ICAO Air Transport Conference and its Implications for Airports', *Air and Space Law*, vol. XX (1995), pp. 76-81.

134. Abeyratne, *op. cit.* (note 132, *supra*), p. 67.

CHAPTER III

The Liability of the Carrier under the 'Warsaw System'

1. Introductory note

It was the Warsaw Convention for the Unification of Certain Rules Relating to International Carriage by Air, dating from 1929, which firmly established and elaborated, as one of its major tenets, the principle of the air carrier's liability for damage caused to passengers, baggage and goods, and also for damage caused by delay.

The rules of the Warsaw Convention[1] are being applied all over the world and have demonstrated their reliability and usefulness. The passenger knows that, wherever and whenever he flies, there is a certain degree of uniformity in the rules governing the carrier's liability, while the carrier, being aware of the extent of his liability, can make arrangements to insure himself against possible losses. It is therefore appropriate to examine the nature and the development of the legal grounds on which the air carrier's liability rests, and their impact on everyday practice. The present chapter will be entirely devoted to these important matters.

As time went by and aviation began expanding on a large scale, the Warsaw Convention had to be amended or added to on a number of occasions in order to be kept up to date. The amendments and/or additions are the following:

1. The Hague Protocol of 1955.[2] It was added to the Warsaw Convention with the aim of adapting it to the demands of modern transport. The Protocol entered into force on August 1, 1963, the ninetieth day after ratification by 30 countries.
2. The Guadalajara Convention of 1961 for the Unification of Certain Rules Relating to International Carriage by Air Performed by a Person Other than the Contracting Carrier.[3] This amendment took the form of a Supplementary Convention because it was concluded to deal with an entirely new subject-matter, namely chartering. It has been in force since May 1, 1964.

---

1. Convention for the Unification of Certain Rules Relating to International Carriage by Air, Warsaw, October 2, 1929; hereinafter cited as Warsaw Convention.
2. Protocol to Amend the Convention for the Unification of Certain Rules Relating to International Carriage by Air, The Hague, September 28, 1955; hereinafter cited as the Hague Protocol.
3. Convention Supplementary to the Warsaw Convention, for the Unification of Certain Rules Relating to International Carriage by Air Performed by a Person Other than the Contracting Carrier, Guadalajara, September 18, 1961; hereinafter cited as Guadalajara Convention.

3. The Guatemala Protocol of March 8, 1971[4] was also meant to be an amendment to the Warsaw Convention. This Protocol, however, has yet to come into force.
4. Another four amending Protocols were concluded at Montreal on September 25, 1975,[5] They have not yet entered into force either.
5. Finally, there is the Montreal Agreement of May 1966,[6] a private agreement concluded between IATA carriers and the United States Civil Aeronautics Board, and the so-called 'Malta Agreement', which is a private agreement between a number of air carriers, mostly from Europe.

The basic Convention of Warsaw and the amendments listed above will now be considered in detail in their chronological order. The structure of the 'Warsaw System' is illustrated on page 107.

2. The Warsaw Convention

2.1. APPLICABILITY

The original text of the Warsaw Convention may conveniently be examined first in terms of its applicabilty, and we note immediately, in Article 1, that it applies only when the transportation is international (although many nations apply its rules also to transportation within their borders). Another notable element is that the Convention is applicable to all international carriage of persons, baggage or goods for reward.

Gratuitous carriage by aircraft is also covered by the Convention, but only when performed by an air transport company. Other gratuitous carriage is not included. The reason why an exception has been made for carriage by an air transport company is that free tickets are usually issued with the intention of obtaining something in return, *e.g.* for propaganda purposes. Rules concerning gratuitous carriage, when it occurs, are normally to be found in domestic law.[7]

Naturally, the question arises: what exactly is to be regarded as 'international carriage'? What does the term 'international transportation'

---

4. Protocol to Amend the Warsaw Convention, Guatemala City, March 8, 1971; hereinafter cited as the Guatemala Protocol.
5. Additional Protocol No. 1 (2, [3], 4) to Amend the Convention for the Unification of Certain Rules Relating to International Carriage by Air Signed at Warsaw on 12th October 1929 (as Amended by the Protocol[s] Done at The Hague on 28th September 1955 [and at Guatemala City on 8 March 1971]), Montreal, September 25, 1975; hereinafter to be cited as the Montreal Protocols or Montreal Protocol No. 1 (2, 3 or 4).
6. Agreement Relating to Liability Limitations of the Warsaw Convention and the Hague Protocol, Montreal, May 1966; hereinafter cited as the Montreal Agreement. Agreement on the text was reached on May 4, 1966; the Agreement was accepted by the United States authorities on May 13 and it became effective on May 16, 1966.
7. See also section 2.9 of this Chapter and I.H.Ph. de Rode-Verschoor, 'Liability Arising from Gratuitous Carriage by Air' (1966) 1 *EVR* 490-534.

really mean? Article 1 provides the answer: for the purposes of the Convention the expression 'international carriage' means any transportation in which, according to the agreement made by the parties, the point of departure and the point of destination, whether or not an interruption in the carriage or a transhipment occurs, are situated either within the territories of two High Contracting Parties, or within the territory of a single High Contracting Party if there is an agreed stopping place within the territory of another state, even if that state is not a High Contracting Party. The applicability of the Convention is not affected by incidental occurrences like an emergency landing.

In the case of *Grein* v. *Imperial Airways*[8] 'agreed stopping place' was defined as a place 'where according to the contract the machine by which the contract is to be performed will stop in the course of performing the contractual carriage, whatever the purpose of the descent may be and whatever rights the passenger may have to break his journey at that place'.

It should be noted with regard to 'agreed stopping places' that it was deemed sufficient for them to be referred to, for instance, in the timetables of the carrier, even if they had not been specifically mentioned in the documents.[9] In the same case it was ruled that 'an intermediate place at which the carriage may be broken is not regarded as a "place of destination"'.

The international character of the contract is determined by the intention of the parties as expressed in that contract. There are three exceptions to the applicability of the Convention, namely:

a. the Convention does not apply to international carriage by air performed by way of experimental trial by air navigation enterprises with a view to the establishment of regular air services on a certain route, as for instance when airline companies were planning to fly over the North Pole (Art. 34);
b. the Convention does not apply to carriage performed in extraordinary circumstances outside the normal scope of an air carrier's business, as for instance when an accident occurred to an aircraft bringing a new engine to a ship that had developed engine trouble while out fishing for sardines (Art. 34)[10];
c. the Convention does not apply to carriage performed under the terms of any international postal convention (Art. 2, para. 2).

8. *Grein* v. *Imperial Airways*, Court of Appeal (England), July 13, 1936; *Avi*, Vol. 1, p. 622; [1936] USAvR, 211.
9. *Rotterdamsche Bank* v. *BOAC (and Aden Airways)*, High Court of Justice, Queen's Bench Division (United Kingdom), February 18, 1953; [1953] USAvR 163; *IATA Law Reporter*, No. 1. See also section 2.2.1 of this chapter.
10. See also *Vanderburg* v. *French Sardine Company and Souby*, California Superior Court, October 29, 1953; [1953] USAvR 423.

Unlike other Conventions, the Warsaw Convention mentions explicitly that its terms do apply to carriage performed by the state. It is, however, possible to make a reservation excluding this type of carriage. Only the USA has made use of this option.

The question whether or not the Warsaw Convention has been suspended as a consequence of the Second World War is a matter of great practical importance, as is illustrated by an accident near Frankfurt in 1952 involving a KLM plane flying from Johannesburg (South Africa) to Amsterdam (The Netherlands) via Kano (Nigeria), Rome (Italy) and Frankfurt (Federal Republic of Germany).[11]

Analysing the case in terms of the applicability of the Warsaw Convention one must carefully bear in mind the following facts: the Union of South Africa had not acceded to the Convention at the time of the accident, so it did not apply to the passengers who had boarded the plane in Johannesburg. The Netherlands and Nigeria had both ratified the Convention (the UK had done so on behalf of Nigeria), and both states had reconfirmed the validity of the Convention with the German Federal Republic. Accordingly, it did apply to passengers who had boarded at Kano with Frankfurt or Amsterdam as their destination. Italy had ratified, but not reconfirmed with the Federal Republic of Germany, so the Convention applied to passengers Rome-Amsterdam, but not to passengers Rome-Frankfurt.

An additional problem in the relationship between Nigeria and the German Federal Republic was that, although both states had ratified the Convention, a state of war formally still existed between them, no peace treaty having been concluded as yet. The question arising here was whether the Warsaw Convention, a non-political agreement, had been cancelled due to the state of war, or just suspended, and, in the latter case, whether it had become operative again after hostilities had ended.

In an American court case[12] the judge ruled that the question whether a Convention is reconcilable with the political needs or the security of a state had to be decided from case to case. On the one hand there is support for those who argue that the Warsaw Convention has fully remained in force between the nations at war, and indeed the theory that non-political agreements had only been suspended by the hostilities has been amply vindicated in post-War international practice. Against this theory it may be argued that after the War several states exchanged notes about reviving the Convention, but this may also be interpreted as a move to reconfirm the validity of the Convention. Seen in that light, no law-making effect can be attributed to such exchanges of notes. The fact that they have also taken place with neutral states like Sweden, Switzerland and Spain seems to

---

11. See for this case the articles listed in note 13, *infra*.
12. *Techt* v. *Hughes*, 229 NY 222; 128 NE 185. See Drion (note 13, *infra*), at p. 304.

favour the latter interpretation. No similar exchange of notes has taken place in respect of the 1933 Convention of Rome concerning precautionary attachment.[13]

Is a signatory state which has not ratified a party to the Convention? In a decision by the House of Lords in the case of *Philippson* v. *Imperial Airways* this question has been answered in the affirmative.[14]

The Convention does not cover the entire relationship between the carrier and the passengers or the consignors of goods. Supplementary rules are to be found in the IATA Conditions based on the Convention, about which more will be said later.

To what types of aircraft will the Warsaw Convention be applicable? As the Convention itself provides no clue we shall have to rely on the general definition found in the Annexes to the Chicago Convention, a definition which in turn had its origin in the Paris Convention, namely: 'Any machine that can derive support in the atmosphere from the reactions of the air'. A very wide definition indeed, since it comprises also helicopters, gliders, balloons, etc. The fact that ICAO has altered this definition by adding the words 'other than the reactions against the earth's surface' is a clear sign of the inapplicability of the Convention to carriage by hovercraft.[15]

Another question requiring an answer is: who precisely is a 'passenger'? A passenger within the meaning of the Convention is a person who is carried by aircraft by virtue of a contract of carriage. Is an airline employee to be regarded as a passenger within the meaning of the Convention? Opinions are divided on this point. On the one hand there are those asserting that the Convention applies exclusively to the legal relationship between the carrier and the passenger who has a contract of carriage with him. There is nothing in the Convention on obligations with regard to persons who have no contract of carriage with the carrier. Other writers, however, hold the view that an employee is not only bound by the terms of his contract, but also by those of the contract of carriage.[16] It is interesting to compare this matter with the Rome Convention of 1952, which may not be applicable when there is a contract of employment.

13. See on this subject H. Achtnicht, 'Luftrechtliche Betrachtungen anlässlich des Absturzes eines Flugzeuges der Königlich Niederländischen Luftverkehrsgesellschaft (KLM) am 22. März 1952 bei Frankfurt-am-Main' [1952] Zfl 323-346; H. Drion, 'Kritische Bemerkungen zum Anwendungsbereich des Warschauer Abkommens' [1953] Zfl 303-313; see also the annotation on the *Wucherpfennig* case (note 64, *infra*) [1955] Zfl 233 *et seq*. See also P.H. Kooijmans, 'State succession and the 1929 Warsaw Convention—A case study', in Air and Space Law: *De Lege Ferenda* (1992), pp. 113-133.
14. *Philippson* v. *Imperial Airways*, House of Lords (Great Britain), March 2, 1939; [1939] USAvR 63.
15. See also Chap. 1, section 5 of this book.
16. Also on this subject: I.H.Ph. Diederiks-Verschoor, *et al.*, 'Die Rechtsstellung des Personals der Zivilluftfahrt' [1972] ZLW 107-132.

2.2. DOCUMENTS OF CARRIAGE

2.2.1. The passenger ticket

For the carriage of passengers the carrier is under an obligation to issue a ticket containing the following details:
- place and date of issue;
- points of departure and destination;
- intermediate stops, if any;
- name and address of the carrier; and,
- a notice that carriage is subject to the provisions of the Warsaw Convention.

When no ticket is issued or when it gets lost or contains an inaccuracy the contract of carriage stands and the Convention remains applicable.[17] However, the consequences for a carrier accepting a passenger without issuing a ticket are far-reaching: he will not be able to invoke the exclusion or limitation of liability laid down in the Convention, and he will be fully liable. It is for the domestic legislation to decide under what conditions a valid contract of transportation comes into being. As regards tickets, there are two problems:
1. what has to be included in tickets and documents? These elements have been referred to above;
2. what is the penalty for the carrier's non-compliance with the requirements of the Convention?

As mentioned earlier, the carrier will, according to the Warsaw Convention, be exposed to unlimited liability when no ticket has been issued to the passenger. Under the Hague Protocol this rule has been made to apply also when the ticket does not include the notice referring to the possible applicability of the Warsaw Convention.

In an American courtcase, where a theatrical director had been holding all the tickets of his employees, it was ruled unnecessary for the ticket to be issued to the passenger personally.[18] A very different attitude now prevails in United States courts: the delivery of the ticket to the passenger is now considered mandatory to enable him to take adequate notice of the liability limitations.

An illustration of this principle is to be found in the case of *Mertens* v. *Flying Tiger Line*,[19] where it was held that 'the ticket be delivered to the passenger in such a manner as to afford him reasonable opportunity

---

17. See e.g. *Manion* v. *Pan American World Airways*, New York State Supreme Court, Appellate Division, May 12, 1981; 16 *Avi* 17,473
18. *Ross (Jane Froman)* v. *Pan-American Airways*, Court of Appeals, New York State, April 14, 1949; [1949] USAvR 168; *Avi*, Vol. 2, p. 14,911.
19. *Mertens* v. *Flying Tiger Line*, US Court of Appeals (2nd Circ.), February 16, 1965; *Avi*, Vol. 9, p. 17,475; [1965] USAvR 1; IATA ACLR. No. 169. See also *Newsome* v. *Trans International Airlines*, Supreme Court of Alabama, March 28, 1986; 20 *Avi* 17,360.

to take measures to protect himself against the limitation of the liability. Such self-protecting measures, for example, could consist of deciding not to take the flight, entering into a special contract with the carrier, or taking out additional insurance for the flight'. In this case the ticket had not been delivered until after Mertens had boarded the plane.

In the case of *Lisi* v. *Alitalia*[20] the relevant clauses in the conditions of carriage printed on the ticket had been rendered 'unnoticeable and unreadable' due to 'Lilliputian typography', hence the passenger's attention had not been properly drawn to the liability limitations and, consequently, he had not really been able to protect himself by taking out additional insurance. The court ruled that no adequate notice had been given to the passenger and that no proper issuing of the ticket had taken place.

An interesting situation arises when the passenger is unable to understand the foreign language in which the notice is printed. The Greek High Court of Justice ruled that the fact that the plaintiffs did not know English and so did not understand the notice concerning the applicability of the Warsaw limits was irrelevant.[21] In a case of carriage not covered by the Warsaw Convention rules it was held by a French court that, in France, issuing a ticket entirely made out in English was contrary to the law.[22]

As indicated above, the ticket must mention the scheduled intermediate stops, and a strict interpretation of Article 3 would require them all to be listed individually on the ticket. In *Grey* v. *American Airlines* the court ruled that the ticket need not mention the intermediate stops, but that it was sufficient for it to refer to the official timetable of the airline.[23] The same applies to the air waybill as a consequence of the judgment in *Kraus* v. *KLM*.[24]

While on the subject of ticketing a new trend must be noted which is emerging lately in the extremely competitive world of civil aviation:

20. *Lisi* v. *Alitalia Linee Aeree Italiane*, US District Court, Southern District of New York, April 1, 1966; *Avi*, Vol 9, p. 18,120; IATA ACLR, No. 188. Affirmed: US Court of Appeals, December 16, 1966; *Avi*, Vol. 9, p. 18,734; IATA ACLR, No. 209. Affirmed by an equally divided Court: US Supreme Court, 1968; Avi, Vol. 10, p. 17,785. See also *Montreal Trust Co. et al.* v. *Canadian Pacific Airlines et al.*, Supreme Court of Canada, December 20, 1976; *Avi*, Vol 14, p. 17,510; [1976] USAvR 469. See also R.H. Mankiewicz, 'the US Supreme Court finally overrules Lisi v. Alitalia?', Air Law, vol. XV (1989), pp. 45-47.

21. *X and Y* v. *Olympic Airways*, High Court of Greece, date not indicated; IATA ACLR, No. 475; Schoner's case law digest, Air Law, vol. I (1976), p. 259.

22. *Vandelay and the Association Générale des Usagers de la Langue Française* v. *Roberts and British Airways*, Tribunal de Grande Instance de Paris, February 8, 1978; [1979] RFDA 97; Schoner's case law digest, Air Law, vol V (1980), p. 42.

23. *Grey et al.* v. *American Airlines*, US District Court, Southern District of New York, December 21, 1950; [1950] USAvR 507; *Avi*, Vol. 3, p. 17,404. Affirmed: US Court of Appeals, November 7, 1955; IATA ACLR, No. 30; *Avi*, Vol. 4, p. 17,811; [1955] USAvR 626. See for a case centering on the consequential use of flight coupons (starting the journey at an intermediate stop), *Malibu Travel* v. *KLM*, District Court Amsterdam, December 20, 1995; *Air and Space Law*, vol. XXI (1996), pp. 161-164.

24. *Kraus* v. *KLM Royal Dutch Airlines*, New York Supreme Court, October 3, 1949; [1949] USAvR; *Avi*, Vol. 2, p. 15,017.

'flying without a ticket'. In view of the high costs involved in issuing tickets and boarding cards a number of air lines have decided to replace them by a new, simpler type of procedure: bookings are dealt with directly by the airline by telephone, a booking reference number is quoted and the passenger simply turns up at the airport paying his fare at the airline's desk. Upon quoting the reference number the passenger receives a docket containing his name, flight number and destination. Printed on the back of this simple slip of paper is the usual notice concerning the possible application of the Warsaw Convention. The docket may carry headings like 'Conditions of Carriage', 'Boarding Information' or other titles. It may, however, be more prudent to entitle it: 'ticket'.[25]

2.2.2. The baggage check

In Article 4 the Convention requires that a baggage check shall be issued for the transportation of baggage other than the items of which the passenger takes charge himself. The baggage check must be made out in duplicate, and must contain the same particulars as mentioned above for the passenger ticket. It must also contain a reference to the serial number of the passenger ticket, the number and weight of the packages, the amount of value declared in case the passenger has made such a declaration, and, finally, a statement to the effect that the baggage will be delivered to the bearer of the check.

In the case of absence, irregularity or loss of the check the contract stands and the Convention rules remain applicable. The carrier, however, will be subject to unlimited liability if he accepts any baggage without issuing a baggage check. The same applies in the event of inaccuracies in the filling out of the check.[26]

The number of requirements was significantly reduced by the Hague Protocol amendments; following everyday practice, the baggage check may now be combined with or incorporated in the passenger ticket. Only a reference to the possibility of liability limitations being applicable remains mandatory in such tickets.

---

25. See R.Schmid, 'Der Flugschein - seine Bedeutung für Fluggast und Luftfrachtführer', in *Festschrift für Henning Piper* (W.Erdmann, W.Gloy and R.Herber, eds.), 1996, pp. 999-1013; and P.Martin, ' "Phone in, Turn up, Take off", a Look at the Legal Implications of Self-service Ticketing', *Air and Space Law*, vol.XX (1995), pp. 189-195.

26. See also section 2.5 of this Chapter, notably the discussion of the *Rifahi* case (notes 41 and 42). See also J. Barrett and R.A. Lewis 'Failure to comply with documentary technicalities of Warsaw Convention leads to unlimited liability in baggage cases', *Air Law*, vol. XV (1990), pp. 98-99.

As regards baggage, we note further that IATA has inserted in Article I of its General Conditions of Carriage (Passengers)[27] a clause describing the meaning of the term 'baggage', which reads as follows: 'Baggage means such articles, effects and other personal property of a passenger as are necessary or appropriate for wear, use, comfort or convenience with his trip. Unless otherwise specified, it shall include both checked and unchecked baggage of the passenger'.

In Article IX, para. 1(a), IATA provides that the passenger shall not include in his baggage:

'(i) Articles which do not constitute baggage as defined in Article I hereof.

(ii) Articles which are likely to endanger the aircraft or persons or property on board the aircraft,...

(iii) Articles the carriage of which is prohibited by the applicable laws, regulations or orders of any state to be flown from, to or over.

(iv) Articles which in the opinion of Carrier are unsuitable for carriage by reason of their weight, size or character.

(v) Live animals,...' (with certain exceptions listed in other paragraphs of this Article).[28]

The carrier may refuse to transport as baggage any of the articles described above, and he may refuse onward carriage of any baggage on discovering that the passenger's baggage does contain such articles. Moreover, the carrier has the right to request the passenger to permit a search of his person or baggage in order to determine whether he is in possession of such unacceptable articles, or whether his baggage contains any.

The consequences of the crew discovering during the flight that a passenger has brought an unacceptably dangerous article on board are illustrated in a German decision of 1961: the passenger had to pay all the costs involved in an emergency landing made to remove the article (a bottle of ether) from the aircraft.[29]

Article IX, para. 5, gives further provisions with regard to articles unacceptable as checked baggage, such as fragile or perishable articles, money, jewelry, precious metals, negotiable papers, securities and other valuables, business documents or samples. Checked baggage will be carried on the same aircraft as the passenger unless the carrier decides this to be impracticable; nothing is said, however, about other baggage to be transported in the same aircraft as the passenger.

27. See for the 1970 version of the 'IATA General Conditions (Passengers)' [1971] ZLW 214-232. These Conditions were adopted at the 1970 Honolulu Conference of IATA and are merely 'recommended practice', effective from April 1, 1971. See also Shawcross and Beaumont, *Air Law* (1977), Vol. 1, paras. 373 et *seq.* and the references in earlier editions of the said book; see for the 1986 IATA conditions Vol. 2 p. D-29 and also *Air Law*, vol. X (1985), pp. 220-223. Similar 'General Conditions of Carriage' for cargo are no longer 'recommended'. The IATA standard form of 'Conditions of Contract' (see note 68, *infra*) are, however, obligatory.

28. See for a case where a dog was held to be luggage: *Gluckmann* v. *American Airlines*, US District Court for the Southern District of New York, February 9, 1994; 24 *Avi* 17,947; *Air and Space Law*, vol.XX (1995), p.171.

29. Amtsgericht Frankfurt-am-Main, February 3, 1961; [1961] ZLW 205.

Finally, Article IX, para. 9(a), provides that 'The passenger shall collect his baggage as soon as it is available for collection at places of destination or stopover'.

2.2.3. The air waybill

The air waybill is made out in triplicate. By means of Article 6 of the Convention, which gives all three copies the status of originals, the authors of the Convention have intended to stress their equivalence. The first copy contains the mention 'for the carrier' and must be signed by the consignor of the goods. The second copy is marked 'for the consignee'; it must be signed by the carrier and the consignor and it accompanies the goods. The third copy is signed by the carrier and delivered to the consignor after the receipt of the goods.

Following the Second World War the matter of a negotiable air waybill modelled on the bill of lading in maritime law had been given closer attention. Increased goods traffic and long-distance, transoceanic flights were responsible for this initiative. Yet, the air waybill still does not possess the status of the bill of lading.

Does the Warsaw Convention permit the introduction of a negotiable document? The answer is in the affirmative, witness the wording of Article 8(f), which allows for the name and address of the consignee to be left open. The right to take delivery of the goods, which derives from the agreement and is mentioned on the air waybill, may therefore be assigned to the bearer of the document. A positive answer is also in line with the intention of the authors of the Convention.

The advantages of a negotiable air waybill may be summed up as follows:
1. when the air waybill arrives sooner than the goods and the latter are resold, the second buyer can take delivery;
2. it makes it possible for the seller to go to the bank and receive his money before the buyer has paid, and for the buyer not to pay until after receipt of the goods;
3. a negotiable document makes transactions during the transportation period possible;
4. combined air-sea transportation will be easier as the negotiable bill of lading is recognised and well known in maritime transport: the longer the journey, the greater the advantages of negotiable documents.

During the ninth session of the ICAO Legal Committee[30] it was suggested that some provisions covering negotiable air waybills should be included in the Hague Protocol. The following arguments were advanced against the suggestion: (1) introducing a negotiable document would be pointless or of little value in actual practice due to the speed

---

30. See the Minutes and Documents of the 9th Session of the ICAO Legal Committee (Rio de Janeiro, August-September, 1953), ICAO Doc. 7450-LC/136; notably the Report on the subject of the 'Negotiable Air Waybill' by Drion.

of modern air traffic; (2) the position of the aircraft commander would have to be sorted out first; (3) for combined air-rail carriage a negotiable document would also be pointless because transport by rail is not effected with negotiable documents. Nonetheless, the suggestion was accepted, and the Hague Protocol added a new paragraph 3 to Article 15. This paragraph states that nothing in the Convention prevents the issuing of a negotiable air waybill.

Article 10 of the Warsaw Convention makes the consignor of the goods responsible for the accuracy and truthfulness of the indications and the statements he inserts in the air waybill. He is liable for all damage suffered by the carrier or any other person as a result of his inaccurate, incorrect or incomplete declarations or indications. The Article is to be read in conjunction with Article 16 stating that the consignor has the duty to supply the necessary information and that he is liable to the carrier for all damage that might result from the absence, insufficiency or inaccuracy of such information, except in the case of fault on the part of the carrier. The carrier is not obliged to check the accuracy or the sufficiency of the information and documents.

Article 11 deals with matters of evidence in respect of the statements made concerning the goods to be transported. The following distinction must be kept in mind: (a) as regards weight, dimensions and packing of the goods, and the number of packages, the statements on the air waybill constitute *prima facie* evidence; (b) statements relating to quantity, volume and condition of the goods do not constitute evidence against the carrier except insofar as they have been checked by him in the presence of the consignor and mention has been made of this fact in the air waybill, or when they relate to the apparent condition of the goods.

Articles 12, 13, and 14 enumerate the rights of the consignor and the consignee *vis-à-vis* the carrier. According to Article 12, the consignor has the right to dispose of the goods in the following manner: (a) by withdrawing them at the airport of departure or destination; (b) by stopping them in the course of the journey on any landing; (c) by calling for them to be delivered at the place of destination, or in the course of the journey to a person other than the consignee named in the air waybill; (d) by requiring them to be returned to the airport of departure. All this is subject to the carrier's duty to carry out all his obligations under the contract of transportation. Moreover, the consignor must not exercise his right in such a way as to prejudice the carrier or other consignors, and he must repay any expenses occasioned by the exercise of his right. If it is impossible for the carrier to carry out the orders of the consignor the carrier must inform him at once.

When carrying out the orders of the consignor for the disposal of the goods the carrier is required to demand the production of the part of the air waybill delivered to the consignor. Failure to do so will make him liable for any damage that may be caused to any person who is in lawful possession of that part of the air waybill, without prejudice, however, to his right of recovery from the consignor.

The right of the consignor ceases to be effective at the moment when the right of the consignee begins in accordance with Article 13, but if the consignee refuses to accept the air waybill or the goods, or if he cannot be contacted, the consignor will resume his right.

As regards the rights of the consignee, Article 13 states that he is entitled to require delivery on arrival of the goods against payment of the charges due and on complying with the conditions of carriage set out in the air waybill. When the goods fail to arrive at their destination and the carrier admits the loss of the goods, the consignee is entitled to enforce against the carrier the rights which flow from the contract of carriage. The same applies if the goods have not arrived at the expiration of seven days after the date on which they ought to have arrived.

According to Article 14 the consignor and the consignee can both enforce all the rights granted to them by Articles 12 and 13, each in his own name and whether he is acting in his own name or in the interest of another person, provided he carries out the obligations imposed by the contract.

Article 15 states that the provisions of Articles 12, 13 and 14 do not affect the relations of the consignor and the consignee with each other, or the relations of third parties whose rights are derived either from the consignor or the consignee.

2.3. THE LIABILITY OF THE CARRIER

We must now examine the heart of the Convention and explore in what manner the liability of the air carrier has been provided for and how the various elements of liability have been described.

Article 17 of the Convention states that the carrier is liable for damage sustained in the event of death or wounding of a passenger or any other bodily injury suffered by a passenger. Article 18 provides that the carrier is also liable for damage to checked baggage or goods. Moreover, in Article 19, the carrier has been made liable for damage occasioned by delay in the carriage of passengers, baggage or goods by air.

It should be emphasised at this point that the rules of the Convention are applicable exclusively in the sphere of transportation: they do not, for instance, cover manufacturers or air traffic controllers; the liability of the latter will be governed by civil law, or common law, as the case may be.

The contract of carriage puts the carrier under an obligation to effect the transport without damage and without delay, so the carrier is compelled to accomplish the transport within a reasonable period of time. The legal basis of the liability of the carrier is a 'fault liability', but with a 'reversed' burden of proof, which means that the onus of proof lies with the carrier. The arrangement reflects a *quid pro quo* in the sense that the authors of the Convention have chosen to place the burden of proof on the carrier's shoulders in return for the passenger losing the benefit of unlimited liability of the carrier. The fact that in 1929 an aeroplane was still rather a novelty as a means of transport must be taken into account in judging the merits of this arrangement. Of course, the passenger can at all times safeguard his interests by taking out insurance, unlike third parties on the surface who are not in a position to do so (further information on their position will be found in Chapter VI).

2.4. WHEN IS THE CARRIER NOT LIABLE?

Article 20 states that the carrier is not liable if he proves that he and his employees have taken all necessary measures to avoid the damage, or that it was impossible for him, or them, to take such measures. The various types of acts which may be regarded as constituting 'necessary measures' are left to the discretion of the judge. The following case may serve as an example.

In *Rugani* v. *KLM*[31] some expensive furs were stolen from a KLM hangar at Idlewild airport in New York, where they had been placed in storage prior to shipment. The New York City Court ruled that all necessary and possible measures had not been taken. Although there had been a guard on duty, he was unarmed; consequently, the guard was unable to protect the goods, because he had no effective defence in this case of armed robbery.

In a similar case an American court ruled that the words 'all necessary measures' should not be interpreted too literally, but, since the carrier had failed to take all reasonable measures that prudent foresight would have envisaged for the security of high-value cargo, he was held liable to the shipper for the theft of his goods by armed robbers from the air carrier's building.[32]

Under the Warsaw Convention the carrier is not liable if he proves that the damage was occasioned by negligent pilotage or negligence in the handling of the aircraft or in navigation and that, in all other respects, he and his agents have taken all necessary measures to avoid the damage. This provision concerns goods and baggage only. The airline companies have hardly ever invoked these clauses, because they fear claims involving negligence.

The carrier will also be exonerated, wholly or partly, from liability if he proves that the damage was caused by, or contributed to by the negligence of the injured person. A case in point was that of a passenger who ignored the 'Fasten seat belts' sign and, wishing to say farewell to her family, did not notice that the stairs leading to the

31. *Rugani* v. *KLM Royal Dutch Airlines*, City Court, New York County, January 20, 1954; [1954] USAvR 74; *Avi*, Vol. 4, p. 17,257; IATA ACLR, No. 25.
32. *Manufacturers Hannover Trust Company* v. *Alitalia Airlines*, US District Court, Southern District of New York, April 16, 1977; *Avi*, Vol. 14, p. 17,710; IATA ACLR, No. 502.

aircraft had already been removed. She fell out of the aircraft and injured her leg. In this case the carrier was not held liable.[33]

The carrier is only responsible for his equipment insofar as he is required to prove, for instance after an emergency landing or a collision with birds, that the aircraft had a certificate of airworthiness and that it was indeed airworthy, not overloaded, and in good condition. In the light of this fact it is worth examining the problem of liability arising when the cause of an accident cannot be traced and the carrier therefore cannot prove that he has taken all necessary measures. Some experts consider that it is sufficient to prove that the aircraft had taken off well-equipped and with well-qualified personnel on board.[34] Others, however, are of the opinion that the carrier is liable for damages up to the limits mentioned in the Warsaw Convention, because he is unable to prove that he is not to blame and is able to insure himself against liability.[35] The latter view has been followed in practice.[36]

2.5. UNLIMITED LIABILITY

There are two cases in which the liability of the carrier is unlimited:
(1) if the damage is caused by his wilful misconduct, or such default on his part as, in accordance with the law of the court dealing with the case, is considered to be equivalent to wilful misconduct (Art. 25). This point will be examined in more detail when the Hague Protocol is discussed.
(2) a. in the absence of the passenger ticket (Art. 3, para. 2);
b. in the absence of the baggage check, or if it does not contain all the requirements of Art. 4, para. 4;
c. if no air waybill has been made out, or if it does not contain all the requirements of Art. 8 (Art. 9).

In all other cases the carrier will be liable according to the limit fixed by the Convention in Article 22, namely for passengers to the sum of 125,000 francs Poincaré (para. 1), while for checked baggage and goods the liability of the carrier is limited to a sum of 250 francs Poincaré per kilogram, unless the consignor has made, at the time when the package was handed over to the carrier, a special declaration of value at delivery and has paid a supplementary sum if the case

33. *Chutter* v. *KLM Royal Dutch Airlines & Allied Aviation Services International Corporation,* US District Court, Southern District of New York, June 27, 1955; [1955] USAvR 250; [1956] JALC 232; *Avi,* Vol. 4, p. 17,733. Cf. *Richardson* v. *KLM Royal Dutch Airlines,* Court of Haarlem (The Netherlands), May 4, 1971; Schoner's case law digest, *Air Law,* vol. I (1976), p. 261; and also *Charpin et al.* v. *Quaranta et al.,* Cour d' Appel Aix-en-Provence, October 9, 1986, *Air Law,* vol. XII (1987), pp. 205-207.
34. M. Lemoine, *Traité de Droit Aérien* (1947), pp. 544 *et seq.* See also J.-M. Fobe, *Aviation Products Liability and Insurance in the EU,* 1994, p. 13 *et seq.*
35. O. Riese, *Luftrecht* (1949), p. 459.
36. *Wyman and Bartlett* v. *Pan American Airways,* New York Supreme Court, New York County, June 25, 1943; [1943] USAvR 1; *Avi,* Vol. 1, p. 1,093. See on this subject D. Ficht, *Die unbekannte Schadensursache im internationalen Luftverkehr,* 1986.

so requires. In that case the carrier will be liable to pay a sum not exceeding the declared sum, 'unless he proves that the sum is greater than the actual value to the consignor at delivery' (Art. 22, para. 2); more comment on this point will be given in the next section of this chapter.[37]

Paragraph 3 of the same Article 22 provides that 'As regards objects of which the passenger takes charge himself the liability of the carrier shall be limited to 5,000 francs per passenger'.

Article 22, para. 4, defines this (French) franc, the so-called franc Poincaré, as follows: 'The sums mentioned above shall be deemed to refer to the French franc consisting of $65\frac{1}{2}$ milligrammes of gold at the standard of fineness of nine hundred thousandths'.

The amounts fixed by the Convention as the limit of the carrier's liability indicate the maximum claimable sums. As these sums make no reference to national currencies the latter cannot be used in evaluating the damage, and variations in their rates of exchange have no effect on the obligation to pay the full amount of compensation.[38]

As Kennelly shows with great clarity in his article on 'Aviation Law', there are three ways of getting round the Warsaw provisions on limitation of liability for passengers:
'1. Prove that the air carrier was guilty of wilful misconduct.
 2. Prove that tickets were not delivered to the passengers.
 3. Prove that tickets delivered to the passengers did not contain adequate warning of Warsaw Convention limitations.'[39]

Again, the legal ground for the carrier's liability is the fact that he must have committed a fault, but the burden of proof has been reversed, *i.e.* it is up to the carrier to prove that he was not to blame and therefore not liable for damages.

Although the wording of paragraphs 2 and 3 of Article 22 seems perfectly clear, some problems remain, for in everyday practice of airline traffic two situations may occur in which the two paragraphs clash. Verwer has described them as follows:
a. Suppose a passenger presents a piece of baggage for registration but keeps it with him in the aircraft on some excuse, and the carrier agrees. How is that piece of baggage to be classified? Does the (higher) limit for checked baggage apply, or the (lower) standard applicable to cabin baggage?

---

37. See also *Data Card et al.* v. *Air Express International et al.*, Queen's Bench Division (Commercial Court), May 28, 1983, *Air Law*, vol. IX (1984), p.187.
38. *Air Madagascar et al.* v. *Musset et al.*, Court of Appeal, Madagascar, January 11, 1973; (1976) 1 *Uniform Law Review* 236. See also *Swiss Bank Corp.* v. *Brink's MAT Ltd*, Queen's Bench Division (Commercial Court), February 6, 1986; [1986]; 2 All ER 188. In this case it was ruled that the total sum payable, including interest, is subject to the liability limits of Article 22 and that interest cannot be awarded over and above these limits.
39. J.J. Kennelly, 'Aviation Law: International Air Travel – A Brief Diagnosis and Prognosis' (1975/1976) 6 *California Western International Law Journal* 86–109, at p. 103; see also B.J.H. Crans, 'The special contract: an instrument to stretch liability limits?', *Air Law*, vol. XV (1990), pp. 159-175.

b. Suppose a passenger keeps a piece of baggage with him and the carrier fails to ask him to have it registered; but on entering the aircraft the passenger is asked by the crew to hand it over for safety reasons, and the crew places it in a safe place within the cabin, but out of the passenger's reach. Is this piece of baggage still in the charge of the passenger, or does the liability for checked baggage apply because the carrier retains control?[40]

In the illustration under (a), classification as checked baggage has been favoured as a solution; the carrier, however, is not bound to accept a piece of baggage in the category desired (or requested) by the passenger.

In situation (b), a weak spot in the Convention becomes apparent: in most cases this type of baggage is not registered, and therefore the limit for unchecked baggage applies. But that very limit also applies to the baggage the passenger keeps with him. The limit set out in Article 22, para. 3, does not apply in this case, because the words 'of which the passenger takes charge himself' are not in fact applicable to such a situation.

Another consequence of classification becomes apparent in the case of partial damage. When a checked piece of baggage has been partly damaged it is easy to calculate the amount of compensation to be paid: according to the Convention this amount is proportional to the weight of the damaged piece(s) of baggage. But as the weight of the *un*checked baggage is unknown, it is obviously rather difficult to fix the amount in case of partial damage. If the weight were known one could use the same method as in the case of checked baggage.

The whole situation changes, of course, when a special declaration of the total value has been made out. In the absence of any indication as to the weight the burden of proof lies with the passenger.

The carrier's liability may be appreciated more clearly in the following case. After a flight from Rome to Beirut with Olympic Airways the checked baggage was not delivered to the passengers. Mr. Rifahi claimed compensation; Olympic Airways, however, contended that the baggage had been delivered, but with no baggage checks being received in return. According to the conditions of the contract the carrier had to prove that the baggage had actually been delivered. Olympic Airways were unable to furnish adequate evidence to that effect. Furthermore, the receipts submitted by Mr. Rifahi in support of his claim were ruled by the court not to be in conformity with the requirements of the Convention, because they were joined to the passenger ticket. For that reason the carrier was not entitled to avail himself of the liability limitations of the Convention, and he was ordered to pay compensation for all the damage.[41]

---

40. Chr.P. Verwer, *Liability for damage to luggage in international air transport*, 1987. Cf. also the decision of the German Bundesgerichtshof, November 28, 1978; [1979] ZLW 52; *Air Law*, vol. IV (1979), p. 165.

41. *Rifahi* v. *Olympic Airways*, Tribunal de Commerce de Beyrouth (Lebanon), March 12, 1965; [1968] RFDA 227; IATA ACLR, No. 263.

This decision has been severely criticised by several experts, since the Court had based its ruling concerning the invalidity of the baggage checks on the redrafting of Article 4 of the Convention by the Hague Protocol. This redraft however, was made only for linguistic reasons, and it did not involve any new rule of international air law. Moreover, the practice of joining baggage checks to passenger tickets is older than the Hague Protocol itself and has never before given rise to similar rulings.[42]

2.6. THE DECLARATION OF VALUE

The special declaration concerning the value of the cargo or baggage on delivery at destination, made out by the passenger or the consignor, has already been mentioned briefly. The passenger or consignor may have to pay extra, if the case so requires. In the latter case the carrier will be liable to pay a sum not exceeding the declared amount.[43]

A declaration of value may on occasion turn out to be very important, as is apparent from the following case involving a shipment of goods carried by Pan-American Airways from Amsterdam to Johannesburg. This particular shipment contained hat samples. Instead of arriving in Johannesburg on March 10, 1951, as scheduled, the goods did not arrive until April 2, because they had been sent elsewhere by mistake and then flown back to Amsterdam. There was no special declaration of value, but the plaintiff claimed compensation for damages amounting to 10,000 Guilders, contending that he had lost important business due to the delay. Pan-Am exonerated itself by referring to the limits set forth in the Warsaw Convention. The plaintiff accused the carrier of gross negligence. The court at Amsterdam, however, ruled that, in the absence of a special declaration of value, it was not sufficient for the shipper of the goods to merely urge the carrier to speed up delivery. There was, accordingly, no case for gross negligence and unlimited liability, and the court awarded compensation within the limits of the Convention.[44]

Another instance was when in 1978 the Dutch Supreme Court handed down a significant decision in a case in which a German employee of KLM had stolen a box containing platinum. There was a declaration of value, but the Supreme Court, reversing the decisions of lower courts, ruled that the declared amount of the value

---

42. Annotation on the Rifahi judgment by M.L. (Lemoine), [1968] RFDA 228.
43. Cf. *Orlove* v. *Philippine Air Lines and Flying Tiger Line*, US Court of Appeal (2nd Circ.), July 25, 1958; [1958] USAvR 611; *Avi*, Vol. 5, p. 18,103. The shipper recovered the full value although no special declaration of value appeared on the air waybill due to a clerical error of the carrier's agent. The agent had been informed of the value of the goods and the shipper was going to pay freight charges on the basis of this value.
44. *Amstelhoedenfabriek* v. *Pan-American World Airways*, Court of Amsterdam (The Netherlands), January 3, 1953; IATA ACLR, No. 14. See on this subject I.H.Ph. de Rode-Verschoor, 'La responsabilité du transporteur pour retard' (1957) 20 RGA 253-265.

was not a limit for liability in terms of Article 22 of the Warsaw Convention. In the case under review, the carrier had been found guilty of wilful misconduct under Article 25 of the Convention.[45]

2.7. THE DURATION OF LIABILITY

Before examining other aspects of the Convention we have yet to consider the length of time during which the carrier remains liable. Article 17 states: 'The carrier shall be liable for damage sustained in the event of the death or wounding of a passenger or any other bodily injury suffered by a passenger, if the accident which caused the damaged so sustained took place on board the aircraft or in the course of any of the operations of embarking or disembarking'.

The first question to examine in connection with this article is: 'What exactly is meant by the word "accident"?'

In *DeMarines* v. *KLM Royal Dutch Airlines*[46] the court ruled that in contexts other than the Warsaw Convention, 'accident has been defined as an unexpected and sudden event that takes place without foresight'. It follows that the occurence on board must be unusual or unexpected, if it is to be regarded as an accident. In the *Husserl* case, for instance, hijacking was regarded as an accident.[47] In the *Price* case a passenger unsuccessfully sued an air carrier when he was attacked by a fellow passenger during the flight. This was held by the court not to constitute an accident as envisaged by the Warsaw Convention for which the carrier could be liable.[48]

In the case of *Warshaw* v. *TWA*[49] the court ruled that an event was not an accident if it arose exclusively from the passenger's state of health. It also found that an injury resulting from normal, expected and necessary changes in the operation of the aircraft, when such changes were performed by the aircraft's crew in the usual and prudent manner, is not covered by the version of the Warsaw Convention, as amended by the Montreal Agreement, which was effective at the time.

The main element, *i.e.* the duration of the period involving the carrier's liability is not clearly stated in the Convention. Yet, it is generally accepted that the carrier's liability begins when the passenger puts himself in the hands of an employee of the carrier and ends when the passenger enters the arrival hall at the point of destination. The following case may serve as an example.

---

45. *Insurance Company of North America* v. *KLM Royal Dutch Airlines*, Supreme Court (The Netherlands), January 6, 1978; *Air Law*, vol. III (1978), p. 123.
46. *DeMarines* v. *KLM Royal Dutch Airlines*, US District Court, Eastern District of Pennsylvania, June 28, 1977; *Avi*, Vol. 14, p. 18,212.
47. *Husserl* v. *Swissair*, US District Court, Southern District of New York; *Avi*, Vol. 13, p. 17,603 (SDNY, 1975).
48. *Price* v. *British Airways*, US District Court for the Southern District of New York, July 7, 1992; 23 Avi 18,465; *Air and Space Law*, vol. XIX (1994), p. 44.
49. *Warshaw* v. *TWA*, US District Court, Eastern District of Pennsylvania, December 15, 1977; *Avi*, Vol. 14, p. 18,297; IATA ACLR, No. 508.

An aircraft of the defendant airline had been unable to take off on schedule due to thick fog, so the passengers had to wait for some time. When the flight was finally called the plaintiff, who along with other passengers hurried down the steps of the air terminal building in order to board the aircraft, slipped and fell; she boarded the aircraft with bruises on her leg and ankle. The plaintiff then claimed and received compensation for the accident, because the court ruled that when the airline company calls its passengers to board the aircraft it takes full charge of the passengers.[50] This was a rather extensive interpretation. The following instance taken from among cases decided by French courts provides another illustration.

A passenger slipped and fell in an airport entrance hall, while he was in front of the check-in counter before proceeding to the departure lounge. The fall was caused by the passenger slipping over a pool of whisky spilt on the ground by a previous traveller. The fall could not be blamed on the carrier, since the airport entrance hall is a public place and not subject to the carrier's control and management. Consequently, the preparatory stage of air transport could not be considered as having commenced.[51]

A French Court of Appeal has, for good reason, rejected the request for compensation from an airline for injuries sustained by passengers who used the escalator situated in the airport entrance hall; it noted that the people applying for compensation were, at the time when the accident occurred, in airport buildings used by different airline companies and where the carrier's agents had not yet taken over responsibility for those persons.[52]

There have been other significant cases involving the carrier's liability, namely when attacks by terrorists occurred. Passengers who are leaving the aircraft by descending the steps, or who are walking or riding on a bus to the terminal, or who are going through passport control and into the main baggage area, are not in the course of any of the operations of embarking or disembarking in terms of the Warsaw Convention, when terrorists attack the baggage area, as happened in one case. Accordingly, the Convention did not apply to the claims for damages resulting from the attack.[53] In another case, the passengers, who were assembled in an airport transit lounge to undergo the physical and handbag search at the time of a terrorist attack on the

---

50. Kammergericht (Federal Republic of Germany), March 11, 1961; [1962] ZLW 78.
51. *Air-Inter* v. *Sage et al.*, Cour d'Appel de Lyon (France), February 10, 1976; [1976] RFDA 266; Schoner's case law digest *Air Law*, vol. II (1977), p. 229.
52. *Consorts Zaoui* v. *Aéroport de Paris*, Cour de Cassation (1re Ch. Civ.), May 18, 1976; [1976] RFDA 394; Schoner's case law digest *Air Law*, vol. II (1977), p. 229. See also *Maché* v. *Air France*, Cour d'Appel de Paris, June 28, 1963; [1964] ZLW 298; [1963] RFDA 353. For the appeal case see Cour de Cassation, January 18, 1966; [1966] RFDA 228. See also *O'Toole* v. *TWA*, US District Court, District of Massachusetts, November 16, 1990; *Avi* vol. 23, p. 17, 151; *Air and Space Law*, vol. XVII (1992), pp. 172–173.
53. *Re Tel Aviv*, US District Court, District of Puerto Rico, December 9, 1975; *Avi*, Vol. 13, p. 18,166; IATA ACLR, No. 481. Affirmed: US Court of Appeals (1st Circ.), November 19, 1976; *Avi*, Vol. 14, p. 17,421; IATA ACLR, No. 499 (renamed *Hernandez* v. *Air France*).

lounge, were in the course of the operation of embarking within the meaning of the term as used in the Convention. The passengers were under the air carrier's control at that moment.[54]

As regards goods, Article 18, para. 2, states that the period of carriage comprises the period during which the baggage or goods are in the charge of the carrier.[55] The period of carriage does not include transportation outside the airport area. Nevertheless, whenever this transportation takes place in the performance of a contract of carriage for the purpose of loading, delivery or transshipment, any damage is presumed to have occurred during the carriage by air, subject to evidence to the contrary (Art. 18, para. 3).

In international transport of goods by air, carriage includes the period during which they are in the carrier's care, whether on his aerodrome or on board an aircraft, and during this time he is liable for any damage which may occur to the goods. The following case is of interest in this context.

The consignee of the goods, upon arranging for their transportation by air, agreed that they would be stored on arrival in private bonded storage which was acceptable to his agents. The court, however, ruled that goods which are in private bonded storage, the sealing and opening of which must be done in conjunction with another company and the customs authorities, are not in the carrier's care.[56]

An error committed by an airline company while delivering to the consignee parcels which had to be destroyed subsequently, renders the carrier liable under the Warsaw Convention. The Convention applies throughout the duration of the transportation contract which, according to Article 18, para. 2 includes the period during which the goods are in the charge of the carrier at an aerodrome, on an aircraft or in any place whatsoever in case of a landing outside an aerodrome, until the moment of their final delivery to the consignee.[57]

---

54. *Evangelinos et al.* v. *TWA*, US Court of Appeals (3rd Circ.), May 4, 1976; *Avi*, Vol. 14, p. 17,101; [1976] USAvR 1; Schoner's case law digest *Air Law*, vol. II (1977), p. 112. Cf. *Upton et al.* v. *Iran National Airlines*, US District Court, Southern District of New York, May 8, 1978; *Avi*, Vol. 15, p. 17,101; Schoner's case law digest *Air Law*, vol. IV (1979), p. 171.

55. Cf. the decision of the Bundesgerichtshof (Federal Republic of Germany), October 27, 1978; [1980] ZLW 61; *Air Law*, vol. IV (1979), p. 222. See also *Victoria Sales* v. *Emery Air Freight*, US Court of Appeals (2nd Circ.), October 22, 1990; *Avi* vol. 22, p. 18,502; *Air Law*, vol. XVI (1991), p. 202.

56. *Hermes Assurance Company* v. *Pan-American Airways*, Court of Appeal of Buenos Aires Civil and Commercial Court 2-A, June 7, 1973; (1975) V—VI *Novum Forum* (Argentina), 121; Schoner's case law digest *Air Law*, vol. II (1977), p. 113.

57. *Banque Libanaise* v. *SAS*, Cour d'Appel de Paris (5e Ch. Civ.), February 3, 1977; [1977] RFDA 282; Schoner's case law digest *Air Law*, vol. III (1978), p. 126. Further case law to be mentioned here: *Favre* v. *Sabena*, Court of Appeal Brussels, June 10, 1950 USAvR 1950, p. 392; and *Sprinks & Cie* v. *Air France*, Court of Appeal Paris, June 27, 1969, *RFDA* 1969, p. 405.

2.8. DELAY

According to Article 19 the carrier is liable for damage occasioned by delay in the carriage by air of passengers, baggage or goods.[58] The liability of the carrier for delay is the same as for injury and death to passengers and for the loss or damage of goods. IATA has formulated regulations[59] relating to delay, requiring the carrier to use his best efforts to carry the passenger and his baggage with reasonable dispatch. Times shown in the ticket, timetables or elsewhere are not guaranteed. Accordingly, damage resulting from delay cannot be claimed when the scheduled time limit is exceeded, an unreasonable delay being necessary to support such a claim. Article 19 contains many loopholes; it does not indicate the factors constituting such delay. For that reason it has often been suggested that the word 'reasonable' should be inserted in contracts of carriage.

The air carrier was held liable to the limit fixed by the Warsaw Convention for delay in a case involving a selection of goods, including sound and lighting equipment as well as musical instruments, which were to accompany a music hall artist on her way to a town where she was to perform; the delay, added to the fact that one of the parcels was completely lost, adversely affected the success of the artist's tour and caused her a certain amount of damage.[60]

The same happened in a case where the producer of a 'Son-et-Lumière' show was awarded compensation because the airline had cancelled his flight for no valid reason, so that he could not fulfill his obligations.[61]

Another well-known case involving delay is also worth quoting here. A firm of architects, Engeli, Pahud and Bigar, had produced a model in order to compete for a plan to rebuild the Turkish city of Izmir. Swissair was charged with transporting the model; unfortunately, it was not delivered in time for the competition, so that it was no longer of any use. The plaintiff asserted that Swissair had been grossly negligent. He claimed compensation for the loss of working hours, the value of the model, the missing of the first prize, the loss of a contract with Izmir, and also for the damage to the reputation of the architects' firm. Swissair argued that it had taken the necessary measures and that it had all been a matter of misunderstanding and a minor mistake.

The Warsaw Convention was not applicable in this case because it had been ratified only by Switzerland and not by Turkey, and no international transport was involved as defined by the terms of the

---

58. See for a discussion of the relationship between the concept of delay and damage *Transports Mondiaux* v. *Lufthansa and Air France*, Cour d'Appel de Paris, March 14, 1960, RFDA 1960, p. 317.
59. IATA General Conditions, see note 27, *supra*.
60. *UTA* v. *Blain, Air-Mer International, Lufthansa*, Cour d'Appel de Paris (5e Ch.), January 6, 1977; [1977] RFDA 181; Schoner's case law digest *Air Law*, vol. III (1978), p. 127 and 129.
61. *Robert-Houdin* v. *Panair do Brazil*, Tribunal de Grande Instance de la Seine (5e Ch.), July 9, 1960; [1961] RGA 285

Warsaw Convention; accordingly, the case had to be judged in conformity with Swiss law. Swissair was ordered to pay 20,000 Swiss francs plus interest and the cost of litigation.[62]

Delay can have many causes. Drion sums them up with regard to passengers: failure to make a reservation, or making a double reservation for the same seat; delayed departure of an aircraft; suspension of a flight; incorrect information to passengers about the time of departure; failure to stop at the place where the passenger was to disembark; deviation or added unscheduled stopping places. Delays affecting baggage and goods: failure to make an agreed reservation, or general lack of space; failure to put baggage or goods on the aircraft; loading of baggage or goods onto the wrong aircraft; deviations; failure to offload baggage or goods; mislaying of accompanying documents essential for regular delivery.[63]

The following example may illustrate Articles 19 and 20. A group of students had rented a car in Germany from a Mr. Wucherpfennig to make a journey through Italy. In the neighbourhood of Florence an engine part broke down. Mr. Wucherpfennig instructed SAS to fly out a new spare part to Rome, and SAS assured Mr. Wucherpfennig that the spare would be at its destination the next day at noon. The Italian Customs kept the spare in their custody for some time, causing a delay in forwarding. At the students' request Wucherpfennig sent another spare part which arrived without delay. The first spare part had been returned to Wucherpfennig with the request to pay transport charges to the amount of DM 26.54. Wucherpfennig refused to pay, holding SAS responsible for the delay.

The decision of the Amtsgericht was that SAS could not claim payment of the transport charges because the damage caused by the delay had been made up for by the amount of the transport charges. The Amtsgericht ruled that SAS should have informed Customs of the urgency of the case.

SAS appealed to a higher court. The Landgericht was of the opinion that there was no delay *ex* Article 19 of the Warsaw Convention because no specific point in time had been agreed at which the transport was to have been completed. SAS was deemed to have taken all the necessary measures required by Article 20, the delay had been caused by Customs. The claim on Wucherpfennig was awarded and SAS was not held liable.[64]

---

62. *Engeli et al.* v. *Swissair*, Tribunal de 1re Instance de Genève (Switzerland), March 8, 1955; [1955] RFDA 335.

63. H. Drion, *Limitation of Liabilities in International Air Law*, thesis Leiden (The Netherlands, 1954), para. 181. See also R. Schmid, 'Which are the duties of an air carrier who does not execute an air carriage contract as agreed', *Air Law*, vol. XV (1990), pp. 102-104.

64. *SAS* v. *Wucherpfennig*, Landgericht Hamburg, April 6, 1955; [1955] ZfL 226; [1955] JALC 352. See about the subject of carriage of cargo J.L. Magdelénat, *Le Fret Aérien* (1979).

There have been some court cases involving overbooking, for instance in *Osman Erdem* v. *Germanair*,[65] where the carrier was ordered to compensate the passenger for the delay and the cost incurred.

The case of *Heerfur* v. *KLM Royal Dutch Airlines*[66] may serve as an example of the influence of the IATA regulations which supplement the Warsaw Convention.[67] The case involved a shipment of live minks. The minks arrived in a very bad condition, which was caused by a delay in their transport. Heerfur claimed compensation, but the Appeals Court ruled that from Condition No. 5 of the 'Conditions of Contract',[68] printed on the back of the air waybill, it appeared that no specific points in time had been agreed upon for the carriage, and that KLM had not been tied down to a particular flight. Moreover, KLM's actions had been consistent with a *bona fide* performance of the carriage; accordingly, there was no question of any liability for delay.

2.9. DAMAGE AND COMPENSATION

What kind of damage will be considered for compensation? Requirements are that the damages must be assessable with accuracy and that they must be the direct result of the accident.

Mention must be made at this point of the dangers inherent in the transportation of radioactive material. The total number of shipments by air of such material has increased sharply over the past few years, and already some cases of contamination of passengers and crew members have been reported.[69]

Article 17 of the Convention speaks of bodily injury. Does bodily injury also include mental injury? In the American case of *Rosman* v. *Trans World Airlines*[70] it was ruled that only mental injury directly resulting from bodily injury could be compensated. In *Husserl* v. *Swissair*[71] an American court was,, however, willing to award compensation for

65. *Osman Erdem* v. *Germanair*, Landgericht Düsseldorf (Federal Republic of Germany), February 3, 1971; [1971] ZLW 290. This case will be discussed *in extenso* in section 4 of this chapter in connection with the Guadalajara Convention.
66. *Heerfur* v. *KLM Royal Dutch Airlines*, Court of The Hague (The Netherlands), March 8, 1962; *Nederlandse Jurisprudentie* (NJ), (1963), p. 115 *et seq.*
67. See also note 27, *supra*.
68. IATA Conditions of Contract Relating to Air Waybills (IATA Resolution 600-B). There exist similar Conditions of Contract Relating to Passenger Tickets (IATA Resolution 275-B). See for the text of both sets of Conditions, Shawcross and Beaumont, *Air Law* (1977), Vol. 2 (1981), pp. D-21–D-33.
69. See D.K. Eyberg, 'Air Transportation of Radioactive Materials' [1974] JALC 681-703; L.A. Dauphinot, 'Radioactive Material' [1976] JALC 906-919; D.B. Atchley, 'Air Transportation of Radioactive Materials and Passenger Protection under International Law' (1974/1975) 5 *California Western Journal of International Law* 425-445.
70. *Rosman et al.* v. *TWA* and *Herman et al.* v.*TWA*, Court of Appeal, New York State, June 13, 1974; *Avi*, Vol. 13. p. 17,231; [1974] USAvR 1.
71. See note 47, *supra*. Also on this subject G. Miller, *Liability in International Air Transport* (1977), pp. 126 *et seq*. Cf. *Palagonia et al.* v. *TWA*, New York Supreme Court, County of Westchester, December 28, 1978; [1979] USAvR 1285; *Air Law*, vol. IV (1979), p. 102 (this case was eventually settled out of court).

mental injury, irrespective of any link with bodily injury. The following example will show the trend in favour of compensation for mental suffering.

The emotional or mental anguish suffered by a passenger who was trampled underfoot by frightened passengers trying to get out of an aircraft that had made an emergency landing because one of its engines was on fire is claimable under the Warsaw Convention. The American court ruled that, under the circumstances, the assault on the passenger's emotional senses was tantamount to inflicting physical blows upon her body and was to be regarded as if she had suffered additional, actual bodily injuries.[72] A restrictive interpretation of the law, however, was followed in a New York judgment, in which it was ruled that the psychic trauma suffered by passengers who were former citizens of Hungary and who, on a flight from Amsterdam to Budapest, were forced to spend six to eight hours within the confines of Prague airport because of engine trouble, did not constitute 'bodily' injury in terms of Article 17 of the Warsaw Convention.[73]

In Article 26 it is stated that in the event of damage to goods the person entitled to take delivery must lodge a claim with the carrier at the latest within three days from the date of receipt. In the event of delay the complaint must be lodged at the latest within 14 days from the date on which the baggage or goods were placed at his disposal. These complaints must be made in writing.[74]

In a case where the death of a shipment of greyhounds was discovered by the air carrier's employees, failure to give notice in writing, as required under the Warsaw Convention, was held by a United States District Court to preclude the payment of compensation by the air carrier. However, the Court of Appeal ruled that in this case, where the goods were destroyed and not merely damaged or delayed, Article 26 of the Convention requiring shippers to give notice in writing of damage or delay, was not applicable.[75] Article 26, para. 4, states that in the case of fraud on the part of the carrier claims exceeding time limits will be received.[76]

---

72. *Kalish* v. *TWA*, New York Civil Court (Queens County), January 19, 1977; *Avi*, Vol. 14, p. 17,936.

73. *Beck et al.* v. *KLM Royal Dutch Airlines and Ritz Travel*, New York Supreme Court, County of Dutchess, November 2, 1977; *Avi*, Vol. 14, p. 18,210; IATA ACLR, No. 524.

74. Cf. the case of *Sofrinski* v. *KLM Royal Dutch Airlines*, New York City Civil Court, November 11, 1971; *Avi*, Vol. 12, p. 17,267; IATA ACLR, No. 406. The ticket did not give notice of the applicability of Art. 26 (relating to the three-day period in which to make a claim), therefore the Court held the passenger not bound by the requirements of this article. Cf. *Panzer* v. *Aerolineas Argentinas*, New York Appellate Term, Division 1, March 6, 1986, 19 *Avi* 18,228 (notice must be in writing). M. Leshem, 'Article 26(3) of the Warsaw Convention: the extent of judicial interpretation', *Air Law*, vol. XV (1990), pp. 100-101.

75. *Dalton* v. *Delta Airlines*, US District Court, Southern District of Florida, October 24, 1974; *Avi*, Vol. 14, p. 17,219. Reversed: US Court of Appeals (5th Circ.), April 7, 1978; *Avi*, Vol. 14, p. 18,425.

76. Cf. *Air Algérie* v. *Fuller and Cotaufruits*, Cour de Cassation, Febr. 22, 1956, 1956 RFDA 220. See also J.L. Magdelénat, *Air Cargo: Regulation and Claims* (1983), pp. 112-113.

Two more aspects of carriage need mentioning. The differences between carriage for reward and gratuitous carriage are the following: with gratuitous carriage, there is no 'reversal' of the burden of proof, and no contract of carriage is required. The gratuitous carrier does not enjoy the limited liability provided by the Warsaw Convention. More attention should be given to the second aspect, namely successive carriage.

The Convention rules also cover transportation in situations where the passengers or goods are carried to their destination by various successive carriers (Art. 1, para. 3 and Art. 30). Such transportation will be regarded as undivided carriage 'if it has been regarded by the parties as a single operation'. It is therefore of prime importance to know the intentions of the parties to the contract.

In the case of *Parke, Davis & Co.* v. *BOAC et al.* the transportation from Calcutta to Detroit was performed by three successive carriers. The court ruled that the carriers had performed in close cooperation and that the existence of separate air waybills did not affect the legal obligation.[77] The parties had regarded the carriage as a single operation.

Are the provisions of the Warsaw Convention applicable when the carriage is entrusted to a carrier not originally mentioned in the contract? In such a case the issue of substitution plays a role. The decision given in the case of *Caisse Parisienne* v. *Air France and Air Liban*[78] provides a good example of such a situation.

Air France had been contracted by Caisse Parisienne to carry 16 gold ingots from Orly to Beirut. Under a Warsaw transportation contract concluded with Air France, Caisse Parisienne shipped the gold in eight cases to Beirut. Air France flew the shipment to Cairo, where it was taken over by Air Liban and flown to Beirut. Upon arrival the cases were weighed and handed over to the customs agents. With regard to one crate the latter falsely entered a weight shortage of 15 kg. The employees of Air Liban in charge of handling the shipment made no protest, nor did they inform their superiors or the consignee. When the crates were delivered, one ingot was found missing, having probably been stolen while the shipment was in Customs. Caisse Parisienne claimed US$16,370 from Air France, and the latter, in turn, brought an action for recovery against Air Liban.

The court ruled that if a shipment is lost while being transported by the second of two successive carriers, the consignor has a right of action against the first carrier according to Article 30 para. 3, of the

---

77. *Parke, Davis & Company* v. *BOAC et. al.*, New York City Court, January 30, 1958; *Avi*, Vol. 5, p. 17,838; IATA ACLR, No. 63; USAvR 1958, p. 122; Zfl 1959, p. 58. This case concerned the non–arrival of 185 monkeys out of a shipment of 900. A claim for compensation for *damage* was not brought within the 7–day period prescribed by Article 26(2) and was consequently not upheld by the court. A claim based on *loss*, however, ought to have been successful since Article 13(3) does not indicate a period *within* which claims for loss may be made, but a period *after* which this can be done.

78. *Caisse Parisienne de Réescompte* v. *Air France and Air Liban*, Tribunal Civile de la Seine (lre Ch.), January 14, 1955; [1955] RFDA 439; [1955] JALC 88. See for the appeal case: Cour d'Appel de Paris, May 31, 1956; [1956] RFDA 320.

Warsaw Convention, and may charge him with negligence committed by the second carrier's agents, without prejudice to the first carrier's right of recourse against the second carrier. The behaviour of Air Liban's employees at Beirut was ruled to constitute at least 'des fautes lourdes équivalentes au dol' within the meaning of Article 25 of the Convention. We note the court's view that the matter was one of successive carriage, and that Article 30, para. 1, of the Convention was applicable.

As Guldimann observes, there is no doubt that the application of Articles 25 and 30 had been correct. The same cannot be said with regard to Article 18 relating to the duration of the period of liability, because it would seem that after the cases had been delivered to the customs agents they were no longer in the charge of the carrier within the meaning of Article 18, para. 2.[79]

In the case of transportation by various successive carriers, each carrier will be considered to be one of the parties to the contract of carriage in so far as the contract deals with the part of the transportation performed under his supervision. According to Article 30, para. 2, the passenger or his representative can take action only against the carrier who performed the transportation during which the accident or the delay occurred, save in the case where, by explicit agreement, the first carrier has assumed liability for the whole journey.

As regards baggage or goods, the passenger or consignor will have a right of action against the first carrier, and the passenger or consignee who is entitled to take delivery will have a right of action against the last carrier; besides, each may take action against the carrier who performed the carriage during which the destruction, loss, damage or delay took place. These carriers will be jointly and severally liable to the passenger or to the consignor or the consignee.

Summarising the problems that may arise in the case of transportation by successive carriers it can be said that they concern:
a. the relationship between the carriers in the event of substitution, *i.e.* when the carriage is entrusted to a carrier not originally mentioned in the contract, and
b. the relations between the carriers, passengers and cargo owners.[80]

In the case of code-sharing, when there is successive carriage, the carriers could be subject to different liability regimes and there could be uncertainty as to which liability system would apply (when an accident occurs and also in other circumstances, e.g. in case of delay).

---

79. W. Guldimann in his note in [1955] JALC at 88. Similarly: [1955] ZfL 328; E. Georgiades in [1955] RFDA at 328. See also [1956] RFDA at 324. Also on this subject I.H.Ph. Diederiks-Verschoor, 'Considerations on Carriage by Air Executed by Various Successive Carriers' (1970) 5 *EVR* 143-165.

80. See, *e.g. Connaught Laboratories* v. *Air Canada; Aerolineas Nacionales de Ecuador, third party*; Ontario High Court of Justice, October 10, 1978; *Avi*, Vol. 15, p. 17,705; *Air Law*, vol. V (1980), p. 37 (claims against and between successive carriers). Cf. also the United Nations Convention on International Multimodal Transport, signed on May 24, 1980. See G.F. Fitzgerald, 'The UN Convention on Multimodal Transport of Goods (1980). Discussions of the Operations of Pick-up and Delivery with Particular Attention to the Air Mode', *Air Law*, vol. VII (1982), pp. 202-214.

2.10. CLAIMS AND CLAIMANTS

The Warsaw Convention states that claims for damages must be lodged within two years counting from the date of arrival of the aircraft at its destination, or from the date on which it ought to have arrived, or from the date on which the transportation ended. The method of calculating the period of limitation will be determined by the law of the court to which the matter is submitted (Art. 29).

The two-year period has been extended in case law, for instance in an American court case where the plaintiff died while the case was before the court. His heir was granted a further two years to present a claim.[81] In a French court decision in a case involving a minor the period was allowed to be interrupted.[82]

Which persons are entitled to lodge claims for compensation? The matter has been explicitly excluded from the Convention by Article 24, and left for the national law to determine. The following decision provides an example.

An aircraft of the Societa Aviolinee Italiane crashed on May 4, 1949, during a flight from Lisbon to Turin, killing the entire football team of Torino and their technical staff. The Footbal Club Torino claimed damages, but both the tribunal and the court rejected the claim. Their decisions were confirmed by the Court of Appeal (Corte di Cassatione) on the grounds that Article 24 of the Warsaw Convention does not specify which persons are entitled to claim damages, and that this point is left for the national law to decide.

The Court of Appeal was, in my opinion, correct in basing its decision on the denial of a direct causal connection between the damage sustained by claimant and the crash, because the right of the passengers to live (an absolute right) takes precedence over the right of the football club to the performance of its team (a qualified right).[83]

At this point mention should also be made of the fact that the Warsaw Convention does not create in itself a cause of action. In civil law countries this usually does not result in difficulties since here the cause of action would evidently be found either in contract or in tort. A different situation prevails in common law countries; particularly in connection with wrongful death cases, the existence (or lack) of a cause of action is a factor of prime importance.

---

81. *Nicolet* v. *TWA*, US District Court, Southern District of New York, June 17, 1954; [1954] USAvR 177; *Avi*, Vol. 4, p. 17,427.
82. *Consorts Lorans et al.* v. *Air France*, Cour de Cassation (Assemblée Plénière), January 14, 1977; [1977] RFDA 268; IATA ACLR, No. 501. Cf. for a different decision *Kahn et al.* v. *TWA*, NY Supreme Court (Appellate Division, 2nd Dep.), October 5, 1981; M.J. Corrigan, 'Actions on Behalf of Infants are Barred by Two Year Time Limitation of Warsaw Convention' *Air Law*, vol. VII (1982), p. 124. A special declaration of value was in Italy ruled to break the two-year claiming period: *Piscicultura Burrini* v. *Alitalia*, Tribunal of Milan, September 26, 1977; *Air Law* vol. XVI (1991), p. 299.
83. *Footbal Club Torino* v. *Aviolinee Italiane*, Corte di Cassatione, March 9, 1953; [1955] ZfL 70.

In a number of common law countries most of the difficulties which could arise in relation to such cases have been eliminated by legislation implementing the Warsaw Convention (United Kingdom, Canada and Australia). In the United States, however, there is no statutory implementation of the Convention, which meant that the courts had to examine the Convention itself in order to find out whether a cause of action had been created by it. Until recently, a negative answer used to be given to this question; grounds on which to bring wrongful death cases had to be (and often were) found elsewhere.

However, in the landmark decision in *Benjamins* v. *BEA* it was established by the US Court of Appeals that the Warsaw Convention does create causes of action for wrongful death and for damage to baggage rather than only establishing conditions for causes of action. 'Uniformity in international air law can best be recognized by holding that the Convention is the universal source of a right of action.'[84]

In a recent UK case clarity has been established as to the question whether a passenger on international carriage by air may bring a claim against the carrier while relying on common or local law principles rather than the Warsaw Convention. Here, passengers were caught in the Iraqi invasion of Kuwait while stopping over. No claim under the Convention was possible since they did not suffer death or bodily injury, but were 'only' held three weeks prisoner by the Iraqis. The Court of Appeal held that the Convention 'set out an exhaustive code for the liability of international carriers by air'. The effect of this is that remedies available in the various States party to the Convention are replaced by a single cause of action enforceable in all of them.[85]

2.11. JURISDICTION AND FORA

The Convention mentions four courts for submitting claims (Art. 28):
1. the court having jurisdiction at the place where the carrier is ordinarily resident (court of domicile);
2. the court having jurisdiction at the place where the carrier has his principal place of business;
3. the court having jurisdiction at the place where the carrier maintains an establishment through which the contract has been made; and
4. the court having jurisdiction at the place of destination.

The court of domicile offers the advantage of convenience. As for the second option, namely the court at the place where the carrier maintains his principal place of business, the situation is different in that the carrier's office where the major part of his business is being transacted must be proved to constitute the company headquarters

---

84. *Benjamins* v. *BEA et al.*, US Court of Appeals (2nd Circ.), March 6, 1978; *Avi*, Vol. 14, p. 18,370; [1978] USAvR 86; *Air Law*, vol. IV (1979), pp. 27 and 171.
85. *Sidhu* v. *British Airways*, Court of Appeal, January 27, 1995; *Aviation and Space Law Reports*, vol. 2 (1996), part 11, p. 445; *Air and Space Law*, vol. XXI (1996), p. 256.

in terms of the Convention.[86] In *Tumarkin* v. *Pan Am* it was ruled that, according to Article 28 para. 1, of the Convention, a passenger who buys a return ticket in Florida with Cuba as his destination cannot initiate proceedings in New Jersey if the carrier's domicile and headquarters are located in New York.[87]

The court at the place where the office concluding the contract of carriage is located enters on the scene when a ticket is sold by a travel agency or a shipping company. To date, the intermediary of travel agents is of ever increasing importance because of the large number of transactions made by them. A further interpretation of the word '*établissement*' (establishment), used in the authentic French text of Article 28, is necessary. Romang is of the opinion that any office where an agreement is made under the authority of the carrier may be included in this category.[88]

In the case of *Woolf* v. *Aerovias Guest* it was ruled that a passenger injured during a flight of a Mexican airline between Mexico City and Miami (the ticket Mexico-Miami having been purchased in Hollywood, Florida), could not file a claim against the carrier in the State of New York, since the Mexican company had its principal offices in Mexico City.[89]

Another decision involving the place of the carrier's establishment was given in *Herfroy* v. *Artop*. The conclusion was reached that it is not possible, according to Article 28 para. 1, of the Warsaw Convention, to grant the character of an establishment to an agency which, although possessing full authority from the carrier for issuing tickets for payment, has a different organisational structure entirely independent of the carrier and is not the property of the carrier.[90]

The last option for receiving claims provided for in Article 28 is the court located at the point of destination. The destination point of a flight is displayed on the ticket. Carriage which is performed by various successive carriers agreed upon in one or more contracts shall have the last place of carriage as the final destination point.

A decision concerning the destination point has been given in the case of *Galli* v. *Re-al Brazilian Airlines*. The court insisted that the terms of the contract of carriage were decisive as regards the point of destination. No unspecified intentions and considerations, including hidden intentions and motives of the passenger, will affect the written contract of transportation: in this case, on a journey from São Paulo to Miami, New York and back to São Paulo, São Paulo was ruled to

---

86. Cf. *Winsor* v. *United Airlines*, US District Court, Eastern District of New York, June 25, 1957; [1957] USAvR 466; *Avi*, Vol.5, p. 17,509.
87. *Tumarkin et al.* v. *Pan-American World Airways*, Superior Court of New Jersey (Essex County), June 20, 1956; [1956] USAvR 383; *Avi*, Vol. 4, p. 18,152; IATA ACLR, No. 35.
88. W. Romang, *Zuständigkeit und Vollstreckbarkeit im internationalen und schweizerischen Luftprivatrecht* (thesis Winterthur, 1958), at pp. 63 a.f.
89. *Woolf* v. *Aerovias Guest*, Municipal Court of the City of New York, Borough of Manhattan (9th District), October, 1954, [1954] USAvR 399.
90. *Herfroy* v. *Cie. Portugaise Artop et al.*, Cour d'Appel de Paris, March 2, 1962; [1962] RFDA 177.

be the point of destination. The fact that the passenger did not have any intention of returning to Brazil and had purchased the return ticket only to satisfy American immigration requirements did not make New York the destination point.[91]

It is possible for a claimant to influence legal procedure by his choice of a forum. First and foremost that choice should be dictated by practical considerations; but it should be noted that according to Art. 28 the court chosen must be located in the territory of one of the states parties to the Convention.

The first question to be answered in this connection is whether Article 28 is mandatory law or not. This seems to be beyond doubt, as most authors are agreed on the fact that Article 28 of the Warsaw Convention is mandatory by virtue of Article 32, which states that all agreements altering the rules as to jurisdiction shall be null and void.

Mankiewicz says that 'Parties to a damage action under the Convention are not permitted to bring the action before another court than those specified in Article 28 of the Warsaw Convention...'.[92]

Reference may be made to a case tried by the High Court of England where was ruled that Article 28 is binding: the court stated that the effect of Article 28 was to limit the number of the courts in which an action could be brought to those explicitly mentioned in the Article.[93]

Goldhirsch states that even though a fifth jurisdiction, added through a contract made prior to the damage occurring, may benefit the claimant, it will infringe on the rules of Article 28 and thus probably be void under Article 32.[94] He adds, however, that Article 32 implies that parties are allowed to agree to anything, including which law is to be applicable or which court is to have jurisdiction, after the damage occurs.

There is a lot to be said for this last reading of Article 28 in conjunction with Article 32. In principle Article 28 contains mandatory law, but it would seem that there is no reason to assume that parties cannot decide on a more appropriate jurisdiction in an agreement after the accident. This can be concluded from Article 32, which specifically provides that parties cannot alter the rules as to applicable law and jurisdiction before the damage occurred. If the drafters of the Convention had not intended to leave open the possibility of an agreement made by the parties after the event, then why did they insert the clause that it was not possible before the damage occurred?

Another problem is: are parties allowed to agree to arbitration in personal injury cases under the Warsaw Convention? It is once more

---

91. *Galli* v. *Re-al Brazilian International Airlines*, State of New York Superior Court (Queens County, Special Term, Part I), January 31, 1961; [1961] USAvR 58.

92. R.H.Mankiewicz, *The Liability Regime of the International Air Carrier*, 1981, at p.133.

93. See *Rotterdamsche Bank* v. *BOAC (and Aden Airways)*, High Court of Justice, Queen's Bench Division (United Kingdom), February 18, 1953; (1953) USAvR 163; *IATA Law Reporter*, No. 1.

94. L.B.Goldhirsch, *The Warsaw Convention Annotated: A Legal Handbook*, 1988, p.174 *et seq*. See also Bin Cheng, 'A shored-up Warsaw Convention plus a contractual so-called "fifth jurisdiction"?', *The Aviation Quarterly*, July 1996, pp.18-30.

a question of how Article 32 is to be interpreted. It contains a provision in paragraph 2, that arbitration agreements with regard to the transport of goods are allowed, as long as the arbitration is to take place within one of the jurisdictions of Article 28.

Does the wording of Article 32 convey the intention of the drafters of the Convention to exclude the possibility of arbitration for cases regarding the carriage of passengers? Many authors seem to think so. Mankiewicz states that arbitration is only possible in cargo cases, and that the arbitration must always take account of the rules of the Convention.[95] There is also agreement to interpret Article 32 to mean that one can agree to arbitration for cargo before the damage has occurred, and for passengers and baggage only after the event.

3. The Hague Protocol

In 1955, a Diplomatic Conference at The Hague proposed the adoption of a Protocol to amend the Warsaw Convention of 1929. Although the Convention was, at the time, considered to be one of the best agreements dealing with matters of private international law, some practical and legal problems had become evident as aviation expanded rapidly between 1929 and 1955, necessitating a number of improvements in the original text.

As regards applicability, the Hague Protocol allows states to make a reservation only in respect of carriage by military aircraft; the Warsaw Convention allowed this for all categories of state aircraft.

The most conspicuous of all amendments, however, was that the limit of liability for passengers was increased twofold, bringing the ceiling limit for compensation up to 250,000 francs Poincaré. The Hague Protocol provides in Article 22, para. 5, that the conversion from gold into national currencies shall, in case of judicial proceedings, be made according to the gold value of such currencies at the date of the judgment.

For the benefit of the carrier a new provision was incorporated aimed at simplifying the requirements for passenger tickets and baggage checks. The obligations imposed on the carrier in this respect now include:

1. mentioning the place of departure and destination;
2. mentioning agreed stopping places; and
3. giving notice that the carriage is subject to the rules relating to liability as established by the Warsaw Convention.

The Warsaw provision releasing the carrier from liability during the transportation of goods and baggage if he can prove that the damage was caused by negligent pilotage or negligence in the handling of the aircraft or in navigation, was deleted. Instead, a second paragraph was added to Article 23: it now provides, in paragraph 2, that paragraph 1 (stating that any provision tending to relieve the carrier

95. R.H.Mankiewicz, *supra* note 92, at page 133.

of liability or to fix a lower limit than is laid down in the Convention shall be null and void) shall not apply to provisions governing loss and damage resulting from the inherent defect, quality or vice of the cargo carried.

When perishable foodstuffs are carried by air and arrive at their destination with a delay considerably exceeding what could be considered as normal, and which the shipper would probably have taken into account when choosing this way of transportation, the air carrier is liable under Articles 18 and 19 of the Warsaw Convention, if the loss suffered by the consignor of the goods (resulting from the loss of weight during transport) exceeds the shortfall normally accepted in such circumstances. The carrier cannot plead his general conditions of exemption from liability for delay or loss of the goods, because Article 23, para. 2, of the Warsaw Convention declares any exemption clause to be null and void, save where (paragraph 2 of that Article, added by the Hague Protocol) it concerns vice or defects of the goods themselves.[96]

It should be noted also that the length of the period in which a claim may be brought in accordance with Article 26 has been extended to fourteen days instead of seven in the case of cargo, and to seven days instead of three for baggage. The period in which claims for damages resulting from delay may be brought has been extended to twenty-one days instead of fourteen days.

In the case of *Fothergill* v. *Monarch Airlines*, an English court ruled that 'damage' in Article 26, para. 2, of the Warsaw Convention as amended at The Hague did not include 'loss' or 'partial loss'. Accordingly, the requirement of giving notice in writing within seven days was not applicable in this case. This decision was contrary to what was intended by the delegates at the Hague Conference in 1955. The House of Lords, however, basing their decision on the authentic French text of the Convention, reversed this judgment, holding that the word 'avarie' in the French text was applicable to (partial) loss as well.[97]

A very important modification from a legal point of view was made in Article 25. In the original version of the Warsaw Convention, Article 25 stipulated that the carrier cannot have recourse to the provisions limiting or excluding his liability in the event of damage resulting from 'wilful misconduct or by such default on his part as, in accordance with the law of the court to which the case is submitted, is considered to be equivalent to wilful misconduct'.

96. *Ets. Peronny* v. *Ethiopian Airlines*, Cour d'Appel de Paris (5e Ch.), May 30, 1975; [1975] RFDA 395; Schoner's case law digest *Air Law*, vol. I (1976), p. 262. See also *Transports d'Armorique* v. *La Langouste and Cie. Parisienne de Garantie*, Cour de Cassation, May 28, 1974, [1974] RFDA 404.

97. *Fothergill* v. *Monarch Airlines*, Queen's Bench Division (United Kingdom), March 17, 1977; IATA ACLR, No. 491. House of Lords, July 10, 1980; IATA ACLR, No. 531. See also the series of articles on this ease in *Air Law* (1977), Vol. II pp. 223-224; (1980), Vol. V pp. 174-183 and (1981), Vol. VI pp. 40-43. Cf. A.E. du Perron, 'Supreme Court of The Netherlands: Affrètair v. VOB or Fothergill's Dutch Treatment: Decision of 12 February 1982', *Air Law*, vol. VII (1982), pp. 173-177. Cf. also *Deere* v. *Lufthansa*, United States District Court, Nothern District of Illinois, April 26, 1985; *Air Law*, vol. XI (1986), p. 174; 19 *Avi* 18,111.

The authentic text of the Convention is in the French language, where the words 'dol' and 'faute... équivalente au dol' are used. The English and French texts, however, do not cover exactly the same concept, considering that 'dol' is characterised by the intention to inflict a specific injury on another person, whereas in the case of 'wilful misconduct' the perpetrator must be aware of his misbehaviour and the potential damage which may ensue without having necessarily intended to inflict a specific injury. The definition of 'wilful misconduct' is wider than that of 'dol', since it may include cases where no wrong has been committed intentionally.

In civil law countries there is a strong tradition to treat 'gross negligence' as equivalent to 'dol'[98]; in France, however, the prevailing attitude since 1957 is that the fault equivalent to 'dol' is the 'faute inexcusable' (inexcusable fault).[99]

In common law countries the courts have emphasised the specific character of 'wilful misconduct', which is entirely different from negligence and goes far beyond it, however gross or culpable the negligence may have been.[100]

Incidentally, mention must be made here of the so-called 'punitive' damages, a phenomenon notably current in the United States. Punitive damages are to be regarded as quite distinct from the compensation provided for under the Warsaw System. For more details reference may be made to section 4 of the chapter on 'Product Liability in Aviation', *infra*.

Continuing on the subject of wilful misconduct, it should be noted that the term has caused a confusion of terminology which in turn has led to varying interpretations by a number of national courts. In the case of *Goepp* v. *American Overseas Airlines*[101] wilful misconduct has been defined as follows:

'Wilful misconduct, as the Trial Court correctly charged, depends upon the facts of a particular case, but in order that an act may be characterized as wilful there must be on the part of the person or persons sought to be charged, a conscious intent to do or to

98. Drion (note 63, *supra*) in para. 179.
99. See, *e.g. Sontag et al.* v. *Air France et al.*, Tribunal de Grande Instance de Paris (1re Ch.), January 8, 1971; [1971] RFDA 176; IATA ACLR, No. 391. Cf. *Bornier* v. *Air-Inter*, Tribunal de Grande Instance de Paris (1re Ch., 2me Sect.), April 27, 1979; [1979] RFDA 340; *Air Law*, vol. IV (1979), p. 168.
100. G. Miller (see note 71, *supra*), at pp. 194 *et seq.*; R. H. Mankiewicz, *The Liability Regime of the International Air Carrier* (1981), pp. 122 *et seq.* Nicolas M. Matte, *Treatise on Air-Aeronautical Law* (1981), pp. 421 *et seq.* Cf. *Télémontage et al.* v. *Air Canada*, Quebec Superior Court (Canada), February 19, 1976; IATA ACLR, No. 496 and *Newell* v. *Canadian Pacific Airlines*, County Court Judicial District of Peel, Ontario; (1976) O.R. (2d) 752; (1976) 74 D.L.R. (3d) 574. See for the last case also J.-L.Magdelénat, *Air Cargo – Regulation and Claims*, 1983, p. 18 (The plaintiff's pet dogs were carried in a cargo hold which also contained dry ice. As the defendants knew this would give off carbon dioxide at certain temperatures; it did so, killing one dog and severely affecting the other. According to Article 25 it was a probability that something was likely to happen.).
101. *Goepp* v. *American Overseas Airlines* , New York Supreme Court, Appellate Division (1st Dep.), December 16, 1952; [1952] USAvR 486; IATA ACLR, No. 12.

omit doing the act from which harm results to another, or an intentional omission of a manifest duty. There must be a realization of the probability of injury from the conduct, and a disregard of the probable consequences of such conduct. The burden of establishing wilful misconduct rests upon plaintiff'.

In *Hennessy* v. *Air France*[102] it was observed that the pilot's excessive confidence in his own competence and the soundness of his equipment must in no way be considered as constituting gross negligence.

An airline failing to arrange for a substitute aircraft from another airline commits a wrongful act entailing liability for delay in the transport of goods left behind on the ground, when a substitute aircraft would have been necessary to carry the packages which the airline was unable to transport on its own aircraft on the date specified in the air waybill, and when there appeared to be every possibility of securing substitute transport at that date on the route between Paris and Tehran, with its easy and frequent direct and indirect connections. Such failure to act clearly constitutes negligence on the part of the airline, or at least carelessness with regard to the service it is expected to provide.

In such circumstances the airline could not invoke the air waybill conditions of contract as set out in IATA-Resolution 600-B,[103] as it pleaded. This Resolution says in Condition No. 4 that the 'carrier is not liable to the shipper or any other person for any damage, delay or loss of whatsoever nature..., unless such damage is proved to have been caused by the negligence or wilful fault of Carrier...'. In this particular case the airline had obviously been negligent and was therefore fully liable.[104]

In the case of *Gallais* v. *Aéro-Maritime* the French court found that flying too close to the earth's surface was the cause of the accident and that this low flying constituted 'wilful misconduct' according to Anglo-Saxon law, the more so because the fault was equivalent to 'dol' in French law. On that ground the carrier was held liable for damages to the heirs of the deceased in accordance with Article 25 of the Warsaw Convention.[105]

In view of all these varying interpretations the Hague Protocol replaced Article 25 by a new Article stating that the limits laid down in the Warsaw Convention will not apply if it is proved 'that the damage resulted from an act or omission of the carrier, his servants or agents, done with intent to cause damage or recklessly and with knowledge that damage would probably result'.[106]

---

102. *Hennessy* v. *Air France*, Tribunal Civil de la Seine (1re Ch.), April 24, 1952; [1952] RFDA 199. Affirmed: Cour d'Appel de Paris (1re Ch.), February 25, 1954; [1954] RFDA 45; IATA ACLR, No. 21.

103. See note 68, *supra.*

104. *Cie. Générale de Géophysique* v. *Iran Air*, Cour d'Appel de Paris (5e Ch.), November 14, 1974; [1975] RFDA 60; Schoner's case law digest *Air Law*, vol. I (1976), p. 263.

105. *Gallais* v. *Aéro-Maritime*, Tribunal Civile de la Seine, April 28, 1954; [1954] RFDA 184 [1955]JALC 99.

106. See also Bin Cheng, 'Wilful Misconduct: From Warsaw to The Hague and from Brussels to Paris', *Annals of Air and Space Law* (1977), Vol. II pp. 55-102.

The advantage of this new rule is that the elements of both 'dol' and 'wilful misconduct' are included, while at the same time 'omission' has been included as a ground for unlimited liability. In the event of such negligence the claimant is required to prove that the employee has committed the act within the scope of his employment.

There are many court decisions containing interpretations of Article 25. In a case involving a theft of gold bars from a bonded area of the carrier's agents at the airport, inexcusable fault was established as a result of police enquiries, carried out following the carrier's complaint that the agent could not have been unaware of the risk of exposing, at night, the valuable merchandise which he had been keeping in a safe. Moreover, the safe was in a place which was not properly locked while the key to the safe was not sufficiently guarded, thus exposing the merchandise to easy access by criminals. The agent should therefore have been fully aware that in such circumstances his acts and omissions were reckless and that damage would probably result.[107]

When a pilot lands in unfavourable atmospheric conditions with no visibility because of ground fog, while he could not have been unaware of the fact that the type of altimeter with which the aeroplane was equipped could not provide him with sufficiently precise estimates of his altitude, and while he knew that even one radar altimeter (with which his aircraft was not equipped) could have given him precise altitude information, his behaviour constitutes an inexcusable fault in terms of Article 25 of the Warsaw Convention as amended by the Hague Protocol: in doing so, he deliberately and consciously took a risk with knowledge of the damage that might be incurred, making the air carrier liable to compensate in full the loss suffered by the heirs of the victims of the accident.[108]

Under the provisions of Article 25, the problem of deciding whether the person responsible for the act or omission that caused the accident was aware that damage would probably result may be solved in two ways: for the act to be judged objectively, the behaviour of the pilot must be assessed against what a pilot of average competence would have done in similar circumstances. For an act to be judged subjectively, personal circumstances must also be taken into account.

The problem of deciding whether an objective or a subjective test should be applied for a proper assessment of an act or omission 'done recklessly and with knowledge that damage would result' was first

---

107. *Cie. Le Languedoc and 57 other insurance companies* v. *Soc. Hernu-Peron et al.*, Cour d'Appel de Paris (5e Ch.), November 17, 1975; [1976] RFDA 109; Schoner's case law digest, *Air Law*, vol. II (1977), p. 114. See also the decision of the Bundesgerichtshof (Federal Republic of Germany), February 16, 1979; [1980] ZLW 55; *Air Law*, vol. VI (1981), p. 97 (banknotes stolen from an unlocked locker during the transportation).

108. *Morand and Marsaud* v. *Soc. Air-Centre*, Cour d'Appel de Riom (France), 2me Ch., January 24, 1973; [1976] RFDA 138; Schoner's case law digest, *Air Law* vol. II (1977) p. 114. Affirmed: Cour de Cassation (1re Ch. Civ.), December 21, 1976; [1977] RFDA 415; Schoner's case law digest, *Air Law* vol. III (1978), p.127. Cf. also *Grein* v. *Imperial Airways*, Court of Appeal (England), July 13, 1936; 1 *Avi* 622; (1936) USAvR 211 (the pilot chose the least prudent of several courses open to him).

decided by French courts in favour of the objective test. It is, however, submitted by both experts and law courts in various other countries that such an interpretation is contrary to the history of Article 25 as well as the intentions of its authors.[109]

In an appeal case the New York Supreme Court decided that an air carrier's refusal to unload the baggage of two passengers, mistakenly loaded on board another aircraft together with the baggage of the other passengers all of whom were continuing their flights on that aeroplane, constituted wilful misconduct in terms of the Warsaw Convention.[110]

The translation of the French text of the Warsaw Convention has caused other uncertainties, as for instance the text of the official English translation, which has force of law in the United Kingdom, illustrates: Article 8(2) requires that the air waybill shall contain the 'weight, the quantity *and* the volume, or dimensions of the goods', whereas the French text speaks of 'le poids, la quantité *ou* les dimensions de la marchandise'.

This divergence has been interpreted in two ways: according to a strict interpretation, three particulars have to be specifically mentioned on the air waybill; in a more liberal interpretation, only one of the particulars would suffice. The word 'and' between the words 'quantity' and 'volume' would seem to be reason enough to adopt the strict interpretation.

In *Corocraft et al.* v. *Pan-American World Airways* the lower court applied the strict approach and ordered the airline to pay full compensation. The Court of Appeal, however, reversed this decision: it considered that the French text was authentic, and also that the interpretation had to be applicable in everyday practice. In general, the weight requirement was the most important, so compliance with that requirement was sufficient. This decision clearly followed the liberal interpretation.[111] The Hague Protocol replaced Article 8 by a completely new one, omitting the requirements discussed above.

109. The objective test approach of the French Cour de Cassation was expressly approved by the Canadian Federal Court in a case concerning the theft of a parcel of bank-notes sent as valuable cargo. See *Swiss Bank Corp.* v. *Air Canada*, Federal Court of Canada, Trial Division, October 22, 1981; *Annals of Air and Space Law*, vol. VII (1982), pp. 533-538. For a subjective interpretation: Cf. the decision in the case of *Consorts Tondriau and Sauvage* v. *Air India*, Belgian Supreme Court, January 27, 1977; [1977] RFDA 193; Schoner's case law digest, *Air Law*, vol. III (1978), p.128. See also on this subject Bin Cheng (note 106 *supra*); G. Miller (note 71, *supra*) at pp. 203-223 and R.H. Mankiewicz (note 100, *supra*), at pp. 114-121. See for an interpretation of the term 'recklessly' *Goldman* v. *Thai Airways International*, Court of Appeal (England) May 7, 1983, *Air Law*, vol. VIII (1983), p. 171.

110. *Cohen* v. *Varig Airlines*, NY Supreme Court, Appellate Division, May 2, 1978; *Avi*, Vol. 15, p. 17,112; Schoner's case law digest, *Air Law*, vol. IV (1979), p. 228. See also *Kupferman* v. *Pakistan Airlines*, Civil Court of the City of New York, March 27, 1981; 16 *Avi* 17,443.

111. *Corocraft el al.* v. *Pan American Airways*, Court of Appeal, London, November 7, 1968; [1969] USAvR 661; IATA ACLR, No. 257. See about this case R.H. Mankiewicz, 'La Convention de Varsovie et le Droit Comparé' [1969] RFDA 136–150 and by the same author 'Solutions jurisprudentielles des divergences entre le texte authentique d'une convention de droit privé et la loi nationale de sa mise en oeuvre, ou une loi postérieure', *Revue de Droit d'Université de Sherbrooke* (1974), Vol. 5 pp. 276-311.

Another improvement introduced by the Protocol deals with the rights of agents to limit their liability. Under the Warsaw Convention it was not clear if employees of the carrier could avail themselves of the limits provided for in Article 22. The Protocol states explicitly, in a new Article 25A, that the servants or agents of the carrier may also invoke the liability limits *ex* Article 22.[112]

4. The Guadalajara Convention

When the Warsaw Convention was drafted in 1929, charter flights played a relatively small part in international air traffic. No definition of the term 'carrier' was adopted in the Convention, because it was considered undesirable to hamper the development of aviation by doing so.

After the Second World War, the number of charter arrangements increased significantly, which made it urgent to draw up new rules designed specifically for the purpose. These rules were laid down in a Supplementary Convention rather than in a Protocol, since it was not a matter of revising old rules: they extended into an entirely new area not covered by the Warsaw Convention. However, it is to be noted that the Guadalajara Convention covers so-called 'wet-leasing' only.

ICAO had been studying the problem of charter traffic since 1955, and two drafts had resulted: (1) the draft Convention of Tokyo of 1957, relative to charter hire and interchange, and (2) the Montreal draft of 1960, which was submitted to the Guadalajara Diplomatic Conference and led to the Guadalajara Convention of 1961.[113] This Convention distinguishes between the carrier who concludes the agreement, and the carrier who actually carries it out wholly or partly, each with his own obligations of liability.

Following the example of the Warsaw Convention, the Convention of Guadalajara contains no explicit definition of the word 'carrier' as such. In Article I(b) the Convention states: 'contracting carrier means a person who as a principal makes an agreement for carriage governed by the Warsaw Convention with a passenger or consignor or with a person acting on behalf of the passenger or consignor'. In Article I(c) it says: 'actual carrier means a person, other than the contracting carrier, who, by virtue of authority from the contracting carrier, performs the whole or part of the carriage contemplated in paragraph (b), but who is not with respect to such part a successive

---

112. Cf. the decision in *Reed et al.* v. *Wiser*, US Court of Appeals (2nd Circ.), April 26, 1977; *Avi*, Vol. 14, p. 17,841; IATA ACLR, No. 493. In this decision it was held that although the USA did not ratify the Hague Protocol, the reading of the French text of the Warsaw Convention, supported by the principles of many Civil Law jurisdictions and the statements of the various delegates at The Hague require treatment of the corporation and its employees as one.
113. See note 3, *supra*; about this Convention: J.W.F. Sundberg, 'The Guadalajara Convention Live from Cyprus', *Air Law*, vol. I (1976), pp 83-98

carrier within the meaning of the Warsaw Convention. Such authority is presumed in the absence of proof of the contrary'.[114]

From an analysis of Article III, para. 2, it may be concluded that the carrier who actually performs the carriage is not liable to the same extent as the carrier who concludes it. The carrier who actually performs the carriage can never be held liable for an unlimited sum; his liability is restricted to the limits specified in the Warsaw Convention. On the other hand, his acts, and those of his employees, may result in unlimited liability for the contracting carrier.

Article VI provides that the aggregate of the amounts of money recoverable from both the actual carrier and the contracting carrier may never exceed the sum total of the limits specified. An action in court may be brought against the actual carrier, the contracting carrier, or both. When legal action is taken against one of the carriers, the others may also be brought into the case. Jurisdiction follows the same pattern as specified in the Warsaw Convention.

The Guadalajara Convention entered into force on May 1, 1964, after ratification by five states, but some conflicting points between it and the Warsaw Convention have yet to be settled. The settlement of such disputes is left to the law of the country whose court has jurisdiction. There is only a relatively small number of court cases. One of the rare instances in which the Guadalajara Convention has been declared applicable is the following.[115]

Mr. Erdem, a Turkish national, had found employment in Germany. On July 10, 1969, he bought a return ticket Düsseldorf-Istanbul at a travel agency in Cologne. Germanair was mentioned on his ticket as the air carrier. When Mr. Erdem wanted to return on the appointed day, October 25, 1969, he was not allowed to board the aircraft due to overbooking, nor was he on the following day. He therefore booked a flight with KLM and arrived at his work a day late. For the expenses caused by the delay Mr. Erdem sued the travel agency and claimed compensation. The court decided that the Warsaw Convention was applicable, even though Turkey was not a member. In the case under review, there was a return ticket with a place of landing in another country, so the flight was to be regarded as international in accordance with Article 1. The court ruled that the travel agency was responsible for the delay: in this case it could be regarded as the contracting carrier, whereas Germanair was the actual carrier. It was the travel agency that was responsible for chartering the aircraft and accepting the bookings. Germanair was not allowed to make contracts with passengers itself. The travel agency could not prove that it had taken all necessary measures and was ordered to pay compensation for the damage.

Attention should be drawn to the fact that travel agencies usually act in an intermediary capacity only. In some cases, however, they combine such activities with chartering aircraft themselves, acting as 'tour-operators'. This was the position in the German case just quoted.

---

114. Cf. the decision of the Oberlandesgericht Stuttgart (Federal Republic of Germany), July 2, 1979; ZLW 437.

115. *Osman Erdem* v. *Germanair*: see note 65, *supra.*

We note further that Article 33 of the Warsaw Convention gives the carrier the right to refuse to carry a passenger. It says: 'Nothing contained in this Convention shall prevent the carrier either from refusing to enter into any contract of carriage, or making regulations which do not conflict with the provisions of this Convention'. A contract of carriage exists when the carrier promises to transport the passenger and the passenger consents.

In everyday practice all airline companies are overbooking since experience has shown that a number of passengers do not turn up in the end. If they did not overbook they would suffer financially, and the fares would have to be increased in order to recover the losses. As Sundberg observes: 'Whenever overbooking occurs in charter traffic, the passenger is normally hit harder because his only passage back home is with the charter airline'.[116]

Overbooking has also been scrutinised by the EC. In April 1991 a Regulation came into force which entitles EC passengers to a certain sum to be paid by the air carrier in case of overbooking, apart from and additional to any compensation for damage caused by the ensuing delay. In case of flights of 3,500 kilometers or under the amount is set at ECU 150, for longer flights at ECU 300. These amounts are halved if the passenger is offered alternative transportation enabling him to arrive with a delay of no more than two hours in respect of his original time of arrival or four hours in case of flights of more than 3,500 kilometers.[117]

Article VIII, para. 1, of the IATA General Conditions of Carriage (Passengers) of 1971 mentions the circumstances which can provide a ground for the carrier to refuse to transport passengers or to continue the transport. A number of cases relating to this subject have been reported; for instance, there was a decision in 1976 in the case of *Rousseff* v. *Western Airlines*, in which a passenger was 'dumped' from his flight at an intermediate point. He was considered to have no claim when the carrier had organised other transport to bring him to his destination within less than two hours from his originally scheduled time of arrival.[118]

In 1975 a carrier refused to accept a passenger with a ticket paid for by a cheque not covered by his bank account. This was not considered to constitute a breach of contract.[119]

---

116. J.W.F. Sundberg, *Chartering of Aircraft*, General Report (Section III.D) to the Xth International Congress (Budapest, 1978) of the International Academy of Comparative Law.

117. See O.J. No. L 36, February 8, 1991 (Council Regulation No. 295/91). See also B.J.H. Crans and E.M.H. Loozen, 'EC Aviation Scene', *Air Law*, vol. XVI (1991), pp. 178–194 at pp. 185–186.

118. *Rousseff* v. *Western Airlines*, US District Court, Central District of California, March 22, 1976; *Avi*, Vol. 13, p. 18,391; Schoner's case law digest, *Air Law*, vol. II (1977), p. 231. Cf. the decision of the Bundesgerichtshof (Federal Republic of Germany), September 28, 1978; [1979] ZLW 134; *Air Law*, vol. IV (1979), p. 111 (refusal of carriage due to overbooking).

119. *Marshall* v. *Delta Airlines* v. *American Security and Trust Company*, US District Court, District of Columbia, December 15, 1975; *Avi*, Vol. 13, p. 18,165; Schoner's case law digest, *Air Law*, vol. II (1977), p. 231.

In the case of *Adamsons* v. *American Airlines* the plaintiff was awarded compensation exceeding the Warsaw limits for damage to her health. She had been refused passage on unjustified suspicions of the aircraft's crew that her condition was contagious. The resulting two–day delay in surgical intervention had seriously impaired her health. The limits were not applicable, as Article 17 of the Convention was not held to apply to this care: the plaintiff had never been accepted as a 'passenger', no accident had occurred, nor was she (dis)embarking when bodily injury was sustained.[120]

A new development worth mentioning in this context is passengers refusing to board their booked flight. In a case heard before the Amsterdam Court of Appeal in 1996 some 40 passengers were awarded damages. Having experienced a series of agonising technical problems and delays on their outward holiday flight to Faro with Air Atlantis they had refused to board this operator's aircraft for the return flight and had arranged for alternative homeward transportation.[121]

A related problem is discussed by Schmid in connection with the crash of a German charterflight near the Dominican Republic in 1996. In this case the tour-operator, shortly before departure, had switched the airline which was to provide the actual transport. Schmid discusses — referring to German transport law — the rights of passengers as regards transport by the airline and type of aircraft that were designated in their contract with the tour-operator. His conclusion is that such switches to an airline or an aircraft unacceptable to the passenger — e.g. for actually being or being regarded as unsafe — may lead to liability in tort for the tour-operator.[122]

The counterpart of the 'denied boarding' problem is the so-called 'denied entry' problem. This involves persons denied entry into a country, *e.g.* those seeking asylum for unvalid reasons. Such persons are sometimes turned back by immigration officials at the exit of a just-landed aircraft and then have to be flown back to their initial place of departure at the carrier's own, often considerable, expenses. A special complication may arise when these persons no longer possess official identification papers, making it impossible to determine their nationality and repatriate them immediately.[123]

A different situation was the subject of a case decided upon in the USA in 1994. Here an over-zealous air carrier had confiscated a passenger's travel documents believing them to be forged. The passenger subsequently had to spend three days in the transit lounge of the airport while his travel documents were inspected. As the passenger was not held to be in the actual process of embarking he had no claim against the carrier under the Warsaw Convention.[124]

120. *Adamsons* v. *American Airlines*, New York Supreme Court, October 31, 1980; *Avi*, Vol. 16, p. 17,196; IATA ACLR, No. 549. See on the subject of refusal: B. Reukema, *Discriminatory Refusal of Carriage in North America* (1982) (thesis McGill, 1981).

121. *Consumentenbond* v. *Air Atlantis*, Amsterdam Court of Appeal, June 27, 1996, roll-number 1348/94 (not yet published).

122. R. Schmid, 'Die Rechte des Reisenden beim Wechsel der Fluggesellschaft und des Luftfahrzeuges', *Neue Juristische Wochenschrift*, vol.49(1996), pp. 1636-1644.

123. See R. Schmid, 'Is a carrier responsible for passengers arriving without travel documents?', *Air Law*, vol. XVI (1991), pp. 142-143.

124. *Umwagbai* v. *Alitalia Airlines*, US District Court for the District of Massachusetts, January 20, 1994; 24 *Avi* 17,811; *Air and Space Law*, vol. XX (1995), p. 36.

5. The Montreal Agreement of 1966

The Montreal Agreement was concluded between a number of airline companies and the Civil Aeronautics Board of the United States. It heralded the beginning of a revolutionary movement aimed at changing the fault liability of the carrier into a risk liability, a development which eventually led to the adoption of the Guatemala Protocol of 1971 and the four Montreal Protocols of 1975.

The Montreal Agreement was intended as a temporary solution to the impasse caused by the American denunciation of the Warsaw Convention on November 15, 1965. The chief cause of the American move was the 125,000 francs Poincaré limit, prescribed for the benefit of the carriers. The United States did not consider this sum to be commensurate with the compensation paid in cases involving domestic transport: within the USA, unlimited liability is usually applied. The Hague Protocol had not been ratified by the USA because even its limits were not thought to be satisfactory.

According to Article 39, para. 2, of the Warsaw Convention the denunciation would become effective six months after notification, which would have been on May 15, 1966. The ICAO had already called a meeting to discuss a revision of the liability limits. This meeting, which took place in February 1966, produced a resolution requesting the ICAO Council to convene a Diplomatic Conference for the purpose of discussing various proposals concerning maximum liability. In the meantime, however, IATA carriers had drafted the Montreal Agreement, which was approved by the United States Government. Consequently, on May 4, 1966, the United States requested the Polish Government to cancel its notification of denunciation of the Warsaw Convention.[125]

The Montreal Agreement is applicable to all international flights in which a point within the United States is an agreed stopping place, point of departure or destination, but only insofar as passengers are concerned. It is not a Protocol attached to the Warsaw Convention, but a private agreement between the air carriers and the US Civil Aeronautics Board, as explained earlier. The maximum liability of the carrier has been fixed at US$75,000 (US$58,000 excluding legal fees and costs); it is up to the passengers to take out additional insurance. Furthermore, the carrier, in case of death or injury of a passenger, can no longer avail himself of the liability limitation clauses contained in Article 20, para. 1, of the Warsaw Convention stating that the carrier will not be liable if he proves that he and his agents have taken all necessary measures to avoid the damage or that it was impossible to take such measures. The plaintiff no longer has to prove that the carrier was at fault, but only the extent of the injury sustained. Article 25 of the Warsaw Convention concerning unlimited liability in cases of wilful misconduct or gross negligence remains applicable.

---

125. See Nicolas M. Matte (note 100, *supra*), pp. 454-471 and D. Cohen, 'Happy Birthday: Agreement CAB 18900: A Critical Review of the Montreal Interim Agreement and the Authority for its Implementation', *Air Law*, vol. VII (1982), pp. 74 91.

The carrier has to notify every passenger in writing of the possible applicability of the provisions relating to the limitation of liability contained in the Convention and in the Agreement at the time the ticket is issued. However, no penalties for failure to do so have been included in the Montreal Agreement. The text to be used for this printed notice is prescribed in paragraph 2 of the Agreement, as well as details with regard to the ink and the typeface in which it is to be printed.[126]

In this connection the following decision is of interest. The court ruled that the Warsaw Convention, as modified by the Montreal Agreement and particularly the wording of the passenger notice on the possible applicability of the Convention dictated by the Agreement permits compensation for mental injury. The fact that the words 'wounding... or bodily injury', used in the Convention, were replaced by 'personal injury' in the passenger notice suggests an intention to clarify the type of injury which is capable of compensation.[127]

Since 1974 an informal grouping of West-European Governments have held a series of consultations about concerted action to encourage their national flag carriers to adopt higher limits of liability in their contracts. These consultations have resulted in the so-called 'Malta Agreement', a rather misleading title, as no formal agreement has ever been promulgated. The Malta Agreement contained an undertaking by a number of West European countries and Japan to raise the liability limit of Article 22, para. 1 of the Warsaw Convention for death or injury suffered by a passenger to US$58,000. The new limit was to apply in the event of accidents taking place on board aircraft operated by the carriers concerned, or in the course of embarkation on, or disembarkation from, such aircraft. Several non-scheduled air carriers have followed suit and raised their limits of liability accordingly.

Save for the legal fees and costs, the US$58,000 limit equals the limit specified in the Montreal Agreement in respect of international air transport that includes a point within the United States as the point of origin, point of destination or agreed stopping place. It should be noted here, however, that most carriers under the Malta Agreement did not waive their defences under Article 20, para. 1 of the Warsaw Convention concerning transport not covered by the Montreal Agreement. The same applies to carriage under the Hague Protocol.[128]

---

126. See *In re Korean Air Line Disaster*, United States District Court, District of Columbia, July 25, 1985; 19 *Avi* 17,584 (Notice in 8 point type instead of 10 point).

127. *Krystal* v. *BOAC and British Airways*, US District Court, Central District of California, September 10, 1975; *Avi*, Vol. 14, p. 17,128; Schoner's case law digest, *Air Law*, vol. II (1977), p. 113.

128. See about the Malta Agreement: N.R. McGilchrist, 'Special Contracts and the Malta Agreement' [1977] *Lloyd's Maritime and Commercial Law Quarterly*, 366–370 and also *Air Law*, vol. I (1976), p. 285.

6. The Guatemala Protocol

A further addition to the Warsaw System is the Guatemala Protocol.[129] It was signed on March 8, 1971, by 21 nations, including the United States, and it was designed to modify the 'Warsaw Convention as amended at The Hague in 1955' (Art. I).

Only eleven states have ratified the Protocol to date. As the ratifications of 30 nations are required and also the condition has to be met that the scheduled air traffic of five ratifying states, on aggregate and expressed in passenger-kilometres, should represent at least 40 per cent of the 1970 total of international scheduled air traffic of the ICAO member States, the Protocol has not yet entered into force. As a result, airlines to date are, practically speaking, still governed by (1) the Warsaw Convention of 1929; (2) the Warsaw Convention as amended by the Hague Protocol of 1955; (3) the Supplementary Convention of Guadalajara of 1961; and (4) the Montreal Agreement of 1966. Nonetheless, the provisions of the Guatemala Protocol deserve our close attention because they would have meant a definite step forward. Incidentally, the Protocol may enter into force in the future.

The Guatemala Protocol contains some fundamental modifications, but they affect only the rules of transportation of passengers and their baggage. Its main feature is a shift of principle, in that the fault liability at present attaching to the carrier will be changed into a risk liability: accordingly, the carrier will be liable also in cases where he bears no fault or blame, for instance in the event of death or injury resulting from hijacking or sabotage. There is, however, an important provision: his liability with regard to passengers and baggage can never exceed the sum of 1,500,000 francs Poincaré (about US$100,000), not even when it is proved 'that the damage resulted from an act or omission of the carrier, his servants, employees or agents, done with intent to cause damage, or recklessly and with knowledge that damage would probably result'. This limit has been made mandatory: the 1,500,000 francs Poincaré are a maximum limit, a limit not to be exceeded.[130] This amount is, however, subject to periodical review.

The case for the introduction of fixed limits in the Warsaw System becomes apparent if one considers the enormous increase in the risks run by air carriers. Not only has the volume of air traffic movements increased sharply, entailing more likelihood of collisions especially around airports, but also the size of the aircraft, so that the number of passengers involved in accidents is now many times higher than was ever dreamt of in 1929. A striking example is the notorious accident at Tenerife Airport where a collision between KLM and Pan-American Jumbo-jets resulted in the worst disaster ever to occur in aviation. We shall have occasion to revert to this tragic accident later in this treatise.

129. See note 4, *supra*.
130. For a different point of view see W.J. Hickey Jr., 'Breaking the Limit – Liability for Wilful Misconduct under the Guatemala Protocol' [1976] JALC 603–622.

Allowance has been made in the Protocol for states to establish and operate within their own territories a supplementary compensation scheme, provided that the costs involved are not charged to the carrier (Art. XIV).[131]

The carrier will, under the Protocol, be able to exonerate himself wholly or partially:

(1) if he proves that the damage was caused or contributed to by the negligence or other wrongful act or omission of the person claiming compensation (Art. VII); and

(2) if death or injury resulted solely from the state of health of the passenger (Art. IV).

The latter provision is new; no similar rule can be found in any other air law convention.

According to Article IV the carrier will be liable for damage sustained in case of destruction or loss of, or damage to baggage, provided only that the event which caused the destruction, loss or damage took place on board the aircraft, or in the course of any of the operations of embarking or disembarking, or during any period within which the baggage was in the charge of the carrier. But the carrier will not be liable if the damage resulted solely from the inherent defect, quality or vice of the baggage.

In the case of delay involving passengers the carrier's liability will be limited to 62,500 francs Poincaré for each passenger, and the carrier will not be liable for damage caused by delay if he proves 'that he and his servants and agents have taken all necessary measures to avoid the damage or that it was impossible for them to take such measures' (Art. VI). Consequently, fault will still be the legal ground for liability when delay is involved.

Under the Warsaw Convention as amended at The Hague, the carrier's liability in respect of checked baggage and goods is limited to the sum of 250 francs Poincaré per kilogram, whereas for objects the passenger takes charge of himself the liability is limited to 5,000 francs Poincaré per passenger. Article VIII of the Guatemala Protocol, however, establishes a new limit for baggage in general, amounting to 15,000 francs Poincaré; this means that the distinction between checked baggage and baggage the passenger takes charge of personally has been dropped. Furthermore, it should be noted that any reference to the special declaration of value with regard to luggage has been abandoned by the Guatemala Protocol.

Finally, one more innovation to be introduced by the Protocol needs mentioning: Article 28 of the Warsaw Convention is to be amended in such a way that it will become possible to file a suit in the state of domicile or permanent residence of the claimant if the defendant carrier has a place of business in that state and is subject to its jurisdiction.

131. See on this subject M. Bodenschatz, 'Die Fluggast-Unfallversicherung als Möglichkeit der ergänzenden Schadenersatzregelung gemäss Guatemala Protokoll', *Beiträge zum Luft- und Weltraumrecht* (Festschrift zu Ehren von Alex Meyer, 1975), pp. 45-54.

7. The Four Montreal Protocols of 1975

Four 'Additional Protocols' amending the Warsaw System were adopted by a Diplomatic Conference held in Montreal in 1975.[132]

Protocol No. 1 allows payments made within the liability limits originally established by the Warsaw Convention to be calculated in terms of Special Drawing Rights (SDRs) as defined by the International Monetary Fund. Protocol No. 2 replaces the limits set out in the Hague Protocol by limits expressed in SDR. Protocol No. 3 deals in a similar manner with the limits specified in the Guatemala Protocol. Protocol No. 4 changes, for the first time since the Hague Protocol, the liability rules relating to goods and introduces SDRs here as well; it will be examined in more detail later, but first it is appropriate to consider the reasons which have prompted the replacement of the franc Poincaré of the Warsaw Convention by Special Drawing Rights.

Article 22, para. 4 of the Warsaw Convention provides that 'The sums mentioned above shall be deemed to refer to the French franc consisting of $65\frac{1}{2}$ milligrams of gold at the standard of fineness of nine hundred thousandths'. This was the official definition of the franc Poincaré in 1929. The Warsaw Convention was the first to adopt it as a standard unit. Paragraph 4 adds that the sums may be converted into any national currency in round figures. The Hague Protocol added to this the following clause: 'Conversion of the sums into national currencies other than gold shall, in case of judicial proceedings, be made according to the gold value of such currencies at the date of the judgment'.

As long as gold remained the basis of the monetary system there was no problem, and for a considerable period of time it remained the standard value in which all currencies were expressed. In 1944 the International Monetary Fund (IMF) was created. Difficulties then arose from the fact that there was an official price for gold expressed in US dollars, but on the free market the price of gold could be different. An examination of the relevant case law reveals that some law courts relied on the gold value as prescribed in the Warsaw Convention, wereas others adopted the free market price.[133] To eliminate just

---

132. See note 5, *supra*.

133. See, *e.g.* the two following cases: *Association Aéronautique du Centre Inter-Club de Saint-Cyr Beynes et al.* v. *Thierache*, Tribunal de Grande Instance de Paris, February 10, 1973; [1973] RFDA 212; IATA ACLR, No. 463 (official exchange rate to be used). *Olympic Airways* v. *Zacopoulos*, Court of Appeals of Athens, January 21, 1974; IATA ACLR, No. 461; Schoner's case law digest, *Air Law*, vol. I (1976), p. 42 (conversion at the market rate as on the date of the hearing at first instance). See also the series of articles in *Air Law* by Peter Martin, 'The Price of Gold and the Warsaw Convention' in (1979), Vol. IV, pp. 70-76; (1980), Vol. V, pp. 34-35 and (1981), Vol. VI, pp. 246-249. See also L.R. Edwards, 'The Liability of Air Carriers for Death and Personal Injury to Passengers' (1982) 56 *The Australian Law Journal*, 108–118, at 113 *et seq.* See also the following case: *State of the Netherlands* v. *Liberia Giants Shipping Corp.*, Supreme Court of the Netherlands, May 1, 1981 (see A.E. du Perron, 'Supreme Court of the Netherlands: "Blue Hawk" case: conversion of the Gold Franc', *Air Law*, vol. VI (1981), p. 191). See also A. Tobolewski, *Monetary limitations of liability in air law*, 1986.

such anomalies the Special Drawing Rights were introduced, which are a fixed sum based, since January 1, 1981, on a 'basket' of the values of five currencies.

The *Franklin Mint* case in particular has caused quite a stir: here a claimant wanted the free market price of gold to be applied. This was rejected by the Court of first instance in a ruling implying that the Warsaw Convention limits would become unenforceable in the USA. The Supreme Court, though, reversed that decision. Accordingly, the liability limit sanctioned by the CAB (approximately $9 per lb. cargo, based upon the last official gold price) was considered to be consistent with the Warsaw Convention. The case is a clear illustration of the complications arising from the USA not having adhered to the 1975 Montreal Protocols, which introduced the SDR as the monetary unit for quantifying the carrier's liability.[134]

Hostility towards the Warsaw Convention's liability limits is not restricted to USA courts alone. In 1985 the Italian Constitutional Court ruled that the limits of Article 22(1) were in conflict with Article 2 of the Italian Constitution which guarantees 'the inviolable rights of man'. These 'inviolable rights' were held to include a right to proper compensation for damage affecting the safety of the supreme asset of life. In view of the development of aviation since 1929 the Warsaw limits were now at variance with this guarantee according to the Court, and thus the Italian law enacting these limits was declared unconstitutional, opening the way for unlimited liability of the carrier.[135] This situation has however been redressed by the speedy introduction (in 1986) of a new act, which increases the Warsaw limits up to the level envisaged in the Guatemala Protocol of 1971, *i.e.* 100,000 SDR, an amount which appears to be well on its way to becoming universally accepted.[136]

However in an unprecedent move, the airlines of Japan have amended their conditions of carriage, to waive, in effect, the liability limits for death and injury to passengers as provided by Article 25 of the Warsaw Convention/Hague Protocol. The measures affect all passengers carried on aircraft of Japan and have become effective on November 20, 1992.[137]

Following these amendments Martin has pointed out that the Japanese airlines will not plead limitation of liability in respect of claims arising out of the death, wounding or other bodily injury of a passenger.

134. *Franklin Mint* v. *TWA*, US Court of Appeals (2nd Circ.) September 28, 1982; *Annals of Air and Space Law*, vol. VII (1982) p. 601, *Air Law* vol. VIII (1983), p. 79; and *TWA* v. *Franklin Mint*, US Supreme Court, April 17, 1984; IATA ACLR No. 614, *Air Law*, vol. IX (1984), p. 184. See also Patricia Barlow, 'Article 22 of the Warsaw Convention in a state of limbo', *Air Law* vol. VIII (1983), pp. 2–30. Cf. *S.S. Pharmaceutical & Anor* v. *Qantas Airways*, Supreme Court of New South Wales, September 22, 1988; *Air Law* vol. XIV (1989), p. 97 and p. 208.

135. See G. Guerreri, 'The Warsaw system Italian style: Convention without limits', *Air Law*, vol. X (1989), pp. 294-305 (refers to the case of *Coccia* v. *THY*).

136. See *Air Law*, vol. XI (1986), pp. 95-96 and pp. 123-125 for the text of the new act and Notes and Commentary by G. Guerreri and his Article 'Law 274 of 7 July 1988: A remarkable Piece of Italian Patchwork', *Air Law*, vol. XIV (1989), pp. 176-182.

137. See *Lloyd's Aviation Law*, vol. II (1992), No. 22, p. 1

However, in respect of claims with a value of under 100,000 SDR the defence under Article 20(1) will be waived, whereas for claims in excess of that amount the defence will be retained with regard to the portion of the claim exceeding 100,000 SDR.[138]

In practice this means that passengers of Japanese airlines (the rules will be valid for all Japanese airline companies) will gain a considerable advantage over passengers of other airlines. The effect will be to put extra stress on the handling procedures for passengers of different nationalities flying in the same aircraft.

In 1995 IATA even went a step further and proposed to its members an agreement to waive the limitation of liability and recoverable damages in Article 22(1) of the Warsaw Convention as to claims for death, wounding or other bodily injury of a passenger within the meaning of Article 17 of the Convention. Recoverable damages would then be awarded and determined by reference to the law of the domicile of the passenger.

An agreement of this nature, entitled 'Intercarrier Agreement on Passenger Liability', was initially signed by Air Canada, Air Mauritius, Avianca, Egyptair, Japan Airlines and KLM, and it was to come into force not later than November 1, 1996. The introduction of this agreement does not deprive Article 25 of the Warsaw Convention of all its meaning: it remains useful for breaking through the liability limit barrier for luggage and cargo. Martin, however, voices doubts about the universal application of the Intercarrier Agreement and wonders whether it will lead to greater fragmentation.[139]

A further development has been put forward in an European Union press release of December 20, 1995. It proposes a Council Regulation designed to guarantee simple and speedy procedures in order to ensure improved compensation for passengers involved in aircraft accidents. The proposed Regulation would introduce
(a) a waiver of the Warsaw/Hague liability limits for passengers;
(b) a strict liability of up to ECU 100,000 (i.e. an imposed cancellation of the Article 20 defence); and

---

138. P. Martin, 'Japanese Airlines — Looking Forward Rather Than Back', *Lloyd's Aviation Law*, vol. II (1992), No. 22, pp. 2-5 at p. 3. See for the Japanese phenomenon of 'condolence money' which may be additional to any claim for compensation in case of death, E. Tobi, 'The insurer's point of view', *Air Law*, vol. XI (1986), pp. 84-94. See also T. Sakamoto, 'The Fate of Passenger Liability Limitation in the Warsaw System', in *The Use of Airspace and Outer Space for All Mankind in the 21st Century*, Proceedings of the International Conference on Air Transport and Space Application in a New World (Tokyo, June 2-5, 1993), Chia-Jui Cheng, ed., pp. 131-140; Bin Cheng, 'The Warsaw System: Mess up, Tear up, or Shore up?', *ibidem*, pp. 105-130; and I.H.Ph.Diederiks-Verschoor, 'New Developments Around the Compensation Limits of the Warsaw Convention', in *Issues in International Air and Space Law, and in Commercial Law* (Essays in Commemoration of Prof.Dr. Doo Hwan Kim's Sixtieth Birthday), 1994, pp. 3-11.

139. See P. Martin, 'The 1995 IATA Intercarrier Agreement', *Air and Space Law*, vol.XXI (1996), pp. 17-24; F.Lyall, 'Essay: the Warsaw Convention - Cutting the Gordian Knot and the 1995 Intercarrier Agreement', *Syracuse Journal of International Law and Commerce*, vol. 22 (1996), pp. 67-80; and R.I.R. Abeyratne, 'Regulatory Management of the Warsaw System of Air Carrier Liability', *Journal of Air Transport Management*, vol. 3 (1997), pp. 37-45.

(c)   an 'upfront' payment by the carrier of ECU 50,000 in case of death and up to ECU 50,000 in case of injury.

These new European rules would apply to all international and domestic flights of European Union carriers. Third country carriers would not be affected and will have to inform their passengers accordingly. This proposal has come in for even more criticism from Martin.[140]

According to the Montreal Protocols the conversion of sums expressed in SDR into national currencies must, in the case of judicial proceedings, be made according to the value of such currencies in terms of the Special Drawing Rights at the date of the judgment. The value of a national currency of a High Contracting Party which is also a member of the International Monetary Fund must be calculated in accordance with the method of valuation effective at the date of judgment and applied by the IMF for its operations and transactions.

For the benefit of those states which are not members of the IMF and whose law does not allow the use of SDRs, alternative limits have been provided. These limits are expressed in a newly introduced 'monetary unit', corresponding to $65\frac{1}{2}$ milligrams of gold of millesimal fineness nine hundred, a definition deriving from that used in the Warsaw Convention for the franc Poincaré. The conversion of the sums expressed in monetary units must take place in accordance with the law of the state concerned.

Protocol No. 4 regulates the liability of the carrier for the transportation of goods in the same manner as the Guatemala Protocol does for passengers. The legal basis for such liability has been changed into a risk liability, but the carrier has four grounds on which he may exonerate himself, namely:

1. inherent defect, quality or vice of the cargo;
2. defective packing of the cargo performed by a person other than the carrier or his employees or agents;
3. an act of war or an armed conflict; and
4. an act of public authority carried out in connection with the entry, exit or transit of the cargo.

Special Drawing Rights have also been introduced in Protocol No. 4. Fixed limits have been set, which cannot be changed. Requirements for the documentation have been simplified.[141]

The complicated situation arising from the numerous Protocols caused the Montreal Diplomatic Conference to adopt a resolution requesting the ICAO Legal Committee to prepare a consolidated text covering the whole area of the Warsaw System, so as to create a measure of uniformity between the Warsaw Convention and its amendments.[142] This

---

140.   Martin, *op.cit.* (note 139, *supra*) p. 23. See also P.Martin, 'The 1995 IATA Intercarrier Agreement: an Update', *Air and Space Law*, vol.XXI (1996), pp. 126-131, where the texts of the Agreement and the EU proposal are given.

141.   See P.N. Ehlers, *Montrealer Protokolle Nr. 3 und 4 – Warschauer Haftungssystem und neuere Rechtsentwicklung*, Schriften zum Luft- und Weltraumrecht, Band 7, 1985.

142.   See the Minutes and Documents of the International Conference on Air Law (Montreal, 1975); ICAO Doc. 9154-LC/174-1 and 174-2.

consolidated text was never adopted into a formal agreement due to various objections from many quarters. Besides it would have confused matters further by adding another legal instrument to the existing series[143]

It is, however, necessary to mention here also that, inspired by the Intercarrier Agreement, an ICAO Study Group on the Modernization of the Warsaw System has been established in February 1996. Its report was studied by the ICAO Council in its 147th Session later that year. The result was a consensus on the Adoption of a New Consolidated Instrument, recommending that this should in particular

(a) provide for a two-tier liability regime for recoverable compensatory damages in case of injury or death of passengers, comprising: (i) liability of the air carrier up to 100,000 SDR, irrespective of the carrier's fault; (ii) liability of the air carrier in excess of 100,000 SDR on the basis of negligence, the defence of contributory negligence of the passenger or claimant being available in both instances;

(b) revise the limit for liability for checked and unchecked baggage;

(c) modernize the provisions regarding the ticket and other documentary requirements; and

(d) include elements of the Warsaw Convention, the Hague, Guatemala City and Montreal Protocols as well as the Guadelajara Convention, to the extent that they are appropriate, give effect to, and are consistent with the foregoing.[144]

This draft has to be approved by the Legal Committee, after which a Diplomatic Conference will be convened. Moreover the Council urged States which have not done so to ratify Montreal Protocol No.4 relating to cargo liability. A meeting of the Legal Committee has been scheduled for April 1997.

A further complicating factor is the situation as regards the USA. As discussed above, passengers to, from or via this country benefit by the provisions of the 1966 Montreal Agreement. Repeatedly, however, the liability limits in this Agreement have been the subject of discussion.

The US Department of Transportation (DOT) proposed initially to accept the IATA Intercarrier Agreement under a number of stringent conditions which would have resulted in the US liability system being imposed on all carriers worldwide.[145]

Following a lot of objections the DOT changed its position and issued a new Order, in this the IATA Intercarrier Agreement with its far more favourable regime than the 1966 Montreal Agreement was approved unconditionally.[146] However, at the same time a number of conditions were proposed to be applied to that Montreal Agreement in such a way that this too would make air carriers strictly liable to an unlimited amount with regard to accidents under the

---

143. See R.H. Mankiewicz, 'A Galaxy of Unified Laws Will Replace the Uniform Regime Created in 1929 in Warsaw, or the Death-Blow to the Uniform Regime of Liability in International Carriage by Air', (1976) 1 *Air Law* 157-160.

144. ICAO Doc. C-WP/10381, 5/3/96.

145. DOT, Show Cause Order 96-10-7, issued October 3, 1996.

146. DOT, Order 96-11-6, issued November 12, 1996.

Warsaw Convention involving death or wounding of passengers with a ticket to, from or via the USA.[147]

Once again the USA exerted intensive pressure in order to push through its plans and we may safely assume the last word about all this has not yet been said.

Summing up the present situation we cannot but conclude that it presents many unsatisfactory aspects: different limits may apply to passengers travelling on the same aircraft but to different destinations; when travelling to or from a state which is not a party to the Warsaw Convention they may receive full compensation for damage, as the limits of the Warsaw Convention are not applicable; a passenger boarding a plane at Rome for Amsterdam may possibly receive the same compensation as a passenger in the same plane bound for the USA, due to the Malta Agreement; but if the carrier states that he has taken all the necessary measures the passenger for Amsterdam must prove that the carrier was at fault, whereas the passenger flying to the USA is not required to assume this burden of proof; it is not at all unusual for transport to take place between two states, one of which has adhered to the Hague Protocol, whereas the other has only ratified the Warsaw Convention: the application of the two Conventions may then cause complications. Most of these problems relate to the fact that the unification of rules provided by the Warsaw Convention for the carriage of passengers, baggage and goods has been adversely affected by the multitude of amendments. Such adverse effects were heightened by the divergent interpretations of some of its terms in both the Continental and the Anglo-Saxon legal systems, as well as in the judicial rulings in various countries. Meanwhile, notwithstanding all complications, the old Convention is still functioning on a worldwide basis; its rules operate for the benefit of passengers and carriers alike. The carriers are fully aware of their responsibilities, against which insurance can be arranged; the passengers know what to expect in cases of injury or damage. If they are not satisfied with the limits for compensation they can take out their own additional insurance policy.

In conclusion, we feel justified in submitting that the almost 70-year-old Warsaw Convention is still worth retaining, but that meanwhile every effort should be made to reduce the number of discrepancies.[148]

---

147. See R.Schmid, 'The Warsaw Convention — between sunset and sunrise. IATA Intercarrier Agreements as a requiem for a well-proved liability system', *Air and Space Law*, vol.XXII (1997) (forthcoming).

148. See R.H. Mankiewicz, 'L'avenir de la Convention de Varsovie', *ASDA-Bulletin* (Association Suisse de Droit Aérien et Spatial), 1982, No. 1, pp. 5-14; and by the same author, 'From Warsaw to Montreal with certain intermediate stops. Marginal notes on the Warsaw System', *Air Law*, vol. XV (1990), pp. 239-260. See also Bin Cheng, 'Sixty Years of the Warsaw Convention', [1989] ZLW 319–345 (Part I) and [1990] ZLW 3–56 (Part II). See also Doo-Hwan Kim, 'An International Air Carrier's Liability in a Changing Era', *Korean Journal of Air Law*, 1993, pp.31-52, also published in *The Use of Airspace and Outer Space for All Mankind in the 21st Century*, Proceedings of the International Conference on Air Transport and Space Application in a New World (Tokyo, June 2-5, 1993), Chia-Jui Cheng, ed., pp. 89-104; and Sung-Hwan Shin, 'The Warsaw System: Developing Instruments', *Korean Journal of Air Law*, 1993, pp. 265-299.

The Warsaw System

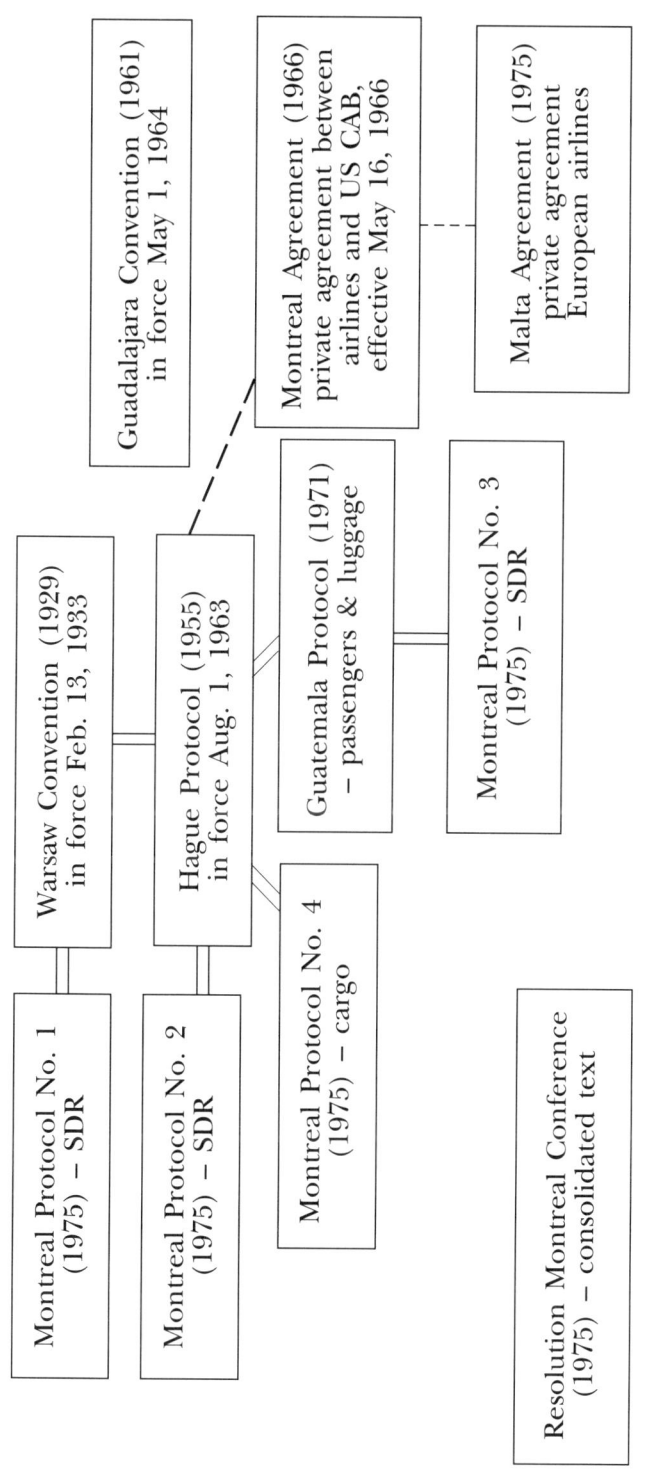

CHAPTER IV

Product Liability in Aviation

1. Introductory note

The area covered by product liability in the broadest sense is so vast that an attempt to analyse all its impact on the aviation world risks going far beyond the scope of this book. Every effort has been made to confine our review of the subject as closely as possible to its place in air law and its influence on aircraft manufacturers, airlines and passengers, in spite of strong connections with other spheres of commercial activity. A brief look at past developments will invariably touch upon these close links, but that is indispensable for a better understanding of modern trends.

Our review is largely based on American practice and American case law. This is not surprising as the idea of product liability originated in the United States.

How is the term 'product liability' to be defined or interpreted? There is more than one answer to that question. It is generally agreed that product liability is the liability resulting from damage caused by defective products. A broader definition is given by Hursh,[1] reading as follows: product liability is 'the liability of a manufacturer, processor or non-manufacturing seller for injury to the person or property of a buyer or third party caused by a product which has been sold'.

There are three grounds for a successful product liability lawsuit: (1) defective design; (2) defective construction; (3) inadequate instructions for handling a product put on the market. Whenever a product turns out to be defective after it has been sold, there are under Anglo-Saxon law two remedies available against the manufacturer: (1) breach of warranty; (2) tort.[2]

It is worth pointing out here that an action for breach of warranty is available only to the direct purchaser on the basis of his contract with the manufacturer, which of course weakens its range and effectiveness. An action for tort offers the advantage of being available also to third parties who have acquired the defective product at a later stage. In tort, obligations are constituted not only by contract, but also by statute and common law.

---

1. R.D. Hursh and H.J. Bailey, *American Law of Products Liability* (2nd ed., 1974 (with supplements)). at pp. 2-3.
2. See for a case centring on the subject of 'warranty': *Helicopter Sales (Australia) Pty. Ltd.* v. *Rotor-works Pty. Ltd.*, High Court of Australia; *Air Law*, vol. I (1976), pp. 189-190.

This point is illustrated by Duintjer Tebbens.[3] He focuses in particular on the obligations affecting professional suppliers of goods and services. Some obligations are usually created by their sales contracts, but others are imposed by law to enhance the general standards of craftsmanship and thus to protect the public at large from inferior or defective products, not only the direct purchaser.

With an increasing number of court cases on their hands American judges and legal critics soon recognised that aircraft manufacturers bore a legal responsibility for product safety and reliability standards similar, or at least comparable, to those imposed by law on manufacturers of ordinary consumer goods. This trend of thought gained a foothold even in California, the home base of giant aircraft industries.

Martin quotes as an early, typical example of product liability in aviation the 1937 case of *Maynard* v. *Stinson Aircraft*.[4] In this case a passenger was awarded damages when she suffered injuries caused by an aircraft catching fire. The manufacturer was held by the court to have been negligent in the design of the airplane on two counts. Firstly, the 'exhaust stacks' were too short to discharge the hot exhaust gases free and clear of the body of the airplane; secondly, the carburettor drain design was such that gasoline escaping from it was likely to accumulate on the underbody of the plane where it was ignited by the exhaust gases.

2. The evolution towards strict liability

As early as 1916 an American court, recognising the limited reach of the breach of warranty action, had opened the way for third party compensation.[5] According to that decision, however, the claimant still had a heavy burden of proof. He had to demonstrate

a. that the damage had been caused by a defect inherent to the product;

b. that the defect already existed when the product left the producer; and

c. that the defect was due to negligence on the part of the producer.

Although the judgment afforded slightly better protection to third parties, the resulting position was still not nearly satisfactory. No redress was available, for instance, in cases involving products of which the defective parts had not been manufactured by the manufacturer/defendant himself. The trend in favour of applying strict liability to manufacturers grew stronger and stronger in the United States, and

3. H. Duintjer Tebbens, *International Product Liability* (thesis Utrecht, 1979).
4. Peter Martin, 'A general view of aviation products liability', *Aviation Products and Grounding Liability Symposium* (Royal Aeronautical Society; London, November 30, 1972), pp. 1-14, at p. 5. The case referred to is *Maynard* v. *Stinson Aircraft Corp.*, State of Michigan, Circuit Court for Wayne County, October 22, 1937; [1940] USAvR 71; *Avi*, Vol. 1 p. 698; [1938] JAL 608.
5. *McPherson* v. *Buick Motor Co.*, 217 NY 382, 111 NE 1050 (1916).

finally, in 1963, it was adopted, for the first time in an American court, in the case of *Greenman* v. *Yuba Power Products*.[6] The court ruled that 'a manufacturer is strictly liable in tort when an article he places on the market, knowing that it is to be used without inspection for defects, proves to have a defect that causes injury to a human being'. Not long afterwards the principle was formally incorporated in the Restatement (Second) of Torts.[7]

The *Greenman* decision did not leave the position of the aircraft manufacturers unaffected, as may be seen from the 1975 decision in the case of *Berkebile* v. *Brantly Helicopter Corp*.[8] On this occasion, the Court decided 'that no current societal interest is served by permitting the manufacturer to place a defective article in the stream of commerce and then avoid responsibility for the damages caused by the defect'.

Under the new doctrine the claimant had to prove that the defect causing the injury existed at the time the product left the seller's hands. The seller was not held liable if the product had been made unsafe by subsequent changes. In practical terms, the law affecting aviation products had by now become a true reflection of the general product liability law.

Yet, it was still not possible to sue successfully on the grounds of defective design regardless of all other circumstances, as is apparent from the case of *Bruce* v. *Martin-Marietta and Ozark Airlines*.[9] An aircraft of the Martin 404 type, built in 1952 by Martin-Marietta, had been chartered to carry a Wichita State University team and supporters to a football match in Logan, Utah. On its way to Logan the aircraft crashed in the Colorado mountains. As a result of the terrific impact the passenger seats broke loose from their attachments and were thrown against the bulkhead of the plane, blocking the exit. Shortly after the crash, the aircraft caught fire, and the accident resulted in 32 out of the 40 passengers being killed. The manufacturers were sued for damages on three counts: 'negligence', 'implied warranty', and 'strict liability'. The Court stated that an aircraft manufacturer was not liable for damage arising from the crash on the grounds just mentioned for alleged defects in the adequacy of the seat fastenings and the lack of fire protection in an aircraft built as long ago as 1952. There was nothing to indicate that the ordinary consumer would expect a 1952 vintage aircraft to have the safety features of one manufactured in 1970. Moreover, the air carrier, who was the intermediate owner and seller of the aircraft, and who had

---

6. *Greenman* v. *Yuba Power Products Inc.* 59 Cal. 2d 57, 377 P2d 897, 27 Cal. Reptr. 697 (1963).
7. American Law Institute, Restatement (Second) of Torts of 1965, Section 402-A, 'Special Liability of Seller of Products for Physical Harm to User or Consumer'. See on this subject S.L. Frank, 'Strict Products Liability under California Law' *Air Law*, vol. V (1980), pp. 195-210, at 199 a.f.
8. *Berkebile* v. *Brantly Helicopter Corp.*, 281 A.2d 707 (Pa. Super 1971); 311 A 2d 140 (Pa. Super 1971). Affirmed 377 A2d 893 (Pa. 1975); *Avi*, Vol. 13, p. 17,878.
9. *Bruce* v. *Martin-Marietta Corp. and Ozark Airlines*, US Court of Appeals (10th Circuit), September 24, 1976; *Avi*, Vol. 14, pp. 17,472.

not made any significant changes in it during its ownership, was not held liable for damages arising from the crash. Thus, the manufacturers were exonerated because the 'design' was regarded as not being defective according to 1952 standards, the year adopted by the Court as the basis of its decision.

The case of *Kay* v. *Cessna Aircraft*[10] provides an instance of adequate instructions playing a crucial role. The pilot of a Cessna Skymaster Model 337 had, quite unforeseeably, misused the aircraft by failing to follow the operating instructions in his 'Owner's Manual'. Had he done so, he would have received a warning prior to take-off that one of the two engines was out of order. The Court admitted that the instructions could have been drawn up more clearly, but found that, had the pilot followed them, he could have averted the accident. The pilot's failure to comply with the instructions was ruled to be not reasonably foreseeable by Cessna, who were exonerated.

The manufacturer may, of course, be granted exoneration if he can demonstrate that the injuries suffered by the plaintiff were not caused by the defect. Contributory negligence on the part of the injured person will also constitute a valid ground for exoneration.

The doctrine of strict liability has been continually extended. The whole evolution one may observe in American case law derives basically from a fundamental rationale, *i.e.* the need to ensure that the costs resulting from defective products are borne by the manufacturers who put such products on the market, rather than by the injured persons who are powerless to protect themselves. An overriding motive behind this consideration has been the fact that the manufacturer is able to arrange for insurance: he can spread his cost among the general public, because such expenditure can easily be offset by a modest price increase.

An important court decision to be quoted in connection with the new trend, but also containing significant qualifications, is the case of *Kaiser Steel* v. *Westinghouse Electric*.[11] Although not relating directly to aviation, its considerations make very interesting reading because they were to affect indirectly airlines suing aircraft manufacturers. The Court of Appeal found that 'although the Californian rule of products liability... encompass(es) situations in which the principles of sales warranty serve their purpose "fitfully at best", the role of products liability does not subsume the entire area of a manufacturer's liability for a defective product'. The Court further noted that tort law is often resorted to as a basis for recovery when sales law, such as the Uniform Commercial Code, does not afford adequate protection to the consumer. Therefore, in an attempt to promote the cost shifting rationale, the Court established the following test to determine

---

10. *Kay* v. *Cessna Aircraft*, US Court of Appeals (9th Circuit), February 24, 1977; [1977] USAvR 375.
11. *Kaiser Steel Corp.* v. *Westinghouse Electric Corp.*, 55 Cal. App. 3d 737; 127 Cal. Reptr. 838 (1976).

whether or not to apply the doctrine of strict liability in a particular situation. It ruled that (strict) '[P]roduct liability does not apply as between parties who:
(1) deal in a commercial setting; (2) from a position of relatively equal economic strength; (3) bargain the specifications of the product; and (4) negotiate concerning the risk of loss'.

The significance of the *Kaiser* decision is evident, considering the fact that the purchase of an aircraft usually involves two companies of relatively equal economic strength. The impact of the strict liability rule was considerably weakened as a result of the *Kaiser* decision.

To illustrate the evolution that took place in practice let us examine a number of cases:

1. In 1964, the dependants of passengers killed in the crash of a Boeing aircraft near Rome sued the manufacturers on the ground of strict liability. Proceedings were based in this case on the law of the State of Washington, the seat of the Boeing Corporation. The issue of Boeing's 'negligence' with regard to the design of a part of the aircraft was, however, decided in accordance with Italian law, because the wrongful act had occurred in that country. It is interesting to note here, incidentally, that never before in Italy had passengers' dependants sued an aircraft manufacturer, and there was no provision in Italian law dealing with matters of this nature. In this instance recourse had to be taken to an article in the Italian Civil Code dealing with the liability of the owner/driver of a vehicle for damage resulting from defective construction. The court decided, in 1971, in favour of the dependants by granting them compensation.[12]

2. An even more dramatic illustration of the consequences of strict product liability is given in the crash of a Turkish Airlines DC-10 near Paris in 1974, where 346 people from more than 10 different countries lost their lives as a result of the catastrophe. Following take-off a door had burst open and the resulting explosive decompression had caused the floor to collapse. The facts made it clear that the manufacturers, McDonnell Douglas, were to blame. In addition, the modifications recommended by the McDonnell Corporation had not been carried out by Turkish Airlines on its plane. In the ensuing proceedings, the manufacturers were sued on the basis of strict liability, the result being that they had to pay great sums of money in compensation for the losses suffered by heirs and dependants.[13]

---

12. *Manos et al.* v. *TWA and Boeing*, US District Court, Northern District of Illinois, February 9, 1969; *Avi*, Vol. 10, p. 18,375; [1969] USAvR 209. US District Court, Northern District of Illinois, January 11, 1971; *Avi*, Vol. 11, p. 17,966.
13. See for this case *Re Paris Air Crash*, US District Court, Central District of California, August 1, 1975, *Avi*, Vol. 14, p. 17,207; US District Court, Central District of California, February 10, 1977, *Avi*, Vol. 14, p. 17,737. See also Judge Peirson M. Hall's 'Memorandum on the Choice of the Law re Damages re Paris Air Crash' (399 F. Supp. 732 (D.C.Cal. 1975)) and his extensive information about the statistics of the settlements in the 'Memorandum' in *Annals of Air and Space Law*, Vol. III, (1978) pp. 615-642.

An interesting point at issue between several authors needs to be mentioned here, namely the question as to what extent the aviation repair stations are liable. Do they incur strict liability, or are they liable only up to certain limits? The trend is for them to be held strictly liable, with no limits, for two reasons: repair stations are involved in the safety of the aircraft, and, moreover, the insurance option is always available to them.[14]

In connection with aircraft maintenance mention must be made of the Chicago DC-10 crash of May 25, 1979. The aircraft crashed shortly after take-off due to losing its port engine and pylon, resulting in 271 passengers and crew being killed. A relationship between the engine tearing loose and improper maintenance techniques was identified by the US National Transportation Safety Board. The accident created a stir due to the US Federal Aviation Administration issuing an 'Emergency Order of Suspension' which prohibited the operation of all US-registered DC-10 aircraft.[15]

Also worth noting is the fine incurred by British Midland Airways on July 25, 1996 for criminal negligence in maintenancing one of its aircraft. A mechanic had omitted to replace certain oil valves in the engines and to test their proper functioning. Only the pilot's consummate skill brought the aircraft to a successful emergency landing, saving the lives of all passengers and crew.

3. The Tenerife accident, which took place in 1977 and is the biggest disaster yet in aviation history, occurred as a result of a series of unfortunate circumstances happening almost simultaneously. In the first place there was a congestion of planes at Tenerife, waiting for departure after being diverted because Las Palmas airport had been closed shortly before due to a bomb-scare. Secondly, during the preparations for take-off visibility deteriorated considerably, so that the PanAm and KLM aircraft were no longer visible to each other and had to depend entirely on radio contact. Thirdly, radio contact was hampered by messages between the control tower and both aircraft being exchanged simultaneously and being unclear. The fog caused PanAm to miss the exit prescribed to leave the runway which was not marked by lights at that moment. Garbled radio messages caused the KLM pilot to assume that both route-clearance and take-off clearance had been given, so that he made what was in fact an unauthorised start, with fatal result.

In the ensuing proceedings liability was conceded by the airline companies; the insurance companies have played an essential part in settling the claims out of court by fixing the sums of money to be paid by the parties involved, including the manufacturer of the aircraft (Boeing) and the Spanish Government.[16]

14. See Tom Davis, 'Aviation Repair Stations and Strict Liability' [1974] JALC 413–424.
15. See Larry S. Dushkes, 'The Chicago Convention: FAA's Action Barring Foreign Carriers DC-10 Aircraft in US Airspace Held Improper', *Air Law*, vol. VII (1982), pp. 92–104; Ghislaine Richard, 'The DC-10 Chicago Crash and the Legality of SFAR 10', *Annals of Air and Space Law*, Vol. VI, (1981) pp. 195-218.
16. See G.C. Sterns, 'Air crash cases in the United States. A consideration of the Tenerife issues', *Nederlands Juristenblad*, vol. 52 (1977), pp. 1109-1119.

The Tenerife disaster is interesting from yet another angle, namely in connection with crashworthiness, as we shall see in the next section of this chapter.

In a number of cases occurring rather more recently the influence of the *Kaiser/Westinghouse* precedent is already apparent:

1. *SAS* v. *United Aircraft* (1979). SAS filed a suit against United Aircraft seeking relief for property damage resulting from the failure of jet aircraft engines manufactured by United Aircraft. The contracts for the purchase of the engines provided for certain limited warranties, express or implied, in addition to an exculpatory clause.[17] After considering the clause which had been incorporated in the contract of sale, the trial judge, following United Aircraft's petition for a summary judgment on all claims, granted SAS's claims based on warranty and tort, but denied the claims based on negligence. In confirming the trial judge's decision, the Court of Appeals ruled that because of the lack of public policy the doctrine of strict liability was not applicable in this case. The decision found strong support in the *Kaiser/Westinghouse* case.[18]

2. *Tokio Marine* v. *McDonnell Douglas* (1980). On November 28, 1972, a DC-8 aircraft manufactured by McDonnell Douglas and owned and operated by Japan Airlines (JAL), crashed during take-off at Moscow, killing 52 passengers and seriously injuring 10 others. Tokio Marine, the insurers for JAL, sought relief from McDonnell for the loss of the aircraft, basing its action on grounds of strict liability. The Court of Appeals decided, however, that the doctrine of strict liability in tort was not to be applied in California in a case where the sales contract was between two large corporations, negotiating from a position of relatively equal economic strength.[19]

3. Crashworthiness

Apart from the aforementioned grounds for supporting claims, there is also the additional factor of 'crashworthiness' to be taken into account in court cases involving product liability. Crashworthiness is a comparatively new element in the game, which has been defined in at least three different ways:

1. 'Crashworthiness is the characteristic of a vehicle which protects its occupants from death in a survivable crash and otherwise protects its occupants from injury or cumulative injury.'[20]

---

17. See on this subject H. DeSaussure, 'Product Liability and the Use of Disclaimer Clauses by Aircraft Manufacturers', *Die Produkthaftung in der Luft-und Raumfahrt/Product Liability in Air and Space Transportation*, Proceedings of an International Colloquium (Cologne, 1977), edited by K.H. Böckstiegel, pp. 157-164.

18. *SAS* v. *United Aircraft Corp.*, US Court of Appeals, (9th Circuit), July 24, 1979; [1979] USAvR 316; *Avi*, Vol. 15, p. 17,699.

19. *Tokio Marine and Fire Insurance Co. Ltd. et al.* v. *McDonnell Douglas Corp.* v. *Japan Air Lines Co. Ltd.* (Third-Party Defendant-Cross-Appellee), US Court of Appeals (2nd Circuit), March 6, 1980; [1980] USAvR 89; *Avi*, Vol. 15, p. 18,050.

20. D. Donnelly, 'Aircraft Crashworthiness – Plaintiff's Viewpoint' [1976] JALC 57–71

2. Crashworthiness is 'The ability of the aircraft structure to maintain living space for its occupants'[21]; and

3. A lack of crashworthiness is 'a design that aggravates the injuries caused by the original accident'[22].

The term 'lack of crashworthiness', for instance, was used in connection with a crash involving a United Airlines Boeing 727 near Salt Lake City in 1965, where the death of most of the passengers had been caused not by the impact itself, but by toxic gases and disabling smoke forming as a result of the cabin interior catching fire.[23] In a second case, the Tenerife accident of 1977 referred to earlier, it also played a role. The Boeing Corporation, being the manufacturer of the older PanAm aircraft, paid 10 per cent. of the compensation on account of insufficient crashworthiness and for not taking adequate measures to prevent damage by fire.

To complete the picture it is appropriate to summarise the various types of damage usually claimed from manufacturers. They have been aptly categorised by Coie as follows.

'1.   personal injuries resulting from an accident;
2.   damage to property other than the aircraft arising from an accident;
3.   damage to the aircraft arising from an accident or incident;
4.   failure of the aircraft to meet the commercial expectations of the airline; and
5.   the airline's damages for loss of use of the aircraft while it is being repaired or replaced'.[24]

With changing attitudes towards product liability strongly affecting the position of aircraft manufacturers and airline companies alike, the position of the passengers did not remain unaffected either. Indeed, one might go as far as saying that it improved considerably. In the past, these persons could only sue the carrier, and their claims had to be based on one of the international Conventions on air law, which often offered the disadvantage of imposing strict limitations of the extent of the liability for compensation. For a passenger to sue the manufacturer was virtually impossible because the burden of proof was too difficult.

The *Greenman* doctrine changed all this, and simultaneously the general attitude of American courts in the last few years became more favourable towards an extension of the rights of the ordinary consumer, including the airline passengers. Unlike the previous situation,

---

21.   *Glossary of Aeronautical Terms*, cited by G.I. Whitehead Jr., 'Some comments on aircraft crashworthiness' [1976] JALC 73–83, at 75.

22.   S.J. Levy, 'The Rights of the Passengers – A View from the United States', *Die Produkthaftung* (note 17, *supra*), pp. 77–89, at p. 85.

23.   Levy (note 22, *supra*), at p. 85.

24.   I.P. Coie, 'The present State of the Law in the United States from the Standpoint of Industry', *Die Produkthaftung* (note 17, *supra*), pp. 109–123, at p. 113.

in which the passenger had to prove negligence on the part of the manufacturer, he can now confine himself to claiming that the product was defective at the time it left the manufacturer's hands and that the defect was the direct cause of the damage. There is no longer a need for him to prove fault. The manufacturer is liable even if he has taken all necessary precautions. The fact that products are so sophisticated nowadays that it is extremely hard for a passenger to prove his case against the manufacturer has undoubtedly played an important role in the recent changes. There is a tendency nowadays away from negligence as the main criterion for liability, and in favour of shifting the burden of compensation onto the shoulders of those best able to pay and to insure themselves, *i.e.* the persons or companies with 'deep pockets'.

Such tendencies would converge ultimately in a state liability. Under international law no person or corporation may, according to Article 31 of the Chicago Convention, operate an aircraft without a certificate of airworthiness issued or rendered valid by the state, and regular inspections by governmental authorities are a prerequisite. Consequently, when there is an accident claimants will try to sue and obtain compensation from the state, being the 'deepest pocket' of all, and it is to be expected that liability will be attached more and more to the state.

4. Punitive damages

While discussing liability and compensation attention should be given to the so-called 'punitive damages'.[25] What are punitive damages? Punitive damages are considered to be related to misconduct that is intentional, malicious, or consists of action or inaction that is so grossly wilful, or indicates such a conscious and aggravated disregard of others that a jury could conclude that the conduct takes on a criminal character, regardless of whether it is punishable as an offence.[26] In the USA, they are occasionally awarded in civil cases by juries upon request by claimants when injury has been claimed and proved. They are subsequently added to the compensation to be paid. In this manner, manufacturers have had to pay enormous sums of money during the past few years. It must be pointed out in this context that in nearly all states of the USA the standard of strict liability is being applied to product liability. French law has also adopted strict liability in such cases, while English, German, Dutch and Canadian law are not far behind. Manufacturers may, of course, resort to insurance: to my knowledge, no insurance policy excludes coverage for punitive damages.

---

25. See Ian Awford, 'Punitive Damages in aviation products liability cases', *Air Law*, vol. X (1985), pp. 3-9.
26. D.M. Haskell, 'The Aircraft Manufacturer's Liability for Design and Punitive Damages – The Insurance Policy and the Public Policy' [1974] JALC 595–635, at 610.

Haskell[27] mentions three reasons for their origin, furnished by case law. They may be summarised as follows:

1. the refusal of early (Anglo-Saxon) courts to grant new trials when excessive compensation had been awarded in cases involving some form of malice, oppression or fraud;

2. the courts' failure to recognise certain injuries (*e.g.* mental anguish) as a proper measurement of damages;

3. punitive damages became the vehicle to reimburse the plaintiff for damages not otherwise legally compensable (*e.g.* litigation expenses).

It should be expressly recorded here that punitive damages are not awarded in connection with product liability only: they are equally applicable in relation to other liability cases. This practice is, however, confined to the United States.[28]

5. Codification of product liability

In sharp contrast with the rulings of the American law courts, we note the opinions of experts who argue that product liability should really be based on standards laid down in laws or regulations rather than leaving it to be decided case by case, which results in a multitude of varying standards.[29]

Regulations of product liability on a national level have been devised in a number of countries, like the Model Uniform Product Liability Act in the United States.[30] Not being directly relevant to our subject they will not be considered here further. As for international rules, we must point out at once that no universal treaty or convention has been adopted by the international community of nations as yet. There are, however, agreements of a slightly more restricted range, such as the Strasbourg Convention of 1977, sponsored by the Council of Europe, which covers product liability in case of personal injury or death.[31] In addition, there is the Hague Convention of 1973 on the Law Applicable to Products Liability, which traces its origins back to the Hague Conference on Private International Law.[32] The

---

27. Haskell (note 26, *supra*), at p. 609.
28. See however, *In Re Disaster at Lockerbie, Scotland,* US Court of Appeals (2nd Circ.), March 22, 1991; *Avi* vol. 23, p. 17, 714; *Air and Space Law,* vol. XVII (1992), pp. 317-318. In this case it was ruled that because the purposes for which the Warsaw Convention was created were not consistent with an award of punitive damages, such damages were not recoverable in actions governed by the Convention, even assuming that an air carrier committed wilful misconduct.
29. Cf. Duintjer Tebbens (note 3, *supra*), at p. 41 *et seq.*
30. See about this Act R.R. Craft Jr., 'La responsabilité des fabricants en droit Américain', [1981] RFDA 21–37 and also the various contributions in [1981] JALC 349–479 ('Special project – The Model Uniform Product Liability Act').
31. European Convention on Products Liability in Regard to Personal Injury and Death, Strasbourg, January 27, 1977. See about this Convention Duintjer Tebbens (note 3, *supra*), pp. 143 *et seq.*
32. The Hague Convention on the Law Applicable to Products Liability, The Hague, October 2, 1973. See Duintjer Tebbens (note 3, *supra*), pp. 333 *et seq.*

Hague Convention is aimed at unifying rules of reference and rules of conflict, *i.e.* at creating a body of rules determining which law shall be applicable to the substance of a given relationship. The Convention does not apply, however, to cases where the injured person has acquired the product directly from the liable party. The motive behind this important exception was that the Convention was not supposed to clash with another Convention, namely the Hague Convention on the Law Applicable to International Sales of Goods.[33]

Finally, the European Economic Community has, for its part, also published some regulations in a 'Proposal for a Council Directive relating to the Approximation of the Laws, Regulations and Administrative Provisions of the Member States concerning Liability for Defective Products'. An Amendment to this proposal was adopted on October 26, 1979, widening the definition of 'damage' to include damage for pain and suffering and other non-material damage. Moreover, indemnity ceilings for total liability were made to include damages related to death and personal injury.[34]

33. Convention on the Law Applicable to International Sales of Goods, The Hague, June 15, 1955. See also the Final Act of the 13th Session of the Hague Conference on Private International Law, *Netherlands International Law Review* (1976), Vol. XXIII p. 404.
34. See for this proposal O.J. 1976 C.241/9 and *Bulletin of the EEC* Supp. 11/76. See for the 1979 amendment O.J. 1979 C.271/3. See for the text of the final Directive: O.J. No. L210 of October 7, 1985. See on this Directive J.-M. Fobe, *Aviation Products Liability and Insurance in the EU*, 1994. See also C. Mannin, 'The effects in aviation of the EEC Directive on product liability', *Air Law*, vol. XI (1986), pp. 248-252.

CHAPTER V

Automation and Air Law

1. Introductory note

Automation ranks high among the major industrial innovations of this century. Its rise, during the period immediately preceding World War II, followed the spectacular mechanisation explosion that had characterised the latter half of the 19th century and subsequent decades. As technology forged ahead, with advanced electronics culminating in electronic computers, the term 'automation' acquired several different meanings, varying from 'simple mechanical device' to 'complicated electronic system'. To avoid confusion it is employed here in a broader sense, namely to indicate an integrated system whereby many or all production operations are performed and/or controlled by machinery or electronical devices.

There are few technological inventions, if any, that can lay claim to a greater impact on modern society than automation. Virtually all sections of society are affected by it, and certainly the world of aviation has not remained immune from its inexorable advance. Indeed, it would be no exaggeration to say that, without it, aviation could not play its present key role in world affairs. No matter whether we are discussing aircraft design, construction, the pilot's performance, weather reports, seat reservations or despatching cargo by air, automation has become the standard method enabling these operations to be carried out not only with accuracy but also with a minimal waste of effort and time. And there is every likelihood of this evolution being far from reaching its full potential.

To many observers of the scene it might appear as if the introduction of integrated systems and other high-tech devices could not have failed to produce an equally revolutionary effect in the legal sphere. There is, for a start, the historical perspective of the matter: large-scale automation was not introduced in aviation until years after the conclusion in 1929 of the Warsaw Convention. As I have indicated in an earlier chapter its rules, taken in conjunction with those of a number of subsequent Conventions and Protocols, form the so-called 'Warsaw System', which is to this day the basic structure defining in some detail an air carrier's duties and liabilities. It is worth examining whether this structure has been affected by the startling new techniques of the last fifty-odd years and, if so, to what extent. The question arises, for instance, whether the links between the acts of an air carrier's personnel and their ultimate effect may perhaps have become so remote or obscured as to raise doubt about the liability aspects involved. Another point at issue is the vexed problem surrounding electronically transmitted data in cases where specific documents are mandatory. These and other automation-related matters will be reviewed in the present chapter.

Faced with an environment of cut-throat competition and vast volumes of traffic no modern airline can hold out much hope of economic survival without maximum efficiency in all its operations. This cannot be achieved without the integrated approach made possible by automation, whose functioning is most evident in the following operations:

1. aircraft handling (the pilot's responsibilities);
2. air traffic control;
3. aircraft design, construction and maintenance;
4. passenger handling; and
5. cargo handling.

2. Aircraft handling

The Warsaw Convention makes it clear that an air carrier's liability may be involved as a consequence of the action (or inaction) of his aircraft's pilot. It is beyond all question that with increasing traffic density and a similar growth ratio in capacity and speed of present-day aircraft the captain's duties have become so much more involved that most flights can only be performed adequately with the aid of automation. This may take various forms such as an automatic pilot, a computer for monitoring and correcting an aircraft's course, apparatus for avoiding collisions, a system for determining the aircraft's exact position, telecommunication systems including an automatic hijack alarm, automated landing instruments for adverse weather conditions, etc.

Thanks to modern navigational assistance provided by satellites, aircraft can determine their position largely independently and yet with accuracy. Nearly all important airports worldwide are already equipped with the 'Instrument Landing System', using radio signals and enabling safe landings. An improved version is the so-called 'Enhanced Vision System', which enables aircraft to land round the clock without any ground control assistance. Needless to stress the importance of these navigational aids in regions where the infrastructure is not yet sufficiently developed.[1]

There can be little doubt that all these devices have gone a long way towards reducing the burden of a captain's responsibilities. A long way, but not entirely, and the temptation of regarding all the high-tech hardware at his disposal as a panacea for all his actions and problems must be resisted. We must not, for instance, minimize the fact that the sheer volume and variety of instruments may well enhance the risk of errors being committed or extremely hazardous situations

---

1. See on the subject of air navigation satellite systems and the role of ICAO, I.H.Ph. Diederiks-Verschoor, *An Introduction to Space Law* (1993), notably chapter VII.

arising: the memory of the tragedy involving Korean Airlines flight KE007 in 1983, which inadvertently strayed into Soviet airspace probably due to faulty computer programming is still with us!![2]

Another implication not to be disregarded is that the continuous availability of so much informative data may lead to an inadequate performance on the part of the pilot. Such considerations clearly demonstrate that it would be wrong to completely rule out the human factor: the captain's personal assessment and handling of the situation, his timely intervention remain paramount for a proper discharging of his duties and, consequently, the deciding element when it comes to determining his responsibility. It may therefore be safely concluded that as far as the pilot's legal position is concerned, the new technology has brought no changes.

3. Air traffic control

For air traffic control to reach the highest degree of safety an orderly movement of flights under the guidance of a control tower is an absolute prerequisite. The control officers' duties may be compared with those of a ship's pilot: they issue instructions to all aircraft within range of their control area.

The Chicago Convention, in its Annex 2 entitled 'Rules of the Air' specifies that an aircraft commander must follow the instructions of the control tower. But it also states that the ultimate responsibility for a flight rests with that same commander. This is quite obviously a legal position which in certain circumstances may cause considerable uncertainty and confusion as to where to lay the blame in the event of an accident. Current practice has found a way out of this problem by interpreting the relevant provisions to mean that the commander is bound to follow the tower's instructions except in an emergency.

While we are on the subject it is worth noting that, apart from the Chicago Convention, no other internationally agreed rules exist in relation to this matter, which is so eminently suitable for that purpose. Indeed for any further rules or regulations one has to look in the domestic legislation of various nations.

Domestic law implies in most cases that control tower personnel enjoy the status of civil servants, a status which will determine their position in terms of rights, duties, working conditions, calls for strike actions, etc. But, quite apart from this important point, control tower officers also carry an extremely heavy burden of responsibility in their daily duties, depending in their operations almost entirely on advanced electronic equipment, arguably even more so than a pilot: they cannot observe their entire control area nor the movement of all aircraft with their own eyes!! And yet, situations may arise in which, at least under the prevailing legal rules, a control officer may be held responsible

---

2. See Bin Cheng, 'The destruction of KAL flight KE007, and Article 3 *bis* of the Chicago Convention', in *Air Worthy*, pp. 47-74.

rather than the pilot.[3] Furthermore that decision would stand quite irrespective of the role their equipment may or may not have played. Again, modern technology does not seem to have altered the legal position essentially.

4. Aircraft design, construction and maintenance

For those comparing the methods of aircraft construction in the beginning of this century with modern techniques the difference is simply staggering. The earliest planes were laboriously put together from wooden components and linen fabric, rather in cottage-industry style. Modern construction methods rely to an extremely high degree on automation. Computer-Aided-Design (the CAD technique) is vital for aircraft designing. The manufacturing of parts is done by robots capable of transforming pieces of metal into specific components. In maintenance operations computer-aided apparatus is used for quality control and final checks. Even the lifespan and recommended replacement dates for components are calculated with the aid of computers.

Have all these changes led to similar upheavals in the legal position? Here we are thinking, of course, especially of the product liability side of the matter.

The answer to our question must be in the negative. It is common knowledge that product liability is the determining factor in the relationship between the manufacturer of an aircraft and its subsequent owner. Mutual obligations and liabilities are governed by warranty rules and guarantees; in some cases manufacturers may even be held liable to third parties such as passengers. There is a continuing shift in legal opinion in favour of absolute liability, and this has already brought with it a substantially increased risk for the manufacturer: it has become vital for him to make sure that his product leaves the factory in perfect condition in terms of safety and reliability. But the question of whether these essential prerequisites have been achieved by way of automation or otherwise makes no difference to him, from a purely legal point of view: it leaves his liability at law completely unaffected.

5. Passenger handling

The Warsaw Convention of 1929 has given us a large number of rules defining the legal status of the passenger in civil aviation, but in the present context the rules relating to the passenger ticket are of special interest. Article 3 makes it clear that the absence of a ticket, the non-issuing by the carrier himself, or faulty issuing all have direct implications for the carrier's liability.

---

3. Cf. *infra*, Chapter VI, paragraph 2.

Documentation and data required for proper ticketing have become more and more complicated over the years, certainly when compared with the days of the stage coach or early railways. Airline ticketing was at first subjected to rather stringent rules contained in the Warsaw Convention, but as time went by and the increasing popularity of air travel demanded simplification the number of requirements was reduced in the Protocol of The Hague of 1955.

One of the most important changes introduced by the Protocol was the abolition of the rule making it mandatory for the ticket to be issued by the carrier himself (Article 3). Further simplification is fore-shadowed in the Guatemala Protocol of 1971, but this Protocol has, unfortunately, not yet entered into force. In Article 3 it not only introduces collective tickets, but also the possibility of a 'substitute' document. It is obvious that this would clear the way for ticket-issuing by automatic slotmachines.[4]

Computer-aided processes and techniques have greatly benefited airline booking offices and travel agents in obtaining the wide range of information they need, but here again progress has not been altogether painless. For one thing, complications may still occur due to programming errors or faulty equipment. For another there is also a far more serious implication, *i.e.* the danger of biased booking systems. It is worth adding a little more detail concerning this most undesirable side-effect of automation.

It is no longer an exception for a travel agent or a bank to have an electronic booking system provided and funded by an airline. This happens today on rather a large scale, and it may well result in the passengers being given biased information when enquiring about a particular route they wish to travel. It is obviously possible to manipulate a computer in such a manner that not all the relevant information is made available to a customer enquiring about flight departures of a specified route, day and time: a rival company's flight might have been left out purposely, for fear of competition or otherwise. What this implies is the passenger being restricted in his choice and getting preselected information, which may not be in his best interests.[5]

But it is not only when booking his flight that the passenger gets confronted with automated processes: he is subjected to its omnipresent influence the minute he starts out on his journey. Automation determines his fate at the check-in counter and in the registration of

---

4. See on this subject P. Martin, '"Phone in, Turn up, Take off", a Look at the Legal Implications of Self-service Ticketing', *Air and Space Law*, vol. XX (1995), pp. 189-195.

5. See on this subject Richard J. Fahy, Jr., 'Regulation of computerized reservation systems in the United States and Europe', *Air Law*, vol. XI (1986), pp. 232-241; G.O. Eser, 'Impact of automation on the airline business', *Annals of Air and Space Law*, vol. XI (1986), pp. 3-16; F.A. van Bakelen, 'Aviation wizards – terminal hazards', *Air Law*, vol. XIII (1988), pp. 77-91; and P.N. Ehlers, *Computerized reservation systems in the air transport industry. How to optimize the passenger's benefits*, 1988. See also R.I.R. Abeyratne, *Legal and Regulatory Issues of Computer Reservation Systems and Code Sharing Agreements in Air Transport*, 1995 (Forum for Air and Space Law, vol. 3)

his luggage. This happens again, soon afterwards, at the passport control officer's desk, with more and more countries introducing 'machine-readable' passports. Automation can also be a valuable asset in tracing individual passengers and their movements, although this may have undesirable effects in that it may constitute an infringement upon their privacy. Such awkward side-effects, however, are largely offset by the advantage of suspected persons or terrorists becoming much more easily traceable.

Whatever the blessings or dangers of automation our conclusion must be that in the light of the legal position as at present, automated processes in airline passenger handling cannot be said to affect the carrier's liability in any way. However, a different situation may occur where national and/or regional (EEC!) rules on competition may be infringed upon by biased reservation systems.[6] This could lead to criminal liability of the carrier, a subject lying beyond the scope of this book.

6. Cargo handling

The Warsaw Convention which determines the liability of the air carrier also includes a set of rules concerning the air waybill: Articles 5 to 16 inclusive deal with this document. Article 8 details the requirements the air waybill has to meet. Failure to observe them has implications for the carrier culminating in the form of unlimited liability. Article 6 states that the air waybill has to be made out in three copies: one for the sender, one for the receiver, one for the carrier.

The Hague Protocol of 1955 has introduced a number of changes relating in particular to the requirements of Article 8. Further simplifications were not introduced until about 20 years later, when the Fourth Protocol of Montreal (which has not yet entered into force) brought the carrier's liability for cargo in line with his liability *vis-à-vis* the passengers.

For our present purpose the key provision is to be found in Article 3 of the Montreal Protocol just mentioned: it opens the way to using any other 'means' suitable for the proper handling of air cargo. It would appear that in doing so all the previous barriers on the road to automation have been removed. But there is one important snag: the crucial point to be decided from a legal point of view, is whether automated data exchange offers parties the same level of accuracy and

---

6. See for an example of EEC action, e.g. *Ehlers* (note 3, *supra*) at p. 49. See for EEC legislation on reservation systems: Council Regulation 2299/89 of July 24, 1989 (O.J. No. L220) and Commission Regulation 83/91 of December 5, 1990 (O.J. No. L10). The passenger's position is heavily influenced by the fairness of the competition. Many organisations, not only governmental but also from the industry, like *e.g.* IATA, are studying whether to issue special rules relating to computerized reservation systems, or have done so already. For instance the US CAB did so in 1984 (see for the text of these rules *Ehlers*, at pp. 83-88).

reliability as the documents hitherto in use. For it is a fact that most regulations currently in force are based on the use of 'documents'. Replacing such documents with electronically transmitted data might possibly have repercussions on the proper functioning of such regulations, and end up with the users finding themselves in a legal quandary.

For a proper assessment of this problem we must, for a start, make mention of a number of practical differences in the handling of cargo as distinct from passengers. It is not usually of vital importance for a firm wishing to airfreight a certain cargo to be informed about the full range of possibilities on offer: more often than not it will be a regular customer 'who knows it all'. Also, for air cargo to make a return journey will be most unusual, so information about return tariffs will hardly ever be required, unlike for passenger traffic where such information is essential for bookings. Thirdly, there are fewer special cargo flights as there are not that many airlines flying the same cargo routes. What is vital, however, for the cargo customer, is reducing 'red tape' to the minimum. That saves time and money!! Unfortunately, the days when an air cargo taking an hour's flying time ended up with a couple of days delay in customs formalities and handling procedures are still not entirely a thing of the past!!

There is another aspect that needs to be taken into account: passenger traffic basically involves only two parties, the passenger himself and the carrier (in some cases also the travel agent). Airfreighting cargo, however, always involves at least three parties, the sender, the carrier and the consignee. But for an airfreighting operation to be completed three more participants must be added to this number, namely the forwarding agent, the consolidator/bulkbreak agent and, last but not least, the customs authorities. They all have their specific role to play before and/or after the actual flight, and they all need to be well informed about every detail relevant to the cargo, information which is usually required in several copies. The normal procedure is for the sender to approach an agent, who makes a suitable offer for the consignment and undertakes to organize it accordingly once his offer is accepted. The formalities are then performed on the basis of the information supplied by the sender, whereupon the cargo is transferred into the care of the handling agent. The latter collects several other consignments until he has sufficient numbers to form a unit suitable for shipment on board a cargoflight.

For several years the various parties involved have been pondering over the problems connected with air cargo data transmission, and this has already brought into being a number of electronic air cargo handling systems on a nationwide scale. In the Netherlands, for instance, the CARGONAUT system has been operational for some time. Originally this was an initiative taken by the forwarding agents, but it has since been brought under the supervision of Schiphol Airport Ltd. The system is based on electronic exchange of data supplied by *all* the parties concerned, in such a way that information put in by one partner in the game is automatically available to all others who need it at any time. Everybody, at any moment in time, has therefore access to all the information he needs about a consignment or item of cargo. A link-up with a similar data-exchange system run by the Netherlands Customs is being planned.

There is every reason for welcoming this form of automation and the great promise it holds for the future. It is particularly important in view of the fact that most consignments nowadays consist mainly of general cargo which are grouped by the so-called consolidator/ bulkbreak agents before reaching the carrier.

The advantages of the modern data exchange techniques may be summed up as follows:

1. instantaneous transmission and access to all relevant information; avoiding waste of time;
2. avoiding misunderstandings and different interpretations between parties as long as standard procedures and formats are followed;
3. diminishing the risk of incomplete or inadequate information as a result of writing or keyboarding errors;
4. electronic recording and storage of information in the consignee's data system helps avoid repeats; and
5. smoother flow of information as peaks unavoidable under the paper document system no longer occur.

From all this it would appear that in the cargo handling business, like in the other sectors discussed earlier, automation had brought immense benefits but has nevertheless little effect, if any, on the carrier's liability. All that has happened is that he obtains, earlier than previously, a complete picture of every consignment on offer for airfreighting supplied by the sender or his agent. As indicated earlier there is, however, a possibility of problems arising due to the present regulations still relying on 'documents'. Especially when legal proof is required an uncertain situation may result.

7. Concluding note

If the emergence of automation in civil aviation does not appear to have had much impact as far as the legal position of the carrier is concerned, this does not take away from the fact that there are a number of important related issues requiring closer attention in the near future. The first of these is the problem of the jurisdiction with regard to border-crossing data exchange. The second is the time-lag between the moment of transmission and that of the actual receipt. Thirdly, who is to be held liable for faults occurring during the exchange? Will it be possible to exclude liability in such cases?

Apart from all these emerging issues we must also bear in mind the ever growing dependence on high-tech equipment supplied by third parties. It is imperative that all such apparatus should be absolutely sound and above all serviceable. Failing that, suppliers may have to face serious claims for damages. Perhaps the time has come for a change in the sense that the established 'fault' criterion for liability should be replaced by a system where the cardinal question will not be 'Who is liable?' but 'Who will pay?'. In view of the magnitude of the interests at stake it is suggested that action should be undertaken in order to arrive at an international agreement covering this important matter.

CHAPTER VI

Surface Damage and Collisions

1. Damage caused to third parties on the surface

1.1. HISTORICAL PERSPECTIVE

The problems involved in cases of damage caused to third parties on the surface, as distinct from the kind of damage covered by the Warsaw Convention, were recognised as early as 1927. Several studies on the subject were undertaken, culminating eventually in the Rome Convention of 1933 and its Brussels Insurance Protocol of 1938.[1] Neither effort can be regarded as particularly successful; the rules of the Rome Convention were soon found to be lagging behind the rapid developments in aviation, and the Convention drew only a very limited number of ratifications.[2] After the Second World War the matter was once again given attention, and at the instigation of the ICAO Legal Committee a sub-committee was established in 1947[3] to revise the Rome Convention and to determine which objections had in fact prevented states from ratifying.

In June 1948[4] the sub-committee submitted a report on four topics which in its opinion were interconnected. Aside from the subjects of liability and insurance inherent to the Convention and the attached Protocol, the sub-committee also reported on air collisions and on the global limitation of the liability of the operator.

The Legal Committee of ICAO thereupon decided to review the items separately and to see if they could be combined into a single convention. Moreover, questionnaires[5] were sent to all ICAO members and under the direction of Professor S. Iuul, who was elected as rapporteur by ICAO, a new text was drafted to replace the 1933 Convention.

---

1. International Convention for the Unification of Certain Rules Relating to Damage Caused by Aircraft to Third Parties on the Surface, Rome, May 29, 1933; hereinafter cited as the 1933 Rome Convention. Additional Protocol to the International Convention for the Unification of Certain Rules Relating to Damage Caused by Aircraft to Third Parties on the Surface, Brussels, September 29, 1938; hereinafter cited as the Brussels Insurance Protocol.
2. Five states signed the Convention; only two the Protocol (see Shawcross and Beaumont, *Air Law* (1981), Vol. 2, pp. A-2 and A-3, respectively).
3. Minutes and Documents of the First Session of the ICAO Legal Committee (Brussels 1947), ICAO Doc. 4635 – LC/71, pp. 154 and 163.
4. Minutes and Documents of the Second Session of the ICAO Legal Committee (Geneva, May 1948), ICAO Doc. 6014 – LC/111, pp. 127–135.
5. Minutes and Documents of the Fourth Session of the ICAO Legal Committee (Montreal, June 1949), ICAO Doc. 6027 – LC/124, pp. 173–229.

A new Convention, based upon Iuul's draft, was devised[6] and finally approved at the Conference on Private International Law held in Rome in September and October 1952. It was opened for signature in October 1952. The new Convention[7] also contained rules originating from the Brussels Insurance Protocol of 1938 concerning the obligation to arrange for insurance against possible injury to third party victims. The old Rome Convention and its Brussels Protocol were superseded by the new Convention.

The Convention of 1952 is still in force, but it did not attract many ratifications either. Only 38 out of the over 180 ICAO members did in fact ratify, and that number did not even include major powers like the United States, the United Kingdom, the German Federal Republic or Canada.[8] The reasons for this rather spectacular lack of interest may be described as follows:

1. the limits for compensation mentioned in the Convention were considered too low;
2. national legislation provided adequate safeguards for the interests of third parties on the surface: it was felt that there was no need for international rules on the subject;
3. the Convention did not deal with problems such as noise, sonic boom or nuclear damage;
4. there were objections against creating only one forum.[9]

The consequences of non-ratification have been dramatically highlighted by an Israelian cargo plane crashing in the Bijlmermeer suburb of Amsterdam on October 4, 1992. Neither the Netherlands nor Israel are parties to the Convention, so Netherlands law was applicable. But Netherlands law has no rules and regulations governing liability for damage caused by air traffic, so general rules regarding negligence had to be invoked. Here, strict liability is the standard rule, but an exception has been made for aircraft: specific regulation of the matter is envisaged in the forthcoming new Netherlands Transportion Act. The final outcome of all this is that someone who suffers damage caused

6. Minutes and Documents of the Fifth Session of the ICAO Legal Committee (Taormina-Rome, January 1950), ICAO Doc. 6029 – LC/126, pp. 329-335.
7. Convention on Damage Caused by Foreign Aircraft to Third Parties on the Surface, Rome, October 7, 1952; hereinafter cited as the 1952 Rome Convention.
8. Canada did ratify the Convention, but denounced it in 1976. This was done mainly because of objections against the limits being too low. See for present parties to this Convention Shawcross and Beaumont, *Air Law* (1981), Vol. 2, pp. A-32 to A-33.
9. See on this subject G. Rinck, 'Schäden Dritter im Internationalen Luftverkehr: über den bisherigen Misserfolg des Römer Haftpflichtabkommens' [1962] ZLW 85–104; by the same author, 'Damage Caused by Foreign Aircraft to Third Parties' [1961/1962] JALC 405–417.

by a remote-controlled model aircraft has the benefit of strict liability of the culprit, whereas victims of a fullscale Boeing 747 crash like the one in the Bijmermeer have to prove negligence.[10]

The Convention came into force on February 4, 1958, but as early as 1964 suggestions were put forward for revision.[11] One of these led to a mandate for a sub-committee of the ICAO Legal Committee to study the matter; the sub-committee started its work in 1965.

Due to the ICAO concentrating on the revision of the Warsaw system and the drafting of two further Conventions on penal aspects of aviation (The Hague Convention and the Montreal Convention), not much progress was made during the late 1960s and the early 1970s. Following the sub-committee's report[12] to the twenty-first Session of the Legal Committee (Montreal, 1974) a new sub-committee was set up to prepare a text, or alternative texts, for the amendment of the Rome Convention of 1952, and a text, or alternative texts, for an instrument on the liability for damage caused by noise and sonic boom, taking into account the discussions in the ICAO Legal Committee, specific proposals made by IATA, decisions of the Sonic Boom Committee of the ICAO and the information that might come in from the International Atomic Energy Agency (IAEA) with regard to nuclear damage. In addition, the question of jurisdiction was to be studied.[13]

At its meeting in 1976 the Legal Committee gave its approval to many minor amendments, but no decision was taken on the matter of the liability limits.[14] In 1978 a Diplomatic Conference was convened by the Council of ICAO, where 58 states were represented, and where IATA, IFALPA and the International Law Association (ILA) also attended as observers.[15] A Protocol was adopted at Montreal aiming at amending the Rome Convention of 1952.[16] No solution, however, could be agreed upon concerning issues such as noise and sonic boom, and it was decided at the Conference that without a considerable amount

10. See C. Stolker, 'Compensation of Damage to Parties on the Ground as a Result of Aviation Accidents', in proceedings (forthcoming) of the International Symposium on the Use of the Air and Outer Space at the Service of World Peace and Prosperity (Beijing, August 21-23, 1995). See also P. Mendes de Leon and S.A. Mirmina, 'The International and American Law Implications of the Bijlmer Air Disaster', *Leiden Journal of International Law*, vol. 6 (1993), pp. 111-122.
11. G.F. Fitzgerald, 'The Protocol to Amend the Convention on Damage Caused by Foreign Aircraft to Third Parties on the Surface (Rome, 1952) signed at Montreal, September 23, 1978', *Annals of Air and Space Law*, Vol. IV (1979), pp. 29–73, at p. 32.
12. See the Report of the Sub-committee in the Documents of the 21st Session of the ICAO Legal Committee (Montreal, 1974), ICAO Doc. 9131 – LC/173–2, pp. 262-297.
13. ICAO Doc. 9131 – LC/173–2, at p. 59.
14. Minutes and Documents of the 22nd Session of the ICAO Legal Committee (Montreal, 1976). ICAO Doc. 9222 – LC/177–1 and 177–2.
15. Minutes and Documents of the International Conference on Air Law, Montreal, September 1978; ICAO Doc. 9357 – LC/183. See about this Conference Fitzgerald (note 11, *supra*) and M. Milde, 'Tenth International Conference on Air Law', *Air Law*, vol. IV (1979), pp. 41-44.
16. Protocol to Amend the Convention on Damage Caused by Foreign Aircraft to Third Parties on the Surface, Montreal, September 23, 1978; hereinafter cited as the 1978 Montreal Protocol.

of additional information it would be premature to undertake the drafting of a new separate instrument.[17] As a result they were, rather reluctantly, left to domestic legislation, but with a recommendation that a separate instrument should, if possible, be created to deal with them.

As regards nuclear damage, Article XIV of the Protocol states explicitly that 'This Convention shall not apply to nuclear damage'. The reason for inserting this provision was that several international instruments on nuclear liability placed the liability squarely on the shoulders of the operator of the nuclear installation.[18] This made it unnecessary to give further rules on the subject in the Rome Convention.

The Montreal Protocol was opened for signature in September 1978. Reading through the preparatory documents one soon realises that amending Article 11 of the Rome Convention, which specifies the limits of the operator's liability, had been the most difficult point to settle. This point will be dealt with at greater length below. Suffice it, for the moment, to mention in this context Milde's opinion, which I fully agree with:

> 'Its is to be hoped that the adoption of the Montreal Protocol of 1978 will lead to a somewhat wider acceptance of the Rome Convention of 1952. However, it is highly unlikely that the Convention as amended will ever attain a wide or nearly universal acceptance because the principle of limitation of liability with respect to third parties on the surface does not appear acceptable in the legislation of many States. In general, since the first Rome Convention of 1933 States have shown considerable reluctance to become parties to a Convention on the unification of law in a field which, fortunately, deals with extremely rare occurrences and where there are no unsurmountable problems of conflicts of law or conflicts of jurisdiction'.[19]

1.2. THE SCOPE OF THE 1952 ROME CONVENTION AND THE 1978 MONTREAL PROTOCOL

The Convention, according to its Article 23, is applicable to damage caused to third parties on the territory of a contracting state by an aircraft registered in another contracting state. It follows that when damage has been caused by aircraft registered in the state where the damage occurred, the national law will apply. The Convention gives no definition of the word 'damage'.

The Montreal Protocol of 1978, which has yet to enter into force, has widened the Convention's scope by providing that it will also apply when damage is caused by an aircraft, whatever its registration may be, whose operator has his principal place of business or, if he

---

17. ICAO Doc. 9357 – LC/183 (note 15, *supra*), at pp. 197 *et seq.*; Fitzgerald (note 11, *supra*), at pp. 61-64 and at p. 72.
18. Milde (note 15, *supra*), at p. 44.
19. Milde (note 15, *supra*), at p. 44.

has no such place of business, his permanent place of residence in another contracting state.[20] This would mean better protection for the injured party.

A ship or aircraft on the high seas shall be regarded as part of the territory of the state in which it is registered, according to Article 23, para. 2. This rule was absent in the 1933 Convention. The fact that the position of aircraft in flights above the high seas has been clarified is undoubtedly a step forward. During the debates concerning the revision of the 1952 Convention some delegates on the sub-committee wondered whether installations like oil rigs should also be expressly mentioned, but the 1978 Conference rejected proposals to insert either the term 'floating construction', or the word 'installation'.[21]

Article 30 defines as a contracting state 'any State which has ratified or adhered to this Convention and whose denunciation thereof has not become effective'. In the same Article, a territory of a state is defined as meaning 'the metropolitan territory of a State and all territories for the foreign relations of which that State is responsible, subject to the provisions of article 36'.

The Montreal Protocol amended these definitions by describing a contracting state as 'a State for which the Convention is in force' and by deleting the definition of 'territory' from the Convention, in deference to the UN General Assembly Resolution 1514 of 1960 concerning the granting of independence to colonial countries.[22] The Protocol also added another definition to Article 30 saying that by 'State of the operator' was to be understood 'any Contracting State other than the State of registry on whose territory the operator has his principal place of business or, if he has no such place of business, his permanent residence'.

Article 25 contains an important exception: it states that the Convention shall not apply if liability for damage on the surface is regulated either by a contract between the person who suffers the damage and the operator, or the person entitled to use the aircraft at the time the damage occurred, or by the law relating to workmen's compensation applicable to a contract of employment between such persons.

We find a familiar provision in Article 26, stating that the Convention will not apply to damage caused by military, customs or police aircraft. The reason for excluding these aircraft was that the majority of states wished to follow as closely as possible the Chicago Convention, which has also excluded these categories of state-owned aircraft. It should be noted, though, that the Rome Convention does apply to state-owned aircraft used for commercial purposes, as well as to

---

20. Art. XII of the 1978 Montreal Protocol.
21. ICAO Doc. 9357 – LC/183 (note 15, *supra*), at pp. 107 *et seq.*; Fitzgerald (note 11, *supra*), at p. 61.
22. Declaration on the Granting of Independence to Colonial Countries and Peoples; UN General Assembly Resolution 1514 (XV) of December 14, 1960.

mail-carrying aircraft. The position in cases where damage has been caused *to* military, customs and police aircraft is not contemplated by the Convention.

Finally, our attention is drawn to the fact that the Rome Convention applies only to damage caused by air collision to the extent that such damage is sustained on the surface of the earth: damage caused in the air is outside the scope of the Convention (Art. 24). One of the reasons was that the principle of risk liability had been adopted in the Convention. This principle could not be made applicable to air collision because such a collision involves two parties of equal strength in similar positions, a situation in which fault liability usually tends to be favoured.[23]

1.3. THE PRINCIPLES AND RULES OF LIABILITY

1.3.1. The principle of risk liability of the operator

The traditional method to assign liability for an act of tort is through fault, *i.e.* the liability attaches to the person causing harm, either intentionally or neglectfully. Another approach, though less common, is through absolute liability, often referred to as risk liability. This is the type of liability incurred upon mere proof that the damage exists and that it has been inflicted by a particular person. No proof of intent or negligence is required here, and the liability is incurred irrespective of the perpetrator's compliance with the required standards of care. It is the latter type of liability which has been adopted in Article 1 of the Rome Convention of 1952.

The discussions which took place during the preparatory stages of the Convention show that the drafters were of the opinion that the liability should attach to the person or entity which took the initial decision to engage in an activity exposing others to risk, even in cases where no amount of care or precaution could have averted damage or injury. It was argued that the person who benefits most from such activity ought to shoulder the risk involved, and not pass it on to a third party.[24]

The Rome Convention, then, embodies the principle of absolute liability, as is apparent from Article 2. This Article attaches the liability to the 'operator' of the aircraft within the meaning of the Convention. It also says, in para. 3, that the owner, easily traceable through the registration markings of the aircraft, shall be presumed to be the operator unless he proves that some other person was in control. In three cases only can the operator exonerate himself from liability, wholly or partially, as the case may be. This will be shown later in the relevant paragraph of this chapter.

23. See about this subject section 2 of this chapter, *infra*, and G.F. Fitzgerald, 'International Review – The Development of International Liability Rules Concerning Aerial Collisions' [1954] JALC 203–210, at 205 *et seq.*

24. See about this subject the Minutes of the Conference on Private International Air Law (Rome, September/October 1952), ICAO Doc. 7379 – LC/34, notably at pp. 12-15 and at pp. 53-60.

It may be mentioned in this context, as a matter of interest, that the principle of absolute liability has been adopted in the legislations of a great many countries.[25]

1.3.2. The requirements of Article 1

The very first prerequisite of Article 1 of the Rome Convention is that the damage must be caused by an aircraft in flight. As the Convention does not give a definition of 'aircraft', we may presume that the original definition of the Chicago Convention is still applicable: 'Aircraft is any machine that can derive support in the atmosphere from the reactions of the air'.[26] Being 'in flight' for an aircraft means the period in time between the moment power is applied for the purpose of actual take-off until the moment when the landing run ends (Art. 1, para. 2).

Article 1, para. 2, also mentions aircraft lighter than air, *e.g.* balloons. They are considered to be 'in flight' from the moment they become detached from the surface until the moment they become again attached thereto.

A causal connection between the damage and the act causing damage or injury is the second prerequisite. What exactly is to be understood by causal connection is for the domestic tribunals to decide, in conformity with the intents and purposes of the Convention: it turned out to be impossible to agree upon a definition for an international Convention acceptable to all parties. The reason lies in the fact that in Article 1, para. 1, damage caused by a person or thing falling from an aircraft is equated to and in fact ranks equal with the damage caused by the aircraft itself. It does not, indeed, seem to be fair to restrict the meaning of 'damage' to damage caused exclusively by direct contact with the aircraft, but this is a point quite open to debate. Here, we touch upon the doctrine of adequate causation, which has been a subject of much controversy and many studies over the years. It would be beyond the scope of this treatise to penetrate further into the matter. Suffice it to say that at the time of the Rome Convention of 1952 it raised a lot of interest and discussion: IATA delegate Cooper regarded it as the most difficult point to settle in the whole Convention[27]; Alex Meyer thought that compensating only direct damage was unfair and wanted damage also to include lost profit.[28] The American delegate Calkins mentioned a few instances not

---

25. See M. Lemoine, *Traité de droit aérien* (1947), paras. 745 *et seq.*; D. Goedhuis, *National Air Legislations and the Warsaw Convention* (1937); Minutes and Documents of the Fifth Session of the ICAO Legal Committee (Taormina-Rome, January 1950), ICAO Doc. 6029 – LC/126, pp. 281–296 (provisions of national law concerning the liability for damage to third parties on the surface).

26. See on the subject of definition of 'aircraft' Chap. I, section 5, of this treatise, *supra.*

27. Minutes and Documents of the Seventh Session of the ICAO Legal Committee (Mexico City, January 1951), ICAO Doc. 7157 – LC/130, at p. 143.

28. A. Meyer, 'Die Bedeutung des Römischen Haftungsabkommens vom 7–10–1952 für die Luftgesetzgebung der Deutschen Bundesrepublik' [1954] ZfL 42–52 (also to be found in *Luftrecht in fünf Jahrzehnten* (1961), pp. 154-163).

covered at all in the Convention: for example, a man who has a heart attack when watching an aircraft crash; a man who stumbles in the dark because of an electricity wire cut in two by a falling aircraft, or potential profits lost in a contract cancelled as a result of an air incident.[29]

There is another point not to be overlooked in Article 1: it states that no compensation is due if the damage results from the mere fact of passage of the aircraft through the airspace in conformity with existing rules of air navigation. To illustrate the point I may quote a few remarkable cases:

1. In the case of *Duchemin* v. *Pan American World Airways*, where there was a causal connection between the flight of supersonic aircraft and the collapse of a building, the court decided that the liability of the aircraft's operator in respect of damage caused by the noise from the aircraft during take-off and landing was limited to damage and inconvenience over and above that normally to be expected in an urban environment.[30]

2. A case in which the causal connection requirement could have played a decisive role was that of the American balloon 'Double Eagle'. This balloon, the first to cross the Atlantic, arrived in France on August 15, 1978. When it landed, thousands of enthusiastic fans ran towards it, damaging a wheatfield. The farmer lodged a claim for US$1,000 with his insurance company. The company refused to pay. The farmer eventually received his US$1,000 from the American Consul General in France, with the result that no legal proceedings were required. It would have been most interesting to have a court's judgment on this case.

3. The keeper of a fruit stall and other persons in a municipal market were injured by a gasoline tank falling from a naval plane participating in an air display over the city. It was ruled that, according to the liability standards obtaining in the state where the occurrence took place, the hazardous nature of the enterprise subjected the operator of the plane to the rule of absolute liability on the surface, and that the adage of *res ipsa loquitur* is clearly applicable in similar situations.[31]

4. In a few instances minks at fur farms became so terrified by overflying aircraft that they killed their young or gave birth prematurely. Yet, no compensation was due, according to the Convention.[32]

5. There is the case of a French winegrower, who filed a complaint against the commander of an airport because hundreds of bottles of

29. Minutes and Documents of the Seventh Session of the ICAO Legal Committee (note 27, *supra*), at p. 143.
30. *Duchemin* v. *Pan American World Airways et al.*, Cour de Cassation (2e Ch. Civ.), December 17, 1974; [1974] RGAE 273; Schoner's case law digest, *Air Law*, vol. V (1980), p. 52.
31. *Vincent d'Anna* v. *United States* (four cases), US Court of Appeals (4th Circ.), April 11, 1950; [1950] USAvR 282; *Avi*, Vol. 3, p. 17, 171. See also J.G. Verplaetse, *International Law in Vertical Space* (1960) p. 372, n. 239.
32. See, *e.g. Nova Mink Ltd.* v. *Trans-Canada Airlines*, Supreme Court, Nova Scotia (Canada), January 5, 1951; [1951] USAvR 40; [1952] Zfl 381.

his fine old burgundy lost their excellent quality ever since jet planes began to use the nearby airport.

6. Finally, in September 1975 a Boeing 727 landed on the back of an alligator sleeping in the sun on a Florida landing strip: the poor animal was killed. No claims were put forward by the alligator's relatives, but the passengers submitted a complaint to the airline because of the rough landing.

1.3.3. Exoneration from liability

The Rome Convention contains three exceptions to the generally accepted principle of liability: the operator can exonerate himself

1. if he proves that the damage was caused solely through the negligence or other wrongful act or omission of the person who suffers the damage or of the latter's servants or agents, unless the person who suffers damage can prove that his servant or agent was acting outside the scope of his authority. In that case liability will be reduced to the extent that negligence or wrongful act or omission contributed to the damage (Art. 6);
2. if the damage is a direct consequence of armed conflict or civil disturbance; or
3. if the operator had been deprived of the use of the aircraft by act of public authority (Art. 5).

These exceptions been left unchanged by the Montreal Protocol.

Under the Convention the operator is liable for damage caused by bombs placed in an aircraft by third parties, notwithstanding the fact that neither the operator nor his servants or agents could have prevented such acts. The United States have had quite some experience with this type of incident. Bombs were generally placed in the aircraft by persons who, either for themselves or for their relatives, were seeking to obtain 'compensation' from insurance policies.[33] At present bombs are usually placed aboard aircraft for political motives; provisions dealing with such unlawful acts are contained in the Montreal Convention of 1971, which will be examined below.

1.3.4. The limits of liability

The reasons leading to the adoption of the principle of limited liability in order to afford some protection to the operator have been discussed earlier, in the chapter on the Warsaw system, and need no further mention here. As for the limits themselves, they are clearly expressed in the Rome Convention in terms of weight, while gold francs are the units of account. A scale of five weight categories has been adopted for this purpose, a number which has later been reduced to four in the Montreal Protocol. The Protocol has basically

---

33. See, *e.g. Graham* v. *People of State of Colorado*, Colorado Supreme Court, October 22, 1956; [1956] USAvR 462. One of the civil lawsuits resulting from this incident was mentioned in Chap. III, note 86, *supra* (*Winsor* v. *United Airlines*).

stuck to the same system as the Rome Convention, but it has made some important changes including a sizeable upgrading of the compensation rates. Indeed, amending Article 11 of the Convention, which deals specifically with the liability limits, proved to be one of the most difficult obstacles facing the experts engaged in drafting the changes. No economic or statistical data were made available to the drafting committee, in spite of urgent requests made to the various states. It may be assumed, however, that such data were not available at all, there being no incident on record of case law concerning damage caused by foreign aircraft on the surface. The instances on record all concerned 'national' cases.

The magnitude of the changes accomplished at Montreal should not be underestimated, as may be appreciated from the following table:

1. First Category: aircraft weighing 2,000 kilograms or less. The limit for this lowest category, which is up to 1,000 kilograms only in the Rome Convention, was raised ninefold. The Rome limit of 500,000 francs Poincaré became 300,000 SDR (Special Drawing Rights of the International Monetary Fund), or 4,500,000 Monetary Units, equivalent to the franc Poincaré, for countries that are not members of the International Monetary Fund.

2. Second Category: aircraft ranging in weight from 2,000 up to 6,000 kilograms (the upper limit would include light transport aircraft of the type DHC-6 Twin Otter, which weighs 6,000 kilograms). The limit was raised sixfold, from 2,500,000 francs Poincaré to 1,000,000 SDR (or 15,000,000 Monetary Units).

3. Third Category: aircraft weighing between 6,000 and 30,000 kilograms (which would include for instance a Fokker F-28, weighing 30,000 kilograms). The limit was increased fivefold, from 7,500,000 francs Poincaré to 2,500,000 SDR (or 37,500,000 Monetary Units).

4. Fourth Category: aircraft weighing over 30,000 kilograms. For instance, for the heaviest type of civil aircraft until now (the Boeing 747, weighing 352 metric tons) the limit was raised about eight and a half times by increasing it to 23,400,000 SDR, an equivalent of circa US$29,300,000 at US$1.25 per SDR.

The clear differentiation between the various categories reflects the concern of the Conference that operators of small aircraft (weighing from 2,000 up to 30,000 kilograms) should be enabled to secure adequate compensation. It may be recalled, in this context, that developing countries usually operate a fleet of aircraft coming within this category.

As regards the limits of compensation for loss of life or personal injury, these were raised 375 per cent over those set forth in the Rome Convention, namely to a maximum of 125,000 SDR (or 1,875,000 Monetary Units), a maximum which previously had been fixed at 500,000 francs Poincaré.

In comparison to the Convention of 1952 the limits have indeed been raised substantially, but the United States still consider these sums to be far too low, especially in relation to large transport aircraft. Moreover, the United States are opposed to the principle of risk liability altogether: they did not sign the Rome Convention because in the event of damage being caused in a state party to the Convention an American operator would be absolutely liable. The United States also objected to the special limits provided with regard to liability for death and injury. Other states shared these objections, *e.g.* The Netherlands. They could see no reason why the operator of an aircraft should have the benefit of yet another area of limited liability, except in cases of a major catastrophe.

The intricacies of calculating the amounts of compensation in the event of persons being killed or injured, and the global limit per aircraft to be applied to these cases have been aptly illustrated by Drion, to whose thesis I may refer the interested reader.[34] Another problem is the timing element. Should the moment the Convention becomes applicable be decisive, or the date of the judgment? The fact that Article 11, para. 4, explicitly mentions the date of the judgment as being applicable to the conversion of the sums into national currencies other than gold, might be a pointer. The Montreal Protocol has not changed this provision. The limits of compensation include statutory interests, but not the costs of legal proceedings.[35]

Besides the schedule of limits of Article 11, there are two more instances of liability limits in the Convention. One of these refers to collision cases according to Article 13, para. 2, and will be dealt with in the relevant section of this chapter. The other applies in cases where two or more persons are liable. Article 13, para. 1 provides that, whenever under the provisions of the Convention two or more persons are liable, or a registered owner who was not the operator is made liable, the persons who suffer damage shall not be entitled to total compensation greater than the highest indemnity which may be awarded under the Convention against any one of the persons liable.

Further to this, Article 14 states that if the total amount of the claims established exceeds the limit of liability applicable under the provisions of the Convention the following rules will apply, taking into account Article 11, para. 2:

'(a) If the claims are exclusively in respect of loss of life or personal injury or exclusively in respect of damage to property, such claims will be reduced in proportion to their respective amounts.

(b) If the claims are both in respect of loss of life or personal injury and in respect of damage to property, one half of the total sum distributable shall be appropriated preferentially to meet claims in respect of loss of life and personal injury and, if insufficient, shall be distributed proportionately between the claims concerned. The remainder of the total sum distributable shall be distributed proportionately among the claims in respect of damage to property and the portion not already covered of the claims in respect of loss of life and personal injury'.

---

34. H. Drion, *Limitation of Liabilities in International Air Law* (thesis Leiden, 1954), para. 153.
35. Art. 20, para. 10 of the Rome Convention. See also Drion (note 34, *supra*), para. 102.

For speedier dispatch of claims, Article 19 provides that if the claimant has not brought an action to enforce his claim or if notification of such claim has not been given to the operator within a period of six months from the date of the incident which gave rise to the damage, the claimant will only be entitled to compensation out of the amount for which the operator remains liable after all claims made within that period have been met in full.

Taken as a whole, the limitation provisions may be regarded as an attempt to create a system affording the highest possible degree of legal security.

1.3.5. Unlimited liability

The liability of the operator is, according to Article 12, unlimited if the person who suffered the damage proves that it was caused by a deliberate act or omission of the operator, his servants or agents, done with intent to cause damage, provided the servant or agent was acting in the course of his employment and within the scope of his authority. This rule remained intact when preparations were under way to revise the Convention. Drion observes, correctly, that the Convention does not contemplate the case of an operator giving instructions to his servant or agent while he is not familiar with certain circumstances liable to cause damage as a result of his orders, and the servant or agent then taking advantage of such instructions in order to cause damage. In such a case the operator's liability will be unlimited, although he personally did not intend to cause any damage. Such a result would, according to Drion, not be in line with the meaning of the Convention.[36] Employees of the operator are persons whose duty it is to fly the aircraft, and persons performing services on the ground.

1.3.6. The liability of the operator

Under Article 2 of the Rome Convention, liability for compensation attaches to the operator of the aircraft. While the drafting of the Convention was in progress it had been suggested to make the registered owner of the aircraft liable because he would be easy to trace through registration, but the proposal was rejected.

The Convention states in Article 2, para. 3, that the registered owner of the aircraft shall be presumed to be the operator and shall be liable as such unless, in the proceedings for the determination of his liability, he proves that some other person was the operator. This provision demonstrates that the Convention places the burden of liability upon the operator rather than the registered owner. The operator is defined in the same Article as 'the person who was making use of the aircraft at the time the damage was caused'. A

---

36. Drion (note 34, *supra*), para. 215.

person is considered to be making use of the aircraft, again according to Article 2, when he is using it personally or when his servants or agents are using the aircraft in the course of their employment, whether or not within the scope of their authority. The operator will usually be an airline company, but he may also be a private person using the aircraft for private purposes. Owner and operator are mostly the same person.

In spite of the broad definition of the term 'operator' third parties are still exposed to the risk that their claims might be illusory, for instance when the charterer or the lessee of the aircraft turns out to be insolvent. For this reason the Convention states that 'if control of the navigation of the aircraft was retained by the person from whom the right to make use of the aircraft was derived, whether directly or indirectly, that person shall be considered the operator'.[37] This means in practical terms that when use and control of the aircraft are not exercised by the same person, the one who supplies the aircraft and crew will be liable. A good example of this situation would be a manufacturer who undertakes a world tour with an airline providing the aircraft and the crew.

The Convention further provides, in Article 3, that if the person who was the operator at the time when the damage was caused did not have the exclusive right to use the aircraft for a period of more than fourteen days, dating from the moment when the right to use commenced, the person from whom such right was derived shall be liable jointly and severally with the operator. In Article 4 it is added that if 'a person makes use of an aircraft without the consent of the person entitled to its navigational control, the latter, unless he proves that he has exercised due care to prevent such use, shall be jointly and severally liable with the unlawful user...'.

A third instance of joint and several liability is when two or more aircraft collide or interfere with each other in flight (Art. 7).

1.3.7. Persons entitled to claim

The question as to which persons are entitled to submit claims is one which has to be decided in accordance with national law. The number of persons entitled to claim in case of death varies considerably from country to country. In nearly all cases, the husband or wife of the deceased person, the children and the parents are recognised as lawful claimants. Differences appear when claims are brought by brothers and sisters, illegitimate or adopted children, or by grandparents. The fact that the claimant was financially dependent or supported by the deceased usually constitutes an important element in qualifying for recognition.

---

37. Art. 2, para. 2(a) of the 1952 Rome Convention.

The decision as to which national law to apply is in the hands of the court where the action has been submitted. It may be noted, incidentally, that no rules are given in the Rome Convention on how the damage is to be assessed, and it must be assumed that this affords the courts ample latitude to interpret the term 'damage' in a generous manner.

1.3.8. Security for the operator's liability

The 1952 Convention has abandoned the rigorous 1933 Convention rule of full liability applying in case of inadequate insurance cover.[38] The Convention contains detailed rules covering the requirements considered to be satisfactory for insurance against claims. It is not explicit on sanctions in case of failure to comply with its stipulations, particularly so with regard to Article 15, para. 1, whereby any contracting state may require the operator of an aircraft registered in another contracting state to be insured up to the limits of Article 11.

Article 15, para. 2, states that the insurance will be accepted as satisfactory if it conforms to the provisions of the Convention and has been effected by an insurer authorised to effect such insurance under the laws of the state where the aircraft is registered, or of the state where the insurer has his residence or his principal place of business and whose financial responsibility has been verified by either of those states. The Montreal Protocol has dropped most of the paragraphs of Article 15, including paragraphs 1 and 2, but replaced the latter two by the following new paragraph 1:

> 'Any contracting State may require that the operator of an aircraft referred to in paragraph 1 of Article 23 shall be covered by insurance or guaranteed by other security in respect of his liability for damage sustained in its territory for which a right of compensation exists under Article 1 up to the limits applicable according to the provisions of Article 11. The operator shall provide evidence of such guarantee if the State overflown so requests.'

In a following paragraph, the Montreal Protocol adds that a state overflown may at any time require consultation with the state of the aircraft's registry, with the state of the operator, or with any other contracting state where the guarantees are provided, if it believes that the insurer or other person providing the guarantee is not financially capable of meeting the obligations imposed by the Convention.[39]

If the security expires during a flight, it shall be continued in force until the next landing specified in the flight plan, but no longer than 24 hours.[40] This is because on flights lasting into a new day the security might expire during the flight although it was still valid on the day of

---

38. Cf. Art. 14 of the 1933 Rome Convention on surface damage.
39. Art. VI of the 1978 Montreal Protocol. Note also the introduction of the term 'guarantee'.
40. Art. 16, para. 1(a) of the 1952 Rome Convention.

departure. If security ceases to be effective for any reason other than the expiration of its term or a change of operator, it shall be continued until 15 days after notification to the appropriate authorities.[41]

According to Article 16, para. 5, the person suffering damage may, without prejudice to any right of direct action which he may have under the law governing the contract of insurance or guarantee, bring a direct action against the insurer or guarantor only in the following cases:
a. where the security is continued in force under the provisions of paragraph 1 of Article 16; and
b. bankruptcy of the operator.

The security will be deemed sufficient, according to Article 17, if, in the case of an operator of one aircraft, it is for an amount equal to the limit applicable under Article 11, and, in the case of an operator of several aircraft, it is for an amount not less than the aggregate of the limits of liability applicable to the two aircraft subject to the highest limits. As soon as notice of a claim has been given to the operator, the amount of security shall be increased up to a total sum equivalent to the aggregate of the amount of the security then required and the amount of the claim not exceeding the applicable limit of liability. The increased security shall be maintained until every claim has been disposed of. According to Article 18, the insured sums due to an operator from an insurer shall be exempt from seizure and execution by creditors of the operator until claims of third parties under this Convention have been satisfied.

The provision in Article 15, para. 8 stating that 'Any requirements imposed in accordance with this Article shall be notified to the Secretary General of the ICAO, who shall inform each Contracting State thereof', has been maintained in the Montreal Protocol.

According to Article 16 of the Convention, the insurer or other person providing security may, in addition to the defences available to the operator and the defence of forgery, set up the following defences:
a. that the damage occurred after the security ceased to be effective; and
b. that the damage occurred outside the territorial limits provided for by the security, unless flight outside of such limits was caused by *force majeure*, assistance justified by the circumstances, or an error in piloting, operation or navigation.

Apart from these two exceptions the insurer may not, under the provisions of the Convention, invoke any other grounds to nullify a contract, nor may he withdraw from a contract or avail himself of any right of retroactive cancellation. This does not, however, preclude recourse against any other person, if circumstances allow him to do so.

Like Article 15, Article 16 has not been left untouched by the Montreal Protocol. Firstly, the word 'security' has been replaced by 'guarantee' throughout the Article; secondly, paragraphs 2 and 3 are deleted; thirdly, in paragraph 1 the sub-paragraphs (a) and (b) are replaced by the following defences:

41. Art. 16, para. 1(a) of the 1952 Rome Convention.

a. that the damage occurred after the guarantee ceased to be effective. However, if the guarantee expires during a flight, it should be continued in force until the next landing specified in the flight plan, but not longer than 24 hours.
b. that the damage occurred outside the territorial limits provided by the guarantee, unless flight outside of such limits was caused by *force majeure*, assistance justified by the circumstances or an error in piloting, operation or navigation.

1.3.9. Jurisdiction

Article 20, para. 1 of the Rome Convention designates the courts of the state where the damage occurred as the only forum before which actions under the Convention may be brought.[42]

When the Convention was under review in recent years the question of a single forum was brought once again into the discussions. It was proposed, and finally decided, that jurisdiction ought not to include the courts of the state in which the operator of the aircraft causing the damage maintained his principal place of business or, if he had no such place of business, his permanent residence, as had been suggested.

The objections raised against assigning more than one forum have been generally motivated by the danger of conflicting judgments and liability limits being exceeded if claims could be brought before several national courts.[43] Moreover, there would be less certainty that judgments would be executed in actual fact, which would jeopardise the position of the claimant.

Although one of the objections against the Rome Convention was directed at the establishment of a single forum, not too much weight ought to be attached to it, in my opinion, especially as the Rome Convention still allows claimants to take action before the courts of any other contracting state, following agreement between the parties in dispute. However, no such proceedings shall have the effect of prejudicing in any way rights of persons who bring actions in the state where the damage occurred. Article 20 further provides that parties may also agree to submit their disputes to arbitration in any contracting state. My point of view seems to be supported by the fact that during the discussions at the Montreal Conference of 1978, the objection was not mentioned again, at least not with any emphasis.

42. Cf. the 1950 proposal for the establishment of a special *ad hoc* international court for the consideration of cases requiring adjudication under the terms of the Convention, which was later redrafted into a proposal for the establishment of an International Court of Appeals. See the Minutes of the Seventh Session of the ICAO Legal Committee (note 27, *supra*), at p. 367. Also on this subject R.P. Cleveringa, 'Proposal to Establish an International Court of Arbitration on Maritime and Air Law', Second Conference of the International Bar Association (The Hague, 1948); the 'Rapport' by P. Chaveau to the 48th Conference of the International Law Association (New York, 1958), published in the *Report* of this Conference, pp. 331-337; and W.P. Heere, 'Some Observations Concerning the Desirability of Creating an International Court for Aeronautical Disputes', *Air Law*, vol. I (1976), pp. 229-252.
43. See Fitzgerald (note 11, *supra*), at p. 37 and at pp. 59-60.

1.3.10. Limitation of actions

Rules of limitation are mainly dealt with in Article 21 of the Convention. Under it, actions under the Convention will be subject to a period of two years from the date of the incident which caused the damage. The right to institute an action will lapse on the expiration of three years from such date, and grounds for suspension and interruption will be determined by the law of the court trying the case. According to Article 20, para. 12 an application for execution of a judgment must be made within five years from the date when such judgment became final. In the Montreal Protocol this period has been reduced to two years.

1.3.11. Execution of judgments

Execution of a judgment may be applied for either in the contracting state where the judgment debtor has his residence or his principal place of business, or, if the assets available in that state and in the state where the judgment is pronounced are insufficient to satisfy the judgment, in any other contracting state where the judgment debtor has assets. Thus it is stated in paragraph 4 of Article 20 of the Convention, which continues in paragraph 5 by providing that the court to which application is made for the execution may refuse to issue execution if it is proved that any of the following circumstances exist:

'(a) the judgment was given by default and the defendant did not acquire knowledge of the proceedings in sufficient time to act upon it;
 (b) the defendant was not given a fair and adequate opportunity to defend his interests;
 (c) the judgment is in respect of a cause of action which had already, as between the same parties, formed the subject of a judgment or an arbitral award which, under the law of the State where execution is sought, is recognized as final and conclusive;
 (d) the judgment has been obtained by fraud of any of the parties;
 (e) the right to enforce the judgment is not vested in the person by whom the application for execution is made.'

In addition, execution shall also be refused in the following situations:
a. the court to which the application is made, shall refuse execution until final judgment has been given on all actions filed in the state where the damage occurred, if the judgment debtor proves that the total amount of compensation which might be awarded by such judgments might exceed the applicable limit of liability under the provisions of the Convention;

b. the court applied to shall also refuse execution of any judgment rendered by a court of a state other than that in which the damage occurred until all judgments rendered in that state have been satisfied.[44]

If, in proceedings under paragraph 4 of Article 20, execution of a judgment is refused, the claimant shall be entitled to bring a new action before the courts of the state where execution has been refused. The previous judgment shall cease to be enforceable as soon as the new action has been started.[45]

In the event of the death of the person liable, an action in respect of liability shall lie against those legally responsible for his obligation.[46]

Finally, it should be noted that according to Article 20, para. 7, the court may also refuse to issue execution if the judgment is contrary to the public policy of the state in which execution is requested.

In assessing the merits of Article 20 the point will inevitably be made that the state where the damage occurs is usually not the state where the operator has his principal place of business or residence. This is indeed a fact, and it means that actions brought by persons who have suffered damage can only be successful if a system is provided whereby the judgment can be enforced. Article 20 reflects an attempt to achieve such a system. According to Wilberforce,[47] this is the first time that states have attempted to introduce a multilateral system for the enforcement of judgments.

The Berne Railway Conventions[48] provided at that time the nearest precedent, but it must be pointed out that these Conventions were adopted by a group of European States with homogeneous legal systems, and adherence to them was possible only by means of special consent on the part of the member states. The Rome Convention, on the other hand, is open for signature to any state, irrespective of whether it is a member of ICAO or not. In the light of this situation the attempt to create a uniform system of legal proceedings and mutual enforcement of judgments must be greeted as a major step forward on the way towards providing effective international remedies at law.

---

44. Art. 20, para. 9 of the 1952 Rome Convention.
45. Art. 20, para. 8 of the 1952 Rome Convention.
46. Art. 22 of the 1952 Rome Convention.
47. R.O. Wilberforce, 'Convention on Damage Caused by Foreign Aircraft to Third Parties on the Surface' (1953) 2 *The International and Comparative Law Quarterly*, 90–94.
48. International Convention Concerning the Carriage of Goods by Rail (CIM), Berne, February 7, 1970; International Convention Concerning the Carriage of Passengers and Luggage by Rail (CIV), Berne, February 7, 1970. Note that both Conventions have been regularly amended and redrafted; the current versions date from 1980 (in force 1985).

1.3.12. Final provisions

For the 1952 Rome Convention and the 1978 Montreal Protocol to come into force, five of the signatory states must have deposited their instruments of ratification. No reservations may be made to either the Convention or the Protocol. Under the Convention (Art. 36) territorial reservations may be made by a state declaring that the Convention's provisions are not to apply to any one or more of the territories for the foreign relations of which such state is responsible. This provision has been deleted by Article XVIII of the Montreal Protocol.

The texts in English, French and Spanish of both the Rome Convention and the Montreal Protocol are equally authentic. In the Montreal Protocol, the same status has been accorded to the Russian text. Although the Rome Convention of 1952 eventually did become effective it has not found wide acceptance: only relatively few countries have ratified it, as I had occasion to mention earlier. At the moment it seems that the Montreal Protocol will not attract many more ratifications either. It could be argued that if the Rome Convention were to be simplified, with only its basic rules retained and at the same time its liability rules extended to cover all damage resulting from the operation of the aircraft (including damage on the surface before take-off and after landing as well as damage during flight, and also including damage resulting from collision), it might secure additional ratifications.[49]

1.4. DAMAGE CAUSED BY NOISE AND SONIC BOOM

The spectacular developments in aviation since the end of the Second World War have been highlighted previously on several occasions, and the great benefits they have brought to the world are obvious and there for all of us to see and enjoy. They must, however, be weighed against the discomfort and the damage caused by some of its side-effects, particularly noise and sonic boom. With industry and motorised transport contributing their share to endangering the environment in the densely populated areas, the incidence of noise caused by aircraft is specially harmful and detrimental. Although in some countries legislative measures against excessive noise have already been introduced, common standards and arrangements sanctioned by the international agreements are still sadly lacking. In the following pages this problem will be given due attention.

It is an old principle of law dating from Roman days and referred to earlier in this treatise which forms the backdrop against which the problem of noise must be set: the rule of *Cujus est solum, ejus est ad coelum et ad inferos.* This old adage has been upheld in law courts all over the world until as recently as the 1960s. Meanwhile, international

---

49. M. Bodenschatz, 'Rome Convention: *Quo Vadis?*', Report of the 55th Conference of the International Law Association (New York, 1972), pp. 742-e to 742-j.

agreements had been concluded to cover damage caused by aircraft on the surface, notably the Rome Conventions of 1933 and 1952. In the latter Convention the operative term related to our problem is in Article 1, which refers to 'aircraft in flight', it being understood that 'in flight' is to be interpreted as 'normal flight', *i.e.* a flight in accordance with the rules of the air. Pursuant to this interpretation it is clearly impossible to apply the Convention to sonic boom, because supersonic aircraft may cause damage even when flying in conformity with the rules of the air.

Excessive noise may be caused by (1) aircraft passing through the airspace; (2) take-offs and landings affecting areas adjacent to airports; and (3) test flights affecting those areas. In 1952, the year in which the Rome Convention was concluded, the damage jet aircraft might cause on the surface could not be predicted, which is one of the reasons why that Convention is not an appropriate instrument to deal with the problem.

To solve the problem on an international level two procedures have been contemplated. One was to amend the Chicago Convention; the other suggestion for a way out was to modify the 1952 Rome Convention.

An amendment to the Chicago Convention could have been brought about on the basis of Article 94: it would have involved modifying the Annex 8 on airworthiness in such a way as to make the issuing of certificates of airworthiness contingent upon meeting certain standards of noise level. Such a solution would, however, be hampered by the fact that in order to become effective the amendments to the Convention would have to secure ratification by a two-thirds majority.

A similar obstacle would have to be overcome in attempts to revise the Rome Convention. Admittedly, the number of states is much smaller here, but the opportunity would probably be seized upon to open discussions on other controversial matters concerning the Convention. Amending the Convention would have been of little use in any case, because it excluded liability for damage caused by the noise of aircraft in 'normal flight'. The matter was discussed in the Legal Committee of the ICAO General Assembly in 1980. Having noted the work of the Sub-committee on the Revision of the Rome Convention in 1975 and also that the Sub-committee on the Problem of Liability for Damage Caused by Noise and Sonic Boom in 1978 had not considered this subject ripe for consideration, the Legal Committee recommended that the subject should be 'relegated to Part B of the General Work Programme', which meant in fact that consideration was to be postponed for an indefinite period.[50]

---

50. See the Documents of the 23rd Session of the ICAO Legal Committee (Montreal, February 1978), ICAO Doc. 9238 – LC/180-2, at pp. 133-134, and M. Milde's report on the 23rd Session of the ICAO Assembly (Montreal, September–October 1980), *Air Law*, vol. VI (1981), pp. 53-56, at 55.

Another procedure to solve the problem would be to create a new instrument on noise and sonic boom. This suggestion was amply considered at the 1976 session of the ICAO Legal Committee, where opinions turned out to be strongly divided on the subject. After lengthy debates it was decided that the question of whether or not to adopt an entirely new instrument was to be referred to a sub-committee specially extended for the purpose, and that its terms of reference were not to include vibrations but only noise and sonic boom. In the meantime, information on the subject was going to be collected from states and from various other sources. This information would be commented on by states and then submitted to the sub-committee in the form of recommended solutions.[51]

In order to combat the effects of aircraft noise, specially in densely populated areas, legislative measures have already been introduced in several countries. Besides, case law has played a useful role in providing relief for those suffering from excessive noise. Once again, there is a notable difference in legal practice between European countries on the one hand and the United States on the other. The following examples may illustrate the point.

In Nice (France) a high-rise apartment building had been constructed on the outskirts of the city, but the apartments were difficult to sell because of the noise produced by jet aircraft using Nice airport. An action was filed against the operator of the airport, the Chamber of Commerce. The court ruled that it had no jurisdiction to hear the case because the Chamber of Commerce was a public corporation set up by the French Government. The case should therefore have been brought before the *Conseil d'Etat*. The builder of the apartment building subsequently filed a claim against Air France, although that company was only one of the many users of the airport, and the residents also sued for compensation. Air France was required to assume the burden of proof and to demonstrate that the noise caused by its aircraft did not in fact exceed legal limits. The court decided eventually that the operator of the aircraft was liable for the damage caused by manoeuvrings of the aircraft.[52] On the whole, the attitude of the French courts towards compensation for damage of this kind seems to be more lenient than in common law countries, notably the

---

51. See the Minutes and Documents of the 22nd Session of the ICAO Legal Committee (Montreal, October–November 1976), ICAO Doc. 9222 – LC/177-1 and 177-2.
52. *Cie.Air France* v. *Sté ERVE et al.*, Cour de Cassation (2e Ch. Civ.), May 8, 1968; [1968] RFDA 327. Also on this case A.F. Lowenfeld, *Aviation Law, Cases and Materials* (2nd ed., 1981), pp. 6-82 to 6-86, and R.H. Mankiewicz, 'Airport Noise – Compensation of Adjoining Landowners under French Law: A Report on a Case and Some Further Considerations' [1969] JALC 238–244.

United States.[53] In the United States, proceedings have generally been based on one of the following three grounds: (1) trespass; (2) nuisance; (3) unconstitutional taking.

Court actions have frequently been based on trespass in cases of direct overflight of the plaintiff's property. Their advantage was that trespass is actionable *per se*, contrary to nuisance, where abnormal discomfort has to be demonstrated. The idea of trespass in the airspace above someone's land stems from the Roman adage quoted earlier which has played such a significant part in air law in general. However, in the *Hinman* case[54] it was ruled that this was not the law and had never been. The court's considerations are interesting enough to quote here in more detail:

'We own so much of the space above the ground as we can occupy or make use of, in connection with the enjoyment of our land. This right is not fixed. It varies with our varying needs and is coextensive with them. The owner of land owns as much of the space above him as he uses, but only so long as he uses it. All that lies beyond belongs to the world.'

'The case differs from the usual case of enjoining a trespass. Ordinarily, if a trespass is committed upon land, the plaintiff is entitled to at least nominal damages without proving or alleging any actual damage. In the instant case, traversing the airspace above the appellant's land is not, of itself, a trespass at all, but it is a lawful act unless it is done under circumstances which will cause injury to appellant's possession'.

Clearly, the particular advantages of trespass as a basis for obtaining compensation in cases of overflight had been undone by this judgment.

In the *Causby* case[55] trespass was not upheld either. The court ruled that private ownership of the airspace was not acceptable in the modern world and that airspace formed a part of the public domain, except within a few feet of the surface of the land: the landowner owns at least as much of the space above the ground as he can occupy or use in connection with the land.

---

53. See Lowenfeld (note 52, supra), Chap. 6; R.R. Wright, *The Law of Airspace* (1968); D.P. Reichenbach, *Haftpflicht und Versicherung des Luftfahrzeughalters für Lärmschäden* (thesis Zurich, 1971); H.J. Martin, *Die eigentumsrechtliche Stellung des Luftraumes, Fluglärm und Überschallknall, Haftungsfolgen und Ansprüche nach deutschem, englischem, amerikanischem, kanadischem, französischem und internationalem Recht* (thesis Würzburg, 1968); E. Alvarez-Correa, *La responsabilité civile pour les dommages causés aux tiers à la surface par le bruit et les ondes de choc des aéronefs, étude de droit français* (thesis Lausanne, 1972); I.H.Ph. Diederiks-Verschoor, 'Haftung für Schäden durch Überschallflüge', [1970] ZLW, 235–240; and the various reports on damage caused by supersonic flights, VIIIth International Congress of Comparative Law (Pescara, 1970).

54. *Hinman* v. *Pacific Air Transport; same* v. *United Airlines Transport Corp.*, US Court of Appeals (9th Circuit), July 20, 1936; *Avi*, Vol. 1, p. 640; [1936] USAvR, 1; [1936] JAL, 624.

55. *United States* v. *Causby*, US Supreme Court, May 27, 1946; *Avi*, Vol. 2, p. 14,189; [1946] USAvR, 235.

'Nuisance', another ground used in connection with damage caused by aircraft noise, 'may be defined as any act or omission which interferes with the enjoyment by another of his health, comfort, or convenience in the occupation of his land'.[56] Nuisance caused by noise is usually recognised by the courts only if it is continuous or repetitive and provided that sensible discomfort and annoyance have been caused to the owner of the property. The economic interests of the community as a whole are so considerable and air traffic has become such a common feature of modern life that it will be extremely difficult for a private action of an individual against aircraft operators causing him abnormal discomfort to be successfully upheld in court. Here again the law varies from country to country.

The main legal ground used in the United States to obtain compensation is 'unconstitutional taking.' It was used in 1946 in the case of the *United States* v. *Causby*.[57] The court held that frequent flights and the interference they caused equalled the taking of an easement for which compensation was due, but added that: 'The airspace, apart from the immediate reaches above the land, is part of the public domain. We need not determine at this time what those precise limits are. Flights over private land are not a taking, unless they are so low and so frequent as to be a direct and immediate interference with the enjoyment and use of the land'.

The line taken in the *Causby* case was further qualified in the *Batten* case,[58] where direct overflight was made a requirement before compensation could be obtained. In only a very few states, notably Washington – the 1964 *Martin* case[59] – and in Oregon – the 1962 *Thornburg* case[60] – has compensation been granted for excessive noise affecting landowners.

Whether repeated overflights do or do not constitute 'unconstitutional taking' on a particular property depends on three factors, according to the *Causby* judgment: (1) the character of the land itself; (2) the altitude of the flights; (3) the frequency of the overflights. Claiming unconstitutional taking has been successful in American courts when the inconvenience was so serious that it was considered to equal the taking of an easement for which compensation was due. Regular low overflights in the airspace over the plaintiff's property have been construed as such. While considering these cases it must not be forgotten that physical damage may be caused purely incidentally as a result of aircraft noise. To quote a few instances: minks killing their young in fright,[61] mules panicking from the noise of a

---

56. E. Jenks, *The Book of English Law* (1967), at pp. 343 *et seq.*
57. *Supra*, note 55.
58. *Batten* v. *United States*, US Court of Appeals (10th Circuit), July 10, 1962; *Avi*, Vol. 8, p. 17,101.
59. *Martin* v. *The Port of Seattle*, Washington Supreme Court, April 23, 1964; *Avi*, Vol. 8, p. 18, 324.
60. *Thornburg* v. *The Port of Portland*, Oregon Supreme Court, November 7, 1962; *Avi*, Vol. 8, p. 17,281; [1962] USAvR, 448.
61. See, *e.g.* the *Nova Mink* case (note 32, *supra*).

low-flying aircraft,[62] or glass damage caused by sonic boom.[63] The chances of obtaining compensation in such cases will depend on the liability laws in force in the various states, because the principles outlined in this paragraph obviously do not apply.

Against whom may an action for compensation be directed? As shown in the case of Nice, France, and also in cases in the United States, it is possible to sue an airline company successfully for damages caused by aircraft noise. It is questionable, however, whether this is always the case, because airlines are obliged by law to land on specially designated airfields (Chicago Convention). Another option would be to sue the operator of the airport, but he might defend his case by arguing that he is compelled by law to allow air traffic to use the airport, and that it is not the airport that has caused the noise anyway.

A third possibility would be to sue the state, but this is obviously not a simple matter. Here we touch upon the problem of whether the state can be or ought to be forced to grant compensation for acts that are perfectly lawful in themselves. Similar claims could arise in connection with pollution.

As for persons wishing to claim compensation, they have to do so in accordance with the rules of general law, the Rome Convention not being applicable to such claims.

Finding insurance for the risk of damage resulting from aircraft noise and sonic boom is not as easy as it seems, because insurance caters for uncertainties whereas the fact that noise can cause damage may be regarded as virtually certain. The very high premiums payable in view of the great many claims to be expected will constitute another obstacle for insurance to play its proper role here. From case law it is already evident that the insurance companies have never wished to consider sonic boom under the heading 'explosions'.[64] Most policies therefore specifically exclude claims arising from noise, sonic boom and associated risks. As Margo observes, this is done either in the wording of the printed standard policy, or by incorporating such risks in a special exclusion clause. Nevertheless, it is still possible to arrange for coverage in the London insurance market.[65]

---

62. *Long* v. *United States*, US District Court, Western District of South Carolina (Greenwood Division), May 14, 1965; [1965] USAvR, 421. Cf. the case of *Brunt* v. *Chicago Mill & Lumber Co. and Blythe Huntley*, Mississippi Supreme Court, April 2, 1962; [1963] USAvR, 63 (cattle stampeding due to aircraft taking off in pasture).

63. See for a striking illustration of this type of damage R. Burkhardt, *CAB – The Civil Aeronautics Board* (1974), third page with illustrations between pp. 86 and 87.

64. See, *e.g. Bear Bros. Inc.* v. *Fidelity and Guaranty Insurance Underwriters Inc.*, Alabama Circuit Court (Montgomery County), May 8, 1959; [1959] USAvR, 146; *Avi*, Vol. 6, p. 17,497 (sonic boom is not an 'explosion' within the wording of the policy). Cf. *Alexander* v. *Firemen's Insurance Co.*, Texas Court of Civil Appeals (Waco), October 23, 1958; [1959] USAvR, 431; *Avi*, Vol. 5, p. 18,218 (a court may not, as of this time, take judicial notice that a sonic boom, as a scientific fact, constitutes an explosion so as to invoke the explosion provisions of the policy).

65. R.D. Margo, *Aviation Insurance* (1989) at pp. 173-174. See also on the subject of insurance Reichenbach (note 53, *supra*).

In order to offset at least in part the discomfort of those suffering from the effects of noise and sonic boom, and at the same time to guarantee proper compensation, it is submitted that perhaps indemnisation funds should be set up on a national level. Considering the great number of parties that might be involved in the matter it would not be unreasonable to oblige all concerned to contribute to the funds needed for relief of the victims, rather than to continue trying to get compensation from one party only.

With aircraft nowadays being regarded as an ordinary means of transport, some measure of tolerance may be expected from the public at large. Nonetheless, there is no denying that the present situation is hardly satisfactory, in spite of the fact that a few countries have already introduced legislation to cope with the problem, while others are preparing for it. Some countries have introduced 'zoning', whereby building in the vicinity of airports has been made contingent upon noise levels in the area; other measures include restricting nightflying, or making the use of certain runways conditional upon the wind direction, etc. However, in the absence of international rules for the foreseeable future the best way out of the problem is probably to concentrate all efforts on the technical and scientific level in order to reduce the noise of the aircraft themselves.

2. Air collisions

Given the increased cruising speed and the density of air traffic, the introduction of suitable measures to prevent air collisions is of the greatest importance. This conclusion is still valid, considering the increase in the number of near-misses during the past few years.

A tragic example of an air collision is the accident that took place near Zagreb, Yugoslavia, in 1976, when both crews and all the passengers lost their lives. The accident occurred at a time when the air traffic controllers were neglecting their duties, and their negligence was proved to be the cause of the collision which involved a Yugoslavia Airlines DC-9 and a British Airways Trident.[66]

Air collisions have practical as well as legal repercussions. From a practical point of view they result in extensive damage in terms of persons and goods. In the legal sphere one would perhaps expect to find rules or guidance in the international Conventions on the liability of the carrier with regard to passengers and goods towards third parties on the surface of the earth.

Unfortunately, there is only one rule in international law referring to this knotty problem: we find it in Article 7 of the Rome Convention of 1952, which provides that

---

66. See for the ensuing trial of the relevant air traffic controller and the international action on his behalf the various references in the 1976 to 1978 volumes of *Flight* and *Aviation Week & Space Technology.*

'When two or more aircraft have collided or interfered with each other in flight and damage for which a right to compensation as contemplated in Article 1 results, or when two or more aircraft have jointly caused such damage, each of the aircraft concerned shall be considered to have caused the damage and the operator of each aircraft shall be liable, each of them being bound under the provisions and within the limits of liability of this Convention.'

It is clear that this provision, the only one with any relevance to the matter, is hardly adequate for the purpose. Comprehensive regulations on the subject do not exist, and will not be achieved until agreement is reached on an international level.[67]

De Juglart[68] is right in saying that, although Article 7 of the Rome Convention covers the subject only in very general terms, the operator of the aircraft may be held liable even when he is not guilty of causing the collision: the Article is completely in line with the risk principle embedded in the Convention, and it affords maximum protection to third parties on the surface.

The position of third parties suffering damage on the surface of the earth as a result of an air collision is quite different from that of persons involved in the collision itself. A third party on the ground is in a less favourable situation because he cannot protect himself by means of insurance: he does not participate in the risk involved in travelling by air.

As for persons involved in the collision itself, their interests are covered by the liability of the operators of the colliding aircraft. As a collision between aircraft involves two parties of relatively equal strength, it would be unreasonable to impose risk liability on the operators of both aircraft. For that reason fault liability has been given preference in the CITEJA and ICAO draft Conventions on air collisions as the guiding principle.[69] This is, of course, the very same standard of liability as adopted by the Warsaw Convention, but there is a slightly different emphasis in the burden of proof between the two.

The latest draft of this kind came up for review during the 1964 meeting of the ICAO Legal Committee.[70] In it, the operator was named as the party liable for damages, but limits of liability were also

---

67. See on the subject of collisions M.D. Werro, *Die Haftung aus Zusammenstoss von Flugzeugen, unter besonderer Berücksichtigung des schweizerischen Rechtes* (thesis Zurich, 1978); and R. von der Lieth, *Die Haftung beim Zusammenstoss von Luftfahrzeugen* (thesis Cologne, 1964).

68. M. de Juglart, *La Convention de Rome du 7 octobre 1952* (1955), paras. 70 and 71.

69. See on this subject Fitzgerald (note 23, *supra*). Cf. the Draft Convention adopted at the XIth Session of the CITEJA (Berne, September 1936), as reproduced in [1937] JAL, 320–325. See for the first ICAO Draft the Minutes and Documents of the Tenth Session of the ICAO Legal Committee (Montreal, September 1954), ICAO Doc. 7601 – LC/138.

70. Minutes and Documents of the Fifteenth Session of the ICAO Legal Committee (Montreal, September 1964), ICAO Doc. 8582 – LC/153-1 and 153–2. The final draft is also reproduced as Appendix XXII in Nicolas M. Matte, *Treatise on Air-aeronautical Law*, (1981). See on this Draft Convention R.H. Mankiewicz, 'The ICAO Draft Convention on Aerial Collisions' [1964] JALC, 375–389.

mentioned. The ICAO draft does not give a clear indication as to what is meant by the word 'collision'. In principle it must be taken to mean an actual material contact between two or more aircraft in flight.[71] It was suggested that the word 'interference' be defined as follows on that occasion: 'Interference refers to a situation where the manoeuvre of an aircraft causes damage to another aircraft without there being a material contact of these aircraft'.[72]

Among the causes of collision may be mentioned navigation errors, faulty construction, natural causes like icing and turbulence, interception and air traffic control errors. We must not lose sight either of the investigation into aircraft accidents, an aspect which is covered by the terms of Article 26 of the Chicago Convention.[73]

An interesting situation arises when a collision takes place between an aircraft and a different type of transport vehicle, for example a ship. Which law is to be applied? The case is not covered by the draft Conventions mentioned earlier. It could be brought under the Rome Convention because the damage is inflicted on a party on the surface, but it could also be argued that perhaps maritime law should be applied instead of air law. Ambrosini[74] has suggested the following solution: when an aircraft in motion collides with a ship or another transport vehicle, maritime and transport law should be applied, respectively, whereas air law should be applied when aircraft collide in flight. Maritime law experts are strongly opposed to the application of air law in collision cases involving an aircraft and a ship. They assert that in all such cases maritime law should prevail.

While on the subject of collisions between aircraft and other means of transport, the following case is worth mentioning: a KLM aircraft which was coming in to land at the airport of Aruba (Netherlands Antilles) hit a small van with one of the wheels of the undercarriage. The driver of the van was injured and the van itself heavily damaged, but the pilot had not noticed the accident and learnt of it only after landing. A civil case was started between KLM and the Antillean authorities, the point at issue being the question of whether the aircraft or the van had the right of way. The judge started from the assumption that an air pocket just above the runway had affected the

71. The adopted definition of 'in flight' (Art. 1, para. 2 of the Draft Convention) closely follows that of the 1952 Rome Convention, and also covers lighter-than-air aircraft (balloons, etc.).

72. See the 'Comments of the Delegation of the Polish People's Republic', Minutes of the Fifteenth Session of the ICAO Legal Committee (see note 70, *supra*), at p. 238. During the discussions, however, it was not found necessary to include a definition of 'interference' in the Draft Convention (Minutes, p. 25).

73. See *e.g.* A.A. van Wijk, *Aircraft Accident Enquiry in the Netherlands* (thesis Amsterdam, 1974); see also by the same author 'The Investigation of Aircraft Accidents and Incidents. Some Notes and Documentation on Recent Developments', *Proceedings Luchtrecht Symposium* (Rotterdam, October 2, 1981), pp. 71-144. See also J.W.E. Storm van 's Gravesande, 'Some observations on fifty years of aircraft accident investigation in the Netherlands', *Air Worthy*, pp. 151–168; and section 7 of chapter II, *supra*.

74. A. Ambrosini, '*Deuxième rapport sur l'avant-projet de convention sur l'abordage aérien*' [1934] RGDA, 474–483 at 476–477 and at 481–482.

aircraft's movements, but also found that the pilot should have coped better with the situation since the runway was long enough for him to come in at a slightly steeper angle. In this ruling, no special right of way for either aircraft or the ground vehicle was recognised. KLM lost their case and were ordered to pay compensation.[75]

Before the Second World War there was little case law relating to air collisions. The few instances that have occurred since have been easily settled, but in the present-day circumstances more and better rules are urgently needed.

---

75. *KLM* v. *Nederlandse Antillen*, Netherlands Antilles Court of Justice, Curacao, January 12, 1954; [1954] JALC, 477; IATA ACLR No. 16. References to further cases resulting from collisions of aircraft with other means of transport are to be found in Shawcross and Beaumont, *Air Law*, (1977), paras. 598 and 599.

CHAPTER VII

Insurance

1. Introductory note

Insurance provides relief for a whole range of liability risks currently associated with modern society. In the public transport sector, risks involving the transportation of passengers and goods as well as those connected with the equipment used in their carriage are nowadays insurable. From a financial point of view, a comprehensive insurance policy has become indispensable to air carriers, given the high market value of aircraft and the great financial risks involved in aviation. Equally recommendable, if not necessary, is proper insurance coverage for the persons entrusting themselves or their goods to the carrier's care.

Is insurance compulsory in aviation? The answer to that question is that there is no direct obligation in air law to arrange for adequate insurance. All we can find is an indirect sanction by way of the Chicago Convention (Art. 9). This Article prohibiting or restricting flights of foreign aircraft 'for reasons of public safety' could be made applicable to operators failing to insure their aircraft in accordance with the provisions of the 1952 Rome Convention.

Domestic legislation has made proper insurance mandatory in a large number of countries. This often refers to insurance against the air carrier's liability up to the limits provided in national laws and international Conventions. In some countries, however, this refers to additional insurance for the benefit of the passenger.[1] In the United States, extensive research has been conducted into this matter.[2] Other states grant their governmental authorities the right to make the registration of aircraft and the right to engage in aviation activities contingent upon insurance cover, without making it mandatory in either case. There are also a number of states where the domestic legislation is completely silent on the matter.

---

1. For example Austria, the German Federal Republic, Italy, Spain and Switzerland. See also R.D. Margo, *Aviation Insurance* (1989), pp. 1-18 and Shawcross and Beaumont, *Air Law* (1977), para. 685.
2. See on this subject P.H. Sand, 'Die USA und das Haager Protokoll: Zum Plan einer gesetzlichen Fluggastversicherung' [1963] ZLW 12-34.

2. History

Opinions differ as to when the very first aviation insurance policy was drawn up.[3] Before the First World War such policies were scarce, and they were primarily issued to cover Zeppelins. After the First World War air traffic expansion started off an increased demand for insurance, but insurers were reluctant to respond to this challenge because of the variety and magnitude of the risks involved in this new means of transport. In a way, insurance acted as a check on aviation expansion, because a tight rein was kept on undue energy displayed by carriers. On the other hand, it also provided a stimulant by reducing premiums in return for better safety conditions made possible by modern technology.

Aviation insurance became a new branch of business activity for various insurance companies after the First World War. Underwriters at Lloyd's of London were notable pioneers. Two conflicting tendencies soon began to make themselves felt in the market. On the one hand, a greater spreading of risks became more and more urgent. On the other hand, the market remained rather restricted on the suppliers' side for some time. The insurers needed a considerable amount of technical knowledge to assess accurately the safety aspects of new inventions. Besides, the number of companies offering insurance for aviation was much smaller than that dealing in the normal types of insurance business. But although the type of risks to be insured and the size of them were initially an obstacle in the way of expansion of the aviation insurance business, the situation changed when improved safety conditions gradually reduced those risks. The better the safety record a company could show, the better the terms it could get in the insurance market. A corresponding expansion of the aviation insurance market, marked by strong competition, was triggered off due to the great expansion in air traffic following the Second World War.

The spreading of risks is made possible by pooling arrangements concluded between a number of insurance companies. Under a pooling arrangement capital is put up according to a certain ratio by the contracting insurance companies and the risks are then shared by participants in proportion to each company's holding in the pool. A pool is, in fact, a common insurance department of the contracting companies. In this manner the advantages of risk-sharing are safeguarded, while at the same time the specialisation of this special branch of insurance remains unaffected.

Initially, there were some misgivings about pooling arrangements, for it was feared that some pools might manoeuvre themselves into a position of monopoly and thereby exercise an unfavourable influence on premium levels, but these misgivings proved groundless. The majority

---

3. See on this subject Margo (note 1, *supra*) and *A Short History of Aviation Insurance in the United Kingdom*, Report H.R. 10 of the Historic Records Committee of the Insurance Institute of London (2nd ed., 1968).

of airlines are in actual fact government enterprises, and the state itself became the principal client in the insurance market. The threat of aviation enterprises turning to foreign insurers because of unfavourable terms at home resulted in pools being forced to compete with the terms offered in foreign markets, in spite of their monopolist position at home.

The United Kingdom and the United States have large insurance markets on which a number of aviation insurance pools operate. Belgium, France, the German Federal Republic, Italy, The Netherlands, the Scandinavian countries, Spain and Switzerland have large and important aviation insurance pools as well.[4] A part of these European pools is reinsured by Lloyd's underwriters and/or insurance companies in the London market. On the other hand, quite a few Lloyd's syndicates place their reinsurance on the European market. There is thus an exchange of risks at reinsurance level, resulting in a wider spreading of risk. Outside Europe and the USA, aviation insurance pools existed as well.

The international interests of the insurers led in 1934 to the creation of the International Union of Aviation Insurers (IUAI), an organisation which, as we have seen earlier, plays a role in the drafting stages of international conventions on air law in an advisory capacity. The IUAI, a non-political association, is open to registered insurance companies from all parts of the world. Its objects are to 'speak and negotiate on behalf of aviation insurance interests, to provide a central office for the circulation of information between members, to cooperate for the better regulation and conduct of aviation insurance, and generally to do anything which may be beneficial to the development and conduct of aviation insurance.'[5] The IUAI is not a cartel. In order to be eligible as a member an insurance company has to show it insures such a large share of its domestic market that it can be regarded as representative for that market. Premium levels are never discussed in the IUAI, neither specifically nor in more general terms.

3. Risk evaluation

For the purpose of risk evaluation, three phases may be distinguished in aviation insurance: (1) the normal hazards encountered by aircraft; (2) situations in which potential dangers have become imminent and continue to present mounting threats to the aircraft; (3) the phase where damage-causing factors and the consequences thereof are either removed by natural causes or brought under control. Quite a number of points need to be made in this context.

The nature of air traffic is such that a catastrophe may occur within a matter of seconds: a sudden shift in the risk factor may be occasioned

4. Cf. Margo (note 1, *supra*), at p. 2
5. Margo (note 1, *supra*), at p. 43.

by a highly safe situation changing suddenly into a very dangerous one. Serious consequences may result from a slight disturbance or incident. It is more difficult to lend effective assistance to passengers, crew and aircraft than in situations involving other means of transport.

In gas and hot air balloons, the danger of fire is never absent due to the presence of inflammable gases. Balloons, however, do not play a significant role in aviation.

Total loss, which in other areas of transport occurs only sporadically, is quite common in aviation accidents. Aircraft therefore carry a special risk.

The circumstances in which flights are carried out must also be taken into account. Flying by night, over mountains, etc. is no longer considered a special hazard nowadays, although landings at very high altitude (*e.g.* at Lima airport) or dangerous fields (for instance Anchorage with its ill-famed fog) are taken into account.

A factor of the utmost importance in any risk evaluation exercise is the qualification of the aircraft commander. The supervision of aircraft personnel is entrusted to government authorities who issue certificates of competency. International conventions and domestic legislation alike contain a large number of technical rules and traffic regulations all aimed at improving safety.

Scheduled airlines on the whole find it easier to secure coverage, as they are widely known and recognised as being reputable; besides, their business operations are well known. In charter business, companies are usually smaller and their capital holdings somewhat less.

Aircraft factories take out special policies against the risks involved in test and delivery flights. Similarly, aircraft carrying out aerial surveys, crop spraying or dusting and rescue operations involving low-flying over unfamiliar territory carry more risks and consequently higher premiums.

The greatest risks are associated with military aviation. Military aviators are required to fly in circumstances where concern for safety plays a secondary role.

Most accidents occur during take-off and landing: in the air, risks are not nearly as great. From aviation statistics it is apparent that in most accidents the pilots are to blame. Yet, errors committed by the ground services such as negligent personnel and insufficiently equipped airports have been a contributory factor in a number of cases.

4. Types of insurance

Aviation insurance may conveniently be divided into three categories:
1. insurance of the equipment, *i.e.* the hull of the aircraft;
2. insurance of the carrier's liability; and
3. insurance of flying personnel.

In aviation insurance the general principles of insurance law are largely applicable. This is not altogether surprising in view of the many similarities between aviation hull insurance and marine hull insurance. Aviation liability insurance has much in common with automobile liability insurance, while cargo and personal accident insurance in aviation show a close affinity to marine cargo and accident insurance.[6] Nonetheless, it was considered appropriate or even necessary to have some special rules for aviation insurance, as we shall see *infra*, when dealing with the insurance policies.

The aviation insurer caters for all three types of insurance described above; his principal activities, however, are concerned with aircraft hull insurance and liability insurance. With personal accident insurance his involvement is on a more reduced scale. Life insurance connected with aviation is still being taken care of by the life insurance companies.

We shall now deal first with aviation hull insurance and its rules as commonly laid down in that most important document, the insurance policy.

4.1. AVIATION HULL INSURANCE

Risks affecting aviation hull insurance may be divided into (1) flight risk, (2) taxiing risk and (3) ground risk. In the insurance policies, the term 'in flight' is defined in conformity with Article 1, para. 2, of the 1952 Rome Convention, namely as the period in time from the moment when power is applied for the purpose of actual take-off until the moment when the landing run ends. The taxiing risk does not constitute a separate item for insurance purposes: it is usually included under in-flight risk.

The following contingencies come under the heading ground risk: (1) loss or damage caused by collision or malevolence; (2) damage caused by fire, self-ignition or explosion; (3) damage resulting from larceny, theft or attempts thereat. In the ground risk sector, insurers are sooner prepared to cover all risks than in the flight risks sector. At present, all-risks coverage is customary in ground risk insurance policies. Note, however, that ground risk cover is only applicable until the moment the engines are started. Use of the propulsion units necessitates the usual complete cover and premium.

Aviation insurers usually limit their liability to the most common form of damage, *i.e.* damage resulting from collision. The meaning of the term 'collision' is given a very broad interpretation in the policies: any sort of physical contact with an external object comes within

---

6. As far as liability for damage by cargo is concerned next to standard policies and clauses, drawn up by, *e.g.* Lloyd's, for ordinary aviation insurance, the shipper of the cargo can obtain financial protection for damage caused by his cargo to the carrier or a third party through three types of insurance policies: the general liability policy (public liability policy), the product liability policy and the pollution liability policy. These policies also exist in marine insurance.

range of this word, and even damage caused by fire or ice formation may be included. Loss or damage caused by fire is sometimes brought under the heading of flight risks. In general, it is required for an 'incidence' or 'occurrence' to have taken place.

The duration of the validity naturally forms an integral part of all policies, and reference may be made here to the provisions of the 1952 Rome Convention, which state that when the validity expires while the aircraft is in flight, insurance continues to be valid until the next point of landing. Insurance coverage may also be taken out for the duration of a single flight. Duration currently averages twelve months.

In most countries the insurer is not liable in law for damage resulting from inherent vice or defect, latent or apparent, of the aircraft, unless otherwise agreed. Damage is taken to mean in this context any damage arising from the aircraft itself and its components. Note, however, the one-recorded-incident theory: wear and tear due to ingestion of dust and sand is not covered but damage caused by ingestion of a single large stone is. Insurance policy terms usually compel the insured to ensure that the aircraft is completely airworthy before each flight.

Aviation supervision and control is regulated by the Chicago Convention, and every aircraft must possess a certificate of airworthiness certifying that the aircraft fulfils the safety requirements in force. Such a certificate does not prove that the aircraft is airworthy at the start of each flight. In the event of a dispute the possession of a certificate may be regarded by the courts as evidence in favour of the insured, but when, for instance, the maximum weight stipulated in the certificate is exceeded, the aircraft will not be considered as airworthy, irrespective of the presence of the certificate.

The certificate of airworthiness does not extend to defects the insured cannot be aware of, like latent defects or faulty construction: most policies contain a clause to the effect that broken-down machinery or defective engines will not be refunded, but that the damage resulting from it will. A similar clause may be written into the policy in respect of faulty construction. As for wear, tear and depreciation, these are explicitly excluded in the policies, not being unforeseeable contigencies.

In some countries loss or damage resulting from the insured's own fault have been excluded from the insurer's liability; in others he may be held liable. Insurance against wilful misconduct or gross negligence is unlawful in some countries. According to a few authors, the absence of the element of uncertainty rules out such an insurance.

Different standards are being applied in cases of wilful misconduct or gross negligence on the part of the insured's agents or employees. Most policies include liability in such cases for the flying risk, but exclude it for the period when the aircraft is not airborne. In general, insurers do not compensate for loss or damage resulting from (1) starting the aircraft's engines without first making precautionary checks and procedures; (2) revving up the engines in the hangar;

(3) leaving the aircraft unattended while in the open; (4) leaving the aircraft outside the hangar insufficiently guarded and secured, unless such omission is due to *force majeure*. Lately, the wilful misconduct theory has been slightly modified: examples (1) and (2) would probably be paid by the insurer.

Most policies exclude liability for experimental flights, aerobatics and other unusual activities such as record attempts, racing, etc. It is possible to find coverage for experimental flights by special agreement.

The latest addition to the long list of exclusion clauses was occasioned by the Israeli raid on Beirut airport in 1968: it is the 'War, Hijacking and Other Perils Exclusion' clause. This clause was first introduced in the London insurance market and later went on to form part of every hull and liability insurance policy: the 'AVN.48B clause'.[7] However, through the 'AVN.52B' clause cover for the liability of the airline may be 'written back' into the policy. Cover for war, hijacking, etc. damage to the hull is usually brought under a separate policy, although this too may be written back by clause 'AVN.51' which, however, gives only a reduced cover.

One final point worth making here is that in matters involving exclusion clauses it is up to the insurer to demonstrate that a causal relation between the injury or death and the activity proscribed by the clause did exist. This rule has been upheld several times in court cases in USA.[8]

When concluding a policy agreement parties may agree on the value in terms of money of the object to be insured. For a new aircraft the value usually equals the manufacturer's price, for older aircraft the replacement value is the criterion. Nowadays a third value is often selected, namely the value of the aircraft to the lessor, the banks. This value bears sometimes no relationship with the actual market value due to currency exchange fluctuations (for instance: financing in Japanese yen which subsequently rose sharply in value against the US dollar). In the absence of any agreement in the policy the market value at the date of the loss is commonly taken as a standard, or failing that, the real value.

There are two arguments in favour of letting the insured bear part of the risk himself: (1) it saves the insurers having to bother about all sorts of small claims often more costly to settle than the compensation involved; and (2) it saves the insured premium money.

The premium may be calculated in two different ways:

(1) as a fixed sum or a percentage of the total value, which is customary in airline insurance; or

(2) from case to case, which may be used in short-term cover transactions.

---

7. Margo (note 1, *supra*), at pp. 222 *et seq.* The clause referred to is reproduced in the Appendix to Margo's book on p. 417.
8. See M.R. Callagher and A.L. Stephens, 'Recent Developments in Aviation Case Law' [1978] JALC 231–260, at 254-257.

In aircraft hull insurance the second procedure is customary: it is very difficult to calculate the amount of the premium on the basis of fixed standards because variable factors such as the pilot's competence, the availability of the ground facilities, the choice of the route, etc., play such an important role. The premium is usually calculated on an annual basis, but in special cases like test flights the hourly basis is customary.

The insured is obliged to notify the insurer immediately in the event of loss or damage. Most policies also include an obligation for the insured to undertake action to avoid or diminish any loss or damage.

The insurers are not obliged to pay until such time as the extent of the damage has been established to their satisfaction by experts.

4.2. CARRIER'S LIABILITY INSURANCE

The carrier's liability insurance covers not only the liability of the carrier for passengers, luggage and cargo, but also third party liability. In most policies covering third party liability two limits are inserted, one for liability resulting from death or bodily injury, the other for liability resulting from loss or damage to property. Most policies nowadays contain a fixed limit for each and every occurrence. Rating is sometimes done by charging a flat rate, while in other cases an amount per Revenue Passenger Kilometer is charged.

Neither the Warsaw Convention nor the Hague Protocol contains any rules on insurance binding upon the carrier; The Guatemala Protocol does not mention any obligation either for the carrier, but it does provide for a system of supplementary compensation operating under certain circumstances. Article XIV of the Guatemala Protocol declares that:

'No provision contained in this Convention shall prevent a State from establishing and operating within its territory a system to supplement the compensation payable to claimants under the Convention in respect of death, or personal injury, of passengers. Such a system shall fulfil the following conditions:

a) it shall not in any circumstances impose upon the carrier, his servants or agents, any liability in addition to that provided under this Convention;

b) it shall not impose upon the carrier any financial or administrative burden other than collecting in that State contributions from passengers if required so to do;

c) it shall not give rise to any discrimination between carriers with regard to the passengers concerned and the benefits available to the said passenger under the system shall be extended to them regardless of the carrier whose services they have used;

d) if a passenger has contributed to the system, any person suffering damage as a consequence of death or personal injury of such passenger shall be entitled to the benefits of the system'.

With his liability under the Warsaw Convention in mind the carrier used to arrange for automatic and collective personal accident coverage for passengers. On the basis of such a policy passengers were automatically compensated for the damage they had suffered as a result of the accident up to the maximum amount enunciated in the policy, provided that the beneficiaries renounced all claims they might have against the carrier, who is the insured party.[9] The amounts mentioned in the policies used to equal the Warsaw Convention limits, but recent policies carried much higher insured amounts. The following instance may be quoted here to illustrate the advantages of automatic personal accident insurance.

An American singer who was making a tour of Europe died in an air crash while being a passenger on a scheduled flight in one of the Scandinavian countries. The dependants wished at first to claim an enormous amount of compensation in an American court but changed their mind when they found that an American court had no jurisdiction in this case according to the Warsaw Convention. Judging legal proceedings in Europe too cumbersome, they finally declared themselves satisfied with the compensation offered by the carrier on the basis of the automatic personal accident policy, which was an amount even lower than the Warsaw maximum.[10]

At present, automatic personal accident insurance is no longer customary due to its high costs. Exceptions occur, however, in certain areas of the world and for airline crews in certain countries. In general the carrier is now relying completely on his ordinary liability insurance.

The question of who can qualify as an heir/claimant under the policy is to be resolved in accordance with domestic law.

Our review of the matter shows that in spite of a multitude of exclusion clauses the injured passenger may still find adequate compensation deriving from his carrier's liability, but for those preferring a more direct and simple way of obtaining compensation there is always the option of taking out a personal accident insurance policy privately and individually for each flight.

4.3. FLYING PERSONNEL INSURANCE

For their flying personnel airline companies usually take out a collective personal accident policy.

---

9. Margo (note 1, *supra*), at pp. 218–219. For an illustration of this type of policy see *Caisse Régionale de Sécurité Sociale du Sud-Est* v. *Air France*, Cour d' Appel d'Aix-en-Provence (France), March 13, 1959; [1959] RGA 194 (in English: [1959] USAvR 427). See also J.G. Sauveplanne, 'Les rapports entre responsabilité et assurance en droit aérien international', *Contributions Neérlandaises au VI-ème Congrès international de Droit Comparé* (Hamburg, 1962), 1963, pp. 121-132.
10. See for this 'Grace Moore case' also A.A. van wijk, *Aircraft Accidents Enquiry in the Netherlands* (thesis Amsterdam, 1974), at p. 102 in note 2, where different aspects of this well-known tragic accident are discussed.

The policies taken out for the benefit of pilots are accident insurance policies. When the insured persons disappear this fact may constitute a presumption of death in relation to an accident covered by the policy.

Amongst the risks usually excluded by the insurers are accidents resulting from drunkenness, the use of narcotics, or the mental or physical conditions of the insured.

5. Hijacking

Aircraft hijacking has had a strong impact on aviation insurance, as well as on other aspects connected with aviation. The risks involved can no longer be assessed realistically. Hijacking has faced aviation insurers with tremendous problems. In a catastrophe due to weather conditions, a defective aircraft, or an error made by the pilot, the risk may be assessed with a reasonable degree of accuracy, but hijacking is such a relatively new phenomenon that insurers have not really had enough time and experience to be able to predict its probable frequency. Conversely, hijacking is not a major problem for the life insurance companies as it concerns relatively few people so that the amount to be paid out in compensation would be negligible. As an illustration of the impact of hijacking on matters of aviation insurance the following case is worth noting.

After hijacking by two men working for the Popular Front for the Liberation of Palestine a Boeing 747 aircraft belonging to Pan American World Airways was ordered to fly via Beirut to Cairo where it was blown up and destroyed. Pan American, the plaintiff in court, carried all-risk policies written by private insurers and war-risk policies written by the US Government. All the insurers denied liability.

It was ruled in court that the all-risk insurers, rather than the war-risk insurers, were liable to pay for loss of the aircraft. The court found that under New York law, the loss of the plane was not due to or resulting from insurrection, rebellion, civil war, a taking by a military or usurped power, war or warlike operations, riot or civil commotion as those terms were used in the exclusions contained in the all-risk insurance policies. It was also recalled that under New York law ambiguity in a term of exclusion will be resolved in the manner least favourable to the insurer. All-risk insurers must demonstrate that an interpretation favouring them is the only reasonable reading of at least one of the relevant terms of exclusion. The judgment was upheld in the US Court of Appeals.[11]

11. *Pan American World Airways* v. *Aetna Casualty and Surety Co. et al.*, US District Court, Southern District of New York, September 17, 1973; *Avi*, Vol. 12, p. 18,069. Affirmed: US Court of Appeals, October 15, 1974; *Avi*, Vol. 13, p. 17,340. Also reported in Schoner's case law digest, *Air Law*, vol. I (1976), pp. 194-196. See also on this case M.J. Corrigan, 'Hijacking Coverage', *Air Law*, vol. I (1976), pp. 35-39. Note that apart from the PanAm airplane another three aircraft were hijacked and diverted to the Middle East, while an attempt at a fifth hijacking failed. All these events happened in September 1970. Currently, war policies are underwritten in the open market without government backing. The socalled 50/50 clause solves possible disputes between the underwriters of the war policy and those of the risk policy: the damages are shared equally.

The Israeli raid on Beirut airport in 1968 has already been mentioned earlier in connection with the introduction of the AVN.48B exclusion clause which was a sequel to it; various instances of hijacking took place in the following years. These events caused a considerable increase in the insurance premium rates, which used to be based on a small percentage of the value of the aircraft. The increase was all the more considerable because war-risk and associated perils had to be covered by a special policy by that time.

An illustration of the sums at stake: for a Boeing 747 comprehensive insurance (hull, liability to passengers, third part liability and personal accident insurance for the crew) can easily top US$1,000 million. Incidentally, the value of the PanAm aircraft blown up at Cairo was about US$24 million at the time.[12] Today's average value of a large plane is about US$150 million.

6. Concluding note

The way aviation insurance developed is closely connected with the evolution in aviation technology. It is a notable fact that, as technology progresses, insurance premiums are reduced and the number of clauses excluding the insurer's liability decreases. Initially, insurance pools completely dominated the market, but as people became more familiar with the risks involved in aviation their predominance began to wane. In the area of personal accident insurance coverage they are being outflanked by the traditional accident insurance companies. Pools nowadays are used mainly for reinsurance.

Another point worth exploring is how new inventions in aviation affect the insurance market. They would probably cause a temporary increase in premiums, but when they are finally accepted and found to be safe premiums will come down. The legal basis for insurance, however, will not be affected. However, accident statistics seem to indicate that nowadays progress in aviation safety is becoming marginal. Besides, the increase in accident costs (both as regards the damage to the hull and liability) clearly outweighs this progress. Mention should also be made of the ever-increasing number of flight movements worldwide. It is therefore forecasted that the costs for the insurances companies will sharply rise in the future and that room for premium reductions will be limited.

It is to be noted that all attempts to codify the whole subject matter on an international level have failed so far, even though ICAO and the former CITEJA have made laudable efforts in that direction.[13]

---

12. Margo (note 1, *supra*), at p. 237 in note 97. See also E. Tobi. 'The insurer's point of view', *Air Law*, vol. XI (1986), pp. 84-93.

13. See about the earlier attempts and discussions M. de Juglart, *Traité élémentaire de droit aérien* (1952), paras. 335 *et seq.*

To conclude this chapter, let us express the hope that aviation insurance can develop freely and technological development settles down to a stable level. As long as aviation remains subject to violent fluctuations the problem of creating an adequate international standardisation of insurance rules will not be an easy one to solve.[14]

14. For literature on aviation insurance see S.Z. Ipekoglu, *Les assurances aériennes et les conventions internationales* (thesis Fribourg, Switzerland, 1949); E.A. Kubli. *Luftfahrtversicherung, unter besonderer Berücksichtigung des Luftpools* (thesis Zürich, 1952); Adel Salah El Din, *Aviation Insurance Practice, Law and Reinsurance*, circa 1971 (year of publication not indicated); H. Matouk, *Les assurances aériennes* (1971); and the various references by Margo (note 1, *supra*).

CHAPTER VIII

Rights in Aircraft

1. Precautionary attachment of aircraft

Although its importance is perhaps not evident at first glance, the Convention for the Unification of Certain Rules Relating to the Precautionary Attachment of Aircraft, signed at Rome on May 29,1933,[1] plays a useful and preventive role in safeguarding aircraft from precautionary attachment. In essence, the Convention enumerates the categories of aircraft not liable to attachment, besides indicating the way in which such action may be prevented.

Article 3 provides that the following categories of aircraft are exempt:

'a. aircraft exclusively appropriated to a state service, including the postal service, but excluding commercial service;
b. aircraft actually in service on a regular line of public transport, together with the indispensable reserve aircraft;
c. every other aircraft appropriated to the carriage of persons or goods for reward, where such aircraft is ready to start on such carriage, unless the arrest is in respect of a contract debt incurred for the purposes of the journey which the aircraft is about to make, or of a claim which has arisen in the course of the journey'.

In Article 4, the Convention points out the way in which attachment may be prevented. This may be done by pledging an adequate guarantee. A guarantee will be considered to be adequate if it covers the amount of the debt and costs and is assigned exclusively to the payment of the creditor, or if it covers the value of the aircraft in the event that this is less than the amount of the debt and costs.

The Convention has been ratified or adhered to by 22 states. This number does not include the United Kingdom or the United States.

The *Kozubski* case provides one of the rare instances where the Convention has been applied.[2] Kozubski was forced to liquidate her English air transport company in 1961. In order to continue her activities on the Continent she entered into an agreement with Aero-Transport, an international carrier based in Austria and in possession

---

1. Convention for the Unification of Certain Rules Relating to Precautionary Attachment of Aircraft, Rome, May 29, 1933 (also known as the Convention on Precautionary Arrest of Aircraft). See about this Convention Nicolas M. Matte, *Treatise on Air-Aeronautical Law*, (1981), pp. 497-501. This Convention should not be confused with the 1933 Rome Convention relating to Damage to Third Parties on the Surface which was signed also on May 29, 1933 (see Chap. VI of this book, *supra*).
2. *Marian Kozuba Kozubski* v. *Aero-Transport*, Court of Haarlem (The Netherlands), March 25, 1964 and July 8, 1964 (unpublished)

of all the documents required for a charter company. By 1964 Kozubski was indebted to Aero-Transport to the sum of 1,920,783.37 Austrian shillings. On February 17, Aero-Transport requested and obtained permission from the court at Haarlem (The Netherlands) to put a precautionary attachment on a Lockheed Constellation stationed at Schiphol airport and belonging to Kozubski. Kozubski was notified of the precautionary attachment and summoned to appear before the Haarlem Court on April 7, 1964. She reacted by requesting the court to lift the measure with immediate effect, or, alternatively, to delay its execution for a short period of time. Moreover, she applied for an immediate decision on a counterclaim she lodged against Aero-Transport, alleging that Aero-Transport owed her an amount larger than she was owing Aero-Transport. The latter claim was dealt with by the Haarlem Court in summary proceedings on March 25, 1964, and Kozubski's claim was rejected for lack of proof. On July 8, 1964, the court decided at the request of the claimant that Aero-Transport was to be allowed to sell the Lockheed Constellation at any time after August 31, 1964. The money was to be deposited with a specially designated notary until such time as the financial claims would be finally settled by the court.

2. International recognition of rights in aircraft

2.1. THE GENEVA CONVENTION

2.1.1. The history of the Geneva Convention

The issue of international recognition of rights in aircraft was one of the subjects examined during the International Conference on Private Air Law, held in 1925. It was the first time consideration was given to this problem on an international level. A CITEJA Commission subsequently formulated two drafts which were accepted at the sixth plenary session of the CITEJA in 1931,[3] but an international convention to settle the matter never materialised at that stage.

The International Civil Aviation Conference held at Chicago in 1944 reopened the discussions on the basis of the two earlier texts, and a final consolidated draft was presented to the second ICAO Assembly, meeting in Geneva in the month of June 1948. On June 18, the draft convention was approved, though with a few reservations. The Convention has since been ratified or adhered to by 53 states; it entered into force on September 17, 1953.[4] Chile and Mexico both made reservations. but Chile later withdrew hers. The substance of the reservations will be considered later in this chapter.

---

3. See B. Hofstetter, *L'hypothèque aérienne* (thesis Lausanne, 1950), pp. 211 *et seq.*
4. Convention on the International Recognition of Rights in Aircraft, Geneva, June 1, 1948; hereinafter cited as the Geneva Convention. See for present status Shawcross and Beaumont, *Air Law* (1977), Vol. 2 (1981), pp. A-31 to A-32.

2.1.2. The need for a Convention

Following the end of the Second World War, the need for a Convention on mortgage of aircraft became urgent due to pressure from several quarters aimed at facilitating the export of aircraft to developing countries while at the same time safeguarding the position of the seller by means of some form of security.[5] The reason why this Convention had a better chance of securing adoption than the previous drafts may well be attributed to the drastic changes in the social, economic and political environment prevailing at the time. Some of the new elements in the post-War situation may be recalled here: (1) the valuable functions performed by aircraft had become more widely appreciated, and their value as a security increased accordingly; (2) aviation safety had improved considerably; (3) insurance policies reducing the risks of aviation had been perfected; (4) special rules governing the ownership of aircraft were more readily accepted.

2.1.3. The special characteristics of the Convention

During the preliminary discussions an approach to the problems was made which contrasted sharply with the methods applied to earlier air law conventions. In trying to achieve a certain degree of unification in what were basically rules of private international law, experts had to contend with the salient points of difference between continental and Anglo-Saxon law. Although American delegates had always been present at the preparatory sessions of earlier international conventions, it was not until transatlantic travelling had become an everyday occurrence that they began to exert considerable influence. Elements of both legal systems were very much in evidence during the preparatory sessions of the Geneva Convention.

It is perhaps appropriate to recall at this point the main tenets of the two systems. The cornerstone of continental law is written law, *i.e.* legal rules promulgated in the form of statutes, often codified. Whenever a ruling is given by a judge in a particular case, he does not always keep strictly to the letter of the law, but he may also rely on his own interpretation of it. Anglo-Saxon law also includes written law, the so-called statutory law, which, like the common law, is considered to be one of the principal sources of law, but not ranking on quite the same level. The common law may be described as law moulded or created by the judges out of the original customary rules of England. Its principles are embodied in case law, where judicial precedent is applied wherever possible. Another striking point of difference lies in the fact that under continental law it is standard practice for judges to explore the historical background of a statute and the intentions of its authors. They may also choose to rely on literary sources like the opinions of experts or treatises of scholars. Under Anglo-Saxon law the substance of a dispute is not addressed in such a more or less detached manner on the basis of the relevant legal

5. Cf. Hofstetter (note 3, *supra*), at pp. 218 *et seq.* Matte (note 1, *supra*), pp. 543-546.

rules: legal practice here is overwhelmingly relying on definitions which are supposed to cover as many cases and contingencies as possible, designed to suit individual contracts, pieces of legislation and other legal documentation.

For those brought up in the traditions of Roman law, the continental system seems to be preferable. Conversely, the Anglo-Saxons will probably regard their system as superior. It is not just the foundation and the basic principles, but also the techniques employed to solve the problems that are so very different under the two systems.[6] In the future, a balance between the two will have to be struck. In England there has been a tendency towards accommodating the continental system. By Act of Parliament the Law Reform Contributory Negligence Act was introduced in 1945, which broke away from the common law by requiring that the fault of the plaintiff which had contributed to the damage must be taken into account as well in court cases and settlements. This is an encouraging sign because it shows that uniformity in matters of private international law is not altogether unattainable.

As pointed out earlier, it is so not much the basic thinking on fundamentals which is divergent in the two systems as the very different techniques employed by them. As to the future course to follow, I am inclined to share Riese's opinion that the continental methods ought to be retained as a basis for drafting treaties and conventions. Such a procedure would allow countries embracing the Anglo-Saxon system to enact more detailed regulations by domestic legislation. The reverse procedure would be pointless, because conventions based on Anglo-Saxon principles cannot easily be brought in line with the domestic law of continental states.[7]

In the days of the Warsaw Convention efforts had always been concentrated on finding formulas to cover exhaustively as many subjects and contingencies as possible. Now, selected rules were put forward designed to obtain practical solutions in conflict situations: in other words, the Geneva Convention was intended to deal with conflicts of law only. Accordingly, what we find here is an impressive enumeration of legal rights, including several typically Anglo-Saxon rights such as the 'rights to acquire aircraft by purchase coupled with possession of the aircraft' (Art. I(b)), or the 'rights to possession of aircraft under leases of six months or more' (Art. I(c)). Anglo-Saxon law, unlike continental law, always tends to rely on a multitude of definitions, and this approach is unmistakably reflected in the Geneva Convention.

As pointed out just now, the Geneva Convention merely provides rules relating to or designed to avoid conflicts of law. The underlying objective of its authors being to achieve ratification in the shortest possible term, it probably was the best result attainable in the circumstances.

6. See on this subject E. Jenks, *The Book of English Law* (6th rev. ed., 1967).
7. See O. Riese, *Luftrecht* (1949), pp. 46 *et seq.*

2.1.4. The scope of the Convention

'The provisions of this Convention shall in each Contracting State apply to all aircraft registered as to nationality in another Contracting State.' This rule, formulated in Article XI, implies that states are not required to apply the Convention to aircraft registered in their own territory. Nonetheless several exceptions have been provided for:

a. Article II: 'All recordings relating to a given aircraft must appear in the same record' (this requirement is aimed at preventing double registration);
b. Article III: 'The address of the authority responsible for maintaining the record must be shown on every aircraft's certificate of registration as to nationality' (this stipulation is designed to ensure that the record entry can be traced by the public);
c. Article IV, in conjunction with Article XI, paragraph 2(b) relative to compensation due for salvage of the aircraft or for extraordinary expenses indispensable for the preservation of the aircraft; these are awarded unless the salvage or preservation operations have been terminated within the state's own territory;
d. Article IX, stating that 'Except in the case of a sale in execution in conformity with the provisions of Article VII, no transfer of an aircraft from the nationality register or the record of a Contracting State to that of another State shall be made, unless all holders of recorded rights have been satisfied or consent to the transfer';
e. Article XII, stipulating that 'Nothing in this Convention shall prejudice the right of any Contracting State to enforce against an aircraft its national laws relating to immigration, customs or air navigation'.

Aircraft used in military, customs or police services are excluded from the scope of the Convention, according to Article XIII.[8]

2.1.5. The definition of aircraft

From the statements made by the French and British delegates during the preparatory stages of the Convention it is evident that the authors intended to create means of financial support for the air carrier in the form of real security. Their idea was to create safeguards for the rights in aircraft intended to participate in *international air traffic*. Cable balloons, free balloons and gliders do not come under this category and the category of aircraft intended to be covered by the Geneva Convention is thus confined to aircraft meant to be used in international air transport.

8. Cf. *supra* Chap. II, section 11.2 of this book.

2.1.6. The basic principles underlying the Convention

The main principle is the protection of the interests of the creditors. The creditor would normally be the aircraft industry which, thanks to the Convention, has better sales opportunities, while the carrier benefits by being able to purchase on easier terms, having to put up less capital himself.

According to Wilberforce,[9] three subsidiary motives must not be left out of account either: (1) the protection of third parties dealing in or with aircraft; (2) the definition and protection of priority rights; (3) facilitating the transfer of aircraft from one nationality to another. I do not feel inclined to share Wilberforce's point of view, for the reason that all these arguments derive from the one supreme motive, which is the protection of the creditors. To demonstrate the point I would like to refer to Article I(d) of the Convention reading as follows: 'mortgages, hypotheques and similar rights in aircraft which are contractually created as security for payment of an indebtedness...'.

Under the Convention, contracting states undertake to recognise the following rights:

- a. 'rights of property in aircraft'; although the right of property is a universally recognised right, the provision is not without relevance in connection with the registration of aircraft;
- b. 'rights to acquire aircraft by purchase coupled with possession of the aircraft'; this covers not only options, but also hire-purchase and conditional sale agreements, both being a form of real security. They are common practice in the United States;
- c. 'rights to possession of aircraft under leases of six months or more'; such rights have all the characteristics of an equipment trust whereby one party (the lessor) rents out to another party (the lessee) an aircraft purchased with money borrowed from third parties, it being understood that the lessee will acquire the ownership by paying the price of the aircraft. This formula reflects American practice, like the previous one.
- d. 'Mortgages, hypotheques and similar rights in aircraft which are contractually created as security for payment of an indebtedness ...'. Here, the exact meaning of the term 'mortgage' must be explored. Article 1 of the CITEJA draft for a Convention on Mortgages, Other Real Securities and Aerial Privileges[10] offered the following definition: 'In the meaning of the present Convention, by aerial mortgage is understood a real security, whatever may be its name and origin, which is inscribed on the register for the publicity of rights and which assigns the aircraft to the payment of a debt the amount of which is equally inscribed thereon.'

---

9. R.O. Wilberforce, 'The International Recognition of Rights in Aircraft' [1948] *The International Law Quarterly*, 421–458, at 424.
10. This Draft Convention was adopted at the Sixth Session of CITEJA (Paris, October 1931); see [1933] JAL 403–407.

Article I further stipulates that the rights must:
a. be constituted in accordance with the law of the contracting state in which the aircraft is registered as to nationality at the time of their constitution; and
b. be regularly recorded in a public record of the contracting state in which the aircraft is registered as to nationality.

From the preparatory work of the Convention it is clear that the rights must comply with the substantive requirements of national law. These relate to the substance of the agreement between the parties, whereas formal requirements are concerned with registration procedure.

2.1.7. The record

There is no obligation for states to keep a record, but in actual practice states without such a record will not be able to benefit from the Convention. During the preparatory stages it had been suggested that states failing to keep a record would be obliged to recognise rights originating and recorded in other states, but would receive nothing in return.

The Convention does not provide detailed rules concerning the record: Article II merely stipulates that:
'1. All recordings relative to a given aircraft must appear in the same record.
2. Except as otherwise provided in this Convention, the effects of the recording of any right mentioned in Article I, para. (1), with regard to third parties shall be determined according to the law of the Contracting State where it is recorded.
3. A Contracting State may prohibit the recording of any right which cannot validly be constituted according to its national law'.

Unlike maritime law, where there is a central register separate from the national registers, air law only recognises national records.

In Article II, para. 3, particular attention should be paid to the word 'may', as this may have the effect of nullifying the preceding provisions. By virtue of this formula the Convention will only have effect provided national law has been complied with; for example, in countries where the equipment trust is not known, it may be inapplicable. Opposition to this rule initially came from IATA, which felt that it introduced a new element.[11] The Convention contains no indication at all as to the evidence value of the record, leaving yet another issue to be decided by national law.

It may be pointed out in this context that the English text of the Convention makes a distinction between the terms 'register' and 'record'. The *register* designates the aircraft nationality register and has

---

11. See Minutes and Documents of the ICAO Legal Committee, 2nd Assembly, ICAO Doc. 5722 at pp. 180 *et seq.*

a public law character, whereas the *record* has a private law nature. The equally authentic Spanish and French texts make a less clear distinction. The legislative provisions in the various states are widely divergent on the subject of who may register an aircraft. In some states registration is accepted provided the owner is a resident. Other states allow registration by foreigners only on certain conditions.

2.1.8. The procedure for creating mortgages

The procedure for creating mortgages is left to the national law of the state where the aircraft is registered at the time of their creation, on the ground that 'registration equals nationality equals national law'. From the preparatory discussions it might be inferred that the drafters intended no deviation from this rule except for considerations of reasonableness or effectiveness. Several authors contend, however, that the municipal law of a state includes rules of private international law as well, which may include provisions making the law of another state applicable. Hofstetter,[12] on the contrary, rules out any such possibility. My feeling is that the majority view deserves support.

The manner in which rights in aircraft are constituted varies from country to country. In some instances they are established by agreement between the parties, *e.g.* in the United States; in others they are created through registration, as is the case in the Netherlands. The Convention presupposes that the rights are established by contract, irrespective of the recording.

When a mortgage is constituted by agreement, the holder of the rights will have to prove that the requirements of the national law have been complied with. In the case of creation through registration such proof is obviously dispensable as the state would not permit rights to be established in contravention of its own laws.

The notion of creating rights in aircraft does not have the same interpretation everywhere. It would have been preferable to include some rules on the subject in the Convention, as was unsuccessfully attempted by the ILA.[13]

No solution has been provided in the Geneva Convention for situations in which mortgage rights or liens attaching to aircraft have not been registered at the time they were created. During the preparatory discussions Cooper mentioned by way of an illustration the case of an aircraft registered in the United States.[14] According to American law a non-registered mortgage or lien is perfectly valid. What would happen if the aircraft were bought by, *e.g.* a French national and registered in France without the Frenchman having any idea of the existence of a non-registered but valid mortgage on his aircraft?

12. Hofstetter (note 3, *supra*), at pp. 227 *et seq.*
13. R.O. Wilberforce, 'Report on Recognition of Rights in Aircraft', Report of the 44th Conference of the International Law Association (Copenhagen, 1950), pp. 233-254.
14. See ICAO Doc. 5722 (note 11, *supra*), at p. 178.

Wilberforce may argue that the existence of non-registered rights is highly improbable and unlikely, but the example just quoted does seem to indicate that this kind of difficulty is not at all imaginary.[15]

To conclude this section it must be mentioned that aircraft are regarded as movables; Ripert, however, prefers treating them as immovable property in a legal sense, to counterbalance the mobility of the aircraft itself.[16]

2.1.9. Priority claims

Contrary to the 1967 Convention on ship's mortgages,[17] the Geneva Convention recognises only two priority claims, described in Article IV as:

a. claims in respect of compensation due for salvaging the aircraft, and

b. claims in respect of extraordinary expenses indispensable for the preservation of the aircraft.

Such rights, and the priority they take, have to be respected by contracting states only if the law of the state where the salvage or preservation operations took place recognises them as such, in other words, their own forum must recognise them as priority claims. The wording here was chosen so as to interfere as little as possible with the national laws, on which the creation and substance of the claims remain dependent. It should be borne in mind that the claims referred to above are rights *in rem* (property rights) unlike the other rights mentioned in the Convention.

Salvage, in terms of the Convention, is not restricted to salvage at sea, although the American delegation would have favoured such a restriction. It argued that the provision was introduced in an analogy with maritime law: applying salvage law to land-based situations would create an element of uncertainty in the Convention, which would have repercussions on national legislations and give rise to a great variety of claims under the pretext of the Convention.[18] On the whole this priority claim faced objections mainly from states with great land masses.[19]

As mentioned above, the law applicable to the priority claims is the *lex rei sitae, i.e.* the law of the place where the salvaging and preserving operations occurred. There is some doubt as to the applicable law in cases

---

15. Wilberforce (note 9, *supra*), at p. 429.
16. See G. Ripert, 'Hypothèque et transfert de la propriété de l'aéronef', RJIdeLA (1922), pp. 157-162.
17. International Convention for the Unification of Certain Rules Relating to Maritime Liens and Mortgages, Brussels, May 27, 1967; Art. 4 of this Convention mentions five priority claims.
18. ICAO Doc. 5722 (note 11, *supra*), pp. 136 *et seq.*
19. ICAO Doc. 5722 (note 11, *supra*), p. 133.

where the operations were carried out at sea; the general opinion seems to be that in such cases the law of the 'port of refuge' should be applied.[20]

According to Article IV, para. 4(a) and (b), prerequisites for the exercise of the priority are (a) that the claim must have been noted on the record within three months of the date of the termination of the operations, and (b) that within that period the claim has been settled out of court, or an action in court to enforce it has been commenced. In the latter case, the grounds for interruption or suspension of the three months' period will be determined by the law of the forum.

Hofstetter has pointed out the difficulties that may arise in case of failure to register a priority claim for salvage; he takes as an example an American aircraft that is salvaged in Switzerland and later returned to America, and is then sold. When the aircraft lands again in Switzerland it may be seized, even though the purchaser was unaware of the existence of a lien.[21]

What precisely is to be understood by the expression 'extraordinary expenses indispensable for the preservation of the aircraft'? During the discussions on this Article it was agreed that preservation would mean keeping the aircraft in the condition in which it was found. The expenditure may include the costs of transport to a safer place, or the costs of guarding the aircraft, but not the costs of repairs to put the aircraft in a better condition than it had been before the accident. In addition, the expenditure must be of an exceptional nature. According to Riese and Hofstetter the costs of repair may be included into this category provided they are of an exceptional character.[22]

A major point of discussion has been whether or not a third type of priority claim needed to be created for fiscal claims. The United States strongly opposed this suggestion, advancing the following reasons for its rejection:

1. The Convention was intended to deal with the rights of individuals: the proposal would introduce the rights of states into the Convention;
2. the Convention rules allow every state to impose such restrictions as would provide adequate safeguards for fiscal claims;
3. the proposal would increase the risk for the creditor to such an extent that he would not be prepared to lend substantial sums on mortgage. Fleet mortgage would become practically pointless as well, as each aircraft forms a security for payment of the total amount advanced on mortgage; and

---

20. See Matte (note 1, *supra*), p. 570; Hofstetter (note 3, *supra*), pp. 239 *et seq.*
21. Hofstetter (note 3, *supra*), p. 242.
22. Hofstetter (note 3, *supra*), p. 237; Riese (note 7, *supra*), p. 293.

4. fiscal claims are adequately protected not only in the Chicago Convention, but also in bilateral agreements; besides, priority status for fiscal claims would be contrary to the general principles of international law.[23]

Strong support for including priority status for fiscal claims in the Convention came from France, which resented being unable to claim this privilege even when the aircraft in question was registered in France.

Mexico was prepared to ratify the Convention only on condition that priority status be given to fiscal claims and claims arising from employment contracts. It made a reservation to that effect, as did Chile, which claimed the privilege for the salaries of the crew, a point which had not even come up for discussion during the preparatory meetings. Some states (*e.g.* the USA) held the view that such far-reaching reservations invalidated the ratification of the two countries concerned. Brazil, on the other hand, accepted it, which resulted in the following situation: the Convention is in force between the various contracting states (including Brazil), but not *vis-à-vis* Mexico (Chile withdrew its reservation on ratifying the Convention). The same Convention, with fiscal claim priority, is valid between Mexico and Brazil.[24] Clearly this is a most unsatisfactory state of affairs: the fact that it still continues to exist may be attributed, indirectly, to changing ideas on treaty reservations being put into practice since 1948, and it shows beyond doubt the complications the present practice may lead to.[25] It is equally attributable to the Vienna Convention on the Law of Treaties concluded on May 23, 1969,[26] which left a legacy of uncertainty with regard to the right of states to make reservations upon adherence to multilateral treaties.

According to Article 2, para. 1(d) of the Vienna Convention, 'reservation' means 'a unilateral statement, however phrased or named, made by a State when signing, ratifying, accepting, approving or acceding to a treaty, whereby it purports to exclude or to modify the legal effects of certain provisions of the treaty in their application to that State'. The effect

---

23. ICAO Doc. 5722 (note 11, *supra*), pp. 98 *et seq.* (notably pp. 100–103).

24. See S.A. Bayitch, *Aircraft Mortgage in the Americas*, University of Miami School of Law Interamerican Legal Studies, No. 5 (1960), at p. 69 in note 346 (also published in (1959) 13 *University of Miami Law Review* 152–188 and 424–446); R.J. Goldstein, Esq., 'Aircraft Title Registration and Perfection of Lien Rights in Aircraft', *Air Law*, vol. IV (1979), pp. 2-7, at 6. See *e.g.* the United States refusal to accept the Mexican reservation [1951] USAvR 131.

25. Cf. UN General Assembly Resolution 598 (VI) of January 12, 1952, in which the UN Secretary-General is requested to communicate the texts relating to reservations 'to all States concerned, leaving it to each State to draw legal consequences from such communications.' See on this subject J.L. Brierly, 'Reservations to Multilateral Conventions', Report to the International Law Commission, *Yearbook of the International Law Commission* (1951 - II), pp. 1-27 (UN Doc. A/CN.4/41); G.G. Fitzmaurice, 'Reservations to Multilateral Conventions' [1953] *The International and Comparative Law Quarterly* 1–26.

26. Vienna Convention on the Law of Treaties, Vienna, May 23, 1969.

of a reservation depends on whether it is accepted or rejected by the other states concerned (Art. 20). Traditionally, a state could not make a reservation to a treaty unless it was accepted by all the states concerned. This rule, however, was undermined by a decision of the International Court of Justice[27] to the effect that a state making a reservation is likely to be regarded as a party to the treaty by some states, but not by others. At that time it was felt that a slight lack of uniformity was a price worth paying for a larger number of ratifications of multilateral Conventions.[28] It should be noted that no reservations can be made which are incompatible with the object and purpose of the relevant Convention.[29]

2.1.10. Implied (concealed) priority claims

Not counting the claims contemplated by Article IV, the Convention recognises four claims carrying an implied (concealed) priority and listed hereunder:

a. a claim amounting to 20 per cent of the execution sale price for persons suffering injury or damage on the surface in the state where the sale takes place, unless adequate and effective insurance is available (Art. VII, para. 5(b));
b. claims in respect of costs legally chargeable in the state where the execution sale took place (Art. VII, para.6);
c. claims arising from national laws 'relating to immigration, customs or air navigation' (Art. XII);
d. claims in respect of the sale of spare parts (Art. X, para. 3).

No terms in the Convention itself confer priority status on the claim referred to under (a), but the Convention does allow the law of the state where the sale takes place to do so. This provision was dictated by the fact that third parties having suffered damage on the surface of the earth are not in a position to protect themselves in the same manner as creditors who have been forewarned by the entries in the record. As for passengers, they can protect their interests by taking out insurance.

When the aircraft is properly insured against this type of liability the provision becomes superfluous and the entire proceeds of the sale goes to the creditors. An aircraft is considered to be properly insured if the insured sum amounts to the value of the aircraft when new (Art. VII, para. 5). This provision is particularly important with regard to fleet mortgage, where each aircraft is a part of the security for the total amount of the mortgage. Hofstetter considers it wrong

---

27. 'Reservations to the Convention on the Prevention and Punishment of the Crime of Genocide', Advisory Opinion of May 28, 1951; [1951] ICJ Reports 15–69, at 18-19.
28. Cf. J. Sztucki, 'Some Questions Arising from Reservations to the Vienna Convention on the Law of Treaties', *German Yearbook of International Law*, Vol. 20 (1977), pp. 277-305; W.W. Bishop Jr.,'Reservations to Treaties', (1961 - II) 103 *Recueil des Cours* 245–341.
29. Art. 19(c) of the Vienna Convention (note 26, *supra*).

to make priority status dependent upon insurance being proper or adequate.[30]

The Convention leaves the operator free to choose his own type of insurance. Riese feels it is superfluous for the Convention to give rules on damage to third parties on the surface as the matter is sufficiently covered by the 1952 Rome Convention; this opinion is shared by other experts.[31] These rules will not be invoked very often since:

1. insurance will cover a whole series of cases before seizure ever occurs;
2. legal and factual conditions must be met before priority can be claimed;
3. damage to third parties on the surface is rather a rare occurrence: when it does happen, the consequences for the injured are often such as to exceed the value of the aircraft at sale.

Under the Geneva Convention actions can be brought against the operator of the aircraft, just like in the Rome Conventions of 1933 and 1952. It may be recalled at this point that the registered owner will be presumed to be the operator unless he furnishes evidence to the contrary and involves the other party in the proceedings.[32]

In a thesis in the Dutch language a clear and practical summary of the various claims is given in their order of priority: this order is particularly relevant because Article IV creates a strong impression that its claims have priority over all others. The correct order is:

1. claims based on Article XII (customs fines, etc.);
2. claims based on Article VII, para. 6 (costs of execution, etc.);
3. claims based on Article X (spare parts);
4. a. claims based on Article IV (salvage and preservation costs);
   b. claims based on Article VII, para. 5 (third parties on the surface);
   c. claims based on Article I.[33]

It should be kept in mind, however, that the above claims hold their ranking only in so far as they were created validly and have fallen due.

Article V of the Convention provides: 'The priority of a right mentioned in Article I, paragraph 1(d), extends to all sums thereby secured. However, the amount of interest included shall not exceed that accrued during the three years prior to the execution proceedings together with that accrued during the execution proceedings.'

---

30. Hofstetter (note 3, *supra*), p. 253.
31. Riese (note 7, *supra*), p. 300.
32. See Art. 2 of the 1952 Rome Convention.
33. K. Rijks, *Het Verdrag van Genève* (thesis Leiden, 1952), pp. 181-182.

2.1.11. The attachment of an aircraft

Attachment of an aircraft in execution is covered by Article VI reading:

> 'In case of attachment or sale of an aircraft in execution, or of any right therein, the Contracting States shall not be obliged to recognise, as against the attaching or executing creditor or against the purchaser, any right mentioned in Article I, paragraph (1), or the transfer of any such right, if constituted or effected with knowledge of the sale or execution proceedings by the person against whom the proceedings are directed.'

It should be noted here that the debtor's awareness of the sale in execution is a prerequisite: a notice on the record is not sufficient. The party against whom execution procedures have been brought must be aware that they have commenced. The Article tries to prevent the fraudulent transfer of an aircraft, viz. the creation of a claim by a debtor who knew that the aircraft was under execution.

Article VI concerns not only the attachment of the aircraft itself, but clearly refers to the execution of a right in an aircraft as well. Hofstetter takes mortgage as an example of such a right.[34] With regard to the insertion of the words 'any right therein', it should be noted that in some countries, *e.g.* Norway and Portugal, execution procedures may take place against a person other than the owner. In such a case it is not the right of ownership that is sold or transferred, but the right held by a debtor. An obvious requirement here is that the sale involves a right *in rem*, a property right, and not a right *in personam*, a right enforceable only against the owner personally. For states which do not recognise the execution of a right the provision of Article VI is of course without relevance.[35]

Attachment and sale in execution are both subject to the law of the country where they take place. Article VII gives some provisions to be observed in connection with the sale: the date and the place of the sale shall be fixed at least six weeks in advance; the executing creditor shall supply to the court or other competent authority a certified extract of the recordings concerning the aircraft; he shall give public notice of the sale at the place where the aircraft is registered as to nationality, in accordance with the law there applicable, at least one month before the day fixed, and shall concurrently notify by registered letter, if possible by air mail, the recorded owner and the holders of recorded rights in the aircraft and of rights noted on the record under Article IV, para. 3, according to their addresses as shown on the record. The legal consequences of failure to observe these rules shall be determined by the national law of the contracting state where the sale took place.

---

34. Hofstetter (note 3, *supra*), p. 246; cf. the annotation on Art. VI in [1949] JALC at 81.
35. ICAO Doc. 5722 (note 11, *supra*), pp. 190-199.

An exception to Article VII, para. 4 is to be found in the earlier Montreal Draft of the Convention with regard to fleet mortgage, a form of security mentioned earlier in this chapter.[36] In the USA, fleet mortgage is standard practice: it provides more security for the creditor and so makes it possible to borrow larger sums of money. On the part of the USA, serious objections were raised against excluding fleet mortgage: exclusion would have meant the end of it, as the difference between it and the usual aircraft mortgage would be eliminated. In view of the importance of fleet mortgage for international aviation the proposed exclusion was rejected.[37]

It is useful to draw a comparison between air law and maritime law, in particular the 1952 Convention of Brussels on the arrest of sea-going ships.[38] The main impact of this Convention was that every creditor in all contracting states should be able to effect precautionary attachment on all ships belonging to his debtor, but only in respect of certain specified claims. Riese maintains that when a non-contracting state does not respect the rules of a sale in execution, creditors risk losing their rights. The only remedy would be for all states to join the Convention.[39]

How to divide the 80 per cent sales proceeds? Article VII, para. 5 gives no indications. It has been suggested that it should be done on the basis of the order of priority, but this would mean that claims having a low priority might receive nothing.[40]

Article VIII provides that the execution sale of an aircraft in conformity with the provisions of Article VII shall effect the transfer of the property free from all rights which are not assumed by the purchaser. Article VII, para. 4, however, reduces the impact of Article VIII by providing that no execution sale can be effected unless all rights having priority over the claim of the executing creditor in accordance with the Convention which are established before the competent authority, are covered by the proceeds of the sale or assumed by the purchaser. Hofstetter observes that through Article VIII, the creditors run great risks: their rights after registration are definitively lost, and they must be satisfied with the proceeds of the sale.[41]

American delegates first objected to these rules. They would have preferred to see the rights in aircraft remain attached to it, as this would more or less force the holder of the mortgage to buy the aircraft himself. Moreover, it would not be fair if priority rights could be rendered illusory as a result of a sale in a country where foreign exchange control regulations prohibit the transfer of his money.[42]

---

36. Cf. Art. 8, para. 4 of the Draft of Commission No. 4 of the 1st Assembly; see the Minutes and Documents of the First Session of the ICAO Legal Committee (Brussels, September 1947), ICAO Doc. 4635, pp. 197-201.
37. ICAO Doc. 4635 (note 36, *supra*), pp. 95-100; Matte (note 1, *supra*), pp. 564-565.
38. International Convention for the Unification of Certain Rules Relating to the Arrest of Sea-going Ships, Brussels, May 10, 1952.
39. Riese (note 7, *supra*), p. 297.
40. ICAO Doc. 5722 (note 11, *supra*), p. 64.
41. Hofstetter (note 3, *supra*), p. 248.
42. ICAO Doc. 4635 (note 36, *supra*), p. 110.

2.1.12. The transfer of a registration

Article IX provides that, except in a sale in conformity with the provisions of Article VII, no transfer of an aircraft from the nationality register of one contracting state to that of another shall be made, unless all holders of recorded rights have been satisfied or consent to the transfer.

The Article was formulated in the light of the risks a mortgage creditor may have to face when the mortgaged aircraft is sold to another country; this had been the subject of much discussion during the preparatory sessions of the Convention. The British delegation objected to the stipulation that consent to the transfer had to be obtained from the creditors before transfer could be effected. It was argued that it was not the duty of the state to look after the security of the creditors: in addition, the Article was considered to constitute too much of an infringement on the freedom to contract. In spite of these objections the inclusion of the Article was held to be indispensable for an adequate protection of the creditors.[43]

The Convention, in Article IX, sets up a double barrier for aircraft to clear before reaching the nationality and private law registers. On the one hand the Article requires the state of the creditor's nationality to prevent deleting an aircraft from the nationality register until all conditions have been fulfilled; on the other hand it requires the state of the purchaser's nationality to refuse entry on the record until it is evident that the prescribed procedures have been completed. Hofstetter would have preferred a system whereby the lien would have followed the aircraft regardless of the changes of its nationality.[44] This idea was rejected because of the uncertainties surrounding it.

The Convention contains no explicit obligations to delete an aircraft from the register or record. This enables double registration of an aircraft sold in execution in another state; this is against the law according to Article 18 of the Chicago Convention[45] and, besides, would lead to considerable difficulties. An apt conclusion was reached in the report to the Air Law Committee of the International Law Association (ILA), which noted that 'A practical difficulty of some gravity seems to arise, because there is no provision for transferring the aircraft from the old record to the record of the State of the new purchaser; a provision seems certainly to be required by which, on notice of a judicial sale, the authority in charge of the old record is obliged to effect the transfer.'[46]

An enquiry into the matter by the Netherlands Government showed that several signatories of the Convention were prepared to delete the

---

43. ICAO Doc. 4635 (note 36, *supra*), pp. 112-114 and p. 118.
44. Hofstetter (note 3, *supra*), p. 254.
45. Art. 18 of the Chicago Convention reads: 'An aircraft cannot be validly registered in more than one State, but its registration may be changed from one State to another'.
46. Wilberforce (note 13, *supra*), at p. 240.

entry in the name of the previous owner, provided that the requirements of Article VII had been complied with. This means that in practice complications will arise mainly in cases involving transfer to the record of a non-contracting state.

2.1.13. The spare parts

Spare parts form a part of an aircraft, according to Article XVI of the Convention. Their value amounts to about 25 per cent of the total value of the fleet in some cases. Article X, para. 4, specifies that 'spare parts' means 'parts of aircraft, engines, propellers, radio apparatus, instruments, appliances, furnishings, parts of any of the foregoing, and generally any other articles of whatever description maintained for installation in aircraft in substitution for parts or articles removed'.

The Swiss delegate raised strong objections against Article X, which extends rights in aircraft to spare parts. He argued that in Switzerland only parts permanently attached to an object could share the same rules as the principal object and that spare parts that were not even connected with the aircraft could not be subject to the rules applying to the aircraft itself. As these legal objections were outweighed by practical advantages they were rejected.[47]

Spare parts owned by airline companies are usually stored in various depots along their routes. They are movables and the *lex rei sitae* applies to them, apart from special regulations. Rights in spare parts are to be created in accordance with the domestic law applicable to the aircraft.

Article X, para. 1, specifies a number of formalities to be fulfilled when security for an indebtment extends to spare parts. Third parties must be given due notification of such encumbrance on a public notice exhibited at the place where they are located. The notice must specify the name and address of the holder of the right and the record in which it is recorded. Paragraph 2 provides that 'A statement indicating the character and the approximate number of such spare parts shall be annexed to or included in the recorded document. Such parts may be replaced by similar parts without effecting the right of the creditor'.

Sale in execution is provided for in Article X, para. 3; Article VII, paras. 1 and 4, as well as Article VIII are declared applicable. We note that Article VII, paras. 2 and 3, governing the formalities of the sale and the sanctions, do not apply to the sale in execution of spare parts. Riese and Hofstetter strongly object to these rules which, in their opinion, are difficult for European legal minds to accept, while the American creditor still lacks adequate protection.[48]

Rights in spare parts need only be recognised in so far as they are an extension of similar rights in an aircraft, the reason being that spares have

---

47. ICAO Doc. 4653 (note 36, *supra*), pp. 119-121.
48. Riese (note 7, *supra*), at p. 304; Hofstetter (note 3, *supra*), at p. 262.

no nationality of their own and that it would be difficult to determine their origin. Entering rights in spare parts separately in the records would cause problems because most records only allow entries of rights in aircraft.[49] Accordingly, parties are forced to arrange for a separate mortgage on spare parts.

2.1.14. Applicable law

When the point is raised: 'Which law is applicable under the Convention?' the answer is that it is, generally speaking, the law of the state where the aircraft is registered. Hofstetter feels that this is appropriate, considering the extreme mobility of an aircraft and the need to accommodate this feature in a single body of law. Aircraft cannot be included into the same category as ordinary movables, to which the *lex rei sitae* is nearly always applicable.[50]

A number of exceptions to the rule have nonetheless been incorporated in the Convention:
1. Article IV, para, 1, providing that the rights referred to in that paragraph have priority provided that they are enforceable according to the law of the contracting state where the operations of salvage or preservation were terminated, regardless of where the aircraft might find itself;
2. Article IV, para. 4(b), providing that the grounds for interruption or suspension of judicial action shall be determined by the law of the forum;
3. Article VII, para. 1, stipulating that the proceedings of a sale in execution of an aircraft shall be determined by the law of the contracting state where the sale takes place;
4. Article X, para. 3, containing a provision making Article VII, para. 1, also applicable to the sale in execution of spare parts.

The exceptions listed above have clearly been inserted in order to ensure a more flexible application of the Convention's provisions.

2.1.15. Aircraft under construction

No indication is given in the Convention as to the law applicable to aircraft under construction that have not yet been registered. It was thought impracticable to impose rules on aircraft even before they were able to operate internationally.

2.1.16. Miscellaneous provisions

An interesting provision is given in Article XIV of the Convention which states: 'For the purpose of this Convention, the competent judicial and administrative authorities of the Contracting States may,

---

49. ICAO Doc. 5722 (note 11, *supra*), p. 94.
50. Hofstetter (note 3, *supra*), pp. 209–210; cf. Riese (note 7, supra), p. 266.

subject to any contrary provision in their national law, correspond directly with each other'. To my knowledge this is the first time such a provision has ever been adopted in an international agreement.

'Contracting States' in the Convention means states which have ratified the Convention. This is apparent from Article XXII, para. 1, stating that 'Any Contracting State may denounce this Convention...': before a state can denounce a Convention it must have ratified first.

The rules for signature, ratification and denunciation have been laid down in Articles XVIII to XXIII of the Convention. Note should be taken of Article XXIII, para. 1, which authorises a state to declare, on ratification or adherence, that 'its acceptance of this Convention does not apply to any one or more of the territories for the foreign relations of which it is responsible'. Failure to do so will make the Convention applicable to such territories. In the event of a reservation being declared the state may adhere separately on behalf of such territories at a later stage. Besides separate accession, separate denunciation is equally allowable under the Convention. As such reservations do not affect the substance of the Convention they are not expected to give rise to complications.

2.1.17. Concluding note

There is no doubt that the Convention has brought about a consensus on a number of important points: the creditor's interests are now adequately safeguarded in all contracting states, priority claims have been defined and their order of priority is determined by the law of the state where they are registered. Nonetheless some gaps remain: to begin with, the precise moment when a right in a registered aircraft is validly created has not been fixed; moreover, the Convention only protects agreements between parties, not the obligations arising by virtue of the law; finally, the Convention contains nothing on execution procedure or on entering an execution in the record of the contracting state of the aircraft's nationality.

Against the background of the circumstances prevailing at the time when the Convention was concluded, no better result could probably have been achieved, and the Convention may certainly be regarded as an important first step towards establishing more adequate rules. In the meantime no effort must be spared to study effective ways of eliminating its remaining imperfections.

The most recent development is the attention of the Unidroit organisation to the subject of rights in mobile equipment in general. A proposal for a convention has already been prepared.[51] Mobile equipment could include not only aircraft but also ships, oil rigs, containers, railway rolling stock and satellites. Although the effort to come to uniform rules, especially a single register, is laudable, it is very doubtful if and when hard results may be expected in view of the different national legislations.

---

51. *First Set of Draft Articles of a Future Unidroit Convention on International Interests in Mobile Equipment*, Unidroit Study LXXII, doc.24, 1996.

2.2. LEASING

The Geneva Convention has lost some of its importance of late due to the increasing popularity and possibilities of leasing.[52] This tendency was in turn dictated by the rapid growth of technical developments and the need for bigger and faster aircraft. The airline companies had to face steeply rising costs and often could not afford to buy the new aircraft. At the same time these larger planes contributed to temporary overcapacity, thereby reducing the profits of the airline companies.

The concept of leasing aircraft was developed in the USA during the Second World War. According to a definition provided by the Equipment Leasing Association in the UK, 'A lease is a contract between lessor and lessee for the hire of a specific asset selected from a manufacturer or vendor of such assets by the lessee. The lessor retains ownership of the asset. The lessee has possession and use of the asset on payment of specified rentals over a period.'[53]

Leasing is basically a form of financing, in other words an economic concept. When the leasing is done by a specialised company it is usually called a 'financial lease' which involves payment over an obligatory period equal to or less than the estimated useful life of the aircraft. But also in circles of aircraft manufacturers there was a growing awareness of the advantages offered by selling aircraft on the basis of a lease. That form of leasing is usually called an 'operational lease', whereby the aircraft is not wholly paid back during the period of the lease.

A characteristic feature of an operational lease is that the economic risk of the aircraft is for the lessor, while in a financial lease the risk is assumed by the lessee. It is obvious that the main economic risk for an aircraft lies in its becoming outdated. Other forms of leasing are mostly derived from the two types described above.

A further term to be mentioned here is 'economic ownership'. Exclusive use of an aircraft does not necessarily constitute this type of ownership; rather a number of conditions have to be fulfilled.

Economic ownership is established (a) when the lessee has the right to take possession of the asset when the lease expires; (b) when the lessee has a contract for a shorter period than the economic life of the asset; or (c) when the lessee has a contract for a period equal to the economic life of the asset.

The economic ownership concept is derived from business economics and is mainly a tax-technical construction. Criteria may vary per fiscal jurisdiction, hence the rising interest in so-called cross-border leases.

---

52. In its Article I, section 1-c, the Convention only refers to leases of six months or more, reflecting the limited importance and occurrence of leasing at the time of the conception of the Geneva Convention.

53. R.S. Sowter, 'Lease Finance for Airlines', *Air Law*, vol. IV (1979), pp. 11–20, at 15. See also W.W. Eyer. 'The Sale, Leasing and Financing of Aircraft' [1979/1980] JALC 217–274.

I would also like to note here in passing that there are three areas in leasing susceptible of causing complications: (1) aircraft registration; (2) aviation safety; and (3) flight licensing. For a discussion of these subjects I would like to refer to Chapter II, *supra*.[54]

Current types of leasing are the 'sale-lease-back' leases which involve the purchase of an aircraft, which is subsequently sold to a leasing company who leases it back to the original purchaser. There is also the 'hire-purchase' type of leasing which has been mentioned before.

At least three rights have to be safeguarded in lease transactions: (1) the title of the owner/lessor in the aircraft; (2) the rights of the lessor's lender as a holder of the chattel mortgage on the aircraft and as assignee of the lease; and (3) the rights of use and quiet enjoyment of the aircraft by the lessee airline user.[55]

As a rule, the laws of the country where the airline utilising the leased aircraft is domiciled will apply. It is therefore important to know that registration in a particular country will afford adequate protection to the aforementioned rights, and also that these will be enforced by other countries so as to give similar protection. It is equally important that the country of registration should be a party to the Geneva Convention, because this Convention is the primary international agreement dealing with the signatories' recognition of both the owner/lessor and the chattel mortgage-holder's rights under the laws of another signatory state. Yet, as we have seen, the Geneva Convention has some limitations: it does not affect in any way the priorities granted by national laws in the case of salvage or in the case of rights of national governments to attach aircraft pursuant to their immigration and customs laws; in some situations it does not grant any rights to governments of states that are parties to the Convention, but only speaks in terms of third party private rights. The type of reservations made by some parties to the Convention must not be overlooked either. In many cases government bank guarantees will be used to protect the rights of the owner and, therefore, of the holder of the chattel mortgage. In order to protect certain rights, dual registration has even been attempted, although the Chicago Convention does not permit registering an aircraft in more than one country.[56]

In order to accommodate the increasingly popular practices of chartering and leasing a special Article 83-*bis*[57] was inserted in the Chicago Convention in 1980. This article makes it possible for a State of

---

54. See I.H.Ph.Diederiks-Verschoor, 'Le financement des aéronefs', in Part III of *Recherches et Réalisations, Mélanges Pierre Vellas*, 1995, pp.551-562 (also separately published under the title *Transport Aérien et Activités Spatiales*, 1995).
55. Goldstein (note 24, *supra*), at p. 3.
56. See note 45, *supra*.
57. See F. Videla Escalada, 'Nationality of Aircraft: a Vision of the Future', in *Air and Space Law, De Lege Ferenda*, (1992), pp. 71-80 and R.D. van Dam, 'Lease, Charter and Interchange of Aircraft and the Chicago Convention - Some Observations', *Air and Space Law*, vol. XIX (1994), pp. 124-130.

registration to transmit its functions and duties in aviation safety to another Contracting State, subject, however, to agreement being reached between the States concerned. Such an agreement has to be registered with ICAO, failing which it will have no effect against third parties. At least 99 ratifications are needed for the 83-*bis* amendment to enter into force, but that number has not yet been reached. The USA are among the States having ratified.[58]

The difference between short-term leasing and hire or charter is often very difficult to discern.[59] As the practice of leasing is growing rapidly, new rules on nationality and registration of leased aircraft will probably have to be devised.[60]

58. See A. Kotaite, 'ICAO's concern and recent work in the legal field to meet the present requirements of international air transport', *Annals of Air and Space Law*, vol. 3 (1978); and J.T. Stewart Jr., 'Aircraft leasing in the USA - a few observations', *Air Law*, vol. VIII (1983), pp. 58-78.

59. Cf. G.F. Fitzgerald, 'The Lease, Charter and Interchange of Aircraft in International Operations: Amendments to the Chicago and Rome Conventions', *Annals of Air and Space Law*, Vol. II (1977), pp. 103–137; M.J. Lester, 'Aircraft Interchange', *Air Law*, vol. IV (1979), pp. 8–10.

60. Cf. Goldstein (note 24, *supra*), at p. 4. For further, recent information on leasing see the special issue of *Air and Space Law* 'Aircraft Financing', vol. XVII (1992), No. 2 (pp. 42 - 128) and *Aircraft Financing: Recent Developments and Prospects*, proceedings of a Conference (Amsterdam, January 17, 1992) held by the law–firm De Brauw Blackstone Westbroek.

CHAPTER IX

Assistance and Salvage

1. Introductory note

In any analysis of assistance and salvage in air law a sharp distinction is to be made between the period preceding the Second World War and the post-War era. Before the War, legal thinking and procedure used to be based on concepts of private law; after the War the subject was approached from a public law angle, because it had come to be regarded as a government responsibility.

This difference in approach is clearly reflected in the two conventions dealing with the subject matter, *i.e.* the Convention for the Unification of Certain Rules relating to Assistance and Salvage of Aircraft or by Aircraft at Sea, concluded at Brussels on September 29, 1938,[1] and the Chicago Convention of 1944.

The Brussels Convention, had it become effective, would not have been the first international instrument to be dedicated to the problem: as early as 1919 an Article had been included in the Paris Convention of the same year reading as follows: 'Le sauvetage des appareils perdus en mer sera réglé, sauf conventions contraires, par les principes du droit maritime'.[2] On the basis of that article provisions on assistance and salvage were subsequently adopted in the domestic laws of various countries.

Only assistance and salvage operations *at sea* were contemplated by the Brussels Convention. During the preparatory stage a separate draft had been prepared to cover similar operations on land, but it never got beyond the drafting stage.[3] The Convention was concluded but not ratified, due to the outbreak of the War and scores of objections from maritime circles. Yet its rules were adopted by the Italian Codice della Navigazione of 1942. After the War, an entirely new legal basis was found in Article 25 of the Chicago Convention, while technical regulations in considerable detail were added in Annex 12 to that Convention, which elaborates Article 25 and bears the title of 'Search and Rescue'.

---

1. Convention for the Unification of Certain Rules Relating to Assistance and Salvage of Aircraft or by Aircraft at Sea, Brussels, September 29, 1933; hereinafter cited as the Brussels Convention. This Convention is not in force; for present status see Shawcross and Beaumont, *Air Law* (1977), Vol. 2 (1981), p. A-3.
2. Art. 23 of the Paris Convention. In English: 'With regard to the salvage of aircraft wrecked at sea the principles of maritime law will apply, in the absence of any agreement to the contrary' (Shawcross and Beaumont, *Air Law* (1st ed., 1945)).
3. See [1938] JAL 603–606, 'Second preliminary draft of convention for the unification of certain rules relative to assistance and salvage of aircraft or by aircraft on land'.

2. The Brussels Convention

Although the Brussels Convention has never become operative, its rules are worth analysing for the purpose of this chapter. The fundamental principle laid down in the Convention is the obligation for both aircraft commanders and ships' captains to render assistance to persons at sea in danger of being lost.

In commenting on this matter the fact should never be overlooked that (1) the conditions under which aircraft operate differ significantly from those affecting ships; (2) the obligation to render assistance is much harder to fulfil for an aircraft commander than for a ship's captain. The Convention has, however, reduced the burden of this obligation to acceptable proportions: it does not apply in the following cases:

1. when the aircraft or ship is in the course of a trip or ready to depart;
2. when it is not reasonably possible for it to render useful aid;
3. when the commander is aware that assistance is being rendered by others under similar or better conditions than it could be by himself;
4. when rendering assistance seriously endangers the aircraft, its crew, its passengers or other persons.

The penalties to ensure the commander's compliance with his obligations are left to domestic legislation.

The payment of an indemnity by the operator of the assisted aircraft is another basic rule recognised and made mandatory by the Convention. It draws a distinction between compulsory assistance and non-compulsory assistance. In the cases of compulsory assistance the indemnity is based on the expenses justified by the circumstances and the damage suffered during the operations. As for non-compulsory assistance, the rule here is: 'no cure, no pay' (Art. 3, paras. 1 and 2).

Apart from indemnity the Convention, in Article 4, lays down another fundamental rule. It states that an aircraft or ship, having rendered assistance, is entitled to a 'remuneration' based on several factors like (1) the measure of success achieved; (2) the efforts of those who have rendered assistance; (3) the dangers run by the aircraft or ship, persons and cargo involved in the operations; (4) the value of the salved objects. The remuneration can never exceed the value of the salved goods at the end of the operations.

An interesting point that might be raised in connection with this matter is whether a set of rules similar to those of general average in maritime law ought to be introduced in air law. The suggestion is nothing new. It had, even before the Second World War, been given a tangible legal form in Article 9 of the Brussels Convention under discussion. Due to cargo transport by air playing until recently a relatively minor role in the aviation business there has not been much pressure to revive that rule. Article 9 differs from the general average rules in maritime law in that there is no *pro rata* apportionment in accordance with the contributory interests involved: it imposes on the operator of the assisted aircraft or the owner or *armateur* of the vessel the obligation to pay the remuneration, but gives him the right of recourse against the owners of the salved goods up to the value of those goods. With air cargo becoming an ever more important business the revival of some general average rules in air law remains as urgent as ever.[4]

Turning next to assistance and salvage on land, we observe a different and rather more complex situation due to the variety of means of transport which may be involved in land salvage operations, whereas at sea they are generally carried out by ships and aircraft only.[5] Besides, in land operations state sovereignty may turn out to be a complicating factor.

In the preliminary draft on assistance and salvage on land it was intended to introduce certain exceptions for assistance in dangerous zones where no adequate organisational facilities are available, such as deserts and Arctic regions. The draft further confined itself to assistance and salvage procedures between aircraft themselves in order to avoid the complications of a multiplicity of means of transport.

The need to create international rules on assistance and salvage of aircraft is essentially dictated by the following considerations: (1) their very existence gives moral support to the passengers; (2) airline companies can assess more accurately their financial obligations and insure themselves against losses; (3) modern developments in aviation have made the introduction of such rules desirable.

3. Search and rescue (Chicago Convention, Article 25 and Annex 12)

In the days when assistance and salvage was still being handled on a private law basis, assistance was usually provided by the local authorities. This was done not in the form of an organised or permanent service, but always on an incidental basis. At the meetings of CITEJA[6] the idea of an organised permanent rescue service was considered on several occasions, and it was often suggested that setting up such an organisation was really the responsibility of the state.

4. Cases with typical general average features involved aircraft having to jettison a petrol tank and oil rig components, in the interest of the safety of the flight. The incidents took place in New Guinea and Surinam, respectively. See on this subject I.H.Ph. de Rode-Verschoor, 'Quelques remarques sur l'utilité d'une réglementation de l'avarie grosse dans le droit aérien' [1952] RFDA 275–277; H. Schadee, 'Für die grosse Havarie im Luftrecht', [1954] ZfL 331–334; E. du Pontavice, *Les épaves maritimes, aériennes et spatiales en droit français* (thesis Paris, 1960).

5. See on this subject A.W. Knauth, 'Salvage as between vessels and aircraft' [1937] JAL 159–190; I.H.Ph. de Rode-Verschoor, 'Le développement de l'assistance et du sauvetage des aéronefs sur terre et sur mer', *Studi in onore di Antonio Ambrosini* (1957), pp. 711-721.

6. See for historical information the various reports on the preliminary proceedings of the Brussels Convention in RGDA, Vols. 1932–1936, and the Reports of the American delegates to CITEJA meetings in USAvR, Vols. 1936–1938 and JALC, Vol. 1939 (pp. 147 *et seq.*).

During the Second World War, a 'Search and Rescue Service' was established in Britain, mainly of course to assist in saving military aircrews. A second organisation called 'Repair and Salvage Service' was responsible for locating and repairing aircraft. The United States and Canada set up similar services. After the War the 'Search and Rescue Service' was retained, and assistance and salvage became a government responsibility.

Article 25 of the Chicago Convention entitled: 'aircraft in distress', reads as follows:

> 'Each contracting State undertakes to provide such measures of assistance to aircraft in distress in its territory as it may find practicable, and to permit, subject to control by its own authorities, the owner of the aircraft or authorities of the State in which the aircraft is registered to provide such measures of assistance as may be necessitated by the circumstances. Each contracting State, when undertaking search for missing aircraft, will collaborate in coordinated measures which may be recommended from time to time pursuant to this Convention.'

As mentioned earlier, this Article is elaborated in Annex 12 which, in its Foreword, makes it clear that it is applicable in almost the entire world, both on land and at sea, unlike Article 25 itself, the scope of which is limited to the national territory of each state.

Chapter 3 of Annex 12 contains standards and recommended practices for co-operation between states. It extends the duty to lend assistance beyond the national borders to neighbouring territories or seas, but fails to specify precisely how far this obligation reaches. Problems arising in connection with this lack of precision are settled by ICAO Regional Air Navigation Agreements; the current international assignment of responsibility for search and rescue is published in ICAO Regional Air Navigation Plans. Rescue co-ordination centres have been established, each of which co-ordinates the operations in a specific area.

Under the present circumstances each co-ordination centre is free to make decisions concerning its own equipment, although it would obviously be preferable to have standardised equipment in all centres. It is essential that rescue equipment can be immediately identified by the crew of an aircraft, whatever its nationality.

In Chapter 2, 3, 4 and 5, detailed rules are given on organisational matters, preparatory procedures, and procedures to be followed during the actual search and rescue operations. The functioning of rescue co-ordination centres has been described in three emergency phases: (1) the phase of uncertainty, when news concerning an aircraft is being awaited; (2) the phase of alert, when rescue services are alerted for action; (3) the phase of distress, when rescue procedures become fully operational. When an accident occurs a centre may appeal for help to other services, such as mountain rescue teams and lifeboat services.

Detailed rules of procedure are prescribed in Annex 12 for the aircraft commander. He is required to keep sight of the aircraft or surface craft in distress, and to spot its exact location. Next, he must report extensively to the co-ordination centre, which will then determine whether or not assistance will be rendered. He is obliged to follow the instructions from the centre. Yet, according to Annex 12, the legal obligation to lend assistance applies only when the commander personally observes that an aircraft or a vessel is in distress.

According to Matte and Kamminga[7] the duty to render assistance does not exist when the commander becomes aware that an accident has occurred but has not actually seen it happen himself. In such a case he is not required to change his course. Kamminga quite rightly maintains that this is a serious flaw in the system which greatly reduces its effectiveness, all the more so as modern aircraft fly at such a high altitude that personal sighting is nearly always a matter of chance.

We would note in this context that the words 'keep in sight the craft in distress' are very restrictive as they stand. Even according to a liberal interpretation this wording would not call for assistance to be given to survivors of an accident. The Brussels Convention was far more explicit on this point: it provided that assistance was to be given 'to any person who is at sea in danger of being lost ...'.

Appendix A of the Annex specifies a number of rules concerning the signals to be used during search and rescue operations.

To conclude this review of Annex 12 we would emphasise that its provisions are effective only to the extent to which they have been incorporated in the domestic legislations of the relevant member states of the Chicago Convention.

It is perhaps useful to list hereunder a few more points of difference between the Brussels and Chicago Conventions:

1. The Brussels Convention contains an obligation for national legislations to provide for penalties (Art. 2, para. 6); the Chicago Convention does not provide for any sanctions on non-compliance with search and rescue procedures. It is therefore impossible to force a state to set up a search and rescue service, or to organise such a service according to the demands of international traffic.

2. The Brussels Convention applies to 'government vessels and aircraft' except military, police and customs craft; Annex 12 relates only to 'civil aircraft', because the Chicago Convention itself is confined to civil aviation.

3. Unlike the Brussels Convention, Annex 12 imposes the obligation to render assistance only on aircraft commanders, not on ships' captains.

4. The Brussels Convention gives rules on indemnity and remuneration: neither the Chicago Convention nor the Annex contain any such provisions.

---

7. M.S. Kamminga, *The Aircraft Commander in Commercial Air Transportation* (1953), p. 73; Nicolas M. Matte, *The International Legal Status of the Aircraft Commander* (1975), p. 86.

4. Financial aspects

The costs involved in search and rescue operations are often quite high, and it is therefore difficult to decide when a search is to be called off. In cases where the expenses are met by a state it would be reasonable to leave the decision to the state in question, but when they are paid for by a private operator the latter should be given the option of continuing the operations or calling them off.

In 1949, aviation insurers met at a conference in Brussels, and drafted the following proposals:

1. An international fund was to be created which would cover partial reimbursements of the costs incurred by states participating in rescue operations.
2. A supplementary charge was to be levied from the owners of international airlines, payable at the moment the aircraft has landed.

To date, these and other proposals have remained without effect.

5. Concluding remarks

It would be most appropriate to modify and improve the existing rules on search and rescue on a number of points, preferably in the following manner:

1. by introducing sanctions into Annex 12;
2. by adding a provision on remuneration on the basis of the 1949 proposals;
3. by including a provision on compensation for salvage of mail bags[8];
4. by imposing a legal obligation on the aircraft commander to start search and rescue operations as soon as he realizes that an accident has occurred within reasonable range, even though he may not have sighted the accident personally, as well as an obligation to assist every person in danger of loss of life;
5. by extending the Convention's provisions applicable to search and rescue operations to include military aircraft, since such aircraft often participate in rescue operations;
6. by arranging for a closer coordination between air law, maritime law and space law in matters involving search and rescue.

---

8. Cf. the 'Report on the contribution by interested parties in the payment for remuneration for assistance and on the contribution of postal cargo to such remuneration', by M. Spanjaard in ICAO Doc. 4526–LC/12 and ICAO Doc. 5335–LC/97. See also on the subject of remuneration the Minutes and Documents of the Third Session of the ICAO Legal Committee (Lisbon, September–October 1949), ICAO Doc. 6024-LC/121, notably the report of the Sub-committee and the Drafting Committee on assistance (pp. 173-187).

With regard to the last point it is relevant to note the importance attached in space law to rescue operations. This is reflected in an international agreement concluded on April 4, 1968, called the 'Agreement on the Rescue of Astronauts, the Return of Astronauts and the Return of Objects Launched into Outer Space'.[9]

9. Agreement on the Rescue of Astronauts, the Return of Astronauts and the Return of objects Launched into Outer Space, April 4, 1968. See on this subject I.H.Ph. Diederiks–Verschoor, 'Assistance et sauvetage en droit maritime, aérien et spatial. Nécessité d'une coopération', *Annuaire de Droit Maritime et Aérien* (1976). Vol. 3, pp 93-101 and by the same author *An Introduction to Space Law* (1993).

CHAPTER X

Penal Law and Aviation

Three international conventions govern this province of law, where introduction of new rules and sanctions had become so very urgent in the past few decades. They are:

1. the Convention on Offences and Certain Other Acts Committed on Board Aircraft, signed at Tokyo on September 14, 1963[1];
2. the Convention for the Suppression of Unlawful Seizure of Aircraft, signed at The Hague on December 16, 1970[2]; and
3. the Convention for the Suppression of Unlawful Acts against the Safety of Civil Aviation, signed at Montreal on September 23, 1971,[3]

The Conventions will be analysed hereunder in the order indicated above.[4]

1. The Tokyo Convention

1.1. HISTORICAL PERSPECTIVE

1.1.1. The preliminaries

The international character of aviation and air law makes it necessary to determine which state is competent to exercise jurisdiction in cases of criminal offences committed on board aircraft. Since 1902 this question had been a major point at issue in legal circles.[5] State sovereignty over the airspace above its territory was, and still is, a recognised principle of law: it was expressed in the Paris Convention of 1919, and it reappeared in the Chicago Convention of 1944.

Generally speaking, one can imagine on the one hand a situation in which complications may arise when a state other than the state in which an aircraft is registered attempts to assert its jurisdiction with regard to offences committed on board such aircraft. Alternatively, we may face a situation where no penal laws at all are applicable, *e.g.*

1. Convention on Offences and Certain Other Acts Committed on Board Aircraft, Tokyo, September 14, 1963; hereinafter cited as Tokyo Convention.
2. Convention for the Suppression of Unlawful Seizure of Aircraft, The Hague, December 16, 1970; hereinafter cited as the Hague Convention (also known as the Hijacking Convention).
3. Convention for the Suppression of Unlawful Acts Against the Safety of Civil Aviation, Montreal, September 23, 1971, hereinafter cited as Montreal Convention (also known as the Sabotage Convention).
4. See for a general survey L.C. Morris, 'International Aviation Security Law', *Majalah Ilmu Hukum & Pengetahuan Masyarakat (Journal of Law and Social Sciences)* of the Padjadjaran University (Bandung), 1996, no. 1, pp. 23-52.
5. Cf. the report by Paul Fauchille, 'Régime Juridique des Aérostats', *Annuaire de l' Institut de Droit International* (1902), Vol. 19, pp. 19-114, at pp. 51 *et seq.*

when an offence is committed above territories not subject to the sovereignty of any particular state, like the high seas, or when the place where the offence was committed cannot be determined with any precision.

On a number of occasions the International Law Association has had the issue on its agenda, while the air law section of the Association du Droit Pénal discussed the problem at its 1957 Congress.[6] Draft conventions based on these preparations were worked out by the ICAO Legal Committee in Munich (1959), Rome (1962) and other cities; the final text was adopted at the Diplomatic Conference held in Tokyo in 1963.[7]

1.1.2. Several theories

An analysis of the various drafts reveals five theories:
1. the territorial theory: the law of the state in whose airspace the offence has taken place will be applied by its national courts. Clearly it is not always possible to determine the exact position of the aircraft at the time the offence was committed; for that reason it is impracticable for a state to base its jurisdiction solely on this principle;
2. the national theory: according to this theory the law of state where the aircraft is registered is to be applied under all circumstances;
3. the mixed theory: side by side with the law of the aircraft's nationality the law of the state over which the aircraft passes is enforceable whenever the security or public order of such state is threatened by offences committed on board;
4. the theory of the law of the state of departure; and
5. the theory of the law of the state of landing.

The last two theories confer jurisdiction on the state where the aircraft has departed and landed, respectively. Both have their own particular advantages: the former does not leave the commander any choice of jurisdiction, whereas the latter does allow his direct intervention: the commander can immediately inform the appropriate authorities by radio and alert the airport for assistance so that the necessary measures can be taken and an investigation started. This would preclude unnecessary delay in the flight schedule. A disadvantage of the last theory is that the pilot has full authority in selecting

---

6. See, *e.g.* the numerous references given by Nicolas M. Matte, *Treatise on Air-Aeronautical Law* (1981), pp. 330-331, in note 13.
7. Minutes and Documents of the International Air Law Conference (Tokyo, August–September 1963), ICAO Doc. 8565 – LC/152–1 and 152-2. Note also the Minutes and Documents of various preceding Sessions of its ICAO Legal Committee for preparatory discussions and drafts. See on the Tokyo Convention R.P. Boyle and R. Pulsifier, 'The Tokyo Convention on Offences and Certain Other Acts Committed on Board Aircraft' [1964] JALC 305–354; G.F. Fitzgerald, 'Offences and Certain Other Acts Committed on Board Aircraft: the Tokyo Convention of 1963', *Canadian Yearbook of International Law*, Vol. II, (1964) pp. 191-204.

the state whose law will eventually be applied to the offence. The next place of landing will be that of the normal flight schedule or, if the commander is of the opinion that an emergency exists, the nearest possible place of landing.[8]

1.1.3. Case law

One of the earliest cases involving the jurisdiction issue dates from 1928. Briefly, the facts of the so-called *Loewenstein* case were as follows: Loewenstein, a Belgian banker, was flying in his private aircraft from Croydon airport in the United Kingdom to Le Bourget airport near Paris. At a certain moment he had disappeared. An investigation led to the discovery of his body in the English Channel. As the incident had occurred while the aircraft was flying over British territorial waters only the British authorities, not the French, were competent to deal with the case in accordance with the territorial theory. Both the British and the French held this view, as is demonstrated by the fact that Loewenstein's aircraft was returned to Croydon in order to be inspected by a British commission of enquiry. However, the confusion and uncertainty around the jurisdiction in such cases was clearly demonstrated by the Belgian authorities, who declared themselves competent on account of the deceased's nationality: they rejected the findings of the British commission.[9]

Another illustration of the need for international rules was the notorious case of *United States* v. *Cordova and Santano*.[10] An aircraft belonging to an American airline made a flight from San Juan, Puerto Rico, to New York on August 2, 1948, with 60 passengers and crew members on board, amongst whom were a Mr. Cordova and a Mr. Santano. Prior to take-off they had been given a 'bon voyage celebration' by their friends and relatives, the principal attraction being Puerto Rican rum in large quantities. They also brought bottles of rum on board and continued drinking. After an hour and a half of flying time, and while the aircraft was above the high seas, the two gentlemen became involved in an argument over a missing bottle. The stewardess made an attempt to calm them, but the two continued their fight

---

8. Cf. O. Riese and J.T. Lacour, *Précis de droit aérien* (1951), pp. 316-318 and Nicolas M. Matte (note 6, *supra*), p. 331 *et seq.*

9. See on this subject E. Morpurgo, 'Quelques considérations sur les conflits internationaux de juridiction en matière pénale aéronautique à propos de la mort du banquier Loewenstein', RJIdeLA (1928), pp. 399-414, at p. 404 in note 8. Cf. I.H.Ph. de Rode-Verschoor, 'Les problèmes concernant les délits commis à bord des aéronefs particulièrement quant à la juridiction', *Revue Internationale de Droit Pénal*, Vol. 27, (1957) pp. 431-445.

10. *USA* v. *Cordova (and Santano)*, US District Court, Eastern District of New York, March 17, 1950; [1950] USAvR 1; *Avi*, Vol. 3, p. 17,306. See also Paul Gerhardt, 'Jurisdiction over Crimes Committed in Aircraft while Flying Over the High Seas' [1951] JALC 115–119; W.E. Hilbert, 'Jurisdiction in High Seas Criminal Cases – Part I' [1951] JALC 427–437, at 431 *et seq.*; and B. Reukema, 'Drinking and Flying. Why the two do not mix well on US carriers', *Annals of Air and Space Law*, vol. IX (1984), pp. 133-147.

in the rear section of the aircraft. Other passengers crowded in to watch the fight. This movement caused the aircraft, which was flying on the automatic pilot, to climb steeply because of the weight increase in the rear section of the plane. The pilot took the appropriate measures to regain control of the aircraft, while being informed by the stewardess of what was going on. He thereupon handed control of the aircraft to the co-pilot and went to the cabin to stop the fight. Santano calmed down, but Cordova attacked the pilot, bit him on the shoulder and knocked the stewardess down. He was then overpowered by others and locked up for the rest of the flight. Prosecution was ordered against both Cordova and Santano, but the indictment against Santano was dropped later on. Although the District Court of New York was satisfied that violence on the part of Cordova had been proved it ruled that his acts could not be punished within the admiralty and maritime jurisdiction of the United States: the statute covering such acts was confined to offences committed on a 'vessel' upon the high seas, and the court had to decide that an aircraft was not a 'vessel' within the meaning of the applicable statute. Moreover, the term 'upon the high seas' could not be extended to include an aircraft in flight 'over the high seas'. Consequently, the court, finding Cordova guilty, had to arrest judgment of conviction since there was no Federal jurisdiction to punish him. Cordova was released from custody, and there was no way left to punish an offence committed above the high seas on board an American aircraft. In response to a wave of criticism, domestic as well as foreign, the United States Congress amended the Federal statutes, making maritime law applicable to offences committed on board aircraft over the high seas.[11]

A third case was *R. v. Martin*. This was a case involving unlawful possession of drugs on board a British aircraft during a flight between Bahrein and Singapore. The case was brought before a British court pursuant to Article 62, para. 1, of the British Civil Aviation Act 1949,[12] which reads as follows: 'Any offence whatever committed on a British aircraft shall, for the purpose of conferring jurisdiction, be deemed to have been committed in any place where the offender may for the time being be'. Nevertheless, the court had to dismiss the case because the statutory offences of the law of England did not apply in British-registered aircraft outside British territory, unless specially so enacted. Article 62 of the Civil Aviation Act 1949, does not create offences, it merely asserts jurisdiction in England over offences created by common law or statutes.[13]

---

11. Public Law 514, 82nd Congress; [1952] USAvR 437–439.
12. Civil Aviation Act 1949 (12 & 13 Geo. 6, c. 67), see Shawcross and Beaumont, *Air Law* (3rd ed.), Vol. 2, pp. B-1 *et seq*. This paragraph was repealed by the Tokyo Convention Act 1967, s. 1(3).
13. *R. v. Martin et al.*, Central Criminal Court (London), March 22, 1956; [1956] USAvR 141.

Added to other instances, the cases quoted above provided ample evidence that legislation was urgently needed to help clear up a most unsatisfactory situation.

1.2. SCOPE AND PURPOSE OF THE TOKYO CONVENTION

According to Article 1, para. 1, the Convention applies to
'a) offences against penal law;
 b) acts which, whether or not they are offences, may or do jeopardize the safety of the aircraft or of persons or property therein or which jeopardize good order and discipline on board'.

Article 1, para. 4, contains an exception for aircraft used in military, customs and police services. From the wording of the text it is clear that the main criterion here is the use and not the ownership or registration of the aircraft.[14]
The objectives of the Convention may be described as follows:
a. to determine the penal law applicable when an offence has been committed above territories not belonging to any particular state, such as the high seas, or in cases in which the place where an offence has been committed cannot be precisely located;
b. to define the rights and obligations of the aircraft commander in respect of offences and acts committed on board which jeopardise the safety of the aircraft;
c. to define the rights and obligations of the authorities of the place where the aircraft lands after an offence or an act which jeopardises the safety of an aircraft has been committed.

1.3. JURISDICTION

With regard to the wording of Article 3 dealing with jurisdiction we would in the first place draw attention to paragraph 3 which states that the Convention 'does not exclude any criminal jurisdiction exercised in accordance with national law'. This means that the jurisdictional rules contained in the Convention are of a subsidiary nature.
Bearing in mind this important qualification, we further note in the same Article that it is the state of registration which has been declared competent to exercise jurisdiction over offences committed on board. However, there are also cases in which states other than the state of registration have jurisdiction over such offences, as is apparent from Article 4 of the Convention. This article reads as follows:

14. Cf. H.J. Rutgers, *Conventions on Penal Law Regarding Aircraft* (thesis Utrecht, 1978), pp. 30-31.

'A Contracting State which is not the State of registration may not interfere with an aircraft in flight in order to exercise its criminal jurisdiction over an offence committed on board except in the following cases:
(a) the offence has effect on the territory of such State;
(b) the offence has been committed by or against a national or permanent resident of such State;
(c) the offence is against the security of such State;
(d) the offence consists of a breach of any rules or regulations relating to the flight or manoeuvre of aircraft in force in such State;
(e) the exercise of jurisdiction is necessary to ensure the observance of any obligation of such State under a multilateral international agreement'.

Finally, we would mention Article 2, which reads:

'Without prejudice to the provisions of Article 4 and except when the safety of the aircraft or of persons or property on board so requires, no provision of this Convention shall be interpreted as authorizing or requiring any action in respect of offences against penal laws of a political nature or those based on racial or religious discrimination'.

It should be noted that no such provision appears in either the Hague Convention or the Montreal Convention, both of which will be discussed later.

1.4. DEFINITION OF THE TERM 'IN FLIGHT'

'An aircraft is considered to be in flight from the moment when power is applied for the purpose of take-off until the moment when the landing run ends' (Art. 1, para. 3). Yet, taken in connection with the authority of the aircraft commander, an aircraft is considered to be in flight 'at any time from the moment when all its external doors are closed following embarkation until the moment when any such door is opened for disembarkation' (Art. 5, para. 2). The first definition was taken from the 1952 Rome Convention relating to damage to third parties on the surface, the second was added to the Tokyo Convention for practical purposes.

Under the first definition the time when the aircraft moves across the airfield into position for actual take-off is left out of account: during that period the aircraft is not considered to be in flight, in terms of the Rome Convention. The same interpretation applies to Article 1, para. 3, and so the national law of the state concerned is applicable. It is important that the provisions of Article 5, para. 2, apply to this pre-take-off period, in view of the powers at the disposal of the aircraft commander. Such powers may be exercised immediately after the external doors of the aircraft have been closed. This rule was prompted by the consideration that from the moment the aircraft has become a 'sealed unit', separated from the outside world, the commander should be in a position to take measures, internationally recognised, to protect the aircraft, the persons and the goods therein. The two definitions serve to guarantee and ensure that at no time after the aircraft has become a 'closed universe' will it operate outside the scope of the Convention; it has therefore been provided that either the entire Convention will apply, or at least some of its important provisions like those of Chapter III concerning the powers of the commander.[15]

1.5. THE POWERS OF THE AIRCRAFT COMMANDER

Chapter III of the Tokyo Convention contains Articles 5 to 11 dealing with the powers of the aircraft commander.[16] The place where and the time during which the commander may exercise his authority are defined in the Convention, as is the liability for the measures taken by him or on his behalf. He may take 'measures of restraint' with regard to any person on board suspected of a penal offence, disembark him in any subsequent state of landing or deliver him to 'competent authorities'. Article 6, para. 2, states:

> 'The aircraft commander may require or authorize the assistance of other crew members and may request or authorize, but not require, the assistance of passengers to restrain any person whom he is entitled to restrain. Any crew member or passenger may also take reasonable preventive measures without such authorization when he has reasonable grounds to believe that such action is immediately necessary to protect the safety of the aircraft, or of persons or property therein.'

The action taken by the commander is subject to standards of reason. It may be difficult for him to decide just what constitutes an offence, but the ultimate decision is left to his discretion. The term 'offence' is not defined in the Convention due to the multitude and diversity of the national laws in the states party to it. This obstacle stood in the way of adopting a universally acceptable formula.

Article 10 speaks for itself; it states that: 'For actions taken in accordance with this Convention neither the aircraft commander, any other member of the crew, any passenger, the owner or operator of the aircraft, nor the person on whose behalf the flight was performed shall be held responsible in any proceeding on account of the treatment undergone by the person against whom the action was taken.'[17]

---

15. See Rutgers (note 14, *supra*), pp. 65-66; Boyle and Pulsifier (note 7, *supra*), p. 328.
16. See on this subject Nicolas M. Matte (note 6, *supra*), pp. 341-344 and also pp. 279-321.
17. Cf. Rutgers (note 14, *supra*), pp. 78-81.

1.6. UNLAWFUL SEIZURE

Although this offence is covered in a general manner by Article 1, the Convention, in Article 11, has devoted a special Chapter to unlawful seizure of aircraft, a phenomenon which has become increasingly frequent since the late 1940s.[18] Such emphasis must be seen as a reflection of the deep concern of the authors of the Tokyo Convention and their wish to underscore the importance they attached to it. It may be argued that such emphasis was not quite commensurate with the effect they may have expected: not only does the Article fail to cover all forms of unlawful seizure, it also fails to prescribe any effective counter-measures, confining itself to imposing on contracting states the obligation 'to take all appropriate measures to restore control of the aircraft to its lawful commander or to preserve his control of the aircraft'.

It is evident from the text of the Article just quoted that hijacking is not adequately covered by it; moreover, it fails to prescribe any sanctions against the offence. Some years later this lack of support in law turned out to be one of the reasons for states to conclude a separate Convention on hijacking (The Hague Convention of 1970), which will be discussed in more detail in section 2 of this chapter.

1.7. THE OBLIGATIONS OF THE STATES

In Articles 12 to 15 the powers and duties of the contracting states have been described. The state where the aircraft has landed must take delivery of any person whom the aircraft commander delivers pursuant to Article 9, para. 4, which allows him to deliver any person who he has reasonable grounds to believe has committed on board an act which, in his opinion, is a serious offence against the penal law of the state of registration of the aircraft. The state of landing must immediately undertake a preliminary enquiry into the facts after it has taken into custody or imposed any other measures against a person of whom it has accepted delivery. The state must also notify immediately the state of registration of the aircraft and the state of the nationality of the detained person and, if it considers it advisable, any other interested state. It must promptly report its findings to the said states and indicate whether it intends to exercise jurisdiction. The state may, if the person in question is not a national or a permanent resident of that state, return him to the territory of the state of which he is a national or a permanent resident, or to the territory of the state in which he began his journey by air (Art. 14, para. 1).

---

18. Cf. Sami Shubber, *Jurisdiction over Crimes on Board Aircraft* (1973), Appendix II (pp. 344-353); A.F. Lowenfeld, *Aviation Law*, Documents Supplement (1981), pp. 1181 *et seq.* (Worldwide Hijacking Statistics).

1.8. EXTRADITION

Articles 15 and 16 contain a number of provisions on extradition, of which those of Article 16 are the more significant. It is stated in Article 16, para. 1, that 'Offences committed on aircraft registered in a Contracting State shall be treated, for the purpose of extradition, as if they had been committed not only in the place in which they have occurred but also in the territory of the State of registration of the aircraft'.

Paragraph 2 of the same Article stipulates that 'Without prejudice to the provisions of the preceding paragraph, nothing in this Convention shall be deemed to create an obligation to grant extradition'.

These provisions on extradition merit special attention, as is pointedly illustrated in the *Soblen* case.[19] The Hague Convention of 1970 contains more specific rules on extradition. The problems surrounding this delicate question will be reverted to in more detail in section 2.4 of this chapter.

1.9. JOINT AND INTERNATIONAL OPERATING AGENCIES

Article 18 deals with organisations which jointly operate air transport and with international agencies conducting such operations. The article reads as follows:

> 'If Contracting States establish joint air transport operating organizations or international operating agencies, which operate aircraft not registered in any one State those States shall, according to the circumstances of the case, designate the State among them which, for the purposes of this Convention, shall be considered as the State of registration and shall give notice thereof to the International Civil Aviation Organization which shall communicate the notice to all States Parties to the Convention.'

1.10. SETTLEMENT OF DISPUTES

The key article governing this matter is Article 24, which states in paragraph 1 that in case of disputes between two or more contracting states there are three ways of reaching a settlement: (a) through negotiation; (b) through arbitration; (c) by submitting the case to the

---

19. See on the *Soblen* case C.H.R. Thornberry, 'Dr. Soblen and the Alien Law of the United Kingdom', *The International and Comparative Law Quarterly*, (1963), pp. 414-474, notably pp. 444 *et seq.*; G.F. Fitzgerald, ' The Development of International Rules Concerning Offences and Certain Other Acts Committed on Board Aircraft', *Canadian Yearbook of International Law* Vol. I, (1963) pp. 230-251, at pp. 248-249 in note 36. Cf. the *British Yearbook of International Law* Vol. XXXVIII (1962), pp. 479-483 and the Minutes of the 14th Session of the ICAO Legal Committee (Rome, August–September 1962), ICAO Doc. 8302–LC/150–1, at p. 5.

International Court of Justice. According to paragraph 2, a contracting state may declare a reservation concerning the preceding paragraph.

1.11. CONCLUDING NOTE

The Tokyo Convention entered into force on December 4, 1969. In spite of its imperfections the coming into force of an international Convention on offences and certain other acts committed on board aircraft may be regarded as a significant step towards establishing some moderate degree of legal order. It cannot be denied, however, that the final result shows a number of weak points such as: the absence of a definition of the word 'offence'; and the restrictive approach to extradition.[20]

2. The Hague Convention

2.1. THE NEED FOR A CONVENTION

The reason why hijacking is so difficult to combat lies in the fact that aircraft are so very vulnerable. The hazards involved in such criminal acts are manifold and unpredictable. They have been very aptly summed up by IFALPA as follows: (1) a fight between the crew and the hijackers may cause a complete loss of control of the aircraft; (2) essential damage may be caused if weapons are used in the cockpit; (3) collisions may result from an aircraft being unable to observe traffic regulations; (4) fuel shortage may occur; (5) the crew may be unfamiliar with a particular airport and its approach procedures.[21]

Hijacking activities have tended to focus mainly on the Middle East and the Caribbean area, the latter centering around Cuba. In an attempt to combat hijacking in the Caribbean region a sort of agreement was reached between the United States and Cuba in 1961, whereby US aircraft, crew and passengers would be returned under the responsibility of the United States. The latter stipulation was agreed because the Cubans argued that the runways of their airports were too short for big jet aircraft to take off fully loaded, so that passengers had to

---

20. Cf. Rutgers (note 14, *supra*), pp. 105-112; Nicolas M. Matte (note 6, *supra*), pp. 351-352.
21. Rutgers (note 14, *supra*), p. 122. Cf. A.E. Evans, 'Aircraft Hijacking: its Cause and Cure', (1969) 63 AJIL 695–710, at 701 *et seq*. I.M. Shepard, 'Air Piracy: The Role of the International Federation of Airline Pilots Associations', *Cornell International Law Journal*, Vol. 3, No. 1 (Winter 1970), 79–91. See for IFALPA's actions *in re* hijacking E.E. McWhinney, 'The Illegal Diversion of Aircraft and International Law', (1973 – I) 138 *Recueil des Cours* 261–372, at 287–289 and 335–337.

be sent back with smaller planes, a procedure involving long delays. As a result the US then assumed full responsibility for large jets taking off from Cuban airports with passengers.[22] Following this consensus an agreement was reached in 1973 which contained penal sanctions against hijacking offences.[23]

In a wider context concerted action was also started at the end of the 1960s to counteract hijacking, which was increasing with alarming frequency. This led to the conclusion, in December 1970, of the Hague Convention, which made hijacking an internationally punishable offence.

It is perhaps useful to mention, en passant, an error commonly made these days. The expression 'air piracy' is being used rather indiscriminately, and taken to be interchangeable with aircraft hijacking. In maritime law, in the 1958 Convention on the High Seas,[24] piracy was declared an offence, provided it had been committed for private motives against *another* ship of aircraft, or against persons or property on board such ship or aircraft. Article 1 of the Hague Convention, however, states that the offences must have been committed *on board* an aircraft in flight, which clearly indicates that in hijacking *only one* aircraft is involved.[25]

The Hague Convention further includes in its definition the following elements: (1) the act must be unlawful; (2) there must be some use of force, or threat of force; (3) the act must consist in seizure of an aircraft and exercise of unlawful control over it or attempt thereat.

2.2. THE SCOPE OF THE CONVENTION

The Convention is applicable irrespective of whether the flight is domestic or international (Art. 3, para. 3). The Convention further contains provisions on the pursuit and punishment of hijackers. It is applicable only to persons on board the aircraft in flight, but complicity and attempted hijackings are included as offences. Unlike the Tokyo Convention, there is only one definition of the term 'in flight' in the Hague Convention: an aircraft is considered to be 'in flight' from the moment when all its external doors are closed following embarkation until the moment when any such door is open for disembarkation (Art. 3, para. 1).

22. See E.E. McWhinney, *The Illegal Diversion of Aircraft and International Law* (1975), pp. 67 *et seq.* by the same author 'Hijacking of Aircraft', *Annuaire de l' Institut de Droit International* (1971), Vol. 54, pp. 520-558, at pp. 529 *et seq.*

23. A.F. Lowenfeld, *Aviation Law*, Cases and Materials (1981), p. 8-103 *et seq.* McWhinney (note 21, *supra*), p. 325 *et seq.* (the USA-Cuban Memorandum of Understanding on Hijacking of Aircraft and Vessels and Other Offences, February 15, 1973).

24. Convention on the High Seas, Geneva, April 29, 1958.

25. See on this subject A. Samuels, 'The Legal Problems: an Introduction' [1971] JALC 163–170, at 170; Evans (note 21, *supra*), at pp. 696-697. Note also the various other contributions on hijacking in [1971] JALC 163–233 (Symposium on the Unlawful Seizure of Aircraft: Approaches to the Legal Problems).

2.3. JURISDICTION

Jurisdiction, according to Article 4, has been assigned to the following contracting states:
1. the state of registration, when the offence has been committed on board an aircraft registered in that state;
2. the state of landing, when the alleged offender is still on board;
3. the state where the lessee of an aircraft without crew has his principal place of business or his permanent residence;
4. the state in whose territory the alleged offender is found and apprehended and which does not extradite him to any of the states previously mentioned.

Taking into custody or taking other measures to ensure the offender's presence have been made obligatory for the state where he is present, as well as making a preliminary enquiry into the facts (Art. 6, para. 1 and 2), but the Convention has stopped short of making the actual prosecution and trial mandatory. Given this overall situation it would be appropriate to say that the Hague Convention has indeed introduced the principle of universality of jurisdiction, which implies that an offender is liable to prosecution anywhere in the world, but with an important restriction: instead of fully honouring this principle, it has been made subject to the actual presence of the offender in a particular state.[26]

Note should be taken of the fact that under the Convention (Art. 4) not only hijacking itself, but also the offender's use of force in connection with the seizure is covered by the jurisdiction.

Article 5 of the Convention deals with joint operating organisations and international operating agencies which may be established by the contracting states. The text of the relevant Article reads:

> 'The Contracting States which establish joint air transport operating organizations or international operating agencies, which operate aircraft which are subject to joint or international registration shall, by appropriate means, designate for each aircraft the State among them which shall exercise the jurisdiction and have the attributes of the State of registration for the purpose of this Convention and shall give notice thereof to the International Civil Aviation Organization which shall communicate the notice to all States Parties to this Convention'.

2.4. EXTRADITION

On the face of it, the Hague Convention seems to contain a reversal of the rules of Articles 15 and 16 of the Tokyo Convention on extradition.

---

26. See F. Spörri, *Die Bekämpfung der widerrechtlichen Inbesitznahme von Luftfahrzeuge durch das Haager Übereinkommen vom 16. Dezember 1970* (thesis Zürich, 1979), at pp. 142-143. Cf. J. de Watteville, *La piraterie aérienne* (1978), at pp. 86-88.

This impression could be inferred from Article 7 which reads as follows:

'The Contracting State in the territory of which the alleged offender is found shall, if it does not extradite him, be obliged, without exception whatsoever and whether or not the offence was committed in its territory, to submit the case to its competent authorities for the purpose of prosecution. Those authorities shall take their decision in the same manner as in the case of any ordinary offence of a serious nature under the law of that State'.

The inspiration behind this article is well-known adage of *aut dedere, aut judicare*.[27]

The reversal of policy, however, is not nearly as complete as it would perhaps seem. In Article 8, paras. 2 and 3, it is explicitly stated that extradition shall be 'subject to the other conditions provided by the law of the requested State'. The Convention, by this token, still contains no general rule making extradition obligatory. Extradition can only be effected in accordance with the laws of the requested state which, in turn, will reflect the rules of any extradition treaty that state may have concluded.

Article 8 is designed to provide a legal basis for extradition for all states party to the Convention. A distinction is made between states which make extradition conditional upon the existence of an extradition treaty, and the states which do not. The first category may or may not accept the Convention as a legal basis for extradition, the second shall 'recognise' the offence as an extraditable one.[28]

Another restriction to be noted in the Convention is its being limited to offences as described in the terms of Article 1. This means that unlawful acts committed in connection with such an offence are not covered by the extradition provisions of the Convention.

Article 8, para. 4 prescribes: ' The offence shall be treated, for the purpose of extradition between Contracting States, as if it had been committed not only in the place in which it occurred, but also in the territories of the States required to establish their jurisdiction in accordance with Article 4, paragraph 1'. The number of states to which extradition can be effected is increased accordingly.

As regards offenders claiming political asylum it should be noted that the Convention is silent on that point, although a ban on it had been contemplated during the preliminary discussions. Such a move would of course have meant an encroachment on the right of asylum. The result now is that when it comes to applying Article 7 much, if not all, will depend on the impartiality and integrity of the prosecuting authorities. Should they wish to ignore their obligation either to extradite or prosecute, then there is nothing to stop them. Herein

27. This principle is clearly demonstrated by the curious case of the hijacking of a Polish airliner to West-Berlin (*United States* v. *Tiede*): see the article on this case by D. Schoner in *Air Law*, vol. VI (1981), pp. 43-47.
28. See the Minutes of the International Conference on Air Law (The Hague, December 1970), ICAO Doc. 8979–LC/165–1 at p. 125 *et seq.*

lies the main weakness of the Convention: it cannot prevent states from granting political asylum to hijackers, if they so choose.[29]

However, in 1977, a European Convention on the Suppression of Terrorism[30] was concluded in Strasbourg by Member States of the Council of Europe, some of whom have already ratified. This Convention has widened the range of extradition possibilities for acts of terrorism (including hijacking) by eliminating the area of what may be termed 'political' offences. In addition, the rule *aut dedere, aut judicare*, which has also been included in the Strasbourg Convention, has been strengthened by contracting parties undertaking to enforce their own jurisdiction in the event of their refusing to extradite, for instance on the grounds of prosecution for reasons of race or religion. The Strasbourg Convention thus represents a significant step forward, in that offenders apprehended in the contracting states will not be able to escape trial.

2.5. MISCELLANEOUS PROVISIONS

The Hague Convention has adopted the provision in Article 11 of the Tokyo Convention safeguarding the right of passengers and crew to continue their journey and the return of the aircraft and its cargo to the persons legally entitled to it; this rule has been accentuated in the Hague Convention by adding the words 'without delay' (Art. 9).

Article 10, para. 2, provides that mutual assistance in criminal matters under the Convention will not prejudice obligations of that nature under any other treaty.

According to Article 11, the contracting states are obliged to promptly notify the ICAO Council of any hijacking, the circumstances and the action taken in response to it.

Finally, Article 12 prescribes that all disputes concerning the interpretation or application of the Convention shall be submitted to arbitration. When a settlement cannot be reached the dispute shall be submitted to the International Court of Justice. This is the only provision in the Convention to which reservations may be made.

2.6. CONCLUDING NOTE

It is clear that, for all the improvements achieved by the Convention, a few inadequacies still remain. One has already been referred to

---

29. Cf. Minutes of the Hague Conference (note 28, *supra*), notably the discussions on Art. 7 (pp. 130-137 and pp. 177-182). However, mention must be made of the 1978 Bonn Declaration on Hijacking which may be used to impose an aviation blockade on countries giving asylum to air pirates. See W. Schwenk, 'The Bonn Declaration on Hijacking', *Annals of Air and Space Law*, vol. IV (1979), pp. 307-322.
30. European Convention on the Suppression of Terrorism, Strasbourg, January 27, 1977. See on this Convention also de Watteville (note 26, *supra*), pp. 121-135.

earlier in this section in connection with jurisdiction: there is no obligation to prosecute. Another is that there is no provision on who is liable for damage to persons or goods resulting from a hijacking. To obtain such compensation one has to resort to the Warsaw System which, as has been demonstrated in Chapter III, does not always provide adequate relief.

The case of a 14-year-old girl travelling by air from New York to Tel Aviv may be quoted here to illustrate the point. Her aircraft was hijacked on September 6, 1970, and was forced to land in the desert near Amman, Jordan. The aircraft remained there with the plaintiff and the other passengers as prisoners of the terrorists until September 12, 1970. The New York Court of Appeals ruled that only mental anguish directly resulting from bodily injury was eligible for compensation under the Warsaw System.[31]

The growing rate of hijacking incidents as a weapon of terrorism has on various occasions prompted the suggestion of establishing an International Criminal Court to deal with this aspect of aviation.[32]

An important item not covered by the Hague Convention concerns the position of security agents on board aircraft and their powers to deal with hijackers. The issue has been discussed at the Diplomatic Conference, but IFALPA and the airline companies represented by IATA were opposed to the idea. Their opposition stemmed from their conviction that the presence of armed agents on board was dangerous, considering the vulnerability of an aircraft.[33]

3. The Montreal Convention

As the Hague and Tokyo Conventions were concerned exclusively with offences committed on board aircraft, another agreement was needed to combat other unlawful acts against the safety of civil aviation. These are dealt with in the Montreal Convention concluded in 1971, the year following the adoption of the Hague Convention.

According to Article 1, para. 1, of the Montreal Convention a person commits an offence if
'he unlawfully and intentionally:
(a) performs an act of violence against a person on board an aircraft in flight if that act is likely to endanger the safety of that aircraft; or
(b) destroys an aircraft in service or causes damage to such an aircraft which renders it incapable of flight or which is likely to endanger its safety in flight; or

---

31. *Rosman et al.* v. *TWA, Herman* v. *TWA*, State of New York, Court of Appeals, June 13, 1974; [1974] USAvR 1; *Avi*, Vol. 13, p. 17,231; see also Chap. III of this book for other cases on the subject of mental injury. Cf. F.A. Boyle, 'The Entebbe Hostages Crisis' (1982) XXIX *Netherlands International Law Review* 32–71.
32. Cf. note 42 of Chap. VI of this book, *supra*.
33. See Rutgers (note 14, *supra*), pp. 124-125, on the USA 'Sky-marshals'.

(c) places or causes to be placed on an aircraft in service, by any means whatsoever, a device or substance which is likely to destroy that aircraft, or to cause damage to it which renders it incapable of flight, or to cause damage to it which is likely to endanger its safety in flight; or

(d) destroys or damages air navigation facilities or interferes with their operation, if any such act is likely to endanger the safety of aircraft in flight; or

(e) communicates information which he knows to be false, thereby endangering the safety of aircraft in flight'.

Attempts to commit such acts, as well as complicity, have also been made offences, pursuant to paragraph 2 of the same Article. Unfortunately, the clause 'endangering the safety of the aircraft' in Article 1, para. 1(e), means that false bomb alerts, which cause only delay and no damage to the aircraft are not covered. False alarms thus remain outside the Convention's reach.

By signing the Convention, the contracting states have undertaken to impose severe penalties with regard to the offences listed above, pursuant to Article 3.

Article 5 states that each contracting state must take all such measures as may be necessary to establish its jurisdiction in the following cases:

'(a) when the offence is committed in the territory of that State;

(b) when the offence is committed against or on board an aircraft registered in that State;

(c) when the aircraft on board which the offence is committed lands in its territory with the alleged offender still on board;

(d) when the offence is committed against or on board an aircraft leased without crew to a lessee who has his principal place of business or, if he has no such place of business, his permanent residence in that State'.

In addition, each state must take such measures in the event of the offender being found on its territory and not being extradited, according to Article 5, para. 2. Another duty for contracting states is to take all necessary steps to prevent the offences mentioned in Article 1 in accordance with international and national law (Art. 10).

The Convention is applicable to domestic as well as international flights if the point of take-off or landing, or both are situated outside the territory of the state of registration, or when the offence is committed in the territory of a state other than the state of registration, according to Article 4, para. 2.

Special mention must be made of Article 2, para. (b), which explains the meaning of the words 'in service' for the purpose of the Convention. It is the first time that this expression has been used in a convention. Article 2 states that 'an aircraft is considered to be in service from the beginning of the preflight preparation of the aircraft by ground personnel or by the crew for a specific flight until twenty-four hours after any landing; the period of service shall, in any event, extend for the entire period during which the aircraft is in flight as defined in paragraph (a) of this article'. The provision has been inserted because the Convention is applicable on both domestic and international level.

As for the word 'landing', this word is supposed to cover scheduled, intended and forced landings. A proposal to make the carrying of deadly or dangerous weapons on board without permission from the carrier or his agent punishable was rejected.[34]

According to Article 12, states are required to supply each other with all relevant information when they have reason to believe that an offence mentioned in Article 1 is going to be committed.

Finally, attention must be drawn to the fact that several provisions in the Montreal Convention are identical with those covering the same subjects in the Hague Convention. This applies to:
1. the non-applicability of the Convention to military, customs and police aircraft (Art. 4);
2. the definition of the words 'in flight' (Art. 2, para. (a));
3. joint and international operating agencies (Art. 9); and
4. the final provisions, including settlement of disputes (Arts. 13–16).

4. Concluding remarks

In the interests of safety of aircraft on land and in the air and of the passengers it is important that the three Conventions reviewed in this chapter should be ratified by the majority of states. During the ICAO discussions on how to impose sanctions on states unwilling to participate in the Conventions few results have been achieved due to political and economical implications.[35] In a meeting of the ICAO Legal Committee in Montreal in January 1973[36] proposals were submitted aimed at amending the Chicago Convention in such a way that states not complying with the Hague and Montreal Conventions would either be excluded from ICAO or refused the right of passage by the states party to the Chicago Convention. On the other hand it was proposed to convene a Diplomatic Conference which would set up a commission to monitor the facts and to advise on measures to be taken against states failing to comply. Added to these there was a Russian proposal to add a Protocol to the Hague and Montreal Conventions requiring the extradition of the offender to the state of registration, if so requested, except when the offender is a citizen of the state receiving such a request. All these proposals failed to secure

---

34. Cf. the Minutes of the International Conference on Air Law (Montreal, September 1971), ICAO Doc. 9081 – LC/170–1, notably the discussions on Art. 1 of the draft convention.
35. See Rutgers (note 14, *supra*), Chap. VII, pp. 176 *et seq.*
36. See the Minutes and Documents of the 20th Session of the ICAO Legal Committee (Special Session, Montreal, January 1973), ICAO Doc. 9050–LC/169–1 and 169–2.

a majority at the meeting of the ICAO Assembly held in Rome in 1973.[37] However, it is interesting to note that the United States authorities insist on an undertaking being given by their partners in bilateral agreements to the effect that the provisions of the three penal Conventions will be applied.

More recently, attempts have been made by ICAO to create an 'Instrument for the Suppression of Unlawful Acts of Violence at Airports serving International Civil Aviation'. For that purpose a special sub-committee of the ICAO Legal Committee preferred the form of a Special Protocol to be added to the Montreal Convention. This proposal was adopted at the February 1988 ICAO Conference held at Montreal[38]. This addition was very useful to improve the safety at airports. But lately in-flight violence has also become a major problem. One of its causes is the abuse of drugs and alcohol by passengers. In spite of the existence of various international instruments discussed above problems often arise in these cases regarding criminal jurisdiction. A solution may be found in starting civil proceedings against the offenders. Drawing up a 'black list' by air carriers could, however, give rise to conflicts with laws and regulations protecting privacy.

Further I would like to mention the Convention on the Marking of (Plastic and Sheet) Explosives for the Purpose of Detection adopted by ICAO in 1991.[39]

Finally, I would like to mention that in June 1996 the ICAO Council added to the General Work Programme of the Legal Committee the subject of 'acts and offences of concern to the international aviation community and not covered by existing instruments'.[40]

---

37. See the 20th Session of the Extraordinary Assembly of ICAO (Rome, August–September 1973), ICAO Doc. 9087. See also M.Milde, 'The International Fight Against Terrorism in the Air', in *The Use of Airspace and Outer Space for All Mankind in the 21st Century*, Proceedings of the International Conference on Air Transport and Space Application in a New World (Tokyo, June 2-5, 1993), Chia-Jui Cheng, ed., pp. 141-158.

38. See Bin Cheng, 'International Legal Instruments to Safeguard International Air Transport: the Conventions of Tokyo, The Hague, Montreal and a new Instrument concerning unlawful violence at international airports', in *Aviation Security: How to Safeguard International Air Transport* (proceedings of a Conference held at the Peace Palace, The Hague, January 22–23, 1987), pp. 23-46. See also *Air Law*, vol. XII (1987), pp. 50-51 and *Air Law*, vol. XIII (1988), pp. 95-100.

39. See on this subject the report and the text of a proposed Draft Convention in *Air Law*, vol. XV (1990), pp. 56-59, and also the report in *Air Law*, vol. XV (1990), pp. 162-163. See also I.H.Ph. Diederiks-Verschoor, 'Responsibility for the transportation by the passenger of dangerous materials by air', in *Air and Space Law: De Lege Ferenda* (1992), pp. 101-112. See also R.I.R.Abeyratne, 'Legal aspects of unlawful interference with international civil aviation', *Air and Space Law*, vol.XVIII (1993), pp. 262-274 at pp. 267-268; J.V.Augustin, 'The role of ICAO in relation to the Convention on the Marking of Plastic Explosives for the Purpose of Detection', *Annals of Air and Space Law*, vol. 17 (1992), pp. 33-69; and R.D.van Dam, 'A new Convention on the Marking of Plastic Explosives for the Purpose of Detection', *Air Law*, vol. XVI (1991), pp. 167-177.

40. See *Air and Space Law*, vol. XXI (1996), p. 296.

Bibliography

In this bibliography the various Minutes and Documents relating to sessions of the ICAO Legal Committee and ICAO International Conferences on Air Law have not been listed. References to these publications are to be found in the relevant notes in this book.

Bibliography

Heere, W.P., *International Bibliography of Air Law, 1900–1971 (1972);*
—*Supplement 1972–1976 (1976);*
—*Supplement 1977–1980 (1981);*
—*Supplement 1981–1984 (1985);*
—*Supplement 1985–1990 (1991);*
—*Supplement 1991-1995 (1996).*

From 1985 annual updates published in advance of the four-yearly *Supplements* are to appear in *Air Law* (see *Air Law*, vol. X (1985), p. 227 *et seq.*)

Journals

Air (and Space) Law.
Annals of Air and Space Law/Annales de Droit Aérien et Spatial.
Il Diritto Aereo.
Journal of Air Law and Commerce.
Revue Française de Droit Aérien (et Spacial).
Revue Générale de l' Air (et de l' Espace).
Zeitschrift für Luft (– und Weltraum) recht(sfragen).

Books and articles

Aéroports du Futur/Airports of the Future, 1996, Proceedings of an international symposium (Paris, December 15-17, 1995).
Aircraft Financing in the Pacific Rim, Proceedings of a Conference, held in Sydney (November 1989).
Aircraft Financing: Recent Developments and Prospects, Proceedings of a Conference (Amsterdam, January 17, 1992).
Air Line Mergers and Cooperation in the European Community, Proceedings of a Conference (London, 1990), P.D. Dagtoglou and T. Soames, eds., European Air Law Association Conference Papers, vol. 2 (1991).
Air and Space Law: De Lege Ferenda, Essays in Honour of Henri A. Wassenbergh, T.L. Masson-Zwaan and P. Mendes de Leon, eds., 1992.
Air Transport and the European Community - Recent Developments, Proceedings of a Conference (London, 1989), P.D. Dagtoglou, ed., European Air Law Association Conference Papers, vol. 1 (1990).
Air Transport Law and Policy in the 1990's, Controlling the Boom, P. Mendes de Leon, ed. (1991).
Air Worthy, Liber Amicorum honouring Prof. Dr. I.H.Ph. Diederiks-Verschoor (J.W.E. Storm van 's Gravesande and A. van der Veen Vonk, eds., 1985).
Aviation Security: How to Safeguard International Air Transport?, Proceedings of a Conference held at the Peace Palace (The Hague, January 22–23, 1987), 1987.

219

Beiträge zum Luft- und Weltraumrecht, Festschrift zu Ehren von Alex Meyer (M. Bodenschatz, K.H. Böckstiegel, P. Weides, eds., 1975).

Cabotage in International Air Transport Historical and Present-Day Aspects (Institut du Transport Aérien (ITA), Paris, Study 1969/7).

'Chicago Revisited', Proceedings of a conference (Montreal, December 3-5, 1994), *Annals of Air and Space Law*, vol. XX (1995).

EEC Air Transport Policy and Regulation and their Implications for North America, Proceedings of a Conference held at McGill University, Montreal (September 1989), 1990, P.P.C.Haanappel *et al.*, eds.

Essays in Air Law (A. Kean, ed. 1981).

European Air Law Association Second Annual Conference, Proceedings of a Conference (Brussels, 1990), P.D. Dagtoglou, J.M. Balfour and J. Stuyck, eds., European Air Law Association Conference Papers, vol. 3 (1991).

European Air Law Association Third Annual Conference, Proceedings of a Conference (Berlin, 1991), P.D. Dagtoglou, F. Montag and J.M. Balfour, eds., European Air Law Association Conference Papers, vol. 4 (1992).

European Air Law Association Fourth Annual Conference, Proceedings of a Conference (Rome, 1992), P.D. Dagtoglou, A. Giardina and J.M. Balfour, eds., European Air Law Association Conference Papers, vol. 5 (1993).

Explorations in Aerospace Law, selected essays by John Cobb Cooper (I.A. Vlasic, ed. 1968).

The Freedom of the Air (E.E. McWhinney and M.A. Bradley, eds., 1968).

The Highways of Air and Outer Space over Asia, Proceedings of a Conference (Taipei, 1991), C.-J. Cheng and P. Mendes de Leon, eds. (1992).

ICAO Lexicon (5th ed., 1980), ICAO Doc. 9294 (2 volumes).

International Air Law (in Russian), vol. I and II (A.P. Movchan and O.N. Sadikov, eds., 1980/1981).

International Air Transport in the Eighties (H.A. Wassenbergh and H.P. van Fenema, eds., 1981).

Issues of International Law of the Sea and Air Law (in Russian), (M.I. Lazarev, *et al.,* eds., 1979).

Liber Amicorum en homenaje al Prof. Dr. Luis Tapia Salinas (Ibero-American Institute of Air and Space Law and Commercial Aviation), 1989.

Liber Amicorum honouring/en hommage à Nicolas Mateesco Matte (G. R. Baccelli, ed.), 1989.

Luftrecht in Fünf Jahrzehnten (Alex Meyer, 1961).

Multilingual Aeronautical Dictionary (Advisory Group for Aerospace Research and Development, North Atlantic Treaty Organisation(AGARD/NATO), 1980).

Die Produkthaftung in der Luft- und Raumfahrt (Product Liability in Air and Space Transportation), Proceedings of an international Colloquium (K.H. Böckstiegel, ed., Cologne, 1977).

'The Right to Health as a Human Right', Workshop Hague Academy of International Law/United Nations University, The Hague, July 27–29, 1978, (R.-J. Dupuy, ed., 1979) published in the *Recueil des Cours* series.

A Short History of Aviation Insurance in the United Kingdom, Report H.R. 10 of the Historic Records Committee of the Insurance Institute of London (2nd ed., 1968).

Studi in onore di Antonio Ambrosini (1957).

The Use of Airspace and Outer Space for All Mankind in the 21st Century, Proceedings of the International Conference on Air Transport and Space Application in a New World (Tokyo, June 2-5, 1993), Chia-Jui Cheng, ed.

Wörterbuch des Völkerrechts (K. Strupp and H.J. Schlochauer, eds., 1962).

Abeyratne, R.I.R, 'Legal aspects of unlawful interference with international civil aviation', *Air and Space Law*, vol. XVIII (1993), pp. 262-274.

— *Legal and Regulatory Issues of Computer Reservation Systems and Code Sharing Agreements in Air Transport*, 1995 (Forum for Air and Space Law, vol. 3).

— 'Regulatory Management of the Warsaw System of Air Carrier Liability', *Journal of Air Transport Management*, vol. 3 (1997), pp. 37-45.

Achtnicht, H., 'Luftrechtliche Betrachtungen anlässlich des Absturzes eines Flugzeuges der Königlich Niederländischen Luftverkehrsgesellschaft (KLM) am 22. März 1952 bei Frankfurt-am-Main' [1952] ZfL 323–346.

Adkins, B., *Air Transport and EC Competition Law*, 1994.

Alexander, Y., E. Sochor, *Aerial Piracy and Aviation Security*, International Studies on Terrorism, vol. 5 (1990).

Alvarez-Correa, E. *La responsabilité civile pour les dommages causés aux tiers à la surface par le bruit et les ondes de choc des aéronefs, étude de droit français* (thesis Lausanne, 1972).

Ambrosini, A., 'Deuxième rapport sur l'avant-projet de convention sur l'abordage aérien' [1934] RGDA 474–483.

Atchley, D.B., 'Air Transportation of Radioactive Materials and Passenger Protection under International Law' [1974/1975] 5 *California Western Journal of International Law* 425–445.

Augustin, J.V., 'The role of ICAO in relation to the Convention on the Marking of Plastic Explosives for the Purpose of Detection', *Annals of Air and Space Law*, vol. 17 (1992), pp. 33-69.

Awford, Ian, 'Civil liability concerning unlawful interference with civil aviation', in *Aviation Security: How to Safeguard International Air Transport?*, pp. 47–73.

—'Punitive damages in aviation products liability cases' *Air Law*, vol. X (1985), pp. 3–9.

—*Developments in Aviation Products Liability* (1985).

—'Handling the legal consequences of aviation disasters – Passenger compensation', ZLW 1992, pp. 17–41.

Bai, A., *Luftrecht und Grundeigentum*, (thesis Winterthur), 1955.

Bakelen, F.A. van, 'Aviation sports bound to legal hushkittings. Some administrative regulations on aircraft models in the Netherlands', *Air Worthy*, pp. 15–24.

— 'Aviation wizards — terminal hazards', *Air Law*, vol. XIII (1988), pp. 77–91.

Balfour, J., *European Community Air Law*, 1995.

Baren, W.H. van, 'Recent Aviation Case Law from the Benelux', *Air and Space Law*, vol. XVIII (1993), pp. 29–35.

Barlow, P., 'Article 22 of the Warsaw Convention in a state of limbo', *Air Law*, vol. VIII (1983), pp. 2–30.

Barrell, Y. and R. A. Lewis, 'Failure to comply with documentary technicalities of Warsaw Convention leads to unlimited liability in baggage cases', *Air Law*, vol. XV (1990), pp. 98-99.

Bayitch, S.A., *Aircraft Mortgage in the Americas*, University of Miami School of Law Interamerican Studies, No. 5, 1960 (also published in 13 *University of Miami Law Review* 152–188 and 424–446 (1959)).

Bentzien, J.F., 'Der europäische Luftverkehr und der EWG-Vertrag' [1981] ZLW 258–277.

— 'Die Zuständigkeit des Internationalen Seegerichtshofes für Streitigkeiten der internationalen Luftfahrt', ZLW, vol. 45 (1996), pp. 145-161.

Bishop, W.W., Jr., 'Reservations to Treaties' (1961 – II) 103 *Recueil des Cours*, 245–341.

Böckstiegel, K.-H., 'Competences for civil and military aviation in German law', *Air Worthy*, pp. 25–33.

Bodenschatz M., 'Die Fluggast-Unfallversicherung als Möglichkeit der ergänzenden Schadenersatzregelung gemäss Guatemala Protokoll', *Beiträge zum Luft- und Weltraumrecht* (Festschrift zu Ehren von Alex Meyer, 1975), pp. 45–54.

221

—'Rome Convention: Quo Vadis?' *Report* of the 55th Conference of the International Law Association (New York, 1972), pp. 742–e–742–j.

Bogaert, E. van, 'The Relativity of the Notion of the Law of the Air', *Studia Diplomatica* (Brussels, 1979), Vol. XXXII, No.6, pp. 621–637.

Bogolasky, J.C., 'Air Transport in Latin America: the Expanding Role of LACAC' [1978] JALC 75–107.

Böhme, K.H., *Die internationale Organisation der zivilen Luftfahrt in ihrem geschichtlichen Werdegang* (thesis Göttingen, 1956).

Boyle, F.A., 'The Entebbe Hostages Crisis' (1982) XXIX *Netherlands International Law Review*, 32–71.

Boyle, R.P. and R. Pulsifier, 'The Tokyo Convention on Offences and Certain Other Acts Committed on Board Aircraft' [1964] JALC 305–354.

Brancker, J.W.S., *IATA and What it Does* (1977).

Brierly, J.L., 'Reservations to Multilateral Conventions', Report to the International Law Commission, *Yearbook of the International Law Commission* (1951–II), pp. 1–27 (UN Doc. A/CN 4/41).

Burkhardt, R., *CAB-The Civil Aeronautics Board* (1974).

Callagher, M.R. and A.L. Stephens, 'Recent Developments in Aviation Case Law' [1978] JALC 231-260.

Carroz, J., 'International Legislation on Air Navigation over the High Seas [1959] JALC 158–172.

Chaveau, P., 'Rapport', *Report* of the 48th Conference of the International Law Association (New York, 1958), pp. 331–337.

Cheng, Bin, *The Law of International Air Transport* (1962). Note that an integral photoreprint of this treatise was published in 1984.

—'State Ships and State Aircraft', *Current Legal Problems*, Vol. 11 (1958), pp. 225–257

—'Transport Law of the European Communities' (1963) 16 *Current Legal Problems*, 197–219.

—'Wilful Misconduct: From Warsaw to The Hague and From Brussels to Paris', *Annals of Air and Space Law* Vol. II, (1977) pp. 55–102.

—'The destruction of KAL flight KE007, and Article 3 *bis* of the Chicago Convention', *Air Worthy*, pp. 47–74.

—'International legal instruments to safeguard international air transport: The Conventions of Tokyo, The Hague, Montreal and a new instrument concerning unlawful violence at international airports', in *Aviation Security: How to Safeguard International Air Transport?*, pp. 23–46

—'Sixty Years of the Warsaw Convention', Part I: [1989] ZLW, pp. 319–345 and Part II: [1990] ZLW, pp. 3–56.

—'The Warsaw System: Mess up, Tear up, or Shore up?', in *The Use of Airspace and Outer Space for All Mankind in the 21st Century*, Proceedings of the International Conference on Air Transport and Space Application in a New World (Tokyo, June 2-5, 1993), Chia-Jui Cheng, ed., pp. 105-130.

—'A shored-up Warsaw Convention plus a contractual so-called "fifth jurisdiction"?', *The Aviation Quarterly*, July 1996, pp. 18-30.

Cleveringa, R.P., 'Proposal to Establish an International Court of Arbitration on Maritime and Air Law', Second Conference of the International Bar Association (The Hague, 1948).

Cohen, D., 'Happy Birthday: Agreement CAB 18900: A Critical Review of the Montreal Interim Agreement and the Authority for its Implementation', *Air Law*, vol. VII (1982), pp. 74–91.

Coie, J.P., 'The Present State of the Law in the United States from the Standpoint of Industry', *Die Produkthaftung in der Luft- und Raumfahrt*, pp. 109–123.

Colegrove, K.W., *International Control of Aviation* (1930).

Coninck, F. de, *European Air Law: New Skies for Europe* (1993).

Cooper, J.C., 'The Bermuda Plan: World Pattern for Air Transport', (1964) 25 *Foreign Affairs* 59–71.

—'The International Air Navigation Conference, Paris 1910' [1952] JALC 127–143 (also published in *Explorations in Aerospace Law*, pp. 105–124).

—'National Status of Aircraft' [1950] JALC 292–311.

Corrigan, M.J., 'Actions on Behalf of Infants are Barred by Two Year Time Limitation of Warsaw Convention', *Air Law*, vol. VII (1982), pp. 124.

—'Hijacking Coverage', *Air Law*, vol. I (1976), pp. 35–39.

Craft Jr., R.R., 'La responsabilité des fabricants en droit américain' [1981] RFDA 21–37.

Crans, B.J.H., 'The special contract: an instrument to stretch liability limits?', *Air Law*, vol. XV (1990), pp. 159-175.

—and E.M.H. Loozen, 'EC Aviation Scene', *Air Law*, vol. XVI (1991), pp. 178–194.

—'EC Aviation Scene', *Air and Space Law*, vol. XVII (1992), pp. 217–223.

Cuadra, E., 'Air Defense Identification Zones – Creeping Jurisdiction in the Airspace' 18 *Virginia Journal of International Law* 485–512 (1978/1979).

Dam, R.D. van. 'Licensing as an instrument of deregulation' *Air Worthy*, pp. 75–87.

—'A new Convention on the Marking of Plastic Explosives for the Purpose of Detection; *Air Law*, vol. XVI (1991), pp. 167–177.

—'A new Convention on the Marking of Plastic Explosives for the Purpose of Detection', *Air Law*, vol. XVI (1991), pp. 167-177.

—'Lease, Charter and Interchange of Aircraft and the Chicago Convention - Some Observations', *Air and Space Law*, vol. XIX (1994), pp. 124-130.

Dauphinot, L.A., 'Radioactive Material' [1976] JALC 906–919.

Davis, Tom, 'Aviation Repair Stations and Strict Liability' [1974] JALC 413–424.

DeSaussure, H., 'Product Liability and the Use of Disclaimer Clauses by Aircraft Manufacturers', *Die Produkthaftung in der Luft- und Raumfahrt*, pp. 157–164.

Diederiks-Verschoor, I.H.Ph., 'Assistance et sauvetage en droit maritime, aérien et spatial. Nécessité d'une coopération', *Annuaire de Droit Maritime et Aérien* (1976), Vol. 3, pp. 93–101.

—'Considerations on Carriage by Air Executed by Various Successive Carriers', EVR (1970), Vol. 5, pp. 143–165.

—'Haftung für Schäden durch Überschallflüge', [1970] ZLW 235 –240.

—*et al.*, ' La naissance d'Eurocontrol et les développements à propos des tarifs de cette organisation', EVR (1976), Vol. II, 842–853.

—*et al.*, 'Der Rechtsstellung des Personals der Zivilluftfahrt' [1972] ZLW 107–132.

—'Responsibility for the Transportation by the Passenger of Dangerous Materials by Air', in *Air and Space Law: De Lege Ferenda*, pp. 101–112.

—*An Introduction to Space Law* (1993).

—and Wassenbergh, H.A., 'Dr. J.F.Lycklama à Nijeholt (1846-1947)', *Air and Space Law*, vol. XIX (1994), pp. 8-14.

—'International Co-operation and its Implications for Aircraft Registration and Nationality', *Annals of Air and Space Law*, vol. XIX, Part I (1994), pp. 145-159.

—'New Developments Around the Compensation Limits of the Warsaw Convention', in *Issues in International Air and Space Law, and in Commercial Law* (Essays in Commemoration of Prof.Dr. Doo Hwan Kim's Sixtieth Birthday), 1994, pp. 3-11.

—'The Settlement of Aviation Disputes', *Annals of Air and Space Law*, vol.XX (1995), pp. 335-341.

—'Le financement des aéronefs', in Part III of *Recherches et Réalisations*, *Mélanges Pierre Vellas*, 1995, pp. 551-562 (also separately published under the title *Transport Aérien et Activités Spatiales*, 1995).

Diersch, W., *Der internationale 'Gelegenheits' luftverkehr* (1981), published as Vol. 8 of the series *Bürgerliches, Handels- und Verkehrsrecht* (E. Ruhwedel, ed.).

Din, Adel Salah El, *Aviation Insurance Practice, Law and Reinsurance*, circa 1971 (year of publication not indicated).

Donnelly, D., 'Aircraft Crashworthiness – Plaintiff's Viewpoint', [1976] JALC 57–71.

Draper, G.I.A., *The Red Cross Conventions* (1958).

Drion, H., 'The Council of ICAO as International Legislator over the High Seas', S*tudi in onore di Antonio Ambrosini*, pp. 323–332.

—'Kritische Bemerkungen zum Anwendungsbereich des Warschauer Abkommens' [1953] ZfL 303–313.

—*Limitations of Liabilities in International Air Law* (thesis Leiden, The Netherlands, 1954).

Driscoll, E.J., 'The Role of Charter Transport in International Aviation', *Air Law*, vol. I (1976), pp. 74–82.

Duintjer Tebbens, H., *International Product Liability* (thesis Utrecht, 1979).

Dushkes, Larry S., 'The Chicago Convention: FAA's action barring foreign carriers DC-10 aircraft in US airspace held improper', *Air Law*, vol. VII (1982), pp. 92–104.

Early, S.B., W.S. Garner, M.C. Ruegsegger, S.S. Schiff, 'The Expanding Liability of Air Traffic Controllers' [1973] JALC 599–624.

Ebdon, R., 'A Consideration of GATS and its Compatibility with the Existing Regime for Air Transport', *Air and Space Law*, vol.XX (1995), pp.71-75.

Edwards, L.R., 'The Liability of Air Carriers for Death and Personal Injury to Passengers' (1982) 56 *The Australian Law Journal* 108–118.

Ehlers, P.N. *Montrealer Protokolle Nr.3 und 4 – Warschauer Haftungssystem und neuere Rechtsentwicklung.* Schriften zum Luft- und Weltraumrecht, Band 7, 1985.

—*Computerized reservations systems in the air transport industry. How to optimize the passenger's benefits,* 1988.

El-Hussainy, Khairy, 'Registration and nationality of aircraft operated by international agencies in law and practice', *Air Law*, vol. X (1985), pp. 15–27.

Erdmenger, J., 'A New Dimension to Civil Aviation through European Economic Integration', *International Air Transport in the Eighties* (1981), p. 35–44.

Eser, G.O., 'Impact of automation on the airline business', *Annals of Air and Space Law*, vol. XI (1986). pp. 3–16.

Evans, A.E., 'Aircraft Hijacking: its Cause and Cure' (1969) 63 AJIL 695–710.

Eyberg, D.K., 'Air Transportation of Radioactive Materials' [1974] JALC 681–703.

Eyer, W.W., 'The Sale, Leasing and Financing of Aircraft' [1979/1980] JALC 217–274.

Fahy Jr., Richard J., 'Regulation of computerized reservation systems in the United States and Europe', *Air Law*, vol. XI (1986), pp. 232–241.

Fauchille, Paul, 'Régime Juridique des Aérostats', *Annuaire de l' Institut de Droit International* (1902), Vol. 19, pp. 19–114.

Fenema, H.P. van, 'Het verdrag van Tokio' (1970) 63 *Militair-Rechtelijk Tijdschrift*, 385–406.

—'Substantial Ownership and Effective Control as Airpolitical Criteria', in *Air and Space Law: De Lege Ferenda* (1992), pp. 27–41.

Fennes, R.J., *International Air Cargo Services: Economic Regulation and Policy*, thesis Leiden, 1997.

Ficht, D., *Die unbekannte Schadensursache im internationalen Luftverkehr*, 1986.

Fitzgerald, G.F., 'The Development of International Rules Concerning Offences and Certain Other Acts Committed on Board Aircraft', *Canadian Yearbook of International Law* (1963), Vol. I, pp. 230–251.

—'The International Civil Aviation Organization and the Development of Conventions on International Air Law', *Annals of Air Space Law*, Vol. III (1978), pp. 51–120.

—'International Review – The Development of International Liability Rules Concerning Aerial Collisions', [1954] JALC 203–210.

—'The Lease, Charter and Interchange of Aircraft in International Operations: Amendments to the Chicago and Rome Conventions', *Annals of Air and Space Law* Vol. II, (1977) pp. 103–137.

—'Offences and Certain Other Acts Committed on Board Aircraft: the Tokyo Convention of 1963', *Canadian Yearbook of International Law*, Vol. II (1964), pp. 191–204.

—'The Protocol to Amend the Convention on Damage Caused by Foreign Aircraft to Third Parties on the Surface (Rome, 1952) signed at Montreal, September 23, 1978', *Annals of Air and Space Law*, Vol. IV, (1979), pp. 29–73.

—'The UN Convention on Multimodal Transport of Goods (1980). Discussions of the Operations of Pick-up and Delivery with Particular Attention to the Air Mode', *Air Law*, vol.VII (1982), pp. 202-214.

Fitzmaurice, G.G., 'Reservations to Multilateral Conventions', [1953] *The International and Comparative Law Quarterly* 1–26.

Fobe, J.-M., *Aviation Products Liability and Insurance in the EU*, 1994.

Frank, S.L., 'Strict Products Liability under California Law', *Air Law*, vol. V (1980), pp. 195–210.

Gau, M.S.T., *Governmental Representation for Territories in the International Civil Aviation Organization: A Case Study*, thesis Leiden, 1997.

Gerhardt, Paul, 'Jurisdiction over Crimes Committed in Aircraft While Flying over the High Seas' [1951] JALC 115–119.

Giemulla, E., U.Schmid, *Warschauer Abkommen*, 1986, loose-leaf with supplements.

—, R. Schmid, P.N. Ehlers, *et al.*, *Warsaw Convention*, 1992, loose-leaf with supplements.

—, R. Schmid and W. Mölls, *European Air Law*, 1992, loose-leaf with supplements.

Gil, A., 'The Outcome of the 4th ICAO Air Transport Conference and its Implications for Airports', *Air and Space Law*, vol.XX 1995), pp. 76-81.

Goedhuis, D., 'The Cabotage Concept in Aviation', *Interavia* (Review of World Aviation), 1952, No. 1, pp. 41–44 and No. 2, pp. 97–98.

—*National Air Legislations and the Warsaw Convention* (1937).

—'Problems of Public International Law' (1952 – II) 81 *Recueil des Cours* 205–307.

Goff, M. le, *Manuel de Droit Aérien*, Droit Public (1954).

Goldhirsch, L.B., *The Warsaw Convention Annotated: A Legal Handbook*, 1988.

Goldstein, Esq.,R.J., 'Aircraft Title Registration and Perfection of Lien Rights in Aircraft', *Air Law*, vol. IV (1979), pp. 2–7.

Goudsmit, J.J., *Het internationale ongeregelde luchtvervoer en art. 5 van het Verdrag van Chicago* (thesis Utrecht, 1953) (with an English summary).

Groot, J.E.C.de, 'Code-Sharing. United States' Policies and the Lessons for Europe', *Air and Space Law*, vol. XIX (1994), pp. 62-74.

Guerreri, G., 'Law no.274 of 7 July 1988: A remarkable piece of Italian patchwork', *Air Law*, vol. XIV (1989), pp. 176–182.

Guldimann, W., 'Aerial collisions liability', *Report* of the 53rd Conference of the International Law Association, (Buenos Aires, 1968), pp. 122–135.

Haanappel, P.P.C., *Ratemaking in International Air Transport* (1978).

—'Deregulation of air transport in North America and Western Europe', *Air Worthy* pp. 89–115.

—'The external aviation relations of the EEC and of the EEC Member States into the 21st century', *Air Law*, vol. XIV (1989), pp. 69–87.

—'Recent Regulatory Developments in Europe', *Annals of Air and Space Law*, vol. XVI (1991), pp. 107–125.

Hailbronner, K., *Der Schutz der Luftgrenzen im Frieden*, Beiträge zum ausländischen öffentlichen Recht und Völkerrecht, No.58 (Koln–Bonn, 1972).

—'Der Schutz von Sanitätsflugzeugen im Krieg', *Beiträge zum Luft- und Weltraumrecht*, pp. 127–146.

Hamalian, S.K., 'Liability of the United States government in cases of air traffic controller negligence'. *Annals of Air and Space Law*, vol. XI (1986), pp. 55–85.

Hames, R. and G. McBain, *Aircraft Finance: Regulation, Security and Enforcement* (1988), loose-leaf with supplements.

Hari, J.P., *Les transports aériens commerciaux non-réguliers en Europe* (thesis Lausanne, 1964).

Haskell, D.M,.'The Aircraft Manufacturer's Liability for Design and Punitive Damages – The Insurance Policy and the Public Policy' [1974] JALC 595–635.

Heere, W.P., 'Some Observations Concerning the Desirability of Creating an International Court for Aeronautical Disputes', *Air Law*, vol. I (1976), pp. 229–252.

Heller, P.P., 'Flying Over the Exclusive Economic Zone' [1978] ZLW 15–17.

—'French Bomb Tests and International Law' (1978) 8 *Recent Law* 252–256.

Heymann, C.A., 'Standards of Care for Air Traffic Controllers', *Annual Survey of American Law* (1979), pp. 85–93.

Hickey, Jr., W.J. 'Breaking the Limit – Liability for Wilful Misconduct under the Guatemala Protocol' [1976] JALC 603-622.

Hilbert, W.E., 'Jurisdiction in High Seas Criminal Cases – Part I' JALC 427–437.

Hofstetter, B., *L' hypothèque aérienne* (thesis Lausanne, 1950).

Honig, J.P., *The legal status of aircraft* (thesis Leiden, 1956).

Houtte, B.van, 'Community Competition Law in the Air Transport Sector (II)', *Air and Space Law*, vol.XVIII (1993), pp. 275-287.

Hursh, R.D. and H.J. Bailey, *American Law of Products Liability* 2nd ed., 1974, with supplements.

Ide, J.J., 'The History and Accomplishments of the International Technical Committee of Aerial Experts CITEJA' [1933] JAL 27–49.

Ipekoglu, S.Z., *Les assurances aériennes et les conventions internationales* (thesis Fribourg, Switzerland, 1949).

Itow, Ryohei, *Air Charter Transportation* (1969).

Jenks, E., *The Book of English Law* (6th rev. ed., 1967).

Juglart, M. de, *La Convention de Rome du 7 octobre 1952* (1955).

—*Traité de Droit Aérien* (E. de Pontavice, *et al.*, eds.), 1989 (vol. 1), 1992 (vol. 2).

Kamminga, M.S., *The Aircraft Commander in Commercial Air Transportation* (thesis Leiden, The Netherlands, 1953).

—'Some Aspects of Aircraft Accident Inquiries', *Studi in onore de Antonio Ambrosini* (1957), pp. 577–585.

Kamp, J., *Air Charter Regulations, a Legal, Economic Consumer Study* (1975).

Kehrberger, H.P., 'The German Go-Slow Action', *Air Law*, vol. III (1978), pp. 175–178.

Kennelly, J.J., 'Aviation Law: International Air Travel – A Brief Diagnosis and Prognosis' 6 (1975/1976) *California Western International Law Journal* 86–109.

Kim, Doo-Hwan, 'An International Air Carrier's Liability in a Changing Era', *Korean Journal of Air Law*, 1993, pp. 31-52; also published in *The Use of Airspace and Outer Space for All Mankind in the 21st Century*, Proceedings of the International Conference on Air Transport and Space Application in a New World (Tokyo, June 2-5, 1993), Chia-Jui Cheng, ed., pp. 89-104.

Knauth, A.W., 'Salvage as between Vessels and Aircraft' [1937] JAL, 159–190.

Kooijmans, P.H., 'State Succession and the 1929 Warsaw Convention – A Case-Study', in *Air and Space Law: De Lege Ferenda* (1992), pp. 113–133.

Kotaite, A., 'ICAO's concern and recent work in the legal field to meet the present requirements of international air transport', *Annals of Air and Space Law*, vol. 3 (1978).

Kubli, E.A., *Luftfahrtversicherung, unter besonderer Berücksichtigung des Luftpools* (thesis Zürich, 1952).

Larsen, P.B., 'Arbitration of the United States-France Air Traffic Rights Dispute' [1964] JALC 231–247.

Lemoine, M., *Traité de Droit Aérien* (1947).

Leshem, M., 'Article 26(3) of the Warsaw Convention: the extent of judicial interpretation', *Air Law*, vol. XV (1990), pp. 100-101.

Lessedjina, I.I., *La coopération multilatérale interafricaine en aviation civile* (Presses Universitaires de Zaïre, 1977).

Lester, M.J., 'Aircraft Interchange', *Air Law*, vol. IV (1979), pp. 8–10.

Levert, W.E., 'Gecombineerd en bijkomstig goederenvervoer in het privaatrechtelijke luchtvervoerrecht', *Ars Aequi*, vol.42(1993), pp. 772-780.

Levy, S.J., 'The Rights of the Passengers – A View from the United States', *Die Produkthaftung in der Luft- und Raumfahrt*, pp. 77–89.

Lewis, L., 'Air Cabotage: Historical and Modern-Day Perspectives' [1980] JALC 1059–1088.

Lieth, R. von der, *Die Haftung beim Zusammenstoss von Luftfahrtzeugen* (thesis Cologne, 1964).

Lissitzyn, O.J., 'Freedom of the Air: Scheduled and Non-scheduled Air Services', *Freedom of the Air*, pp. 89–105.

—'The Treatment of Aerial Intruders in Recent Practice and International Law' 47 (1953) AJIL 559–590.

Lowenfeld, A.F., *Aviation Law* (2nd ed., 1981) (2 volumes: Cases and Materials; Documents Supplement).

— *et al.*, 'Agora: the downing of Iran Air flight 655', AJIL, vol. 83 (1989), pp. 318-341.

—'Airline Liability and Terrorism', in *The Highways of Air and Outer Space over Asia* (1992), pp. 139–147.

—'Competition in International Aviation: The Next Round', in *The Use of Airspace and Outer Space for All Mankind in the 21st Century*, Proceedings of the International Conference on Air Transport and Space Application in a New World (Tokyo, June 2-5, 1993), Chia-Jui Cheng, ed., pp.175-184.

Lyall, F., 'Essay: the Warsaw Convention - Cutting the Gordian Knot and the 1995 Intercarrier Agreement', *Syracuse Journal of International Law and Commerce*, vol.22 (1996), pp. 67-80.

McGilchrist, N.R., 'Special Contracts and the Malta Agreement', [1977] *Lloyd's Maritime and Commercial Law Quarterly* 366–370.

McWhinney, E.E., 'Hijacking of Aircraft' 54 (1971) *Annuaire de l' Institut de Droit International* 520–558.

—'The Illegal Diversion of Aircraft and International Law' (1973 – I), 138 *Recueil des Cours* 261–372.

—*Aerial piracy and international terrorism*, 1987.

—*The Illegal Diversion of Aircraft and International Law*, 1975.

Magdelénat, J.L., *Le fret aérien* (1979).

—*Air Cargo, Regulation and Claims* (1983).

Malanczuk, P., *Humanitarian Intervention and the Legitimacy of Force* (1993)

Mankiewicz, R.H., 'Airport Noise – Compensation of Adjoining Landowners under French Law: A Report on a Case and Some Further Considerations' [1969] JALC 238–244.

—'L' avenir de la Convention de Varsovie', ASDA-Bulletin (Association Suisse de Droit Aérien et Spatial), 1982, No. 1, pp. 5–14.

—'La Convention de Varsovie et le Droit Comparé' [1969] RFDA 136–150.

—'A Galaxy of Unified Laws will Replace the Uniform Regime Created in 1929 in Warsaw, or The Death-Blow to the Uniform Regime of Liability in International Carriage by Air', *Air Law*, vol. I (1976), pp. 157–160.

—'The ICAO Draft Convention on Aerial Collisions' [1964] JALC 375–389.

—*The Liability Regime of the International Air Carrier* (1981).

—'Solutions jurisprudentielles des divergences entre le texte authentique d'une convention de droit privé et la loi nationale de sa mise en oeuvre, ou une loi postérieure', (1974) 5 *Revue de Droit d' Université de Sherbrooke* 276–311.

—'From Warsaw to Montreal with certain intermediate stops. Marginal notes on the Warsaw System', *Air Law* vol. XIV (1989), pp. 239-260.

—'The US Supreme Court finally overrules Lisi v. Alitalia?', *Air Law*, vol. XV (1990), pp. 45-48.

Mannin, C., 'The effects in aviation of the EEC Directive on product liability', *Air Law*, vol. XI (1986), pp. 248–252.

Margo, R.D., Aviation Insurance, (second edition) 1989.

—'Insurance Considerations for Airline Operations in the Asia Pacific Region', in *The Highways of Air and Outer Space over Asia* (1992), pp. 149–162.

Martin, H.J., *Die eigentumsrechtliche Stellung des Luftraumes, Fluglärm und Ueberschallknall, Haftungsfolgen und Ansprüche nach deutschem, englischem, amerikanischem, kanadischem, französischem und internationalem Recht* (thesis Würzburg, 1968).

Martin, Peter, 'A General View of Aviation Products Liability', *Aviation Products and Grounding Liability Symposium* (Royal Aeronautical Society, London, November 30, 1972), pp. 1–14.

—'The Price of Gold and the Warsaw Convention', *Air Law*, Vol. IV (1979), pp. 70–76; Vol. V (1980), pp. 34–35; and Vol. VI (1981), pp. 246-249.

—'Japanese Airlines – Looking Forward Rather Than Back', *Lloyd's Aviation Law*, vol. 11 (1992), pp. 2–5.

—'"Phone in, Turn up, Take off", a Look at the Legal Implications of Self-service Ticketing', *Air and Space Law*, vol.XX (1995), pp. 189-195.

—'The 1995 IATA Intercarrier Agreement', *Air and Space Law* vol.XXI (1996), pp. 17-24.

—'The 1995 IATA Intercarrier Agreement: an Update', *Air and Space Law*, vol.XXI (1996), pp. 126-131.

Matte, Nicolas M., *The International Legal Status of the Aircraft Commander*, 1975.

—*Traité de Droit Aérien-Aéronautique*, third edition, 1980.

—*Treatise on Air-Aeronautical Law*, 1981.

Mendes de Leon, P., *Cabotage in Air Transport Regulation*, thesis Leiden (1992).

—and Mirmina, S.A., 'The International and American Law Implications of the Bijlmer Air Disaster', *Leiden Journal of International Law*, vol.6 (1993), pp. 111-122.

Meyer, A., 'Die Bedeutung des Römischen Haftungsabkommens vom 7–10–1952 für die Luftgesetzgebung der Deutschen Bundesrepublik', ZfL 1954, pp. 42–52 (also published in *Luftrecht in Fünf Jahrzehnten*, (1961), pp. 154–163).

Mifsud, P.V., 'Foreign Investment in Air Transport in the Emerging Multilateral Era', in *The Use of Airspace and Outer Space for All Mankind in the 21st Century*, Proceedings of the International Conference on Air Transport and Space Application in a New World (Tokyo, June 2-5, 1993), Chia-Jui Cheng, ed., pp.161-166.

Milde, M., 'Tenth International Conference on Air Law', *Air Law*, Vol. IV (1979), pp. 41–44.

—'Aeronautical Consequences of the Iraqi Invasion of Kuwait', *Air Law* vol. XVI (1991), pp. 63–75.

—'The International Fight Against Terrorism in the Air', in *The Use of Airspace and Outer Space for All Mankind in the 21st Century*, Proceedings of the International Conference on Air Transport and Space Application in a New World (Tokyo, June 2-5, 1993), Chia-Jui Cheng, ed., pp. 141-158.

—'Future Perspectives of Air Law', in *proceedings* (forthcoming) of the International Colloquium on Perspectives of Air Law, Space Law and International Business Law for the Next Century (Cologne, June 7-9, 1995).

—'The International Civil Aviation Organization: After 50 Years and Beyond', *Australian International Law Journal*, (ILA, Australian Branch),1996, pp. 60-69.

Miller, G., *Liability in International Air Transport*, 1977.

Mok, M.R., 'De Haagse Conventie van 16 december 1970 ter bestrijding van het kapen van luchtvaartuigen' (1971) 46 *Nederlands Juristenblad* 281–297.
—'De strijd tegen de luchtpiraterij' (1973) 48 *Nederlands Juristenblad* 837–849 and 879–888.
Morpurgo, E., 'Quelques considérations sur les conflits internationaux de juridiction en matière pénale aéronautique à propos de la mort du banquier Loewenstein', *Revue Juridique Internationale de la Locomotion Aérienne* (1928), pp. 399–414.
Morris, L.C., 'International Aviation Security Law', *Majalah Ilmu Hukum & Pengetahuan Masyarakat (Journal of Law and Social Sciences)* of the Padjadjaran University (Bandung), 1996, no.1, pp. 23-52.
Moussé, J., 'Eurocontrol: The Changes Effected in International Organisation by the Instruments Signed on 12 February 1981', *Air Law,* vol. VII (1982), pp. 22–40.
Murchison, J.T., *The Contiguous Airspace Zone in International Law* (thesis McGill, 1955).

Naveau, J., *Droit du transport aérien international* (1980).
—*International Air Transport in a Changing World,* (1989).
—*Droit Aérien Européen: Les Nouvelles Règles du Jeu* (1993).

Oppenheim, L., *International Law* (8th ed., 1955).

Peng, Ming-Min. *Le statut juridique de l' aéronef militaire* (1957).
Pépin, E., 'The Law of the Air and the Draft Articles Concerning the Law of the Sea adopted by the International Law Commission at its Eighth Session', UN Conference on the Law of the Sea (Geneva, 1958), *Official Records*, Vol. 1, pp. 64–74.
Perron, A.E. du, 'Supreme Court of The Netherlands: Affrètair v. VOB or Fothergill's Dutch Treatment: Decision of 12 February 1982', *Air Law,* vol. VII (1982), pp. 173–177.
—'Supreme Court of the Netherlands: "Blue Hawk" case: conversion of the Gold Franc', *Air Law,* vol. VI (1981), pp. 191–195.
—'Liability of air traffic control agencies and airport operators in civil law jurisdictions', *Air Law,* vol. X (1985), pp. 203–216.
—'Eurocontrol; liability and jurisdiction', *Air Worthy,* pp. 135–149.
Plaisant, R., 'Le CITEJA et son oeuvre' [1946/1947] RFDA 153–162.
Planta, Flavio de, *Principes de Droit International Privé Applicables aux Actes Accomplis et aux Faits Commis à Bord d' un Aéronef* (1955).
Pontavice, E. du, *Les épaves maritimes, aériennes et spatiales en droit français* (thesis Paris, 1960).
—'Le statut juridique des affrètements aériens dits charters,' [1970] RGAE 241–257.
Pradelle, P. de la, 'L'aviation sanitaire en temps de guerre', *Report* of the 45th ILA Conference, (Lucerne, 1952), pp. 138–142.
—'Les frontières de l'air', *Recueil des Cours,* vol. 86 (1954–II), pp. 117–202.
Priyatna Abdurrasyid, 'Towards the new Indonesian Aviation Law', *Air Worthy,* pp. 1–13.

Reichenbach, D.P., *Haftpflicht und Versicherung des Luftfahrzeughalters für Lärmschäden* (thesis Zürich, 1971).
Reifarth, Jürgen, *Internationale Regelungen der Tarife im Linienluftverkehr,* Europäische Hochschulschriften, Reihe II, Rechtswissenschaft. Bd.478, 1985.
Reukema, B., *Discriminatory Refusal of Carriage in North America,* (thesis McGill, 1981), 1982.
—'Drinking and Flying, Why the Two do not Mix Well on US Carriers', *Annals of Air and Space Law,* vol. IX (1984), pp. 133–147.
Richard, Ghislaine, 'The DC–10 Chicago Crash and the Legality of SFAR 10', *Annals of Air and Space Law* Vol. VI, (1981), pp. 195–218.
Riese, O., *Luftrecht* (1949)
—and J.T. Lacour, *Précis de droit aérien* (1951).

Rijks, K., *Het Verdrag van Genève* (thesis Leiden, 1952).

Rinck, G., 'Schäden Dritter im Internationalen Luftverkehr: über den bisherigen Misserfolg des Römer Haftpflichtabkommens' [1962] ZLW 85–104.

—'Damage Caused by Foreign Aircraft to Third Parties' [1961/1962] JALC 405–417.

Ripert, G., 'Hypothèque et transfert de la propriété de l'aéronef', *Revue Juridique Internationale de la Locomotion Aérienne* (1922), pp. 157–162.

Rode-Verschoor, I.H.Ph. de, 'Le développement de l'assistance et du sauvetage des aéronefs sur terre et sur mer', *Studi in onore di Antonio Ambrosini*, pp. 711–721.

—'Liability Arising From Gratuitous Carriage By Air', (1966) 1 EVR, pp. 490–534.

—'Les problèmes concernant les délits commis à bord des aéronefs particulièrement quant à la juridiction' (1957) 27 *Revue Internationale de Droit Pénal* 431–445.

—'Quelques remarques sur l'utilité d'une réglementation de l'avarie grosse dans le droit aérien' [1952] RFDA 275–277.

—'La responsabilité du transporteur pour retard' [1957] RGA 253–265.

—,W.P. Heere *et al.*, 'The Legal Status of State Aircraft' (1963) 2 IDA 115–140.

Rodière, R., *Droit des Transports. Transports terrestres et aériens*, 1977.

Romang, W., *Zuständigkeit und Vollstreckbarkeit im internationalen und schweizerischen Luftprivatrecht* (thesis Winterthur, 1958).

Rudolf, A., 'Die sogenannten Pauschalreise (IT) Charter im Spannungsfeld zwischen Fluglinien- und Gelegenheitsverkehr' [1970] ZLW 110–124.

Ruhwedel, E., *Die Rechtsstellung des Flugzeugkommandanten im zivilen Luftverkehr*, Schriften zum Deutschen und Europäischen Zivil-, Handels– und Prozessrecht, No. 27 (1964).

—*Der Luftbeförderungsvertrag*, 1985

Rutgers, H.J., *Conventions on Penal Law Regarding Aircraft* (thesis Utrecht, 1978).

Sakamoto, T., 'The Fate of Passenger Liability Limitation in the Warsaw System', in *The Use of Airspace and Outer Space for All Mankind in the 21st Century*, Proceedings of the International Conference on Air Transport and Space Application in a New World (Tokyo, June 2-5, 1993), Chia-Jui Cheng, ed., pp.131-140.

Samuels, A., 'The Legal Problems: An Introduction' [1971] JALC 163–170.

Sand, P.H., 'Die USA und das Haager Protokoll: Zum Plan einer gesetzlichen Fluggastversicherung' [1963] ZWL 12–34.

Sauveplanne, J.G., 'Les rapports entre responsabilité et assurance en droit aérien international', *Contributions Neérlandaises au VI-ème Congrès de Droit Comparé* (Hamburg, 1962), 1963, pp. 121–132.

Schadee, H. 'Für die grosse Havarie im Luftrecht' [1954] ZfL 331–334.

Schenkman, J., *International Civil Aviation Organization* (1955).

Schmid, R., 'Which are the duties of an air carrier who does not execute an air carriage contract as agreed', *Air Law,* vol. XV (1990), pp. 102-104.

—'Is a carrier responsible for passengers arriving without travel documents?', *Air Law,* vol. XVI (1991), pp. 142–143.

—'Der Flugschein - seine Bedeutung für Fluggast und Luftfrachtführer', in *Festschrift für Henning Piper* (W.Erdmann, W.Gloy and R.Herber, eds.), 1996, pp.999-1013.

—'Die Rechte des Reisenden beim Wechsel der Fluggesellschaft und des Luftfahrzeuges', *Neue Juristische Wochenschrift*, vol.49(1996), pp. 1636-1644.

—'The Warsaw Convention - between sunset and sunrise. IATA Intercarrier Agreements as a requiem for a well-proved liability system', *Air and space Law*, vol.XXII (1997) (forthcoming).

Schmidt-Räntsch, G., 'Die internationale Luftrechtskonferenz in Tokio (1963) und das Abkommen über strafbare und bestimmte andere Handlungen an Bord von Luftfahrzeugen', [1964] ZLW 75–110.

Schubert, F., *La Responsabilité des Agences du Contrôle de la Circulation Aérienne*, (thesis Opfikon, 1994)

Schwenk, W., 'The Bonn Declaration on Hijacking', *Annals of Air and Space Law*, vol. IV (1979), pp. 307–322.

Shawcross, C.N. and K.C. Beaumont, *Air Law* (4th ed., 1977, 2 vols., with supplements to Volume 2).

Sheehan, W.M., 'Air Cabotage and the Chicago Convention' *Harvard Law Review* (1980) 1157-1167.

Shepard, I.M., 'Air Piracy: The Role of the International Federation of Airline Pilots Associations' *Cornell International Law Journal* Vol. 3, No. 1 (Winter 1970), 79–91.

Shin, Dong-Chun, 'Foreign Ownership of Airlines', *Korean Journal of Air Law*, 1993, pp. 207-263.

Shin, Sung-Hwan, 'The Warsaw System: Developing Instruments', *Korean Journal of Air Law*, 1993, pp. 265-299.

Shubber, Sami, *Jurisdiction over Crimes on Board Aircraft* (1973).

Slot, P.J. and P.D. Dagtoglou, *Toward a Community Air Transport Policy*, 1989.

Slijper, D., 'Recent European Developments Concerning Product Liability', in *The Highways of Air and Outer Space over Asia* (1992), pp. 203–243.

Slijper, D.J., 'Standardization of Safety Requirements', in *The Use of Airspace and Outer Space for All Mankind in the 21st Century*, Proceedings of the International Conference on Air Transport and Space Application in a New World (Tokyo, June 2-5, 1993), Chia-Jui Cheng, ed., pp. 185-193.

Sowter, R.S., 'Lease Finance for Airlines', *Air Law*, vol. IV (1979), pp. 11–20.

Spanjaard, M., 'Report on the Contribution by Interested Parties in the Payment of Remuneration for Assistance and on the Contribution of Postal Cargo to Such Remuneration', ICAO Doc. 4526/LC–12 and ICAO Doc. 5335/LC–97.

Spörri,F., *Die Bekämpfung der widerrechtlichen Inbesitznahme von Luftfahrzeuge durch das Haager Übereinkommen vom 16. Dezember 1970* (thesis Zürich, 1979).

Stabenow, W., 'The International Factors in Air Transport under the Treaty Establishing the European Economic Community' [1967] JALC 117-131.

Sterns, G.C., 'Air crash cases in the United States. A consideration of the Tenerife issues', *Nederlands Juristenblad*, 52 (1977), pp. 1109–1119.

Stewart Jr., J.T., 'Aircraft leasing in the USA - a few observations', *Air Law*, vol.VIII (1983), pp. 58-78.

Stolker, C., 'Compensation of Damage to Parties on the Ground as a Result of Aviation Accidents', in *proceedings* (forthcoming) of the International Symposium on the Use of the Air and Outer Space at the Service of World Peace and Prosperity (Beijing, 21-23 August 1995).

Storm van's Gravesande, J.W.E., 'Some observations on fifty years of aircraft accident investigation in the Netherlands', *Air Worthy*, pp. 151–168.

Straszheim, M.R., *The International Airline Industry* (1969).

Sucharitkul, S., 'Immunities of Foreign States before National Authorities' (1976–I) 149 *Recueil des Cours* 87–216.

Sudre, E., 'Le Comité International Technique d'Experts Juridiques Aériens (CITEJA). Son origine – son but – son oeuvre – son avenir' [1946] RGA 49–65

Sundberg, J.W.F., *Air Charter, A Study in Legal Development* (1961).

—*Chartering of Aircraft*, General Report (Section III.D) to the Xth International Congress (Budapest, 1978) of the International Academy of Comparative Law.

—'The Guadalajara Convention Live From Cyprus', *Air Law*, vol. I (1976), pp. 83–98.

—'The aircraft commander in legal turbulence', *Air Worthy*, pp. 169–194.

Sztucki, J., 'Some Questions Arising from Reservations to the Vienna Convention on the Law of Treaties', *German Yearbook of International Law* (1977), Vol. 20, pp. 277–305.

Thomka-Gazdik, J.G., 'Are Inclusive Tour Charters Scheduled or Non-Scheduled Services?', *The Freedom of the Air*, pp. 106–122.

Thornberry, C.H.R., 'Dr. Soblen and the Alien Law of the United Kingdom' [1963] *The International and Comparative Law Quarterly*, 414–474.

Thornton, R.L., *International Airlines and Politics; a Study in Adaptation to Change* (Michigan International Business Studies, No. 3, 1970).

Tobi, E., 'The insurer's point of view', *Air Law*, vol. XI (1986), pp. 84–94.

Tobolewski, A., *Monetary limitations of liability in air law*, 1986.

Tuuk Adriani, P. van der, 'The "Bermuda" Capacity Clauses' [1955] JALC 406–413.

—Some Observations on the Newly Born Bermuda II', *Air Law*, vol. II (1977), pp. 190–193.

Tzou, C.-K. and C.-J. Cheng, 'New Types of Agreements in International Air Transport', in *The Highways of Air and Outer Space over Asia* (1992), pp. 299–310.

Veenstra, K., '"Special Event Charter Flights" and "Scheduled Air Services": Some problems of interpretation', *Air Law*, vol. I (1976), pp. 294–299.

Vellas, P., *et al.*, *La Vie de l'Avion Commercial*, 1990.

Verdross, A., *Völkerrecht* (5th ed., 1964).

Verplaetse, J.G., *International Law in Vertical Space* (1960).

Verploeg, E.A.G., *The Road towards a European Common Air Market* (thesis Utrecht, 1963).

Verwer, Chr., *Aansprakelijkheid voor bagageschade in het internationaal luchtvervoer* (thesis Amsterdam, 1976).

—*Liability for damage to luggage in international air transport*, 1987.

Videla Escalada, F., 'The international regulation of liability in the field of air traffic control services', *Air Worthy*. pp. 195–213.

—'Nationality of Aircraft: a Vision of the Future', in *Air and Space Law: De Lege Ferenda* (1992), pp. 71–80.

Vlugt, P. de. *'Het begrip "Militair Luchtvaartuig"'* (1956) 49 *Militair Rechtelijk Tijdschrift* 81–85.

Wagner, W.J., *International Air Transportation As Affected By State Sovereignty* (1970).

Wassenbergh, H.A., *Aspects of Air Law and Civil Air Policy in the Seventies* (1970).

—'Innovation in International Air Transportation Regulation (the US–Netherlands Agreement of 10 March 1978)', *Air Law*, vol. III (1978), pp. 138–162.

—*Post-War International Civil Aviation Policy and the Law of the Air* (1962).

—*Public International Air Transportation in a New Era* (1976).

—'The *"Nouvelles Frontières"* case', *Air Law*, vol. XI (1986), pp. 161–166.

—'The "right to fly" and the "right to carry traffic by air", in international air transportation, after 40 years', *Air Worthy*, pp. 215–233.

— 'Iraq/Kuwait and International Civil Aviation Relations', *ITA Magazine* vol. 63 (sept.-oct. 1990), pp. 8–15.

— *Principles and practices in air transport regulations*, 1993.

—' "Open Skies"/"Open Markets": The Limits to Competition', in *The Use of Airspace and Outer Space for All Mankind in the 21st Century*, Proceedings of the International Conference on Air Transport and Space Application in a New World (Tokyo, June 2-5, 1993), Chia-Jui Cheng, ed., pp. 195-204.

—'Future Regulation to Allow Multi-national Arrangements between Air Carriers (Cross-border Alliances), Putting an End to Air Carrier Nationalism', *Air and Space Law*, vol.XX (1995), pp.164-168.

—'World Trends in Air Transport Policies', *Air and Space Law*, vol.XX (1995), pp. 174-178.

—'De-regulation of Competition in International Air Transport', *Air and Space Law*, vol.XXI (1996), pp. 80-89.

—'The "Sixth" Freedom Revisited', *Air and Space Law*, vol.XXI (1996), pp.285-294.

Watteville, J. de, *La piraterie aérienne* (1978).

Weber, L., *Die Zivilluftfahrt im Europäischen Gemeinschaftsrecht* (thesis Heidelberg, 1980), published as Vol. 78 in the series Beiträge zum ausländischen öffentlichen Recht und Völkerrecht (Berlin–Vienna, 1981).

—'Legal Activities of the International Air Transport Association (IATA) 1993-1994', *Air and Space Law*, vol. XX (1995), pp. 32-34.

Werro, M.D., *Die Haftung aus Zusammenstoss von Flugzeugen, unter besonderer Berücksichtigung des schweizerischen Rechtes* (thesis Zürich, 1978).

Wessels, H., 'Haftungsgrenze und Wertdeklaration in Art. 22 Abs. 2 des Warschauer Abkommens bei Teilschäden an Fracht und Reisegepäck', [1960] ZLW 35–40.

Westermann, H., 'Der Großflughafen im Raum- und Nachbarrecht', [1957] ZfL 259–286.

Whitehead Jr., G.I., 'Some Comments on Aircraft Crashworthiness', [1976] JALC 73–83.

Wijk, A.A. van, *Aircraft Accident Enquiry in the Netherlands* (thesis Amsterdam, 1974).

—'The Investigation of Aircraft Accidents and Incidents. Some Notes and Documentation on Recent Developments', *Proceedings Luchtrecht Symposium* (Rotterdam, October 2, 1981), pp. 71–144.

—'Visual and oral signals between aircraft in flight as a means to convey instructions by a State', *Air Worthy*, pp. 235–289.

Wilberforce, R.O., 'Convention on Damage Caused by Foreign Aircraft to Third Parties on the Surface' [1953] *The International and Comparative Law Quarterly* 90–94.

—'The International Recognition of Rights in Aircraft' [1948] *The International and Comparative Law Quarterly* [1948] pp. 421–458.

—'Report on Recognition of Rights in Aircraft', *Report* of the 44th Conference of the International Law Association (Copenhagen, 1950), pp. 233–254.

Wilhelm, A., 'De la situation juridique des aéronautes en droit [international,' *Journal du Droit International Privé* (Clunet, 1891)], pp. 440–452.

Wright, R.R., *The Law of Airspace* (1968).

Zylicz, M., 'Key Problems of the Future International Air Transport Regime', *Air and Space Law*, vol.XIX (1994), pp.185-188.

Index

References are to the pages

235